JDBC

Developer's Resource

2nd edition

JDBC

Developer's Resource

2nd edition

ART TAYLOR

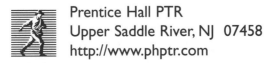

Prentice Hall PTR
Upper Saddle River, NJ 07458
http://www.phptr.com

The Library of Congress has catalogued the first edition of this work as follows:

Taylor, Art
JDBC developer's resource: database programming on the Internet/
Art Taylor.
p. cm.—(Prentice Hall PTR developer's resource series)
Includes index.
ISBN 0-13-842352-0
1. Internet programming. 2. Database management. 3. Java
(Computer program language) I. Title. II. Series.
QA76.625.T39 1997
005.75'6--dc21 97-806
CIP

Editorial/Production Supervision: *Precision Graphics*
Acquisitions Editor: *Mark Taub*
Manufacturing Manager: *Alexis R. Heydt*
Cover Design: *Scott Weiss*
Cover Design Direction: *Jerry Votta*
Art Director: *Gail Cocker-Bogusz*
Marketing Manager: *Dan Rush*

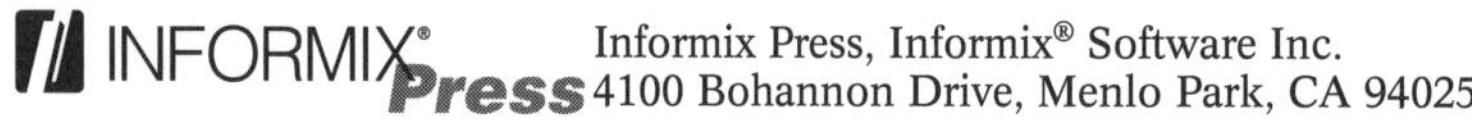
Informix Press, Informix® Software Inc.
4100 Bohannon Drive, Menlo Park, CA 94025

Prentice-Hall, Inc.
A Simon & Schuster Company
Upper Saddle River, NJ 07458

The publisher offers discounts on this book when ordered in bulk quantities. For more information, contact: Corporate Sales Department, Prentice Hall PTR, One Lake Street, Upper Saddle River, NJ 07458. Phone: 800-382-3419; FAX: 201-236-7141; E-mail: corpsales@prenhall.com

Printed in the United States of America

10 9 8 7 6 5 4 3 2 1

ISBN 0-13-901661-9

Prentice-Hall International (UK) Limited, *London*
Prentice-Hall of Australia Pty. Limited, *Sydney*
Prentice-Hall Canada Inc., *Toronto*
Prentice-Hall Hispanoamericana, S.A., *Mexico*
Prentice-Hall of India Private Limited, *New Delhi*
Prentice-Hall of Japan, Inc., *Tokyo*
Simon & Schuster Asia Pte. Ltd., *Singapore*
Editora Prentice-Hall do Brasil, Ltda., *Rio de Janeiro*

For Carolyn
with affection and thanks,
for enduring yet another

CONTENTS

The Java Language and JDBC

Since its inception in 1995, the Java language has generated intense interest in the computer industry. The Java Database Connectivity (JDBC) standard adds a whole new dimension to this capable and multi-faceted language. Rather than simply being used to "bring life to Web pages," Java with JDBC can now fill the role of database-aware applications for a variety of application needs. Where currently common gateway interface (CGI) applications are required to access databases from within Web browsers, Java applets with JDBC now have the potential to provide this functionality with more direct programming and the potential for improved performance.

Using this API, you can now use Java applications for standard database programming tasks such as reports or updates. With Java's flexible network API, you can use Java/JDBC applications for filter programs, to read data from a data stream, and to provide conversion facilities before updating a database.

Java applications written using JDBC are portable both for the hardware platform and the database. You can run a correctly written Java/JDBC program on a variety of platforms against a variety of databases without any code changes. This is possible because JDBC is based on ODBC, which is in turn based on the X/Open CLI specification. The goals of the X/Open group have been met to the extent that database access standards have been accepted by the industry. Access to all major databases is available through ODBC. And JDBC-ODBC bridges are available to provide database access by mapping JDBC calls to their corresponding ODBC calls. Thus, any database that is accessible with an ODBC driver is also accessible with a Java/JDBC driver using the JDBC-ODBC bridge.

JDBC uses the industry standard Structured Query Language (SQL) to communicate with the database. Writing a JDBC application, therefore, requires knowledge of both the Java language and SQL. To provide a refresher, this book includes sections on both of these languages. These chapters are intended to help those who have had moderate exposure to these languages. For those with no experience in SQL, additional training is recommended.

About This Book

This book is designed to provide you with a thorough grounding in the JDBC API. It is divided into two parts: a tutorial and a reference. The tutorial part provides a primer on the Java language and relational databases. This is followed by a set of examples that demonstrate the process of programming database applications using JDBC. This part begins with simple examples and then progresses into more complex applications.

The reference part provides several listings of the methods available in JDBC. A brief, quick reference of the methods is provided, followed by a more detailed description of the methods arranged by JDBC interfaces.

Target Audience

If you use Java and have a need to perform database access, then this book is for you. This book presumes the reader is an experienced programmer, but not necessarily a Java programmer. This book is designed to be a useful resource for both the experienced and inexperienced Java programmer. A programmer just learning the Java language will find the JDBC library is similar in design to the other Java libraries and just as easy to use. This book will provide the guidance and the code samples to easily complete a JDBC application.

Java has intentionally been designed with a syntax similar to C/C++, so a programmer familiar with either of these languages will be able to use Java. And a programmer familiar with object-oriented concepts will be comfortable with JDBC and it's object-oriented design.

If you are one of those individuals very familiar with C but with moderate exposure to C++ or Java, then this book provides a Java overview to present some of the more important Java concepts. Having read these sections, an experienced programmer will have no problem understanding the numerous code samples presented in this book.

Resource

This book is designed to be both a tutorial and a reference combined into a single book: a complete 'developer's resource.' As a reference book, a quick reference section contains all methods in the class library and a short description of the method. A second reference section lists all JDBC interface descriptions and provides a code sample for virtually all JDBC methods.

This book is designed to be a **complete** JDBC resource. A tutorial section is provided to demonstrate how to use JDBC with Java. With the belief that a good code sample is worth a 1000 words, numerous code samples provide a 'picture' of how to access data using JDBC.

A complete reference section is also included. The entire JDBC class library is covered with code samples provided for most of the methods.

An experienced programmer with solid Java experience could read the sections of the tutorial that cover basic JDBC programming, use the reference section as needed, and quickly develop a working JDBC application. A less-experienced Java programmer could read the Java primer section and the tutorial section, and then use the reference section as a reference to develop a JDBC application.

Conventions Used in This Book

You'll notice as you read this book that there are several conventions used to help make especially useful material easier to read and to locate when you're using this book as a reference during your programming sessions.

Source Code

All code fragments and listings that have been set off from the main text of this book have been formatted in the following way:

```
...
StringBuffer DTString = "The answer is ";
int num = 42;
DTString = DTString + num;
System.out.println( DTString );
...
```

As well, coding terms that appear within the main text have been set in a special font for easier reference, like so: "The Java language eliminates this difficulty by extending the capabilities of the `continue` and `break` statements."

Icons

Oftentimes, there is information that deserves special attention because it highlights a particularly useful or important point that might otherwise get lost among all of the other important information in the main text. For this reason, a number of special icons have been created to help this information stand out. These icons are as follows:

This convention highlights information such as an interesting fact about the topic at hand or an important point to keep in mind when using this book.

This convention is used to help useful information stand out for easier reference. Such information might be a pointer to save you time, a particularly useful technique, or just some good old-fashioned programming advice.

This convention is used to flag information that could save you lots of serious frustration in the long run.

About the CD

Several useful tools and programming examples are provided on the CD-ROM enclosed with the book. The tools are as follows:

- The Java JDK, complete with JDBC and this JDBC-ODBC bridge.
- INTERSOLV DataDirect ODBC Pack for Windows 95/Windows NT.
- The OpenLink Data Access Driver Suite.

Also provided are the majority of the programming examples used in this book. Wherever a program is referenced with a program name, that program is available on the CD-ROM. A special Web page has been created as a front-end to navigating the CD-ROM included with this book. To access that Web page, please load the file named `index.html`, found in the root directory of the CD-ROM, into your browser. The directory locations of the programs and instructions on running the various applications are accessible from this Web page. Also included on this Web page are links to various JDBC-related sites, as well as the online supplement to this book, explained in the following section.

The combination of the JDBC-ODBC bridge and the Intersolv DataDirect ODBC drivers allow JDBC applications to be developed under the Windows 95 environment.

The OpenLink Data Access Driver Suite provides a complete set of drivers for database connectivity using a number of different standards, including ODBC, JDBC™, and Universal Database Connectivity (UDBC). The suite may be used with either multitier or single-tier drivers. All OpenLink drivers are provided on the CD for evaluation.

About the Web Site

Finally, this and every book in the Developer's Resource Series is accompanied by a special online Web supplement created especially for each book. You can look for additional information related to the JDBC, as well as other books in the series, at:

`www.prenhall.com/developers_resource_series`

Additionally, you can link to the online Web supplement directly from the Web page included on the CD-ROM accompanying this book.

Changes to JDBC for JDK 1.1

With the release of version 1.1 of the JDK, JDBC will be part of the core Java API. As part of this merge effort, several minor changes have been made to JDBC. These changes are not, unfortunately, backward compatible. They are as follows:

- The `java.sql.Numeric` class has been superseded by `java.math.BigDecimal`.
- The `Connection` class auto close mode has been removed from JDBC. This has the impact of removing the `setAutoClose` and `getAutoClose` methods from the `Connection` class.

Acknowledgments

I would like to acknowledge the contributions of Shekhar Kirani, for a perceptive technical review; and Mark Hapner at SunSoft, for consistently speedy responses to my technical queries.

Part One

Java Tutorial

Colin R. Bänger

This chapter is intended to provide a quick overview of the Java language with a focus on the components that have a bearing on JDBC programming. The base class libraries, Java data types, and exception handling are all covered briefly.

For a C or C++ programmer, Java is not a difficult language to master. Much of the syntax of the C language has found its way into Java, including the much-loved increment operator (++). But probably just as important as what has been included is what has not been included, and these differences are also highlighted in this chapter. And, though this chapter was written with the C or C++ programmer in mind, it is intended to be accessible by any programmer familiar with object-oriented programming.

For the programmer not familiar with C or C++ or object-oriented programming concepts, additional grounding in this material is recommended before programming with Java/JDBC.

History of Java

As most of the computer-savvy world already knows, the Java language originated at Sun. Based on a language that was at one time called Oak, the language had its start in 1991. James Gosling and engineers at Sun needed a language that was small and CPU independent. They considered the UCSD Pascal language and its ability to create intermediate code. But the Unix engineers at Sun preferred the C++ language, so C++ was used as a basis for design. And, possibly considering the fact that caffeine-laden liquids struck a more resonant chord with programmers than trees, the name Oak was rejected and, ultimately, the language was named Java.

The engineers at Sun realized that Web-based applications could benefit from many of the features of Java and they decided to develop a browser with Java to demonstrate its capabilities. In 1994, Patrick Naughton and Jonathan Payne developed a World Wide Web browser that eventually became the HotJava browser. This browser was demonstrated at SunWorld '95, inspiring a great deal of interest in the language.

In the fall of 1995, Netscape announced that the next release of its browser would support Java *applets*—Java code that is downloaded as part of an HTML page and run on the client machine. While the phenomenal growth of the World Wide Web and interest in developing applications for this rapidly growing market continued, interest in Java has also continued to grow. With the introduction of the final JDBC specification in June 1996, there is great potential for this versatile language with database-aware applications.

Features

The Java language provides a number of important features that make it the language of choice for enterprise applications. The language is portable. It is object-oriented (in fact, there is no other way to write a program but as an object-oriented program). It provides a runtime environment that creates a security layer between the application and the client machine. And the language provides a rich API with flexible classes to provide easy access to a number of important features. The following section identifies and explains some of these features.

The Java Runtime Environment

The Java application runs in a runtime environment known as the *Java virtual machine*. The Java virtual machine consists of an interpreter that reads and interprets the byte codes that make up the application. This interpreter dynamically loads classes as they are needed. Additional portions of the virtual machine perform garbage collection, freeing memory when it is no longer needed, and managing other resources.

This architecture provides platform transparency for the application. The Java programmer need not be concerned with porting issues; these issues are solved by the Java virtual machine. As long as the Java programmer writes to the Java portable libraries, the application is portable.

Language Safety

The Java language succeeds on many levels. It is a powerful, yet safe, language. It provides platform independence. It has built-in Web functionality. It uses a familiar C/C++ language syntax. It provides easy language access to its multi-threading support. It is portable. Combined with Netscape's decision to support Java in its browser, these features are an important reason for the intense interest in this language.

Java was intended to overcome many of the limitations and problems of the C language. Java developers considered two of the most significant problems of C to be its poor language safety, and the work it required of programmers to manage memory. These problems have been solved in Java.

Design

The Java language was designed to be used in a networking environment, not only the Internet but the Intranet, where security and portability are still important considerations. The growth of the Internet has increased interest in the language and has forced the industry to reconsider the manner in which software has traditionally been developed and distributed.

The Java language has not only forced developers to reconsider issues such as security and portability, but also language safety. The Java language removes many of the unsafe features of the C language to create a language in which it is difficult, if not impossible, to corrupt program memory. Extensive compile-time checking of array bounds and the elimination of pointers helps ensure language safety. Additional runtime features check for array bounds violations and null pointers.

The Java language was designed with a syntax that is familiar to the C++ programmer. The language contains many of the features of C++, but was designed to overcome many of the shortcomings of that language. Towards this goal, the C language problem of pointer traversal without memory bounds protection is eliminated in Java. Memory allocation only occurs through object instantiation, and the only "pointer" reference is that of an object. The Java runtime environment can therefore protect memory bounds.

Java also performs its own garbage collection; programmers need not concern themselves with memory reclamation. This reduces code and a significant source of memory bounds violation errors.

Multiple inheritance was considered a source of confusion in C++ and was difficult to implement. Multiple inheritance is eliminated in Java and has been replaced in part with the concept of the *interface*.

C++ and Java

The Java language has strong roots in C and C++. Even though the designers felt C++ had many problems, they wanted to design a language similar to C++ to avoid the need for extensive programmer re-training—a C++ programmer can quickly learn Java. For this reason, a significant portion of the syntax of C++ has found its way into the Java language.

The object-orientation of Java is essentially that of C++. Classes, objects, inheritance, and polymorphism all exist in the language and object members have several levels of protection, just as in C++.

Emerging Java Technologies

As this book goes to press, Java technologies continue to evolve. Facilities for added security, code re-use, and enhanced performance are being added to the language. These new facilities, in combination with the other benefits of Java programming, continue to earn converts to the language. Several of the emerging technologies are discussed in the sections that follow.

Java Beans

Java beans is a *component architecture* for Java. The goal is to enable independent software vendors (ISVs) to develop reusable software components that end-users can combine using application builder tools.

Java Beans provides both an architecture and a platform-neutral API for creating and using dynamic Java components. These components can be GUI widgets, non-visual functions and services, and more full-scale applications.

The Java Beans component model has two major elements: *components* and *containers*. A *component* can range in complexity from a simple GUI widget to a complete application. A *container* provides the context for the components. A container can also be a container; in this respect, a container can be used as a component inside another container.

A component can publish or register its interface, thus allowing them to be driven by calls and events from other components or scripts. Event handling and persistence services are also supplied by this model. A facility for application builder support allows an interface to enable components to expose their properties and behaviors to application builder development tools.

Java Database Access Standard (JDBC)

The JDBC standard developed from the need to enable Java applications to connect to SQL databases. Because of Java's features, it is uniquely suitable for network access to a variety of databases. And because Java is itself a platform-independent language, there is a compelling reason to develop applications that are independent of a particular database vendor.

The goal of the JDBC developers was to develop a low-level API that supported SQL access. There was some motivation to use ODBC as the basis for this API because there had been a general acceptance of the ODBC standard at that point. The JDBC specification developers described their design goals in June of 1996:

> Our immediate priority has been to develop a common low-level API that supports basic SQL functionality. . . . We based our work on the X/Open SQL CLI (Call Level Interface) which is also the basis for Microsoft's ODBC interface. Our main task has been defining a natural Java interface to the basic abstractions and concepts defined in the X/Open CLI.

But ODBC was a C-language standard; Java required a standard that could be mapped onto the Java language. JDBC represents a collection of object-oriented classes (in a Java *package*) that can be directly related to similar ODBC functions. (Note that ODBC is not an API for an object-oriented language, so there is a significant difference in that JDBC represents ODBC functionality with a "set of classes," not simply a "collection of functions" as ODBC does.)

The JDBC standard, like its predecessor for the C language, is designed to make the application *database independent*. If applications written with JDBC use only portable SQL statements, statements that are contained in the SQL ANSI 92 Entry Level standard, to access the database, then the application would run with any database that provided the same level of SQL ANSI compliance.

JDBC Driver Types

There are four different types of JDBC drivers. The distinctions between these drivers are based primarily on the components of the driver, where the components must reside, and the language used to develop the components. Each database vendor uses a different set of calls and a different network protocol to access their database. These database vendors offer their own proprietary APIs and drivers to provide access to their database, and with all JDBC driver types, JDBC calls must be *mapped* or converted to the vendor protocol. In the case of the Type 1 driver, this mapping has an additional layer of indirection through the ODBC protocol. The Type 3 driver provides this mapping through a middleware server component that communicates with the client-side driver and provides mapping and database communication. The Type 4 driver provides this mapping through pure Java code written to manage the vendor-specific protocol.

Type 1 and Type 2 drivers require binaries to reside on the client machine. To develop a true *thin-client* solution where no driver code must reside on the client, a Type 3 or Type 4 driver is needed, because

Table 1.1: *JDBC Driver Types*

Driver	Description
Type 1	JDBC-ODBC bridge; JDBC through ODBC binary written in another language; requires software on the client machine
Type 2	Driver is partially composed of Java code with portions mapped to database-specific code for the target database (e.g., Informix, Oracle, Sybase); requires some client-side binary code
Type 3	Pure Java driver; uses middleware to convert JDBC calls to vendor-specific calls and protocol required to access the database
Type 4	Pure Java driver that does not require middleware

with these drivers, no driver code is required on the client. Table 1.1 lists JDBC driver types.

A Type 1 driver, also known as the *JDBC-ODBC bridge*, is one of the more common types of driver currently available. The current release of the JDK is bundled with this type of JDBC driver. (Note that the JDBC-ODBC bridge requires an ODBC driver on the client machine. An ODBC driver is *not* included in the JDK.)

Type 2 drivers require some binary code to reside on the client machine. JDBC calls are converted into vendor-specific protocol for the database vendor, potentially mapping the calls to a database driver (usually provided by the database vendor) written in some other language.

Type 3 drivers do not require client code to communicate with the database. The JDBC driver communicates with middleware, which converts the JDBC calls to server-specific (and vendor-specific) DBMS calls. This is a true thin-client solution since the JDBC driver is pure Java and can be invoked and loaded without having to reside on the client machine.

A Type 4 driver is a pure Java driver that does *not* require middleware to convert the JDBC calls into the vendor-specific protocol required to communicate with the database. This is a driver that can be invoked and loaded without client-side code.

The Java Base System

The Java base system is composed of a set of base utility classes. These base classes are used by developers to develop a variety of multi-platform applications in much the same way that `stdio.h` and `stdlib.h` are used in the C language system. The base system can then be combined with additional Java libraries to add functionality as needed.

The Java base libraries are composed of the libraries listed in Table 1.2: `java.lang`, `java.io`, `java.util`, `java.net` and `java.awt`. These libraries provide the portable features needed for a multi-purpose platform-independent language.

Basic Elements of Java

Everything in Java is an object, with the exception of primitive data types, and they can be encapsulated optionally in Java objects in the base classes. Java is therefore a truly object-oriented language.

Table 1.2: *Java Base Libraries*

Library	Description
`java.lang`	The collection of base types, including declarations for `object` and `class` plus threads, exceptions, and other fundamental classes.
`Java.io`	The rough equivalent of the stdio library in the C language. Contains the streams and i/o libraries.
`java.net`	Network access methods, including support for sockets, telnet interfaces, and URLs.
`java.util`	Container and utility classes such as `Dictionary`, `Hashtable`, `Stack`, encoder and decoder techniques, and `Date` and `Time` classes.
`java.awt`	The *Abstract Windowing Tookit,* which provides an abstract layer to port Java applications from one windowing environment to another. Contains basic components such as events, colors, fonts, and controls.

There are only three groups of primitive data types in Java: *numeric, Boolean,* and *arrays*. These are explained in more detail in the following sections.

Numeric Data Types

Java supplies a complete set of numeric data types, roughly equivalent to the data types of the same name in C (although technically the C language left the length and precision of some numeric data types to the machine implementation). Numeric data types are outlined in Table 1.3.

By default, a floating-pointer literal value is considered a `double` and must be cast explicitly to a `float` in order to assign it to a `float` variable. Real numeric types, and arithmetic operations on those types, are as defined by the IEEE 754 specification.

Character Data Types

Character data types in Java are stored as 16-bit Unicode characters. These 16-bit values range from 0 through 65,535. By adopting the Unicode character set, the Java language and its applications are amenable to internationalization and localization.

Java character arrays are similar to the C language `char[]` data type, but the Java `String` type is probably a more useful data type. The Java `String` allows the strings size to grow dynamically at run time, if needed, thus avoiding the need for memory management.

Table 1.3: *Numeric Data Types*

Numeric Type	Description
`byte`	8-bit integer
`short`	16-bit integer
`int`	32-bit interger
`long`	64-bit integer
`float`	32-bit floating-point number
`double`	64-bit floating-point number

Boolean Data Types

The Java Boolean data type mirrors the C/C++ convention of defining a constant named TRUE or FALSE for appropriate values. In Java, a `boolean` variable assumes a value of true or false. The boolean data type is a distinct data type; it is *not* a numeric data type and cannot be converted to one.

Java's flow of control statements (`if, while, switch`) require boolean targets; this differs from the C language where any expression that returns an integer can be used in these statements.

```
...
   // not evaluating a boolean
 if ( x/2 ) then
   System.out.println( "This won't work" );
// ______________________________

// ok, evaluating a boolean
if ( (x/2) == 10 ) then
 System.out.println( "This works" );
...
```

The first `if/then` statement shown above would not compile because a Java `boolean` value is not returned by the expression `x/2`. The second statement would compile because the comparison statement would return a Java boolean value. Note that in Java the "= =" represents an equality expression between two values; the "=" character is an assignment operator.

Arithmetic and Relational Operators

In keeping with the design goal of making Java familiar to C/C++ programmers, all C and C++ arithmetic and relational operators apply.

Java does not allow operator overloading, so the meaning of an operator is always clear. Java has, however, overloaded the "+" operator for string concatenation and has added the ">>>" operator to indicate an unsigned (logical) right shift.

Arrays

In Java, arrays are language objects. Arrays can be allocated for any data type including objects, and arrays of arrays can be allocated to create multi-dimensional arrays. Access to elements of an array is performed with array indexing as in C or C++, but in Java array references are validated at runtime. A language exception is generated if an array reference is outside of the bounds of an array at runtime.

Strings

Java strings are language objects of the `String` and `StringBuffer` class, with the `String` class for read-only objects and the `StringBuffer` class for strings that can be modified. `String` concatenation can be performed with the "+" operator, and a certain amount of sensible type conversion can be used to convert numbers to string characters, as shown in the following code fragment.

```
...
StringBuffer DTString = "The answer is ";
int num = 42;
DTString = DTString + num;
System.out.println( DTString );
...
```

This code fragment would output "The answer is 42," indicating that the integer value "42" was converted to a `String` and concatenated onto the end of the `String` variable `DTString`.

Labels

The Java language, for a host of reasons that have probably been memorized by most Programming 101 students, has no `goto` statement. The `goto` statement was often used in the C language to overcome the difficulty of breaking out of nested loops. The Java language eliminates this difficulty by extending the capabilities of the `continue` and `break` statements.

In the C language, the `continue` statement can continue only to the immediate enclosing block. The Java language supplies expanded loop branching capabilities with the use of *labels* that are recognized by the `continue` and `break` statements. Labels can be placed on loop or switch constructs and then the `break` or `continue` keyword can be used either to exit the code block or to continue at the start of the code block.

Memory Management in Java

Much time and effort was expended by the programmer to manage memory in C and C++. Java eliminates the need to manage memory by providing automatic garbage collection. The Java programmer needs only to assign a null reference to an object, or let the object go out of scope. The Java virtual machine then performs garbage collection with its low-priority garbage collection thread.

All variables in Java are subject to containership—they are member variables of an object. There are, therefore, no global or module scope variables in existence and no need to manage these global heap references. Paying proper attention to object management and releasing objects when they are no longer needed will lead to effective memory management in Java.

Exception Handling

Errors in Java are trapped using a form of exception handling similar to that of C++. In Java, an exception is an instance of a class derived from `Throwable`. A program exception can be either an *error* or an *exception*. An exception can be either an `IOException` or a `RuntimeException`. An error condition leads to program termination, but an exception can be caught and managed.

Exceptions can be managed in Java code with the `throw` and `catch` statements. JDBC methods throw an `SQLException`. This exception can be caught and managed through a combination of `try` code blocks followed by `catch` exception code blocks that manage the exception being caught. A series of `catch` blocks can be used to catch a variety of exception errors. The following code fragment demonstrates this concept.

```
...
  try {
     Statement stmt = conn.createStatement();
     ResultSet rs = stmt.executeQuery(
                  "select * from customers" );
     processResults( rs );
   }
   catch ( SQLException ex ) {
          System.out.println( "Error on select." );
          System.out.println (
                 "\n*** SQLException caught ***\n");
          while (ex != null) {
          System.out.println ("SQLState: " +
               ex.getSQLState ());
          System.out.println ("Message:  " +
               ex.getMessage ());
          System.out.println ("Vendor:   " +
               ex.getErrorCode ());
          ex = ex.getNextException ();
          System.out.println ("");
        }
      ex.printStack.Trace();
   }
...
```

In this code example, a `try` code block is used to connect to a database and retrieve a row of data. Any `SQLExceptions` generated by the JDBC method calls made in this code block are caught by the `catch` code block following the `try` code block within the same class. The `catch` code block demonstrates the use of a `while` loop to iterate through what could potentially be more than one exception that has been thrown.

C and C++ Features Not Present in Java

The Java language has eliminated a number of features from the C and C++ language because they were not considered safe or because they were redundant. The C and C++ programmer familiar with these features needs to be aware of their absence.

typedefs, defines, and Pre-processor Support

Considered a source of confusion by Java developers, the pre-processor support of the C language has been eliminated from the Java language. Java developers felt that it was difficult to understand the context of a C language program because of the program-specific alterations to syntax supported by pre-processor changes. By doing away with these facilities, much of this confusion has been eliminated.

It is worth noting that the Java language does not supply the oft-used C language `#include` directive. But this does not mean that all pertinent code for an application must be included in a single source file. A Java `package` (which represents a group of classes) is automatically *included* into a Java source file simply by reference. The source code reference in the Java program could include the full name for the package as follows.

```
java.util.Date thisDate = new java.util.Date();
```

This indicates to the Java compiler that it must search for a directory hierarchy of `./java/util` and then for a file named `Date.class`. Use of the `import` directive allows the tedious naming of the class to be avoided, as shown in the following code fragment.

```
import java.util.Date;
Date ThisDate = new Date();
```

The `import` directive should not be confused with the C language `#include` statement; the similarity between these two compiler directives ends with the fact that both are compiler directives. The C language `#include` statement inserts code into a source code module. The Java `import` directive allows naming references for a class to be shortened in the source code and does not direct Java to read an additional source code file. (Without the `import` directive, the Java compiler *includes* the class file implicitly simply because the class was referenced in the source code file.)

With this mechanism, Java does force the programmer into a storage directory hierarchy for source code, but these hierarchies are probably not very different from the C language storage hierarchies and are at least standardized by this Java requirement.

Structures and Unions

Structures and unions have been eliminated from Java. These complex types have been eliminated in the belief that the same effect can be achieved by creating classes with instance variables. The creation of classes further extends the features of structures and unions by allowing the instance variables to be declared public or private, thus allowing these details to be hidden or exposed as needed.

Functions

Functions have been eliminated from Java so that the language is a purely object-oriented language. In lieu of using functions, the more correct object-oriented use of classes and methods is required.

Multiple Inheritance

Multiple inheritance was considered a source of problems in C++. This has been eliminated from the Java language and the feature of *interfaces* has been created. An interface is a definition of a set of methods that one or more objects may implement. Interfaces declare only methods and constants; no variables are declared in interfaces.

Operator Overloading

Operator overloading has been eliminated from Java to avoid confusion. The correct use of class and method declaration can achieve the same effect.

Automatic Coercion

No automatic coercion occurs in the Java language. Code that would assign a variable to another variable and result in a loss of precision results in a compiler error. The programmer would have to re-write the code with an explicit cast that indicates that coercion should take place or alter the assigned type so that no loss of precision would occur.

Pointers

Pointers have long been considered some of the "guns and knives" available to C and C++ programmers. They have been eliminated from the Java language for safety. The only element resembling a pointer in Java is an object reference and its manipulation is tightly controlled in the language.

This chapter provided a brief overview of Java language features pertinent to JDBC programmers. It is also intended to provide a quick overview of the Java language and its features for those who have had only moderate exposure to the language.

For the C/C++ programmer, the Java language syntax will be familiar. But, the C/C++ programmer must be aware of the differences between Java and C/C++ and must program accordingly. These language differences have been highlighted in this chapter. Keep the following points in mind concerning Java.

- *Java data types*—basic data types are provided; data types are consistent over platforms.
- *Java Objects*—all variables *contained* in Objects and Objects are passed by reference.
- *Java Strings* —can be assigned values during declaration and can grow dynamically.
- *Java memory management*—memory management is performed automatically in Java by a low-priority garbage collection thread.
- *Java exception handling*—JDBC invocations throw exceptions that must handled.
- *Java garbage collection*—garbage collection is scheduled automatically in Java when an object reference is null.

- *Java pointers*—Java has no pointers; object variables represent references but memory management is under strict control of the Java virtual machine.

Coming Up

In the following chapters the JDBC interface is discussed in increasing detail through a series of examples. A tutorial section will provide these examples, starting with a simple example of creating a database connection and retrieving data and proceeding with more examples to demonstrate the use of JDBC cursors, positioned updates, and using prepared statements. More complex examples demonstrate the use of a `ResultSet` array to provide the functionality of a *scroll cursor*.

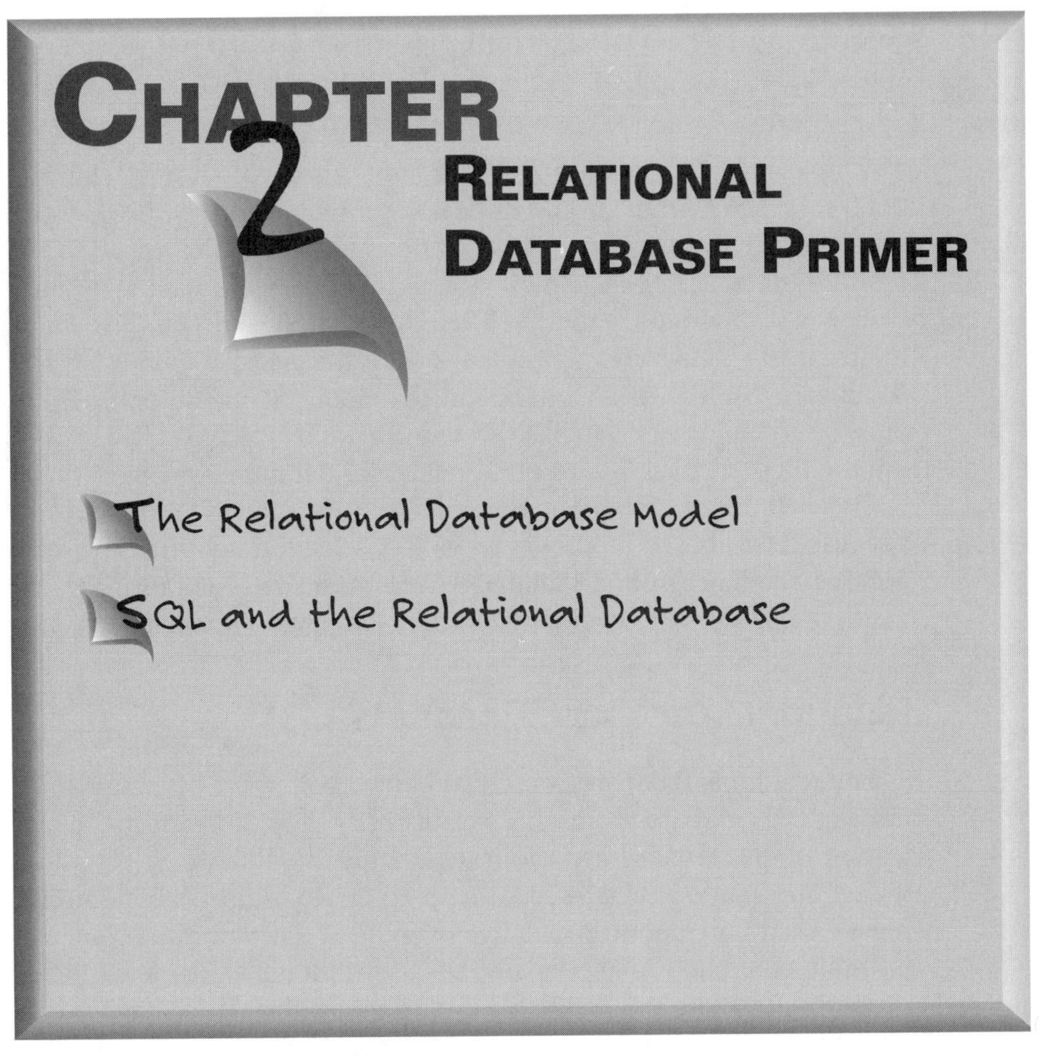

The JDBC API provides an interface to a relational database; some knowledge of relational databases is therefore required to use JDBC. And because the language of relational databases is SQL, understanding this language is also an integral part of using JDBC. A basic understanding of these two components, relational database terminology and SQL, is a solid foundation for JDBC application development.

This chapter will provide a brief overview of these topics. If you are already familiar with relational databases and SQL, then this material can be skipped. If, however, you, have had only limited exposure to relational databases, then this material will help you understand relational database terminology and the basics of SQL.

History of the Relational Database

The relational database model had its theoretical start in the late 1960's. In 1968, while at an IBM research institution, Dr. E. F. Codd began researching the concept of applying mathematical rigor to the world of database management systems. Codd's ideas were later published in a landmark paper, "A Relational Model of Data for Large Shared Data Banks" (Communications of the ACM, Volume 13, No. 6, June 1970). The ideas laid out in this paper had a sweeping influence on the nature of database systems for years to come. Today, they are the theoretical standard of all relational database systems.

The relational database was favored in academic institutions because it was based on provable mathematical foundations. This differentiated the relational database from other database formats and made the process of developing a query language somewhat easier.

Relational Database Concepts

The relational database is conceptually a collection of tables. Each table in the database represents a data *entity*, and each entity is a collection of data *attributes*. An entity is a distinguishable object about which information is to be recorded. An entity is any object (people, place, or thing) about which we want to record information. An example of such an object is a car. An attribute is a characteristic or property associated with the distinguishable object. An example of attributes for a car entity would be the color of the car, the make of the car, the size of the engine, and the age of the car.

Entities, Attributes, and Relationships

The process of designing a relational database involves first identifying the entities (the objects) to be modeled. In the design of a system to take catalog orders, for example, the entities would be objects such as a catalog item, an order for an item or items, the manufacturer of an item, and the customer who purchased an item. The attributes for these entities would be the characteristics—the features of the entity or object. In the case of a catalog item, characteristics would be a description of the item, the cost of the item, the weight of the item, the size of the item, and the manufacturer of the item. The characteristics of another entity, such as the customer, would be the name of the customer and the address of the customer with the zip code. And the order would contain characteristics or attributes for the customer making the order, the item or items being ordered, and the cost of the order.

Entities can have *relationships*. Relationships are the connections between the objects being modeled. An order does not exist in its environment alone. There are customers who have made the order and there are items on the order that represent items the customer has purchased. The customer and item entities are therefore related to the order entity.

Relationships have several forms: *one-to-one*, *one-to-many*, and *many-to-many*. A *one-to-one* relationship indicates that for a particular entity there is one and only one related entity. An example of a one-to-one relationship would be the relationship between a manufacturer and an item. For any particular item record, there is one and only one manufacturer record. (An alternative design could allow multiple manufacturers for an item, but for our purposes, a different manufacturer would entail a different item.)

A *one-to-many* relationship indicates that for a given entity record there are one or more than one related entity records. This would be the case for the orders entity and the line items on the order. For every order record, there could be multiple items purchased and each of these items would be represented by line item records.

A *many-to-many* relationship indicates that for the multiple records in a given entity, there are one or more than one records in a related entity. An example of a many-to-many relationship is the relationship between cars and family members. A single family member can own more than one car and a single car can be owned by more than one family member.

A relational database is often diagrammed using an *entity-relationship diagram* (ERD) as shown in Figure 2.1; these diagrams provide a series of specialized lines, boxes, and symbols to represent the relationships between entities.

Normalization

Once the attributes and entities of the database have been identified, there is usually a process of *normalization* that the database developer must complete. Normalization generally involves the elimination of

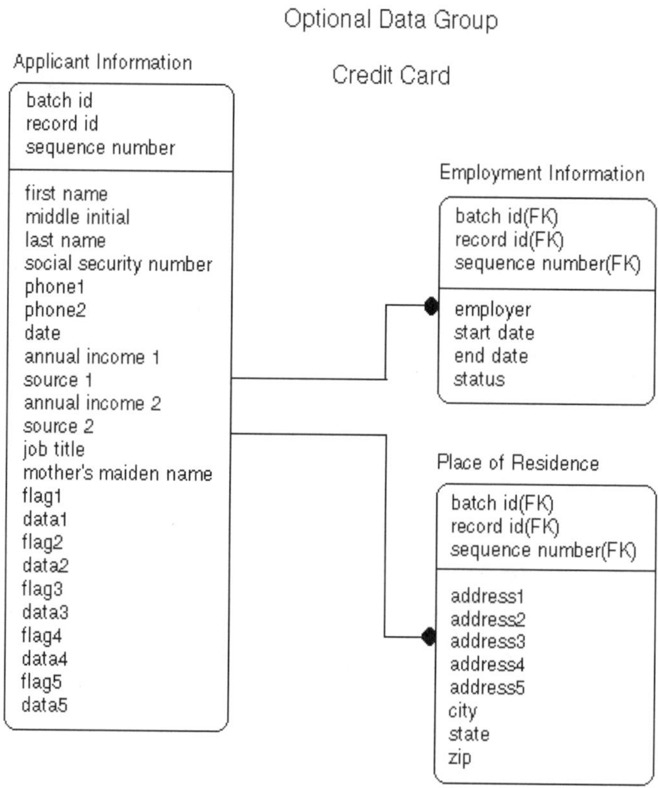

Figure 2.1: *Sample ERD*

repeating attributes in an entity and the identification of attributes that belong in a particular entity and attributes that belong elsewhere. The database developer must usually go through several iterations of review and modification before the proper level of normalization has been achieved.

Several levels of normalization have been defined by Dr. Codd and other academics. Each level provides for examination and review of the entity and its attributes and a determination of what belongs and does not belong to that entity. The most common level of normalization is known as *third-normal form* though a *fifth-normal form* has been defined.

The normalization of a relational database is an important part of the database design process. Normalization reduces data redundancy and thus reduces the amount of data storage required for the data. A normalized design also simplifies the process of making the inevitable modifications required of most databases.

Creating the Database Tables

At the end of the design process, the identified entities become the *tables* of the database and the identified attributes become the *columns* of the tables. These tables and columns are then manipulated using SQL. Each table can contain one or more rows of data.

For each row in the table, a column or a collection of columns should uniquely identify the row. This unique identifier is considered the *primary key*. If this unique identifier is contained in another table, then it would represent the *foreign key* in that table. Figure 2.2 illustrates this concept.

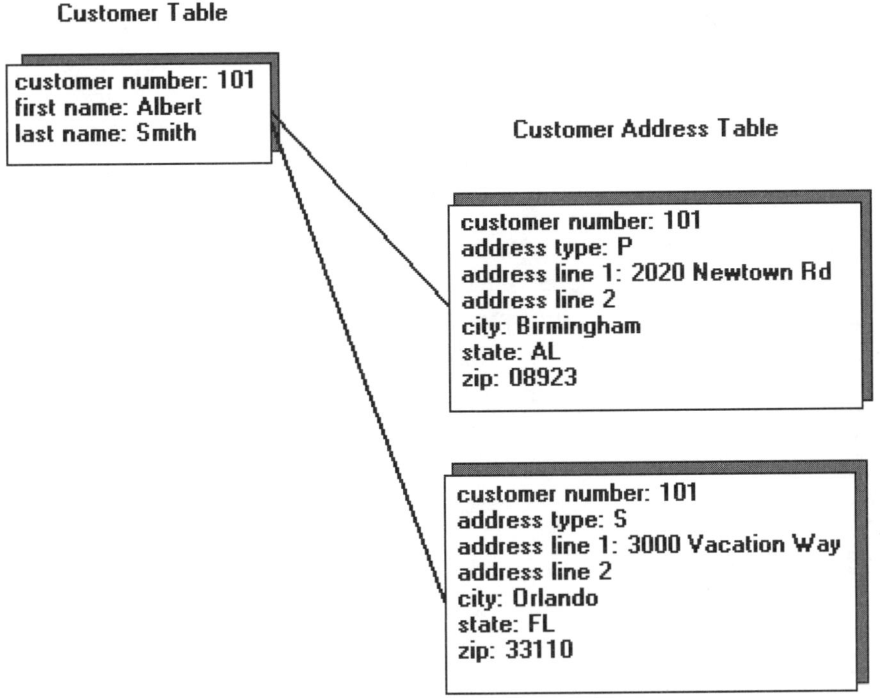

Figure 2.2: *Primary key/foreign key relationship*

Customer Table
Customer number (primary key)
customer first name
customer last name

Customer Address Table
customer number (primary key, foreign key)
address type (primary key)
address line 1
address line 2
city
state

In this example, the primary key for the customer table is the 'customer number'. This number uniquely identifies each row in this table. For the related 'customer address' table, the 'customer number' alone is a foreign key because this number refers to a row in the customer table. Because this example allows for the customer to have more than one address (a primary and secondary residence), the customer number in the customer address table does not uniquely identify each row in this table. If the customer had multiple addresses, with just the customer number as a key, there would be no way to identify which address was the primary residence and which address was the secondary residence.

Another key column is needed to create a primary key for the customer address table; this is the reason for the 'address type' column. This column is a single character that represents the type of customer address being examined. This column would be "P" for primary residence and "S" for secondary residence. This column combined with the customer number column would uniquely identify each row in the customer address table.

Relational Database Terminology

The relational database is firmly planted on the theoretical foundation of relational algebra, thus the terminology of that discipline has found its way into the relational database industry. Some of the common terms and their meanings are explained in the following sections.

RELATION

The term *relation* is a mathematical term for a *table.* A database with three tables would therefore be a database with three relations. The terms *relation* and *table* are often used interchangeably.

DOMAIN

A *domain* is often used to describe a pool of values that are appropriate for an attribute (or column). For example, a single character column that stores the response to a true or false question with a valid answer of 'T' or 'F' would have a domain of 'T' or 'F'. A column that held the years-of-employment for a company that had been in existence for 12 years would have a domain of integer values in the range of 1 to 12 inclusive.

JOINS

In technical terms, a *join* builds a relation from two specified relations. To extract rows from two related tables having a corresponding primary key-foreign key relationship is to *join* the two tables.

Using the SQL `select` statement (which is different than the relational algebra SELECT and provides a number of the relational set operations in a single statement), a join between two tables with no 'join criteria' results in the Cartesian product of the two tables: Every row in table A is joined with every row in table B. This is usually not the desired result, so a join condition expressing an equality condition between key columns of joined tables is usually part of a valid `select` statement.

TUPLES

The term *tuple* is roughly equivalent to a record, but because of the sometimes fuzzy definition of a record in the early days of database management systems, the term tuple was used to apply to a specific *flat record instance.* In the case where a join of multiple tables retrieves specific columns from each table, the result is referred to in relational database terminology as a *tuple* (though it is very likely a programmer would refer to this result as a *record* regardless of academic opinion).

Unions

The union of two relations A and B is the set of all tuples in A, all tuples in B, or both. By default, duplicate rows are eliminated from the result. A '`union all`' operation is sometimes available to preserve duplicate rows in the result. Depending on how the statement is written, the results of a `union` statement can often be duplicated with a SQL `select` statement.

Master-Detail Relationships

A *master-detail* relationship exists when a record in one table relates to several records in another table (see Figure 2.3). Such is the case with an order where a single record contains the order information such as the order number and the order date, and a related table stores the order items with each item being stored as a separate

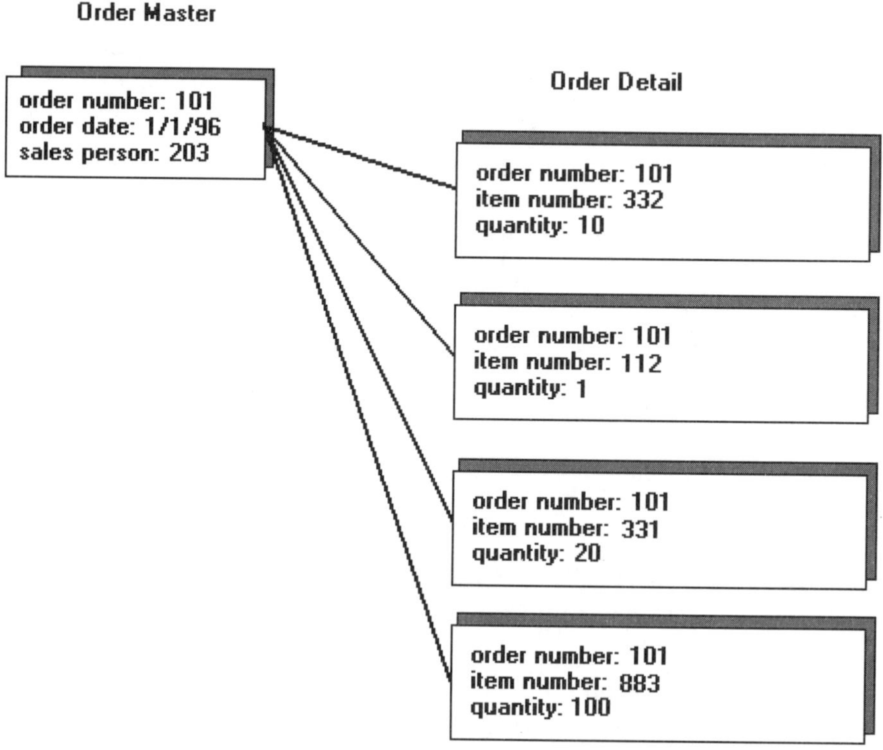

Figure 2.3: *Master-detail relationship*

record. With this example, the order information record would be referred to as the *master* (or *header*) record and the order item records would be referred to as the *detail* records. This is also sometimes referred to as a *parent-child* relationship, with the master record being the *parent* record and the detail records being the *child* records. (The term *record* is used here in lieu of *tuple* because this is the most common usage of these terms.)

Structured Query Language

The language of choice for the relational database is the Structured Query Language, usually referred to as SQL. Originally spelled SEQUEL and still pronounced that way by many, the SQL language was developed by IBM at their San Jose, California research facility. Now widely accepted by the relational database industry, it is essentially the *lingua franca* of relational databases.

One of the strengths of SQL is that it expresses set logic clearly with an English-like syntax. This has enabled relational database users to quickly learn the language. With the knowledge of a few keywords and clauses, a user can quickly learn to access data in a SQL database. And data retrieval and formatting that would require a lengthy program be written in other databases can often be expressed in a single SQL statement. SQL statements are divided into two types: *data definition language* (DDL) statements and *data manipulation language* (DML) statements (see Figure 2.4). The DDL statements include schema definition statements such as `create database`, `create table`, and `create view`. These statements create database tables and allow the creation of views on that data. The DML statements include the `select`, `update`, and `delete` statements used for querying and updating the database.

Using JDBC, DDL statements are executed using the `executeUpdate` method in both the `Statement` and `PreparedStatement` classes. SQL DML statements are executed using both the `executeQuery` method and the `executeUpdate` statements. The `executeQuery` method is used for statements that return values such as the `select` statement. The `executeUpdate` statement is used for statements that do not return values, such as `update` statements and DDL statements (`create table`, `create index`).

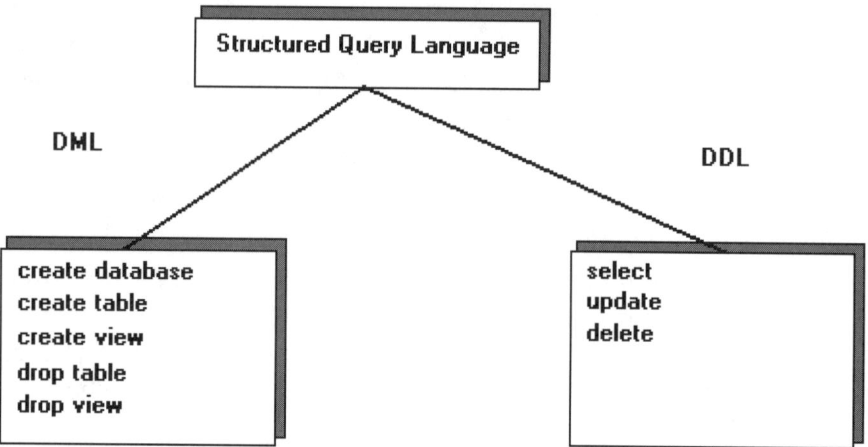

Figure 2.4: *Structured Query Language Statement Types*

Additional SQL statements exist for manipulation of the database. Many of these statements are database-vendor-specific. These statements perform additional functions such as changing the isolation level, the unloading and loading of data from external data sources, the definition of constraints, and the creation and execution of stored procedures.

Basic SQL Statements

There are several core SQL statements that provide the bulk of the functionality of SQL. These statements are `select`, `update`, and `delete`. The `where` clause, which provides filter criteria to specify the specific tuples to extract or update and table join criteria, is a very important clause shared by these statements. These statements are explained in more detail in the following sections.

The Select Statement

The SQL `select` statement is the workhorse of the language. This statement is used to perform all queries for the database and is sometimes used in the `where` clause of the `update` statements to specify the rows to retrieve for update. The format for the `select` statement is as follows:

```
select  <column list>
from    <table list>
where   <filter criteria>
```

The select clause lists the columns that will be retrieved as part of the query. These column lists can sometimes contain expressions so that mathematical calculations can be made on columns. With this same functionality, several columns can be concatenated with other columns or with character string constants.

The from clause contains the list of tables from which the columns will be retrieved. Many versions of SQL support the ability to perform *outer* joins on the tables listed (retrieving partial joined rows even if the related row does not exist).

The optional where clause is used to express the filter and join criteria for the SQL statement being executed. This clause is shared by the query and update statements in SQL. The filter criteria is expressed as a series of Boolean expressions. An example of this statement follows.

```
select  orders.*, items.*
from    orders, items
where   orders.order_num = items.order_num
```

In this example, columns are selected from the orders table and the items table. This query effectively joins these two tables on the order_num column as specified in the where clause.

The Update Statement

The update statement updates rows in a table. Updates can only be performed on one table at a time. Filter criteria may be specified with the where clause using the same format as when this clause is used with other SQL statements with some minor restrictions. The where clause is optional, though without a where clause all rows in the table will be updated; this is not usually the desired behavior for an update statement. The format for the update statement is as follows:

```
update   <table name>
set      <column list>
where    <filter criteria>
```

An example of this statement follows.

```
udpate items
set    price = price * 1.1
where  cost > 10
```

This example updates the items in the `items` table where the price is greater than 10 dollars. It updates each record by increasing the `price` column by 10%.

The Delete Statement

The `delete` statement deletes specified rows from a table. The `delete` statement can only be performed on one table at a time. The `where` clause is optional, though without the `where` clause the `delete` statement will delete all rows in the table; this would have the effect of deleting all rows in the table from the database. If database logging is not in place, then there is most likely no means of undoing the delete statement without resorting to a backup. The format for the delete statement is as follows:

```
delete
from      <table name>
where     <filter criteria>
```

The following is an example of this statement.

```
delete
from   items
where order_num = 123456
```

This example deletes items from the orders table where the `order_num` is equal to '123456'.

SQL Standards

SQL has been standardized by the American National Standards Institute (ANSI). The original standard was issued in 1986 and the most current standard is 1992. This standard defines three programmatic interfaces: the *module language* interface, the *embedded SQL* interface and the *direct invocation* interface. These interfaces are described in more detail in the following sections.

Module Language

The module language interface allows procedures to be developed in compiled programs or modules. These procedures are invoked from traditional programming languages. Parameters are used to return values to the calling program.

Embedded SQL

This standard allows SQL statements to be embedded in the code for a traditional programming language. This specification allows embedded statements in languages such as C, COBOL, and Fortran.

Direct Invocation

Access using direct invocation is implementation-defined. This involves the direct entry of SQL and execution of SQL statements through some type of interface. The specific functionality of the interface is left to the developer.

Call Level Interface

A Call Level Interface (CLI) defines a set of function calls that provide access to a database. This interface provides function calls to control the database, determine the state of the database, and use SQL statements to query and update the database.

The CLI provides all of the functionality of an embedded SQL interface but with some added flexibility, especially in the area of dynamic data access. The CLI does not require the use of host variables as an embedded SQL interface does and is therefore a more familiar form of programming for a programmer familiar with a programming language. And the process of dynamic SQL requires the dynamic creation and traversal of internal data structures. This is difficult to express in an embedded SQL interface, but with a CLI native programming language structures can be used to store the dynamic information, allowing a more natural programming style to be used. Both ODBC and JDBC are CLI definitions. The ODBC CLI definition is based on the SQL Access Group CAE specification (1992) and X/Open CLI definition.

Transactions, Database Logging and Isolation Levels, and Concurrency

When working with a relational database, a series of updates may be made to a set of related tables. In order for database integrity to remain intact, all of these updates must succeed together. Should one of the update statements fail, a master record could exist without all corresponding detail records and the integrity of the database would be compromised.

This is the case when a customer order record is inserted into two tables: an order master table containing the order date, the amount of the order, the customer number and due date, and a series of order detail records containing the items the customer has ordered. This is illustrated in Figure 2.5.

With this example, an order master record is inserted and three corresponding order detail table records are inserted. Because transaction logging is in place, should one of the updates to the detail table fail, the entire transaction would be rolled back and the database would remain in a consistent state. But should one of the updates to the order detail table fail and transaction logging is not in place, then the order amount column in the order master record will not balance

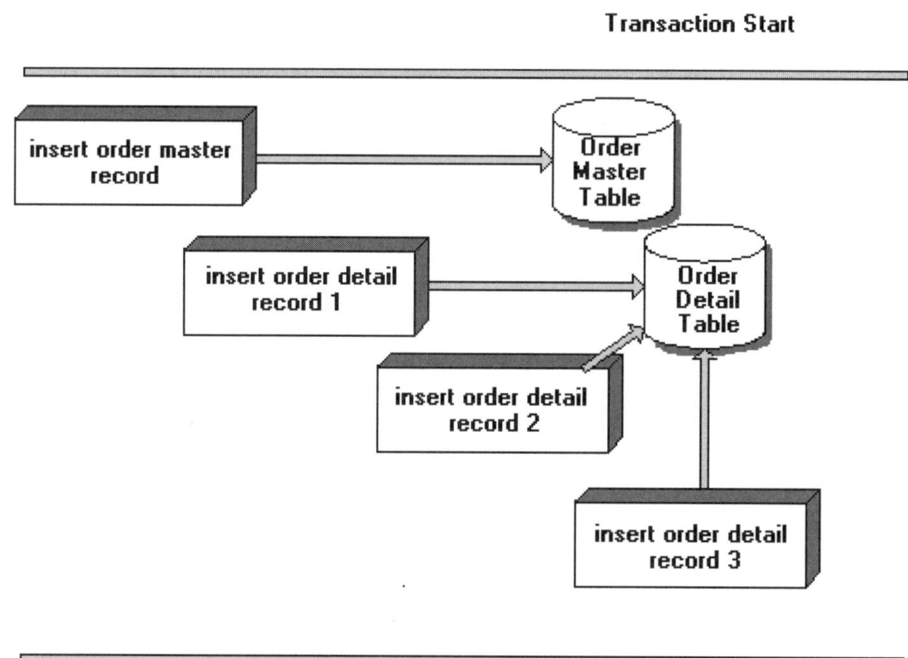

Figure 2.5: *Order entry in a transaction*

with the constituent detail records. This will leave the database in a corrupt state.

Using transaction logging can help alleviate this problem. With transaction logging, a series of updates can be treated as a single *transaction*; should one of the updates fail, all updates will fail. Thus the database integrity is preserved.

Transaction logging requires that the programmer identify what statements comprise the transaction. In the case of the order updates, the order master record update and the order items record updates are one transaction. The JDBC code for a transaction would be as follows.

```
...
try {

          Class.forName ("jdbc.odbc.JdbcOdbcDriver");

          String url = "jdbc:odbc:msaccessdb";

          Connection con = DriverManager.getConnection (
                                   url, "", "");
          // this method must be called with boolean false
          //  else JDBC commits each statement execution
          con.setAutoCommit( false );

          Statement stmt = con.createStatement();

          // begin the transaction
      con.commit();

      int n = 0;

      PreparedStatement prepStmt = con.prepareStatement(
         " insert into transtest values ( ?, 1, 'XXXXXXX' ) " );

      for ( n = 1; n < 20; n++ ) {
          prepStmt.setInt( 1, n );
          prepStmt.executeUpdate();
      }
```

```
        // if at this point, then transaction succeeded
        con.commit();
catch ( SQLException ex ) {
         System.out.println( "Error on update. Rolling back
transaction."  );
         con.rollback();
}
...
```

This example begins a JDBC transaction by issuing a 'commit' to the database. A statement is then prepared and a series of database updates are executed. If an error should occur, an exception would be thrown and the 'catch' code block would be executed. Within this code block, a database transaction rollback is executed. Because the 'catch' code block would only be executed in the event an error had occurred, this code effectively triggers a transaction rollback in the event of an error.

Isolation Levels and Concurrency

When using transaction logging, there are concurrency issues to be considered. Concurrency involves the use of a database by multiple users, by far the most common use of relational databases. When using transaction logging, there are situations where a record may have been updated in a SQL statement but the transaction has not been committed. This would be the case in the previous example where the first `order_detail` record had been inserted but not the second or third; a user reading the order at this point in time would be reading uncommitted records (if that was allowed) and would read an incomplete order.

Transaction *isolation levels* take such issues into account. Using isolation levels, programmers and database administrators can restrict the user's view into the database. A programmer can set an isolation level to a very unrestrictive level that allows any record to be read regardless of whether or not it has been committed. Or an isolation level can be set that only allows committed records to be read. Isolation levels are implementation-dependent—a number of different flavors of isolation levels are available from various database vendors. The code below demonstrates the call necessary to set the isolation level for a database using JDBC.

```
...
con.setAutoCommit( false );
con.setTransactionIsolation( Connection.TRANSACTION_READ_COMMITTED
);
...
```

This is not a trivial issue. The isolation level in effect can directly impact application results. Should an unrestrictive isolation level be in effect that allows incomplete transactions to be read, an application generating a report of active orders could produce an unbalanced report by reading incomplete transactions. Conversely, an application using a restrictive isolation level could be prohibited from reading critical records being accessed by a user who has not yet committed their transaction. (This could be an even more serious problem if the user fails to commit the record before their two-hour lunch.)

The issue is further complicated when developing applications that can potentially be run against different databases over the Internet. The application programmer must be aware of isolation levels and different flavors of transaction logging on the databases to be accessed. Different isolation levels and logging procedures could have an impact on the application.

The Informix database provides four levels of isolation: *dirty read*, *committed read*, *cursor stability*, and *repeatable read*. These isolation levels provide varying degrees of concurrency isolation from virtually unrestricted concurrency with *dirty-read* to very restrictive concurrency with *repeatable-read*. These isolation levels are explained in more detail in the following sections. Different vendors have different variations and terms for isolation levels, but the functionality and restrictions are similar. JDBC supports four levels of isolation mode. These modes and their correspondence to Informix database isolation modes are shown in Table 2.1.

Figure 2.6 illustrates each of these isolation levels.

Dirty Read Isolation

The *dirty read* isolation level provides zero isolation, so this effectively allows full concurrency. This isolation level allows retrieval of uncommitted rows. So a row that has been inserted or modified in a transaction can be retrieved before being committed to the database.

Table 2.1: *Four Levels of Isolation Mode*

JDBC Isolation Mode	Informix Mode	Description
TRANSACTION_NONE	n/a	Transactions are not supported.(Informix **does** allow a database to be created with no logging, but once logging is in place it cannot simply be turned off.)
TRANSACTION_READ_COMMITTED	Committed Read	Only reads on the current row are repeatable
TRANSACTION_READ_UNCOMMITTED	Dirty Read	Dirty reads are done
TRANSACTION_REPEATABLE_READ	Repeatable Read	Reads on all rows of a result are repeatable
TRANSACTION_SERIALIZABLE	Repeatable Read	Reads on all rows of a transaction are repeatable

Committed Read Isolation

This isolation level guarantees that every row retrieved has been committed to the database at the time of retrieval. No exclusive locks are acquired; one user can process a row while another user modifies the row.

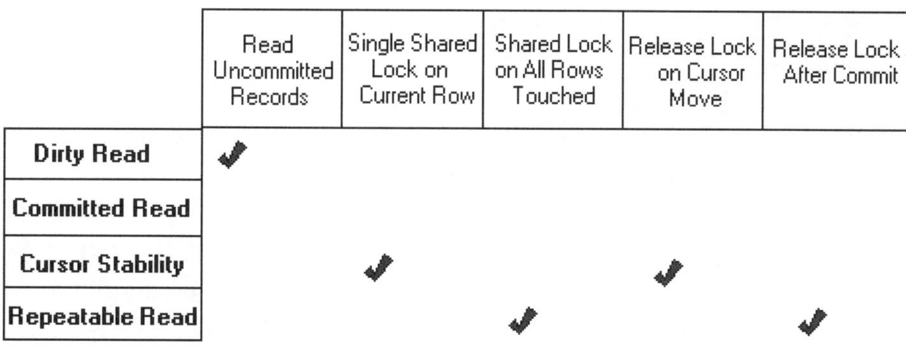

	Read Uncommitted Records	Single Shared Lock on Current Row	Shared Lock on All Rows Touched	Release Lock on Cursor Move	Release Lock After Commit
Dirty Read	✔				
Committed Read					
Cursor Stability		✔		✔	
Repeatable Read			✔		✔

Figure 2.6: *Isolation modes compared*

Cursor Stability

This isolation level acquires a shared lock on each row being examined, thus eliminating the possibility that another user can update the row being processed. A first user can read and update a row and second user can read and acquire a shared lock on the same row, but the exclusive lock needed for an update by the second user cannot be acquired until the first user releases the lock. When the first user moves to the next row, the lock is released.

Repeatable Read Isolation

This isolation level acquires a shared lock on every row *selected* during the transaction. Any row touched by a user in repeatable read isolation will be locked using a shared lock. Another user can read the row but will not be granted the exclusive lock needed to perform an update. The shared locks are released only when the row is committed or rolled back. This differs from committed read in that the entire selected set is locked by the user, not just the current row.

Choosing Isolation Levels

Generally, it is the purpose of the application that drives the decision on which isolation level to use. For report applications, a *dirty read* or *committed read* isolation level may be adequate. A report does not perform updates and would not need to acquire an exclusive lock on a row. The committed read isolation level would access only committed data and would therefore give only a consistent view of the database.

For an application that has to perform groups of updates, such as the data entry application for an order entry system, a cursor stability or repeatable read isolation level would be needed. The application would need to know that no other user has updated a row while they are updating the row, otherwise their transaction may be invalid. With an isolation level of *cursor stability*, a lock would be acquired as soon as the row to be modified is read. When the application was finished modifying the row, the update would be made, the next row accessed, and the lock would be released using the cursor stability isolation level. If a number of rows must be updated together, as is the case with most master detail relationships, then the *repeatable read* isolation level may be desirable.

There are tradeoffs in these choices. With the *repeatable read* isolation level, the application programmer can be confident that their transaction maintained database consistency. But there will be a corresponding loss of concurrency required to maintain this integrity. Other applications that need to update rows already updated by the *repeatable read* process will not be able to acquire the locks needed to update the row, even though their update may not affect the process using the *repeatable read* isolation level. For example, if a process started a transaction at the repeatable read isolation level, then updated a status record and proceeded to begin updating various rows, another application needing to update the same status record would not be able to proceed because it could not acquire the shared lock needed.

SQL Query Optimization

Modern relational databases provide the capability to determine the data access path at runtime. While most vendors provide some ability to store the access paths in the database, the most common mode of access determines the optimal access path at runtime using an *optimizer* (see Figure 2.7).

When a SQL statement is presented to the database, the database engine must first evaluate the statement for correct syntax. The statement is first parsed and the parameters in the statement are evaluated. For instance, a `select` statement must be evaluated to determine if the required clauses are present (the `select` and the `from` clause)

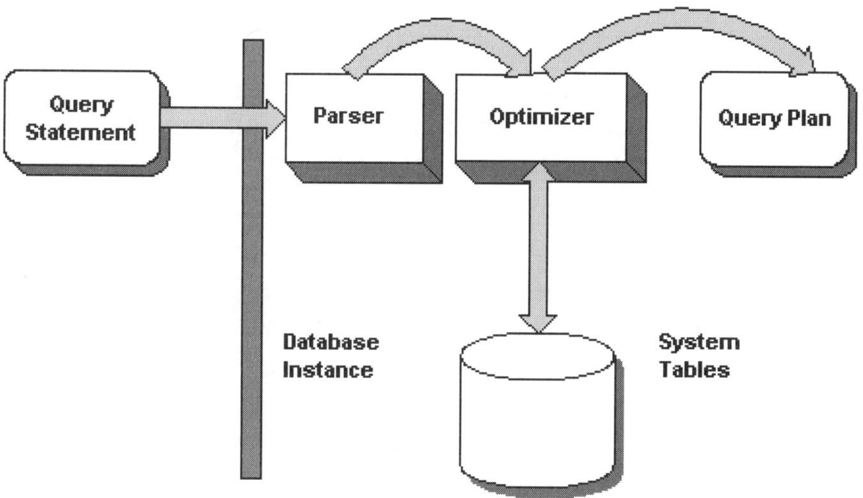

Figure 2.7: *Query optimization*

and the parameters or objects of those clauses are valid database objects.

Once the statement has been parsed, the access path is then determined by the optimizer. There has been a great amount of study performed on optimizers and and how to determine the most efficient query access paths. Some of the factors that are considered by the optimizer are the numbers of rows in the tables, the presence of indexes, the uniqueness of the indexed data, statistical skew of data, the efficiency of a sort or a hash-merge-join operation, and a variety of other factors.

The requirement for valid statistics on the data being queried has led to the expansion of system catalogs in many databases. The Informix-Online database currently contains a number of system tables that store statistical information on the data in the database. Extended SQL statements are available to update these tables using several options that impact the statistical methods used to compute the statistical data.

Dynamic SQL Execution

Most relational databases allow execution of dynamic SQL statements. These are SQL statements where some portion of the query is unknown until runtime. This could require the substitution of parameters or the complete construction of the query statement at runtime.

An example of this would be an ad-hoc report where the user chooses the columns to be returned in the report and the filter and sort criteria. In order for an application to process this report, it must be able to build the `select` statement at runtime. This can be accomplished fairly easily using JDBC; because the query to be executed is a string parameter, the application must merely concatenate an SQL `select` statement into the string parameter for the query. The following Java/JDBC code fragment demonstrates this concept.

```
...
     String tableName = "loadtest";
          if ( argv.length > 0 ) {
             tableName = argv[0];
            whereClause = argv[1];
          }

          String qs = "select * from " + tableName +
 " where " + whereClause;
          Statement stmt = con.createStatement();

          ResultSet rs = stmt.executeQuery( qs );
          ResultSetMetaData rsmd = rs.getMetaData();
     ...
```

In this example, the table name and the `where` clause criteria are not known until the application is run. These values are passed into the Java applications as runtime parameters. The `select` statement is then constructed using the table name and `where` clause parameters. A `Statement` object is created to execute the statement, the statement is executed and a `ResultSet` is returned. Because the application did not know about the composition of the query when it was written, it must discover this information using the metadata classes provided by JDBC. A `ResultSetMetaData` object is instantiated in this example to provide information needed by the application to process the dynamic query.

Summary

Relational databases are the target of JDBC applications; any application written using JDBC will be interacting with a relational database. An understanding of relational database concepts and terminology is a must for JDBC programmers. This chapter covered the basic concepts behind relational databases.

The language of choice for interacting with relational databases is SQL. Some of the more important components of SQL were covered and demonstrated in this chapter.

Important concepts covered in this chapter are as follows:

- Relational databases are databases based on the theoretical foundation of relational calculus. They allow mathematical rigor to be applied to the problem of data storage.
- A relational database is composed of entities and attributes and the relationships between the entities.
- Normalization is the process of reducing redundancy and clarifying the information presented in a relational database.
- A master-detail relationship is comprised of a single master record and, in another database table, multiple related detail records. This is also referred to as a parent-child relationship.
- The SQL language is composed of DDL (Data Definition Language) and DML (Data Manipulation Language) statements.
- The `select` statement is one of the more commonly used SQL statements. It selects records to retrieve data from a database.
- The `where` clause is used to define filter and join criteria for a selection set.
- Transactions allow multiple SQL DML statements to be treated as one; should any single statement in a set of statements fail, the entire set of statements will be rolled back or eliminated from the database, thus preserving the integrity of the database.

Coming Up

The next chapter begins the tutorial section of the book. The tutorials demonstrate the process of programming JDBC applications through the presentation of several code examples. Examples are provided for simple JDBC applications to demonstrate the process of connecting to a database and retrieving data. More complex examples then demonstrate using prepared SQL statements, using a positioned cursor for updates, using transactions with JDBC, and the use of metadata to provide information about the database or a result set. Later examples cover the use of JDBC with applets.

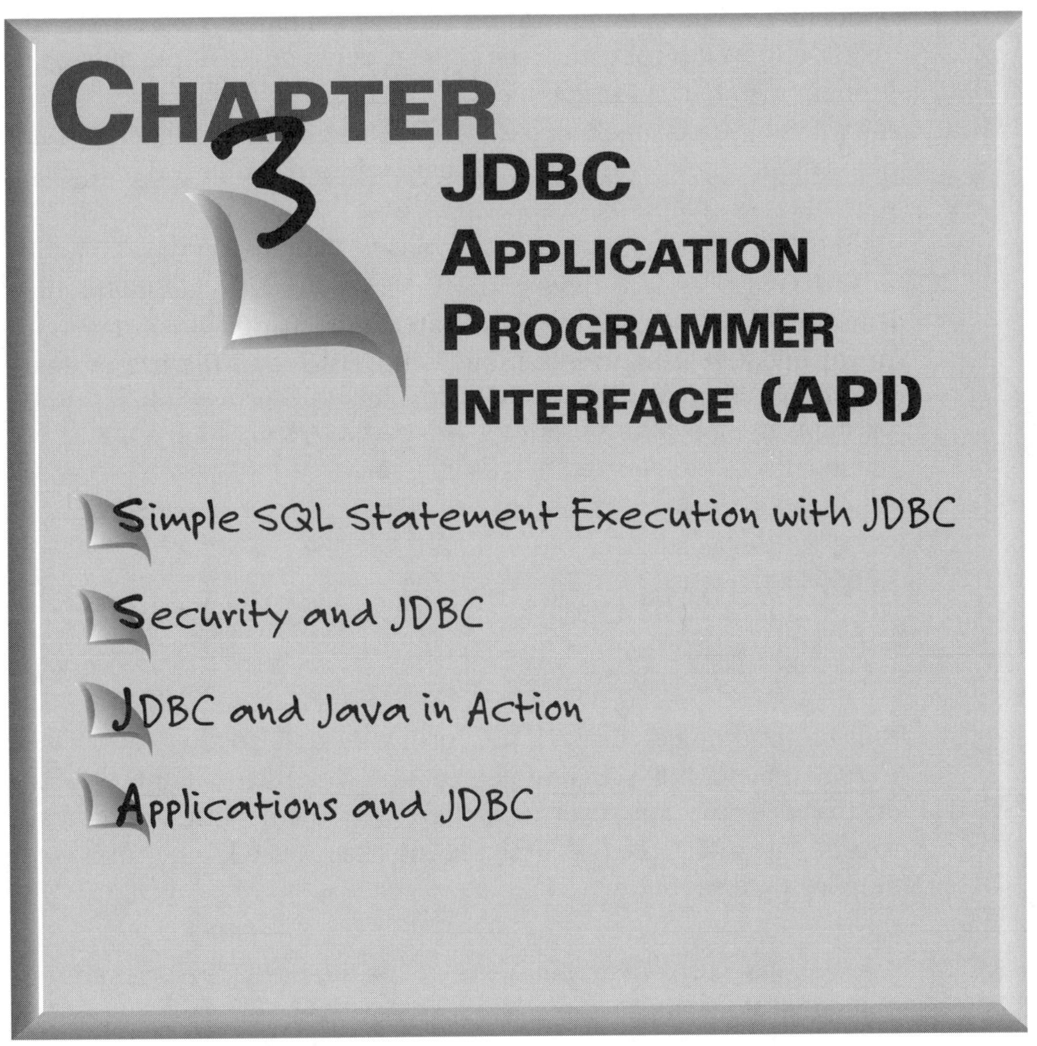

Chapter 3 JDBC Application Programmer Interface (API)

- Simple SQL Statement Execution with JDBC
- Security and JDBC
- JDBC and Java in Action
- Applications and JDBC

This chapter provides an introduction to the JDBC API. It provides an overview of JDBC and, by using a simple application, demonstrates the steps necessary to create and execute a SQL statement with JDBC. The JDBC classes involved in executing this statement are the most commonly used JDBC classes. To help you become more familiar with these classes and their methods, this chapter provides an overview of each of these classes.

One of the most common development architectures in use today is the client-server architecture. This is a two-tiered development architecture with the client being the first tier and the database server being the second tier. With the development of the Internet and object-oriented remote communication facilities such as Java's RMI, the ability to develop robust three-tier or n-tiered applications is quickly becoming a reality. These issues are discussed in this chapter.

To move data from a database via JDBC to a Java application, some data type mapping from the SQL data types to the Java data types is required. This mapping is covered in this chapter.

Transactions allow you to group sets of database updates together as one. They are an important part of database programming. The JDBC implementation of transactions is covered in this chapter.

Cursors provide a pointer to the set of data returned by an SQL statement that has been executed. Java provides serial cursors through an object representing the results returned by the query. These cursors are covered in this chapter.

SQL Statement Execution with JDBC

A Java programmer using JDBC primarily uses four classes. These classes enable the programmer to load a driver, connect to the database, create and execute a SQL statement, and examine the results. The interfaces that describe the classes used to perform these functions are as follows:

- `java.sql.DriverManager`—loads the JDBC driver and manages the database connection
- `java.sql.Connection`—connects to the database
- `java.sql.Statement`—manages an SQL statement on a connection
- `java.sql.ResultSet`—allows access to the results of an executed statement

A simple statement execution with Java would proceed as follows: a JDBC driver is loaded; a database connection is created from the driver; a statement is created from the connection; a SQL statement is executed using the statement and a result set returned; and the result set is used to retrieve additional rows and examine the data (see Figure 3.1). The following code demonstrates this sequence of calls.

DriverManager → JDBC Driver → Connection → Statement → ResultSet

Figure 3.1: *JDBC class relationships*

```
 try {
// load the JDBC driver
Class.forName ("jdbc.odbc.JdbcOdbcDriver");

String url = "jdbc:odbc:msaccessdb";

// connect to the URL and return a Connection object
Connection con = DriverManager.getConnection (
                                url, "", "");
// create a SQL statement
String qs = "select * from loadtest";
Statement stmt = con.createStatement();

// execute the SQL statement and return a
// ResultSet with results
ResultSet rs = stmt.executeQuery( qs );

// step through results in the ResultSet
boolean more = rs.next();
 while ( more  ) {

System.out.println( "Col1: " + rs.getInt( "col1" ) );
                more = rs.next();


  }
}
```

In this code fragment, a database driver is first loaded using the `Class.forName` method. This loads the JDBC-ODBC bridge driver and returns a reference to a `Class` object (which is ignored in this code). A URL for the database is then specified. The URL is composed of the character constant "jdbc," a subprotocol, and subname, as follows:

```
jdbc:<subprotocol>:<subname>
```

The *subprotocol* identifies a database connectivity mechanism that a number of drivers may support. The contents of the *subname* are dependent on the subprotocol. If a network address is to be used as part of the subname, then the naming convention should follow that of standard URL names with the subname named

```
//hostname:port/subsubname
```

Using this scheme, the URL for a local Microsoft Access database would be

```
jdbc:odbc:msaccessdb
```

In this example, the subprotocol is ODBC for an ODBC driver and `msaccessdb` is the subname; in this case, it represents the data source name for the Microsoft Access database.

Once the driver manager has been loaded, a `Connection` object is instantiated. The `Connection` class contains methods to control the database connection. From this object, objects can be instantiated to manage the SQL statements that are to be executed against the database. In this example, the `createStatement` method in the `Connection` class is then used to create a `Statement` object.

The statement object allows the execution of SQL statements. Different methods are used to execute queries (`executeQuery`), updates (`executeUpdates`), and queries with parameters (`executePrepared`). When statements are executed that will return a series of results (such as an SQL `select` statement), a `ResultSet` object is returned to represent the series of rows and columns within the rows. This example shows the execution of the `executeQuery` method of the `Statement` class and the subsequent execution of the `next` method of the `ResultSet` class to obtain data for each of the rows returned.

The commonly used classes identified and demonstrated in this code are an important part of using JDBC. These classes are used consistently throughout JDBC applications. Their usage is explained in more detail in the sections that follow.

DriverManager Class

The `DriverManager` class provides access to the JDBC facilities. The relationship between the `DriverManager` class, the `Connection`, `Statement/PreparedStatement`, and `ResultSet` classes is shown in Figure 3.2.

When instantiated, the `DriverManager` object uses the system `jdbc.drivers` property to obtain a list of class names for the driver classes. The `DriverManager` attempts to load each of these driver classes.

Once the appropriate driver or drivers has been loaded, the `DriverManager` object then manages the connections using that JDBC driver. The `DriverManager getConnection` method will return a `Connection` object, which is then used to instantiate `Statement` objects that produce `Resultset` objects when the `Statement` is executed. A given `DriverManager` can manage multiple connections, and multiple connections can support multiple statements, as shown in Figure 3.2. The most common call to `DriverManager` is to the `getConnection` method, as follows.

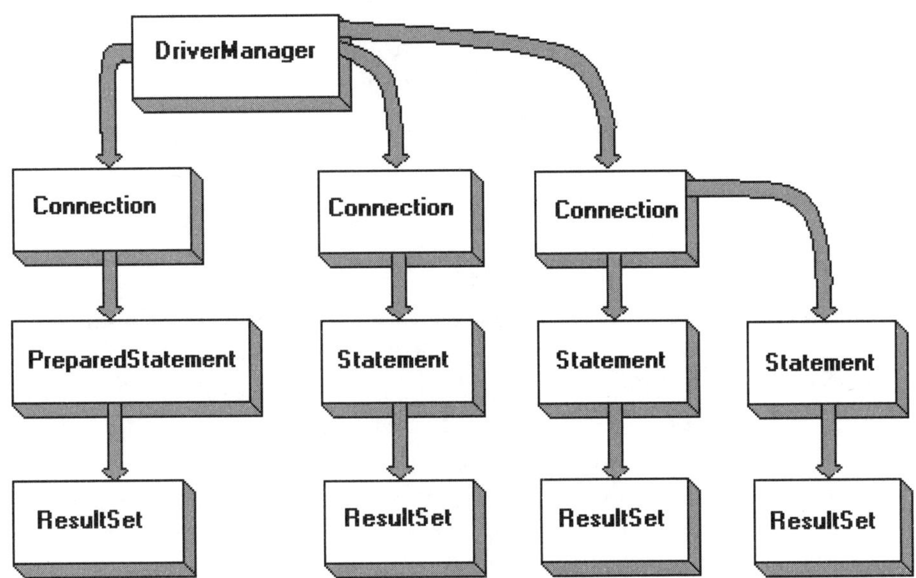

Figure 3.2: *Supporting multiple connections and statements with JDBC*

```
...
// connect to the URL and return a Connection object
Connection con = DriverManager.getConnection (
                                    url, "", "");
...
```

In this code fragment, the DriverManager getConnection method is called to create a Connection object. The getConnection method can be called with arguments for the database URL for the connection, the password, and the user name. Other variations of this method accept different parameters.

A number of methods are available in the DriverManager class to manage drivers. These methods register and de-register the driver, direct logging output, and set login timeout parameters. See Table 3.1 for a description of these methods.

The java.sql.Connection Class

An object of the Java Connection class represents a session with a database. Using a Connection object as a parameter, a Statement object can be created. This Statement object is then used to execute SQL statements and return a set of results.

A Connection can provide information about the tables in the database, the supported SQL grammar, the stored procedures available, and the general capabilities of the database connection using the getMetaData method.

Note that a connection is in AutoCommit mode by default. A transaction *commit* in autocommit mode automatically closes all PreparedStatement, CallableStatement, and ResultSet (but not Statement) objects. With AutoCommit set, each SQL statement executed is automatically committed to the database. In order to group a set of transactions together, the AutoCommit mode must be set off (using the setAutoCommit method) and the commit method must be used at the point that the transaction should be committed (or rolled-back) to the database. Methods are available to determine and set the AutoCommit state for the connection.

Table 3.1: *DriverManager Class Methods*

Method	Description
`getConnection(String url, java.util.Properties info)`	Attempts to establish a database connection to the given URL
`getDriver( String url )`	Attempts to locate a driver that understands the given URL
`registerDriver( java.sql.Driver driver )`	A newly loaded driver should make this call to register with the `DriverManager`
`deregisterDriver( Driver driver )`	Drops a driver from the `DriverManager`'s list
`getDrivers()`	Returns an enumeration of all the currently loaded JDBC drivers
`setLoginTimeout(int seconds)`	Sets the maximum time in seconds that all drivers must wait when attempting to login to a database
`getLoginTimeout()`	Gets the maximum time in seconds that all drivers can wait when attempting to login to a database
`setLogStream( java.io.PrintStream out )`	Sets the logging/tracing `PrintStream` that is used by all drivers and the `DriverManager`
`getLogStream()`	Gets the logging/tracing `PrintStream` that is used by the `DriverManager` and all drivers

Table 3.2 provides a description of the methods in this class. All methods throw an `SQLException`.

Table 3.2: *Connection Class Methods*

Method	Description
`createStatement()`	Creates and returns a new `Statement` object
`prepareStatement ( String sql )`	Pre-compiles a SQL statement and stores the statement for later reference in the `preparedStatement` object
`prepareCall ( String sql )`	Creates an object for calling a stored procedure. The `CallableStatement` class provides methods for managing IN and OUT parameters.
`NativeSQL( String SQL )`	Converts JDBC SQL grammar into the database system's native SQL
`setAutoCommit( boolean autoCommit )`	Allows the default `autoCommit` mode of enabled to be disabled.
`GetAutoCommit()`	Retrieves the current state of the `autoCommit` mode
Method	**Description**
`commit()`	Commits all changes made since the previous commit/roll-back and releases any database locks held by the `Connection`
`rollback()`	Rollback any changes made since the previous commit/roll-back and releases any locks held by the `Connection`

continued

`close()`	Causes an immediate release of a `Connection`'s database and JDBC resources
`isclosed()`	Returns TRUE if the connection is closed and FALSE if the connection is still open

The java.sql.Statement Class

The Java `Statement` class is used to execute static SQL statements and to obtain the results from those statements. Only one `ResultSet` per `Statement` object can be opened at one time; if multiple statements are to be used at the same time, then multiple `Statement` objects must be instantiated and used.

The `Statement` class is best used for an SQL statement that is executed only once and its results iterated through.

```
...
Statement stmt = conn.createStatement();
ResultSet rs = stmt.executeQuery( "select * from table1" );
...
```

As this code sample demonstrates, the `Statement` object is created via the `createStatement` method of the `Connection` class. Once created, the `Statement` object is used to execute a query statement that returns a `ResultSet` to represent the rows returned by the query. This `ResultSet` is then used to iterate through the results obtained by running the query.

> **Tip**
> If a statement is to be executed multiple times, it is better for performance reasons to use the `PreparedStatement` class to execute the SQL statement. A prepared statement is sent to the database engine to be parsed and optimized before being used. Therefore, each time the statement is executed, the overhead of parsing and optimization is eliminated.

The methods for the `Statement` class are listed in Table 3.3. As with the other methods previously described, these throw an `SQLException` when errors are encountered.

Table 3.3: *Statement Class Methods*

Method	Description
`executeQuery( String sql )`	Executes a SQL statement and returns the `ResultSet`
`executeUpdate( String sql )`	Executes the SQL insert, update, or delete statement; returns the row count, or 0 for SQL statements that return nothing
`close()`	Releases a statement's database and JDBC resources
`getMaxFieldSize()`	Returns the `MaxFieldSize` limit—the maximum amount of data returned for any column value
`setMaxFieldSize( int max )`	Sets the `MaxFieldSize` limit
`getMaxRows()`	Gets the maximum number of rows that a `ResultSet` can contain
`setMaxRows( int max )`	Sets the maximum number of rows that a `ResultSet` can contain
`setEscapeProcessing ( boolean enable )`	Sets escape processing for the driver on or off. If escape processing is on, the driver will do escape processing before the SQL is sent to the database

continued

Method	Description
`getQueryTimeout()`	Retrieves the `QueryTimeOut` limit. The `QueryTimeOut` limit is the number of seconds the driver will wait for a statement to execute.
`SetQueryTimeout ( int seconds )`	Sets the `QueryTimeOut` limit
`cancel()`	Executed by one thread to cancel a statement being executed by another thread
`getWarnings()`	Returns `SQLWarnings` for the `SQLStatement`
`clearWarnings()`	Clears the warnings for this `Statement`
`setCursorName ( String name )`	Defines the SQL cursor name that will be used by subsequent `Statement` execute methods
`execute( String sql )`	Executes a SQL statement that may return multiple results
`getResultSet()`	Returns the current result as a `ResultSet`
`getUpdateCount()`	Returns the current result of the update
`getMoreResults()`	Moves to a SQL statement's next result

The java.sql.ResultSet Class

The ResultSet class provides access to the data returned by the SQL statement that has been executed. The rows are retrieved in sequence with the next method used to advance the cursor. A number of methods are available to retrieve the JDBC data types stored.

Currently, result rows can be retrieved only in a serial fashion; the result set cannot move to any previous rows. (Several simple workarounds to this limitation are demonstrated in this text.)

```
...
// retrieve the set of results from the query
ResultSet rs = stmt.executeQuery(
                     "select * from table1" );
// position cursor before the first result element
boolean more = rs.next();
while ( more ) {
        System.out.println( "col1 value : " +
                                  rs.getInt( 1 ) );
          // move to the next row
          more = rs.next();
  }
...
```

This example shows the `Statement` object (`stmt`) being used to execute the query; the result of this action is returned as a `ResultSet` object representing the returned rows. The first time the `next` method is called, the `ResultSet` will be positioned at the first row of the set. Subsequent executions of the `next` method will position the `ResultSet` object to the next row in the set.

It is not an error to execute a query that doesn't return any rows. An empty `ResultSet` is indicated by a boolean false being returned from the first call to the `next` method. Testing and responding to this result provides a graceful method of managing an empty `ResultSet` as shown in the following code.

```
...
ResultSet rs = stmt.executeQuery(
                     "select * from table1" );
```

```
   // position cursor before the first result element
   boolean more = rs.next();

   // if no rows found, print message and return
   if ( !more )
      System.out.println( "No rows returned." );
...
```

Table 3.4 lists the methods available in this class. Methods are available to move to the next row in the `ResultSet` and to retrieve columns by column index (integer number) or column name. Only the methods to retrieve data by the column index are shown below. The corresponding methods to retrieve data by column name merely receive a parameter for the column name as a character string, rather than the integer column index shown in these methods. All methods for the `ResultSet` class are detailed in Part II of this book.

Table 3.4: *ResultSet Class Methods*

Method	Description
`next()`	Moves to the next row in the `ResultSet`
`close()`	Closes the current `ResultSet`
`wasNull()`	Reports whether or not the last column read had a NULL value
`getString ( int columnIndex )`	Returns the value of the column index element as a `string`
`getBoolean ( int columnIndex )`	Returns the value of the column index data element as a `boolean` data type
`getByte ( int columnIndex )`	Returns the value of the column index data element as a `byte`
`getShort ( int columnIndex )`	Returns the value of the column index data element as a `short` integer

continued

Method	Description
`getInt ( int columnIndex )`	Returns the value of the column index data element as an `int`
`getLong ( int columnIndex )`	Returns the value of the column index data element as a `long` integer
`getFloat ( int columnIndex )`	Returns the value of the column index data element as a `float` data type
`getDouble ( int columnIndex )`	Returns the value of the column index data element as a `double` floating-point number
`getNumeric ( int columnIndex, int scale )`	Returns the value of the column index data elements as a Java `Numeric` data type of specified scale
`getBytes ( int columnIndex )`	Returns the value of the column index data elements as a series of `bytes`
`getDate ( int columnIndex )`	Returns the value of the column index data element as a `Date`
`getTime (int columnIndex )`	Returns the value of the column index data element as a `Time`
`getTimeStamp ( int columnIndex )`	Returns the value of the column index data element as a `TimeStamp`
`getAsciiStream ( int columnIndex )`	Returns the value of the column index data element as an ASCII stream
`getUniCodeStream ( int columnIndex )`	Returns the value of the column index data element as a UniCode stream
`getBinaryStream ( int columnIndex )`	Returns the value of the column index data element as a `BinaryByteStream`

The java.sql.PreparedStatement Class

In Java, a statement can be pre-compiled and stored in a statement object. Once pre-compiled, this object will execute faster than a statement that is executed directly without the pre-compile phase.

A prepared statement potentially can have a series of parameters, sometimes called *placeholders*, which can be substituted with values when the statement is executed. A series of methods are available to set these values.

```
...
     PreparedStatement stmt  = con.prepareStatement(
                       " select * from customers " +
                       " where lastname like ? " );
     stmt.setString( 1,
          vectorParams.elementAt( 0 ).toString() );
      ResultSet rs = stmt.executeQuery();

...
```

This code sample demonstrates the creation of a `PreparedStatement` object. The `preparedStatement` object allows placeholders (i.e., a question mark—`?`) to be placed in the query statement. These place holders are used to substitute parameter values when the statement is executed. A number of set methods are available to set the values of parameters for various data types. In this example, the parameter is set using the `setString` method of the `PrepareStatement` class. The `executeQuery` method is then used to create a `ResultSet`.

An object used to store a prepared statement would be an instantiation of the `PreparedStatement` class. The methods in this class are described in Table 3.5.

Table 3.5: *PreparedStatement Class Methods*

Method	Description
`executeQuery()`	Executes a prepared SQL statement and returns the `ResultSet`
`executeUpdate()`	Executes a prepared SQL update statement and returns either a row count for the statement or a zero
`setNull( int parameterIndex, int sqlType )`	Sets a parameter to the SQL null representation for the data type
`setBoolean( int parameterIndex, boolean x )`	Sets a parameter to an appropriate value for the `boolean` data type at the parameter Index
`setByte( int parameterIndex, byte x )`	Sets a parameter to an appropriate value for the `byte` data type at the parameter index
`setShort( int parameterIndex, short x )`	Sets a parameter to an appropriate value for the `short` integer at the parameter index
`setInt( int parameterIndex, int x )`	Sets a parameter to an appropriate value for the `int` at the parameter index
`setLong( int parameterIndex, long x )`	Sets a parameter to an appropriate value for the `long` integer at the parameter index
`setFloat( int parameterIndex, float x )`	Sets a parameter to an appropriate value for the `float` at the parameter index
`setDouble( int parameterIndex, double x )`	Sets a parameter to an appropriate value for the `double` number at the parameter index
`setNumeric( int parameterIndex, Numeric x )`	Sets a parameter to an appropriate value for the `Numeric` at the parameter index

continued

Method	Description
`setString( int parameterIndex, String x )`	Sets a parameter to an appropriate value for the `String` at the parameter index
`setBytes( int parameterIndex, byte x[] )`	Sets a parameter to an appropriate value for the `byte` array at the parameter index
`setDate( int parameterIndex, java.sql.Date x )`	Sets a parameter to an appropriate value for the `Date` at the parameter index
`setTime( int parameterIndex, java.sql.Time x )`	Sets a parameter to an appropriate value for the `Time` object at the parameter index
`setTimestamp( int parameterIndex, java.sql.TimeStamp x )`	Sets the parameter to an appropriate value for the `TimeStamp` variable at the parameter index
`setUniCodeStream( int parameterIndex, java.io.InputStream x, int length )`	Sets the parameter to an appropriate value and size for the UniCode `InputStream` at the parameter index
`setBinaryStream( int parameterIndex, java.io.InputStream x, int length )`	Sets the parameter to an appropriate value and size for the Binary `InputStream` at the parameter index
`clearParameters()`	Clears and releases the resources used by the current parameter values
`setASCIICodeStream( int parameterIndex, java.io.InputStream x, int length )`	Sets the parameter to an appropriate value and size for the ASCII `InputStream` at the parameter index
`setObject( int parameterIndex, Object x, int targetSQLType, int scale )`	Sets the value of a parameter to the `parameter` (several variations `of` parameters are used to call this method—only one is shown here)

This section provided an introduction to JDBC and described some of the most commonly used JDBC classes. Loading an appropriate driver is a necessary step in using JDBC, which essentially implements the driver's functionality with JDBC classes. A connection is then required to interact with a database, as represented by a `Connection` object. Statements can then be created using the `Connection` object, creating a `Statement` or `PreparedStatement` object. Once the statements have been executed, a `ResultSet` is created to represent the results returned by the execution of the SQL statement. Some if not all of these classes will be used in any JDBC program. These classes will be covered in more detail in the following sections.

But creating a connection and retrieving data is not the only concern of the Java/JDBC programmer. One very important concern for any database programmer is security. This concern is heightened further with Internet programming where allowing Internet access to internal databases raises serious security issues. As of this writing, the Java language and JDK continues to evolve and along with it security facilities. Some of the current applet security restrictions are discussed next.

JDBC Security

Security in Java and JDBC is evolving. Facilities to improve the present set of security methods are planned in the next release of the Java SDK.

Most Java security is centered on the applet and its capabilities as code downloaded via the Internet or Intranet. Currently, applets have a very strict set of security rules that must be followed when run through certain browsers. With these browsers, they are restricted in their access to the client machine and cannot read or write to files on that machine. This would preclude JDBC applets from using a local client database such as Microsoft Access or DBase. Applets run in this manner are also restricted in their access to other machines. In fact, the only machine to which they are allowed to make a database connection is the machine from which they were downloaded. And these applets are only allowed to run the code that has been downloaded with the applet. These restrictions are relaxed when applets are run using applet runners such as the Java `appletviewer` or the `HotJava` browser.

The JDK version 1.1 supplies JDBC with a JDBC-ODBC bridge. This library maps JDBC calls to corresponding ODBC calls. Thus a JDBC application can use an existing ODBC driver to communicate with any relational database supported by the ODBC driver. This provides an excellent solution for JDBC applications that are run on the local Intranet. But this solution will **not** work with restricted applets downloaded via the Internet because these applets will not be allowed to run code that was not downloaded with the applet (as would be the case with the local ODBC driver). For these applications, a JDBC driver must be downloaded with the applet or a *three-tier* solution that allows access to databases either on the server or any machine accessible via the server must be implemented.

JDBC Usage

As there are numerous uses for the Java language, so there are a number of valid uses for Java applications that use JDBC. The flexibility of Java and its adaptability to network environments make it amenable to database applications run over a network. The sections that follow present several common uses for Java/JDBC applications.

Applet

A Java *applet* is a small, compact application downloaded as Java bytecodes over the Internet by a World Wide Web browser. These compact programs represent one of the more common uses of a Java application and can perform most of the functions of a regular Java application, though with more restrictive security on the local machine to which it is downloaded.

An applet can be either *trusted* or *untrusted*. A trusted applet has convinced the Java virtual machine that it can be trusted either by providing a cryptographic key or some other means. Once trusted, this applet could be granted access to local data.

An applet that has not provided some means of authentication is considered untrusted and would not have access to any local data. This applet could, however, open a database connection back to the server from which it was downloaded.

Benefits of Applet Programming to JDBC

An applet is designed to be embedded in a Web page and then to supplement the HTML page being rendered by the browser. Because an applet is a Java program, it is much easier to perform complex functions with an applet than with HTML, which is not by any means a complete programming language.

Programming database access with JDBC in a Java applet is a much more natural, straightforward method of programming than using a CGI application. And programming with JDBC in the applet allows database state to be retained; an application can easily browse a set of database tables, a process that is much more difficult with a *state-less* CGI application.

An applet can use a GUI interface. Some GUI facilities are available as part of an HTML page, but Java allows a finer level of programming with GUI controls.

Special-Purpose Applets

Java applets make the programming of special-purpose applications simpler and practically eliminate the software distribution costs for these programs. When combined with JDBC to enable access to relational databases, the possibility for special-purpose Java applets is greatly expanded. Some examples of these are listed in the following sections.

Loan calculator

This application could be developed by a bank to run within their Web page. In order to give accurate amortization costs, the most current loan rate would need to be determined. This could be accomplished with a database connection back to the bank database (in the domain where the applet originated) to retrieve the current loan rates and possibly to access user credit information to determine loan risk. The user could enter her loan parameters and this information, combined with current loan rates, would return the cost of a loan and the monthly payment to the end user.

Catalog browse

A catalog browse window could enable the user to enter a catalog item number and then retrieve the cost, quantity on-hand, and a picture of the catalog item that could be displayed to the applet window. Buttons could exist in the window to query the database, retrieve the data set and retrieve the next or previous set of rows. In the event the user makes an order, the user's order could be written back to the database.

Stock Portfolio

A user could access this applet to see the state of their stock portfolio. The application could retrieve information about the user's portfolio, and the prices of the stocks in that portfolio from the database. If the user wished to make a change to his portfolio, the changes could be entered into the database and could be read later by a stock broker who would then execute the changes.

APPLET ISSUES

While there are numerous benefits to developing applications as Java applets, there are also a number of issues to be considered. These are issues that must be considered with all Web applications, specifically *performance* and *security*.

Access bandwidth over the Internet tends to vary and impacts performance. An application that accesses a database through the Internet most likely will perform worse than the same application run over the local network; such is the nature of the Internet versus an internal (Intranet) network.

Security of an applet is another issue. An applet downloaded over the Internet operates within a fairly restrictive set of security rules. The object of these rules is to protect the interest of the user by protecting their client machine, but the programmer of the applet must consider these rules when designing the application.

In general, normal unsigned applets are considered *untrustworthy* and are not allowed access to any local database or local files. This type of applet could, however, open a database connection back to the server from which it was downloaded. An applet could download a JDBC driver and register this driver with the JDBC `DriverManager`. In this case, the Java runtime environment should allow this untrusted applet, and only this untrusted applet, to use this driver to satisfy connection requests.

An applet that manages to convince the local Java machine that it can be trusted by providing a password or cryptographic key could be considered *trustworthy* and would be subject to different security restrictions.

Java for General-Purpose Applications

The Java language is a multi-purpose, general use language that can be used for a variety of applications. In the short term, Java applications may primarily be Internet applications, but in the long-term Java has the potential to satisfy a variety of programming needs. Java and JDBC combine to expand the capabilities of this flexible language and extend its utility to a variety of applications.

Java/JDBC applications need not run over the Internet; they can be run within a company (an Intranet application) and be used for applications such as data entry, query screens and reports. These applications could begin to fill the role now reserved for C and C++ applications and some specialized 4GLs and database front-end tools.

CGI Application

A CGI application in Java is developed much as it would in C or C++. Parameters are retrieved, parsed, and processed. When processing is complete, data is returned and formatted for an HTML page.

Java with JDBC provides several advantages to writing a CGI script in C/C++ or Perl. Java provides a simpler syntax to perform many of the functions that need to be executed in a CGI program. And Java's JDBC interface provides a database vendor-neutral method for retrieving any data and returning it to the HTML page.

JDBC Application Design

Java JDBC applications can be two-tiered (conventional client-server) or three-tiered (partitioned applications). While it is expected that many applications will make use of two-tiered application development, there are advantages to the three-tiered approach as discussed in the following sections.

Two-Tiered Java Applications (Conventional)

The *two-tiered* approach to database access is the conventional client-server approach. There is a front-end portion of the application

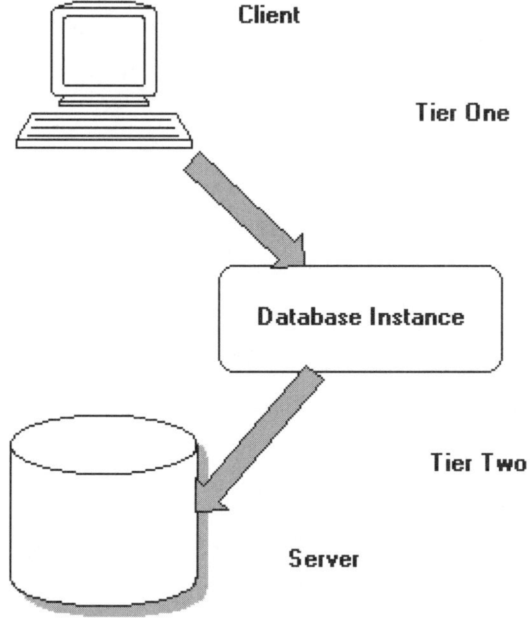

Figure 3.3: *Two-tiered application development architecture*

that requests data (see Figure 3.3). The data is stored on and retrieved from a server.

This approach has the benefit of moving front-end processing off the server. This removes work from the server where there is usually a significant demand for CPU cycles and places processing on the client where there are usually plenty of CPU cycles available.

This works fine for most applications. For data processing, it has the benefit of allowing data collection to be performed in what is usually a rich GUI environment such as Windows. The GUI environment requires CPU cycles and fast access to the display device. To run such an application on the server could require CPU resources that could be scarce on a busy server, and significant bandwidth to the display device.

But this approach begins to fail with some application profiles. When an application must retrieve a large number of rows from the server and process the rows in application memory, then the traditional two-tiered, client-server model begins to suffer performance degradation.

Most large report applications (a report that retrieves and processes a large number of rows) match this transaction profile. If this type of application is running on the client, then the rows must be retrieved over the network. The limited network bandwidth and the speed with which the data must be retrieved could lead to a bottleneck on the network. A *three-tiered* approach to application processing can eliminate this bottleneck.

Three-Tiered Java Applications (Server Interface Approach)

Three-tiered application processing adds an additional layer to the standard client-server model. The processing of the application is split between two portions of code. One portion of code processes on the client and the other on the server. The third remaining component of the application is the database server. An example of this approach to Java/JDBC programming is covered in Chapter 6, "Three-Tiered Programming with JDBC."

With three-tiered applications, a client-side application performs a portion of the processing. An additional server-side portion of the application operates on the server and communicates with the application partition that resides on the client (see Figure 3.4).

Report applications present a classic processing problem that is uniquely suited to application partitioning. Report applications usually retrieve a large number of rows into application memory, process the rows, and then output processed, formatted report data. Programmed with a standard two-tiered client-server approach, these report rows would be retrieved to the client and processed, leading to the network bottleneck that plagues client-server reports.

Programmed with a three-tiered approach, the client-server report retrieves report parameters at the client side. These parameters are transmitted to the server partition for processing. The server partition processes the report as shown in Figure 3.4. Report rows are processed on the server where retrieval of the rows to the server code operates at server *inter-process communication* (IPC) speeds (sockets, shared memory), which are generally much faster than network speeds. When the server partition finishes processing the rows, the results can be returned to the client for output, or output to the printer on the server.

Another approach can be considered a *four-tiered* approach. In the case of firewall machines—machines that restrict Internet access to the corporate network—there is a restriction on making a direct socket connection from the applet to the application server. In this case,

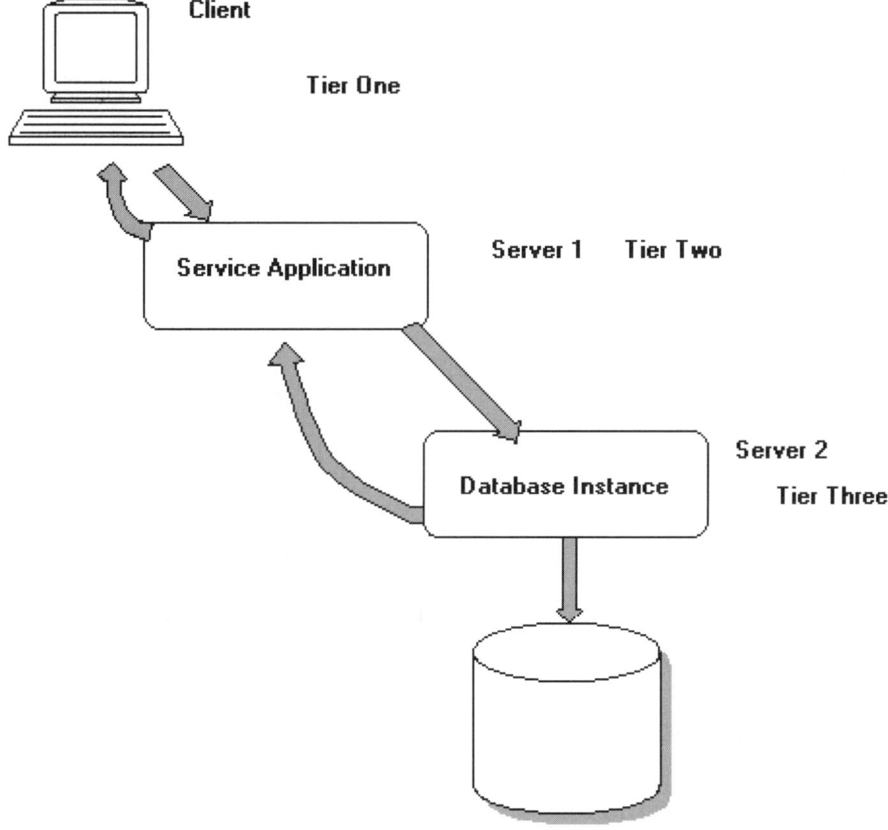

Figure 3.4: *Three-tiered application architecture*

the HTTP/WWW server is used as an intermediary between the application server. The application server interacts with the database, returns data to the HTTP server, which in turn returns the data to the client machine. This approach provides an additional layer of security that many sites require for their Internet access.

JDBC Data Type Mapping

Java is designed to be platform-independent and its data types reflect this. A Java/JDBC developer must be aware of data type mapping and design programs accordingly. The following sections detail the specifics of data mapping.

MAPPING SQL DATA TYPES INTO JAVA

With JDBC, data is retrieved from the database into `ResultSet` objects with correct data type mappings. This occurs automatically with JDBC and is the responsibility of the JDBC driver. It is when the data is retrieved from the `ResultSet` into member variables that data types must be mapped correctly. Various meta-data methods are available to discover data types of returned columns if needed, but most applications will have data type knowledge and simply need to use the correct methods to retrieve the data.

The SQL data types do not map directly into Java data types, but this is not generally a problem. In some cases, a number of SQL data types can be mapped into a single Java data type. In other cases, there are several choices available for storing SQL data types in Java applications.

The reverse operation of storing Java data types in a SQL database involves using the same conversion rules in reverse. Once again, a number of options are available to the programmer for data storage. Table 3.6 lists the SQL data types and the corresponding Java data types. Not all databases will store all of these data types and not all databases may use the SQL names for the same data type.

Table 3.6: *SQL Data Types to Java Data Type Mappings*

SQL Type	Java Type
`CHAR`	`String`
`VARCHAR`	`String`
`LONGVARCHAR`	`String`
`NUMERIC`	`java.math.BigDecimal`
`DECIMAL`	`java.math.BigDecimal`
`BIT`	`boolean`
`TINYINT`	`byte`
`SMALLINT`	`short`
`INTEGER`	`int`
`BIGINT`	`long`

continued

SQL Type	Java Type
REAL	float
FLOAT	double
DOUBLE	double
BINARY	byte[]
VARBINARY	byte[]
LONGVARBINARY	byte[]
DATE	java.sql.Date
TIME	java.sql.Time
TIMESTAMP	java.sql.Timestamp

These data type mappings are discussed in more detail in the following sections.

SQL CHAR Data Type

The SQL CHAR data types all map into the Java `String` data type. Java has no fixed length character string arrays; character string arrays in Java should be treated as `String` data types that can assume a variable length. There is, therefore, no need to distinguish between variable-length and fixed-length character strings with Java. The SQL data types of `CHAR`, `VARCHAR`, and `LONGVARCHAR` all can be stored in a Java `String` data type.

SQL DECIMAL and NUMERIC

The SQL `DECIMAL` and `NUMERIC` data types are used to represent fixed-point numbers. These two data types are represented using a `java.sql.Numeric` data type. This data type is a subtype of the `java.lang.Number` type. This type provides math operations for `Numeric` data types to be added, subtracted, multiplied, and divided with `Numeric` types and other data types.

SQL BINARY, VARBINARY and LONGVARBINARY

These three data types all can be expressed as `byte` arrays in Java. Because the LONGVARBINARY data type can be very large, JDBC allows the programmer to set the return value of a LONGVARBINARY to be a Java input stream.

BIT Data Type

The SQL `BIT` type can be mapped to the Java `boolean` type.

TINYINT, SMALLINT, INTEGER and BIGINT

The SQL TINYINT, SMALLINT, INTEGER and BIGINT types can be mapped to the Java `byte`, `short`, `int` and `long` data types, respectively.

REAL, FLOAT and DOUBLE

The SQL floating-point data types of REAL, FLOAT and DOUBLE can be mapped as follows. The REAL data type can be stored in a Java `float` data type, and the REAL and DOUBLE can be stored in a Java `double`.

DATE, TIME, and TIMESTAMP

SQL provides three date/time-related data types: DATE, TIME, and TIMESTAMP. The `java.util.date` class provides date and time information, but this class does not directly support any of the three SQL date/time data types. To accommodate these SQL data types, three subclasses were declared from `java.util.date`, they are `java.sql.Date`, `java.sql.Time`, `java.sql.TimeStamp`.

The `java.util.Date` class can be used to store SQL DATE data. The `java.util.Time` class can be used to store SQL TIME information. And the `java.sql.Timestamp` can be used to store SQL TIMESTAMP data.

Multi-Threading in Java

The JDBC specification requires that all JDBC class implementations be multi-thread safe. Objects created using these classes are able to support being accessed by several threads simultaneously.

Java provides easy-to-use access to multi-threading facilities. This can be a very useful capability when used for database access. The application need not wait for a long running query to finish—processing can continue and, when complete, the query thread can trigger an event that signals completion of database access.

Because Java is a multi-threaded environment, there is no real need to provide explicit support for asynchronous thread execution. Simply creating a thread separate from the main thread to execute a query will effectively create an asynchronous query.

JDBC developers can assume full concurrent execution, but it is the responsibility of the driver to maintain concurrency. If the driver developer does not maintain full concurrency, but instead processes one query at a time, the developer will be able to execute multiple query threads but will see limited concurrency and throughput because the driver will execute the statements serially.

A common use of multi-threading is to execute a long-running SQL statement in one thread, and in another thread time the query and cancel it using the `Statement` class `cancel` method if it runs too long.

Transactions

A database *transaction* is a series of database updates that are grouped together as a single *atomic* update transaction. In the event any single update in the transaction fails, the remaining updates are *rolled-back;* that is, their effect on the database is removed and any records they may have deleted or updated are restored to the state they were in before the transaction was started.

By default, JDBC classes operate in *auto-commit* mode. This means that each SQL statement executed is considered a separate transaction and a commit is made at the completion of the statement. In order to group a set of transactions together, this auto-commit mode must be disabled using the `Connection` class `setAutoCommit` method and passing the method a `boolean` FALSE value.

With auto-commit disabled, there is always an implicit transaction in place. An explicit commit can be made by calling the `Connection` method `commit`. Alternatively, a rollback can be made by calling the `Connection` method `rollback`. This rolls back the current transaction and restores the database to the state it was in before the start of the current transaction.

Various database-dependent isolation levels can be set. There are methods in the `DatabaseMetaData` class to learn the existing defaults in place in the current session and methods in the `Connection` class to change the current isolation level.

Cursors

A *cursor* is a database facility that represents a set of rows in the database. This set of rows is defined by the SQL statement used to retrieve the rows from the database. A cursor can be used to both retrieve rows of data from the database and optionally update or delete the rows.

JDBC provides cursors for positioned updates and deletes. The `ResultSet` method `getCursorName` returns the cursor associated with the current `ResultSet`. This cursor name can then be used for positioned update and delete. The cursor is valid until the `ResultSet` or parent `Statement` is closed.

Because not all databases support positioned update or delete, the `DatabaseMetaData` methods `supportsPositionedDelete` and `supportsPositionedUpdate` can be used to detect whether or not this functionality is supported.

Note that in the current release of JDBC, *scrollable* cursors (the ability to move forward and backward in the current set) and ODBC-type bookmarks are not supported. Some viable techniques for overcoming these limitations are demonstrated in the tutorial section of this text. (JDBC 2.0 will support scrollable cursors.)

SQL Level

The SQL level specifies the American National Standards Committee (ANSI) standard supported. The ANSI committee has described several levels of SQL syntax compliance. The current standard for SQL is what is known as SQL-2. There are several levels of compliance within this standard, the most common being SQL-2 Entry level. The 1.0 version of the JDBC specification supports SQL-2 Entry Level. The SQL-2 Transition Level is not supported at the present time.

SQL Escape Syntax

JDBC provides syntax for SQL escape for stored procedures, dates, times, scalar functions, and outer joins. This syntax is then mapped to database-specific syntax by the driver. The syntax is provided via an escape clause denoted by curly brackets, as follows:

```
{keyword ... parameters }
```

Stored Procedures, Time and Date Literals and Scalar Functions

The syntax used to call a stored procedure uses the SQL escape sequence, as follows:

```
{call this_proc( arg1, arg2 ...) }
```

If the stored procedure returns a value, it is called as follows.

```
{? = call this_proc( arg1, arg2 ...) }
```

Databases use slightly different syntax for their representation of date and time. An escape clause is used by the driver to format this representation in such a way that the current database understands it. The following is an example of a date and time literal.

```
  // datetime literal

 { d 'yyyy-mm-dd' }
// timestamp literalG
 { ts 'hh:mm:ss' }
```

Scalar Functions

Scalar functions are also available through the JDBC escape clause syntax. JDBC supports numeric, string, date, time, system, and conversion functions on scalar values. These functions are denoted by the keyword "fn" followed by the name of the function.

Some drivers may not support all of these functions. The meta-data method `getNumericFunctions` returns a comma-separated list of the names of numeric functions and `getStringFunctions` returns a comma-separated list of string functions. The functions potentially supported are listed in Appendix A of this book.

Summary

This chapter has covered the basics of JDBC programming. The simple process of creating a JDBC application has been described and the classes involved in that process have been presented. Issues relating to JDBC applications such as security and data type mapping have also been discussed. The use of cursors to iterate through the data returned, database transactions to maintain the integrity of data updates and the impact of multi-threading on JDBC applications were also presented in this chapter. Some of the more important points covered in this chapter are as follows:

- A driver manager (`DriverManager`) must be loaded before a database connection can be made.
- A database connection (`Connection`) must be made before a SQL statement can be executed.
- A SQL statement (`Statement`) returns a result set (`ResultSet`) object representing the results of the executed query.
- Some data type mapping is required from SQL data types to Java native data types.
- JDBC begins data base transactions in `autoCommit` mode—each SQL update statement is automatically committed.
- In the current release, cursors proceed serially through the data—there are no scrollable cursors.

Coming Up

The next chapter marks the beginning of the tutorial section. This section begins with a simple JDBC application that is explained in detail. This example enables you to understand what is required to establish a connection and retrieve rows from a database. More complex examples follow to provide a discussion of positioned cursor updates, using prepared statements to improve performance, transactions, and multi-threaded programming with JDBC.

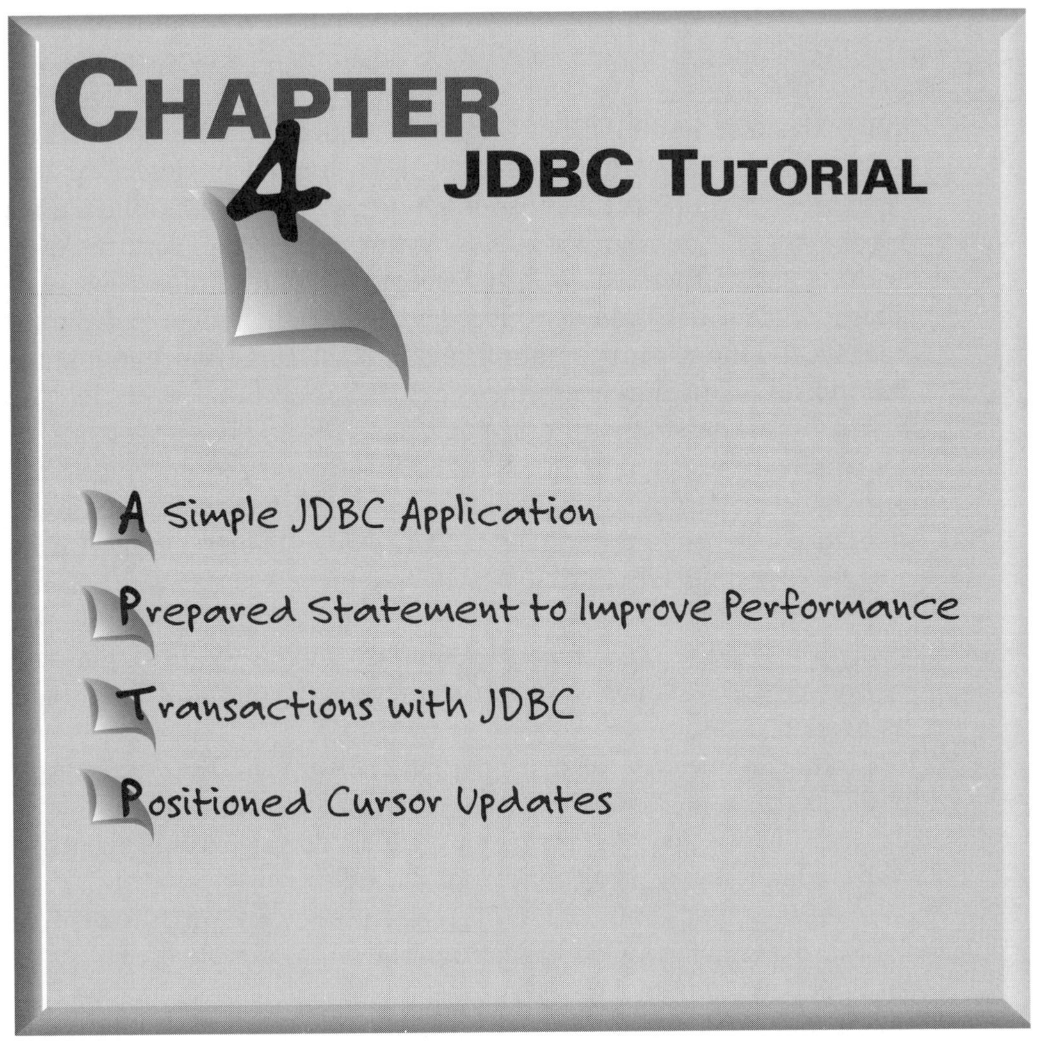

CHAPTER
4
JDBC TUTORIAL
A Simple JDBC Application
Prepared Statement to Improve Performance
Transactions with JDBC
Positioned Cursor Updates

Every program has unique requirements for database access; some need to *browse* a database, selecting a set of rows in order to allow users to move forward and backwards through the set; other applications need to perform a series of updates to a set of related tables that must be treated as a complete, *atomic* transaction, where multiple rows in the update must be treated as a single row.

Some applications contain a fixed set of selection criteria for data, while others require that parameters be provided at runtime. There are yet other applications that may know nothing about the capabilities of the database to which they are connected, so they must discover the capabilities of the database. Demonstrating a single application with JDBC cannot cover the full spectrum of functionality we reference here; a series of JDBC examples is required.

Java applications are now used primarily as applets; this more likely than not represents the most common usage of JDBC applications for the near future. But it is reasonable to expect that over time Java, with its array of features, will be accepted as a general-purpose language. Once it has been accepted, Java with JDBC will be used for a variety of general-purpose applications such as CGI programming, reports, and data entry programs.

This tutorial demonstrates the use of JDBC first in a series of simple applications, then in an applet and CGI application. The simple applications demonstrate the basics of JDBC usage: loading a database driver, creating a `Connection` object, creating a `Statement` object, executing a SQL statement with the `Statement` object and returning a `ResultSet`, and retrieving rows of data using the `ResultSet` object. Database access with JDBC will always represent some variation of these calls and additional calls as needed.

Code examples are also used to demonstrate JDBC usage with applets. This represents a variation on the simple code example; with applets, JDBC methods are usually called during button events to retrieve and display data to the applet window

A very common application currently used with World Wide Web HTML pages is the CGI application. The CGI example in this chapter uses JDBC to retrieve data from a database; it demonstrates a CGI application that receives a set of parameters, parses the parameters, and returns data formatted as an HTML page.

One of the limitations of the current implementation of JDBC is that a `ResultSet` can only be reviewed in serial order—the cursor cannot move backwards. An example demonstrated in this chapter provides a solution that allows rows to be retrieved in any order.

The overall goal of the tutorial section is to demonstrate the use of JDBC to program simple to moderately difficult database access. Complete examples are used to provide a clear understanding of the context of the application.

Tutorials are provided for the following topics:

- A Simple JDBC Application
- Use of the Prepared Statement
- Positioned Cursor Update
- Transaction Modes
- Java Applet
- Metadata Usage
- ResultSet Array

These examples are be explained in more detail in the following sections.

A Simple JDBC Application

This simple tutorial demonstrates the use of JDBC to create a `Connection` object and connect to the database; create a `Statement` object and execute a SQL statement using the `Statement` object; retrieve the results of the `Statement` in a `ResultSet` object; and to display the data in the `ResultSet`.

This example uses a class and a series of methods to

1. Create a database table
2. Insert data into the table
3. Select data from the table
4. Update rows in the table
5. Delete rows from the table

This list of database activities represents a broad spectrum of database functions; most database access programs are required to perform some or all of these functions.

Two types of SQL statements are demonstrated in this tutorial: Data Definition Language (DDL) statements and Data Manipulation Language (DML) statements. The DDL statements are used to create a database table and an index; for JDBC purposes, these statements are update statements executed with the `executeUpdate` method because they do not return data. They do however, return an integer value for the number of rows updated.

Use of the Prepared Statement

Once stored for a statement, this process of parsing and optimizing need not be repeated as long as the structure and database objects in the statement do not change. Since the overhead of parsing and optimizing a statement can be avoided during each execution of a SQL statement, a prepared statement is more efficient than regular execution of a SQL statement.

A JDBC prepared statement allows parameters to be identified within a SQL statement. The parameters are usually limited to those values that vary from execution to execution of the statement.

The prepared statement examples presented here demonstrate the use of a prepared statement to improve performance and allow parameter substitution.

Positioned Cursor Update

In many databases, you can create a cursor to maintain a pointer to a specific row in a table. This pointer or position indicates where the current row pointer is located. When the application needs to update the table being read using the cursor, it uses the cursor to update the record at the current record position; this is known as a *positioned cursor update.*

The syntax for the positioned cursor update, if supported by the target database, is usually a SQL `select` statement clause, which identifies the `select` statement as a statement to be used to create a cursor. Once the statement with the "`for update of`" clause has been declared, the cursor name is retrieved to create the update statement. The update statement SQL string includes the "`where current of`" clause followed by the cursor name.

Transaction Modes

Database transaction modes enable varying degrees of transaction integrity to be used during program execution. An application can switch from a mode where uncommitted records can be read and records updated by the application can be read by other users, to a mode where only committed records can be read by an application and no records that have been updated by an application can be read by other users. This use of granularity in transactions allows for better performance and increased concurrency when an application does not need to limit it (such as a report). But more limited concurrency may be necessary when an application needs to update several tables within a transaction and commit the rows to the database as a transaction.

The transaction example demonstrates the use of transaction modes by creating a database connection and then setting the isolation mode for the database connection through the appropriate `Connection` method. The JDBC API does not provide an explicit "begin work" statement. Using the "`commit work`" statement, all current database transactions from the session are sent to the database when the statement is executed.

This example executes the `commit Connection` method to commit the current updates to the database. A series of statements is then executed followed by another commit method invocation to commit the transaction to the database. Should the transaction fail due to some error, the `catch` code block contains a `rollback` method call to roll back the database to a current state. One of the current shortcomings of the JDBC interface is that it does **not** provide a means of scrolling through a `ResultSet` both forward and backward; this capability is known as *scroll cursors*. This feature is useful for a database browse application for which the user must enter selection criteria and then move backwards and forwards through the returned set of rows

The solution to this problem is to store the `ResultSet` in a Java `Vector` object. The `Vector` has the ability to grow dynamically and provides the ability to address a specific element. The result set array example demonstrates this capability.

Java Applet

The Java applet currently represents one of the principal uses of the Java language. A Java applet can be downloaded off the Internet and run through a browser. This capability has been a large part of the reason for the incredible popularity of the Java language.

A Java applet that can access a database is a powerful programming tool. This application is platform-independent and, when placed at a single location, can be distributed to multiple client computers by simply being downloaded as a Java applet through a link in the HTML page.

But a Java applet run through a browser is currently subject to certain security restrictions depending on the browser being used. For instance, a Java applet that has been downloaded cannot access any local files on the client machine. An application that wants to create a Microsoft Access table and insert rows into the table would fail as a downloaded applet if the Microsoft Access database builds files on the local machine.

The example shown here uses a Microsoft Access database that resides on the local machine. It runs successfully using the Sun `appletviewer` application where security is relaxed. It does **not** run using the more restrictive Netscape browser.

This example will first display an input form to the application window. Using the buttons available in this window, the user can browse the data available in the database. Search criteria can be entered and then used to retrieve rows from the database. Users can optionally move forward or backwards through the ResultSet by pressing buttons in the application window.

CGI Application

In today's world of World Wide Web/Internet application programming, CGI applications are ubiquitous. While use of JDBC in applets can eliminate the need for many of these CGI programs, security restrictions and performance improvements could still make CGI programming a viable alternative. And Java, as a flexible general-purpose language, could fill this role.

If it is desirable to have the applet or a HTML page connect to a database on a server other than the Internet server, there are a number of good reasons why you would not want to expose that machine to the Internet and would prefer to have the HTTP server process and manage the connection.

In order to connect to this machine, a third-tier application is needed as a middle tier between the client applet and the database server. A CGI application is a viable approach to programming this third tier.

Such a CGI application can receive a request, retrieve the data, and then format the data for return as an HTML page. The CGI tutorial application demonstrates a Java program that could provide output for such a CGI application.

Metadata Usage

There is a rich supply of metadata methods available in JDBC. An application can use these methods to discover information about the database to which it is connected—a task that could be a requirement for a Java applet that needs to connect to multiple databases. These examples demonstrate the use of many of the metadata functions available in JDBC.

ResultSet Array Example

One of the limitations of the current release of JDBC is that result sets can only be retrieved in a serial fashion. The `ResultSet` methods only retrieve the next row; the previous row cannot be retrieved. Using a technique that stores retrieved rows in an internal list (a Java `Vector`), data can be retrieved for the current row, the previous row, and for a specific row in the result set. This technique is demonstrated in the `ResultsSet` array example and the three-tiered application example.

Basic JDBC Programming

This chapter presents the basic steps involved in creating JDBC programs. The first example in this chapter demonstrates the basic set of calls required to use JDBC with Java. These steps are:

1. Load driver
2. Create connection
3. Create statement
4. Execute statement and return `ResultSet` or result count
5. Iterate `ResultSet` if returned

The use of JDBC usually involves some combination of these calls in addition to other calls to metadata or transaction control methods. The calls listed here must be made in sequence—you must have a `Connection` object before a `Statement` object can be created, and you must have a Statement object before a SQL statement can be executed.

Results are returned in a `ResultSet`, the JDBC equivalent of a cursor. The JDBC `ResultSet` provides methods for iterating the results and retrieving individual columns. Specific methods are used to retrieve specific data types. In the event an update is executed, an integer result count is returned.

The `ResultSet` retrieved contains, as the name implies, the *set of results* retrieved by the query. These results may be iterated, but only sequentially; there is no capability to move backwards through the result set or to move a specific set of positions. A work-around for this limitation is demonstrated later in this section.

Note

The design of JDBC has kept methods and their arguments simple. To reduce the number of parameters to be passed to methods, additional methods were added to span the functionality needed. So, instead of designing a method with three parameters, one that would indicate the call type and two others that may or may not be needed depending on the call type, JDBC developers would create three separate methods.

To discover some basic information about the `ResultSet`, a `ResultSet` metadata object must be obtained. This metadata object will provide information such as the number of columns in the `ResultSet`, the data type of the columns, and the size and precision of the column. As some of the examples in this chapter demonstrate, it is possible to convert the basic data types from the `ResultSet` to a string and display or manipulate the data in that format.

Note

If you know and are familiar with the database being used, then metadata information probably won't have to be retrieved. In situations where this information is not known, then the database metadata methods are available. Any application that can possibly connect to databases from different database vendors potentially needs metadata information. Such an application might be a general-purpose database query tool that could attach to either an Informix, Oracle, or Sybase database using JDBC drivers. This application would need to discover the database to which it was connected, the version of the database product, and potentially the specific capabilities supported in that version. All of this information is supplied by database metadata methods.

To discover information about the database or the result set, a metadata object can be instantiated using a `DataBaseMetaData` object or a `ResultSetMetaData` object. These objects provide information on the database, data types supported, or the number of columns retrieved and their data types. It is not uncommon to retrieve some metadata information about the database or the result set as is demonstrated in the examples provided here.

Basic JDBC Steps

The following sections outline the basic steps necessary to create and manage a database connection using JDBC. A specific set of methods must be invoked each time a database connection is made and data is retrieved.

Load Driver

The first step in using JDBC is to load the JDBC-ODBC bridge driver. This is usually accomplished using the `forName` static method of the `Class` object (which is part of the base Java system). The call is made as follows:

```
Class.forName ("sun.jdbc.odbc.JdbcOdbcDriver");
```

When this call is made, the Java system searches for the class requested and loads the driver. A class descriptor is returned by this method, but because it is not needed, it is ignored.

Create Connection

The loading of the JDBC database driver does not connect to the database; it merely creates an *environment* in the program where this can be done. Before any database-specific SQL statements can be executed, a *connection* must be established to the database. This is accomplished through a call to the DriverManager getConnection method to find a specific driver that can create a connection to the URL requested.

The DriverManager searches through registered drivers until one is found that can process the database URL that was specified. If a driver cannot be found, an exception is thrown and code execution will not continue for that method. Code that follows this statement can therefore assert that no exception was thrown and a connection has been successfully established. The call is made as follows:

```
String url      = "jdbc:odbc:msaccessdb";
Connection con = DriverManager.getConnection ( url,
"", "");
```

In this example, the getConnection method is invoked with a String containing the URL for the database and two additional String parameters, one for the user name and one for the user password.

The familiar universal resource locator (URL) is used to supply the naming system for the database resource to be loaded. The format of the URL name is:

```
jdbc:subprotocol:subname
```

where *subprotocol* indicates the access method used in addition to JDBC and the *subname* is a name that has significance for the *subprotocol* being used.

In this case, the JDBC-ODBC bridge is being used and ODBC is the subprotocol, the protocol being used as a *bridge* to provide database connectivity. The subname in this case is the *data source* name for the ODBC connection. In this example, the data source name is msaccessdb, a local client Microsoft Access database. The specifics of the database name and location are mapped through the ODBC driver facilities provided.

Create Statement

In order to interact with the database, SQL statements must be executed. This requires that a Statement object be created to manage the SQL statements. This is accomplished with a call to the Connection class createStatement method as follows:

```
Statement stmt = con.createStatement( );
```

This call creates a Statement object using the established database connection. The Statement class provides methods for executing SQL statements and retrieving the results from the statement execution. Note that result sets (or cursors) are not part of the Statement class but are represented through a separate class, the ResultSet class.

Execute SQL Statement and Return ResultSet

The SQL Statement object does not have a specific SQL statement associated with it (unlike the PreparedStatement superclass, which does). The SQL statement to execute is determined when the call to executeQuery is made, as follows:

```
String qs = "select * from orders";
ResultSet rs = stmt.executeQuery( qs );
```

This call sends the query to the database and returns the results of the query as a ResultSet. Should an error be generated during the execution of the query, an exception is generated and caught using the catch code block. Successful execution of the executeQuery moves control to the next line of code following the statement, which in this example begins iterating the query results.

Iterate ResultSet

The ResultSet represents the collection of results from the query. The ResultSet class contains methods that can be used to iterate through these results in a serial fashion. First, you must make a call to the next method in order to position the pointer (or cursor) before the first element of the result set, as follows:

```
boolean more = rs.next();
```

The call to the `next` method returns a `boolean` value. The `boolean` value of *true* indicates that the call was successful and the pointer is positioned, thus there is data to retrieve. A `boolean` value of *false* indicates that the call was unsuccessful and there are no rows to retrieve. Because it is not an error to execute a SQL select statement that returns no rows, this first call to the `next` method reveals whether or not the query returned **any** rows—a value of *false* would indicate no rows have been retrieved.

Next, a `while` loop is executed to step through the results in the `ResultSet`. The loop control is the boolean variable `more` returned by the first call to the `next` method. As long as this value is *true*, the loop continues to execute.

Within the loop, the value of the first column of the result set is displayed and the `next` method is called to position the pointer to the next row. If the `next` method returns false, then the loop does not continue execution and control is passed to the statement after the end of the `while` loop, as follows:

```
            while ( more ) {
             System.out.println( "Col1: " +
rs.getInt( "col1" ) );
            more = rs.next();
           }
```

The complete code for the simple select program is shown in Program 4.1.

Program 4.1 Select1.java

```
import java.sql.*;
import java.io.*;

class Select1 {

     public static void main( String argv[] ) {

       try {

          Class.forName ("jdbc.odbc.JdbcOdbcDriver");
```

continued

```
    String url = "jdbc:odbc:msaccessdb";

Connection con = DriverManager.getConnection (url, "",
      "");

String qs = "select * from loadtest";
Statement stmt = con.createStatement( );
ResultSet rs = stmt.executeQuery( qs );
boolean more = rs.next();
while ( more ) {
           System.out.println( "Col1: " +
                     rs.getInt( "col1" ) );

   more = rs.next();
  }
  }

  catch (java.lang.Exception ex) {

  // Print description of the exception.
  System.out.println( "** Error on data select. ** " );
    ex.printStackTrace ();

            }
        }
    }
```

A Dynamic SQL Select Program

The previous program used a specific SQL `select` statement to retrieve rows and display a single column of data from the database table. The following example presents a more generic approach to processing a SQL `select` statement. The program accepts a single command line argument: the name of the table to query. It uses this table name to build a query for all the columns and all the rows in the specified table. The query is executed and the results are displayed to the terminal screen.

Because the query is built at runtime, the number and names of the columns are not known when the program is compiled. This information must be determined by retrieving metadata information on the `ResultSet` using the `ResultSetMetaData` object for the `ResultSet` returned by the query. This example does not deal with the problem of determining the data type of the column

The next method and data retrieval

Note that calls to the `ResultSet` `next` method do not return data. They merely position the pointer to the next row in the result set. Successive calls to the appropriate "get" method for the data types of the columns must be made to retrieve the data (for example, `getInt`, `getString`, `getNumeric`). The programmer must know the data types of the columns and call the correct method. Alternatively, if simple display of data is required and the programmer does not know the data type of the column being retrieved, each column value can be retrieved as a `String` regardless of data type, as follows:

```
System.out.println( "Col1: " + rs.getString( "col1" ) );
```

In this example, the value of column 1 is retrieved as a `String` even though the column in the database is defined as an integer. This approach obviously has its limitations with data types such as BIT and BINARY, but could be useful with some of the more simple data types.

(which is easily available with the getType ResultSetMetaData method) but simply treats each column as a Java String and displays the data in the column as returned by the getString ResultSet method. The steps used in executing this program are as follows:

1. Load driver and get database connection
2. Retrieve table name from command line argument
3. Build select statement
4. Create statement object and execute SQL statement
5. Create a ResultSetMetaData object
6. Traverse the ResultSet

Each of these steps are detailed in the following sections.

Load Driver and Get Database Connection

The database driver is loaded and the connection is made as shown in the previous example. The same ODBC data source is used for this connection, as follows:

```
Class.forName ("sun.jdbc.odbc.JdbcOdbcDriver");
String url      = "jdbc:odbc:msaccessdb";
Connection con = DriverManager.getConnection (
                                          url, "", "");
```

The forName method is used to load the JDBC-ODBC bridge class. The URL string is created with reference to the ODBC MicroSoft-Access database used in the example. This string is then passed as a parameter to the getConnection method of DriverManager, which then returns the Connection object.

Retrieve Table Name from Command Line Argument

This program retrieves the table name to query as a command line argument. This code determines only whether or not an argument has been passed to the program. A String variable is declared and initialized to the value of a valid table name for the database. If an argument has been passed to the program, it is stored in a `String` variable named `tableName` as shown in the following snippet. If an argument has not been passed to the program, the variable retains the original value of the table name.

```
String tableName = "loadtest";
if ( argv.length > 0 )
     tableName = argv[0];
```

Build Select Statement

The SQL `select` statement is built by concatenating a `select` column list clause with the table name stored in the `tableName` variable. The code for this is as follows:

```
String qs = "select * from " + tableName;
```

No `where` clause is appended to the SQL `select` statement; the query will retrieve all rows from the database table.

Create Statement Object and Execute SQL Statement

Then the `Statement` object is created using the `Connection` object and the SQL statement is executed using the `executeQuery` method, as follows:

```
Statement stmt = con.createStatement();
ResultSet rs = stmt.executeQuery( qs );
```

The `executeQuery` method returns a `ResultSet`, which is then processed as shown in the following steps.

Create a ResultSetMetaData Object

A `ResultSetMetaData` object is then created. This is used to determine the characteristics of the `ResultSet` that has been retrieved. The `ResultSet getMetaData` method is used to retrieve this object, as follows:

```
ResultSetMetaData rsmd = rs.getMetaData();
```

Traverse the ResultSet

The code used to retrieve and display the ResultSet follows. First an integer index variable is created and the next method is called for the ResultSet. Calling the next method positions the pointer for the ResultSet at the first result row and determines whether or not there are any rows to retrieve. The boolean return value from the next method (a Java boolean variable named more) is then used to control a while loop, as follows:

```
int n = 0;
boolean more = rs.next();
while ( more ) {
    for ( n = 1; n <= rsmd.getColumnCount(); n++ ) {
        System.out.println( "Col " + n +
                " Name: " + rsmd.getColumnName( n ) +
                " value: " + rs.getString( n ) );
                 }
        }
```

For each iteration of the while loop, all columns in the row are retrieved and displayed. This is accomplished using an inner for loop that iterates up to the count returned by the getColumnCount method of ResultSetMetaData. For each column value returned, a call to the ResultSetMetaData getColumnName method returns the column name. Each column value is returned as a String value using the getString method of the ResultSet class.

The complete code for the dynamic SQL select program is shown in Program 4.2.

Program 4.2 selectgen.java

```
import java.sql.*;
import java.io.*;

class SelectGen {

     public static void main( String argv[] ) {

       try {
```

continued

```
        Class.forName ("jdbc.odbc.JdbcOdbcDriver");
        String url = "jdbc:odbc:msaccessdb";
        Connection con = DriverManager.getConnection (
                                   url, "", "");

        String tableName = "loadtest";
        if ( argv.length > 0 )
           tableName = argv[0];

        String qs = "select * from " + tableName;
        Statement stmt = con.createStatement();

        ResultSet rs = stmt.executeQuery( qs );
        ResultSetMetaData rsmd = rs.getMetaData();

        int n = 0;
        boolean more = rs.next();
            while ( more ) {
              for ( n = 1; n <=
  rsmd.getColumnCount(); n++ ) {
              System.out.println( "Col " + n +
                                 " Name: " +

    rsmd.getColumnName( n ) +
                                  " value: " +
                                  rs.getString( n )
    );
                   }
         }

     }

     catch (java.lang.Exception ex) {
```

continued

```
    // Print description of the exception.
    System.out.println( "** Error on data select. ** " );
    ex.printStackTrace ();
                }

  }

}
```

Prepared Statement

Each SQL query presented to the database engine must be processed before data can be retrieved or updated. The database engine must determine whether or not the SQL statement presented to it is syntactically correct, whether the database objects referenced exist in the engine, and whether the data type conversions necessary can be performed. These basic operations are known as *parsing* the SQL statement. In addition to parsing the query, the database engine must make decisions about what the best access path is to process the SQL statement. This process is known as *optimizing* the SQL statement. Both of these operations require a certain amount of overhead in the database engine. If a query is to be performed many times with the same structure, then it may be better to perform these operations once and merely substitute parameters for the portions of the query that change with each successive execution. This can be accomplished with JDBC using the `PreparedStatement` class.

The `PreparedStatement` class allows a SQL statement to be *prepared* with place-holders for the parameters. These place-holders are usually the "?" character and they can only be used to create parameters for certain portions of the SQL statement. Many databases do not allow database objects (table and column names) to be substituted with parameters.

(This does not preclude creating queries at runtime where the table names and column names are not known. This can still be accomplished by building a `String` with the query and using the `executeQuery` or `executeUpdate` method of the `Statement` class to execute the SQL statement.)

Using PreparedStatement for data retrieval offers performance improvements over queries executed with the Statement class methods. The code shown in this example was used to test this claim. A version of this program (included at the end of this section) contains the same SQL statement execution but instead of preparing the statement, the SQL statement is created using string concatenation and then is executed using the executeQuery method of the Statement class. This version of the program took 126 seconds to complete 2000 iterations. The same SQL statement executed using a prepared statement completed in 24 seconds.

The use of a PreparedStatement also provides a convenient way to define queries in a single location in the code, and then using the prepared statement (represented by a PreparedStatement object) throughout the program.

The program shown here creates and executes a prepared SQL statement in the following steps.

1. Load driver and create connection
2. Create query string with parameters and create PreparedStatement object
3. Set parameter value and execute query
4. Loop for 2000 iterations

Load Driver and Create Connection

As shown previously, the database driver is loaded and the connection to the database is made. The same ODBC data source is used for this connection, as follows:

```
Class.forName ("sun.jdbc.odbc.JdbcOdbcDriver");
String url      = "jdbc:odbc:msaccessdb";
Connection con = DriverManager.getConnection (
                                            url, "", "");
```

The forName method is used to load the JDBC-ODBC bridge class. The URL string is created with reference to the ODBC MicroSoft-Access database used in the example. This string is then passed as a parameter to the getConnection method of DriverManager, which then returns the Connection object.

Create Query String with Parameters and Create PreparedStatement Object

A String used to hold the query is created and assigned an initial value of the SQL select statement with the placeholder in the where clause, as follows:

```
String qs = "select * from loadtest where col1 = ? ";
PreparedStatement prepStmt = con.prepareStatement( qs );
```

The PreparedStatement object, prepStmt, in combination with the setInt method in the preparedStatment class, is now used to execute the statement throughout the program.

Set Parameter Value and Execute Query

The goal of this program is to demonstrate the performance improvement that can be realized with the execution of prepared SQL statements. The starting time and ending time therefore are tracked using a series of calls to a java.util.Date object, as follows:

```
          Date dt = new Date();
          long seconds = dt.getTime();

          String startTime =
DateFormat.getTimeInstance().format( dt );
          System.out.println( "Start Time: " +
startTime );

          int n = 3;
          boolean result;

          prepStmt.setInt( 1, n );
          ResultSet rs = prepStmt.executeQuery();
```

The value of the prepared statement parameter **must** be set before the query is executed. This is accomplished using the setInt method to set the value of the parameter. The setInt method takes two arguments, an integer value indicating the position of the parameter (starting from position 1) in the query statement and an integer value to set the parameter at that position. Once the parameter is set, the executeQuery method of the PreparedStatement class is called to execute the statement and return a ResultSet representing the results of the query.

Loop for 2000 Iterations

In the next step, the result set is positioned before the start of the first set and the loop is started. In this test, data is not actually retrieved and displayed (this does not significantly affect the results). For each iteration, the previous ResultSet is closed, the PreparedStatement parameter is set to the new value using the index variable for the for loop, and the executeQuery method is called and the new ResultSet is retrieved using the same object container that was previously used.

```
        boolean more = rs.next();
        for (; n < 2000 && more ; n++ ) {

            rs.close();
            prepStmt.setInt( 1, n );
            rs   = prepStmt.executeQuery();
            more = rs.next();

        }

        Date dtEnd = new Date();
        long endSeconds = dtEnd.getTime();
        String endTime =
DateFormat.getTimeInstance().format( dtEnd );
        System.out.println( "End Time:" + endTime );

     // display elapsed time
     seconds = (endSeconds - seconds)/1000;
     System.out.println( "Elapsed time: " + seconds +
                " seconds for " + n + " records." );
```

When the loop is complete, the ending time and the elapsed time are calculated and displayed to the terminal screen.

The complete code for this example is shown in Program 4.3.

Program 4.3 preptest2.Java

```
import java.sql.*;
import java.io.*;
import java.util.Date;

class PrepTest2 {

     public static void main( String argv[] ) {

       try {

          Class.forName ("sun.jdbc.odbc.JdbcOdbcDriver");
          String url = "jdbc:odbc:msaccessdb";

          Connection con = DriverManager.getConnection (
                                         url, "", "");

          String qs = "select * from loadtest where col1 = ? ";
          PreparedStatement prepStmt = con.prepareState-
      ment( qs );

          Date dt = new Date();
          long seconds = dt.getTime();

          String startTime =
      DateFormat.getTimeInstance() .format( dt );
          System.out.println( "Start Time: " + startTime
      );
          int n = 3;
          boolean result;

          prepStmt.setInt( 1, n );
          ResultSet rs = prepStmt.executeQuery();
          boolean more = rs.next();
          for (; n < 2000 && more ; n++ ) {
              rs.close();
              prepStmt.setInt( 1, n );
              rs   = prepStmt.executeQuery();
```

continued

```
            more = rs.next();

        }

        Date dtEnd = new Date();
        long endSeconds = dtEnd.getTime();
       String endTime =
    DateFormat.getTimeInstance().format( dtEnd );
       System.out.println( "End Time:" + endTime );
        // display elapsed time
        seconds = (endSeconds - seconds)/1000;
        System.out.println( "Elapsed time: " + seconds +
                                 " seconds for " + n + "
    records." );

     }

     catch (java.lang.Exception ex) {

    // Print description of the exception.
    System.out.println( "** Error on data select. ** " );
    ex.printStackTrace ();

    }
  }
}
```

The following code example shows the creation and execution of a query statement to process the same number of records but uses a `Statement` object instead of a `PreparedStatement` to process the SQL statement. The query statement is created within the processing loop using the following code.

```
   String qs = "select * from loadtest where col1 = ";
...
   queryString   = qs + n;
   rs  = stmt.executeQuery( queryString );
```

Because the new value for the selection criteria cannot be related to a parameter, with each iteration of the loop the query string must be re-created and then must be executed using the `executeQuery` method of the `Statement` class. The query string has been defined as a string with the column select criteria missing. This information can be appended to the query string to complete the statement and is done for each iteration of the loop, as shown in Program 4.4.

Program 4.4 preptest1.Java

```
import java.sql.*;
import java.io.*;
import java.util.Date;
import java.tsxt.DateFormat;

class PrepTest1 {

   public static void main( String argv[] ) {

      try {

          Class.forName ("sun.jdbc.odbc.JdbcOdbcDriver");
          String url = "jdbc:odbc:msaccessdb";
          Connection con = DriverManager.getConnection (
                                        url, "", "");
          Statement stmt = con.createStatement();

          Date dt = new Date();
          long seconds = dt.getTime();

         String startTime = DateFormat.getTimeInstance()
        .format( dt );
         System.out.println( "Start Time: " + startTime );

          int n = 1;
          String qs = "select * from loadtest where col1 = ";
```

continued

```
        String queryString = qs + n;
        ResultSet rs = stmt.executeQuery( queryString );
        boolean more = rs.next();

        for (; n < 2000 && more ; n++ ) {
            queryString   = qs + n;
            rs  = stmt.executeQuery( queryString );
            more = rs.next();
        }

        Date dtEnd = new Date();
        long endSeconds = dtEnd.getTime();
         String endTime =
      DateFormat.getTimeInstance().format( dtEnd );
         System.out.println( "End Time:" + endTime );

        // display elapsed time
        seconds = (endSeconds - seconds)/1000;
        System.out.println( "Elapsed time: " + seconds +
                                " seconds for " + n + "
      records." );

       }

    catch (java.lang.Exception ex) {

   // Print description of the exception.
   System.out.println( "** Error on data insert. ** " );
   ex.printStackTrace ();
   }
}
}
```

Positioned Cursor Update

It is not uncommon for an application to read data with a cursor and then update rows selectively based on information gathered during the data retrieval process. It is convenient and more efficient simply to update "the current row" of the cursor rather than to create selection criteria and execute another SQL statement to search for and then update the record. The additional statement execution could require an index read and possibly additional data retrieval.

The positioned cursor update (or *update cursor*) provides functionality that eliminates the need to query for an update of a current record. This capability is supported in JDBC provided the database being used supports it. This example performs the following steps:

1. Load database driver and create connection
2. Create `DatabaseMetaData` object and test for positioned update functionality
3. Execute select query
4. Get cursor name and execute update statement
5. Review results

Load Database Driver and Create Connection

The JDBC-ODBC bridge driver is loaded as in the previous steps. The only difference in this case is that the database driver loaded is the Informix database driver. This driver is needed because the Microsoft Access database used in the previous examples does not support positioned update as of this writing.

```
Class.forName ("sun.jdbc.odbc.JdbcOdbcDriver");
String url = "jdbc:odbc:informix5";
Connection con = DriverManager.getConnection (
                        url,      // database URL
                        "usera",  // user name
                        "xxxxx"); // user password
```

The call to create the Connection object includes values for the user name and password. These values are required by the Informix database being used.

Create DatabaseMetaData Object and Test for Positioned Update Functionality

Once the connection is established, the program tests for the ability to perform positioned updates. This is accomplished using the DatabaseMetaData object for the database connection.

```
   // need a database that supports positioned updates
   DatabaseMetaData dmd = con.getMetaData();
   if ( dmd.supportsPositionedUpdate() == false )
{
        System.out.println(
       "Positioned update is not supported by this
database."  );
             System.exit( -1 );
        }
```

The DatabaseMetaData object is created using the getMetaData method of the Connection object. The DatabaseMetaData class contains a supportsPositionedUpdate method that returns true if positioned updates are supported and returns false if they are not. In the previous code snippet, if the supportsPostionedUpdate method returns false then an error message is printed to the terminal screen and the program terminates.

Execute Select Query

Two Statement objects are used to perform the database operations: one Statement to retrieve the data and set the cursor position and the other to perform the update. The statement executed to retrieve the data is created and executed as follows:

```
Statement stmt1 = con.createStatement();
ResultSet rs = stmt1.executeQuery( "select " +
               " * from loadtest where col1 = 5" +
               " for update " );
```

This statement is executed using a `select` statement that ends with the clause "for update." This indicates to the database engine that the cursor may be used later to perform an update.

Get Cursor Name and Execute Update Statement

The common SQL syntax for performing a positioned update is

```
update <table_name>
set    <column_list> = <value_list>
where current of <cursor_name>
```

The cursor name is needed to perform a positioned update. This name is obtained using the `getCursorName` method of the `ResultSet` class as shown:

```
String cursName = rs.getCursorName();
System.out.println( "cursor name is " + cursName );

Statement stmt2 = con.createStatement();

// update stmt2 at col1 = 5
int result = stmt2.executeUpdate(
      "update loadtest set col2 = '1000' " +
      " where current of " + cursName );
```

A second `Statement` is created and the cursor name is used to create the update statement executed with the `executeUpdate` method of the `Statement` class. The cursor name is appended to the clause "where current of" to identify a cursor for the positioned update statement.

Review Results

This example then executes another statement that retrieves data from the updated row. This data is then displayed to the terminal screen to validate that the update has taken place, as shown in the following code:

```
// retrieve row to view updated value
rs = stmt1.executeQuery( "select * from loadtest " +
       " where col1 = 5 " );

 rs.next();
 System.out.println( " col1 = " + rs.getInt( 1 ) +
                     " col2 = " + rs.getInt( 2 ) );
```

The complete code for this example is shown in Program 4.5.

Program 4.5 posupd.java

```
import java.sql.*;
import java.io.*;

class PosUpd {

     public static void main( String argv[] ) {

       try {

          Class.forName ("sun.jdbc.odbc.JdbcOdbcDriver");
          String url = "jdbc:odbc:informix5";
          Connection con = DriverManager.getConnection (
                         url, "usera", "xxxxx");

          // need a database that supports positioned
      updates
          DatabaseMetaData dmd = con.getMetaData();

          if ( dmd.supportsPositionedUpdate() == false ) {
              System.out.println(
          "Positioned update is not supported by this database." );
              System.exit( -1 );
          }

          Statement stmt1 = con.createStatement();
```

continued

```
        ResultSet rs = stmt1.executeQuery( "select " +
                        " * from loadtest where col1 = 5" +
                        " for update " );
        rs.next(); // look at the first row (col1=5)

        String cursName = rs.getCursorName();
        System.out.println( "cursor name is " +
    cursName );

        Statement stmt2 = con.createStatement();

        // update stmt2 at col1 = 5
        int result = stmt2.executeUpdate(

            "update loadtest set col2 = '1000' " +
            " where current of " + cursName );

        // retrieve row to view updated value
        rs = stmt1.executeQuery( "select * from
    loadtest " +
           " where col1 = 5 " );

        rs.next();
        System.out.println( " col1 = " + rs.getInt( 1 ) +
                        " col2 = " + rs.getInt( 2 ) );

     }

     catch (java.lang.Exception ex) {

    // Print description of the exception.
    System.out.println( "** Error on data select. ** " );
    ex.printStackTrace ();

    }
  }
}
```

Transaction Modes

Transactions provide the capability to treat a series of SQL update statements as a single statement; if any statement fails, the entire set of updates is removed from the database. If a database supports transactions, JDBC provides the facilities to use these transactions.

With JDBC, if a database supports transactions and transaction logging is on, then every statement is treated as though a transaction were open. There is no explicit "begin work" to indicate the start of a transaction because the database is always in a transaction. A `commit` method is available in the `Connection` class to commit all current work to the database and begin a new transaction. This effectively executes a "begin work" against the database.

A JDBC connection begins with the database in *auto-commit* mode. This means that every SQL statement executed is treated as an individual transaction; no statements will be grouped together as transactions. This mode must be changed using the `setAutoCommit` method of the `Connection` class. The following steps are involved in the creation of the transaction modes example.

1. Load driver and create connection
2. Set the auto-commit mode
3. Create statement and execute DDL and DML
4. Commit work
5. Create prepared statement and execute updates
6. Rollback work and examine results
7. `catch` code block

These steps are detailed in the sections that follow.

Load Driver and Create Connection

The JDBC-ODBC bridge driver is loaded first. The database driver loaded is the Informix database driver because support for transactions is needed in this example.

```
Class.forName ("sun.jdbc.odbc.JdbcOdbcDriver");
String url = "jdbc:odbc:informix5";
Connection con = DriverManager.getConnection (
```

```
                    url,
                    "usera",
                    "xxxxx");
```

The call to create the `Connection` object includes values for the user name and password. These values were required by the Informix database being used.

Set the Auto-Commit Mode

When the JDBC auto-commit mode is set to true, each SQL statement is executed as a *singleton* transaction; if it completes successfully, there is an implied commit to the database. This mode would preclude the grouping of a set of SQL statements as one single, atomic transaction. Setting the auto-commit mode to *false* disables the auto-commit feature and allows a group of SQL statements to be grouped as a transaction.

```
// will turn off the default auto-commit mode so that statements
// can be grouped as transactions.
con.setAutoCommit( false );
```

Create Statement and Execute DDL and DML

A statement object is required to execute a series of SQL statements to update the database. DDL statements are then executed to create a database table and create an index on the database table.

```
        Statement stmt = con.createStatement();


  int result = stmt.executeUpdate(
      "create table transtest( col1 int, col2 int, col3
char(10) )" );
  result =    stmt.executeUpdate(
      "create index idx1 on transtest( col1 ) " );
```

Commit Work

If an error occurs during the execution of any of the previous SQL statements, a `SQLException` is thrown and caught with the `catch` code block in the method. This code block executes a SQL *rollback*, which rolls back or removes from the database the results of the execution of the statements shown in the previous method. If code execution has arrived at the following line, then no fatal exception has been thrown and the data can be committed to the database. This can be accomplished using the `commit` method of the `Connection` class.

```
con.commit();
```

Note that in some databases, executing a `commit` or `rollback` would close open database statements, requiring database objects to be re-opened after these operations.

Create Prepared Statement and Execute Updates

To demonstrate multiple updates and transactions, a series of updates will be performed as a single transaction. A `preparedStatement` object is created using the `prepareStatement` method of the `Connection` object. This returns a statement with a single parameter which is substituted before the statement is executed as shown below.

```
...
int n = 0;
PreparedStatement prepStmt = con.prepareStatement(
  " insert into transtest values ( ?, 1, 'XXXXXXX' ) " );

for ( n = 1; n < 20; n++ ) {
    prepStmt.setInt( 1, n );
    prepStmt.executeUpdate();
}
```

Within the `for` loop, the single statement parameter is set and the prepared statement is executed using the `executeUpdate` statement. This loop will be executed and the database update performed 20 times. This entire set of updates will represent a single transaction.

Rollback Work and Display Results

To demonstrate the effect of a rollback work statement, the `rollback` method of the `Connection` object is executed. This rolls back the work since the last commit. This means that the database table and the index remain in the database after the rollback method has been executed because these statements were executed before the commit work method had been called.

```
con.rollback();

// validate that rollback succeeded. There should be
//no data in the table
Statement stmt1= con.createStatement();
ResultSet rs = stmt1.executeQuery( "select * from transtest" );
boolean more = rs.next();
if ( more == false )
   System.out.println( "Data was rolled back ");
```

After the rollback work has been executed, a new statement is created and executed to examine the data that remains. If no data is found, this indicates that the table is still there, but there is no data in the table—an indication that the rollback was successful.

catch Code Block

This section of code will be executed if an `SQLException` has been thrown.

This indicates that an error has occurred and all of the statements in the group should be rolled back. This rollback is performed as follows:

```
catch (SQLException  ex) {

// Print description of the exception.
System.out.println( "** Error on database update. Rolling back
... ** " );
con.rollback();
ex.printStackTrace ();

}
```

Program 4.6 provides the complete code for the transaction mode example.

Program 4.6 TransData.Java

```
import java.sql.*;
import java.io.*;
class TransData {

  public static void main( String argv[] ) {

    try {

      Class.forName ("sun.jdbc.odbc.JdbcOdbcDriver");
      String url = "jdbc:odbc:msaccessdb";
      Connection con = DriverManager.getConnection (
                                   url, "", "");

      // will turn off the default auto-commit mode so that
     statements
      // can be grouped as transactons.
      con.setAutoCommit( false );

      Statement stmt = con.createStatement();

      int result =
        stmt.executeUpdate(
             "create table transtest( col1 int, col2 int,
     col3 char(10) )" );

      result =
        stmt.executeUpdate(
          "create index idx1 on transtest( col1 ) " );

      con.commit();
      int n = 0;
      PreparedStatement prepStmt = con.prepareStatement(
```

continued

```
        " insert into transtest values ( ?, 1, 'XXXXXXX' ) " );

      for ( n = 1; n < 20; n++ ) {
           prepStmt.setInt( 1, n );
           prepStmt.executeUpdate();
      }

      con.rollback();

// validate that rollback succeeded.
// There should be no data in the table
      Statement stmt1= con.createStatement();
      ResultSet rs = stmt1.executeQuery( "select * from
     transtest" );
      boolean more = rs.next();
      if ( more == false )
         System.out.println( "Data was rolled back ");

    }
    catch (SQLException  ex) {

   // Print description of the exception.
   System.out.println( "** Error on database update.
      Rolling back ... ** " );
  con.rollback();
  ex.printStackTrace ();

   }
  }
}
```


CGI Application

With the prevalence of the World Wide Web, CGI applications are commonplace. Though currently these are written primarily in C or C++, Java presents an attractive alternative to these languages for the creation of these applications. The code in this section provides an example of a simple CGI application written in Java.

The purpose of the this CGI program is to retrieve the records from the customer's table where the last name is *like* the parameter passed into the CGI program. The CGI application first receives the command line arguments, the CGI token. This token is parsed and used as a parameter in a SQL statement to be executed. The results of the executed statement are formatted as an HTML page and displayed to the terminal screen. The following steps are used in this application:

1. Load driver manager and create connection
2. Create prepared statement with parameter
3. Parse CGI arguments
4. Set parameters and execute query
5. Retrieve results and HTML output

These steps are discussed in more detail in the following sections.

Load Driver Manager and Create Connection

The driver manager is loaded as in the previous examples and the connection is created with the Microsoft Access database. The code for this is as follows:

```
Class.forName ("sun.jdbc.odbc.JdbcOdbcDriver");
String url = "jdbc:odbc:msaccessdb";
Connection con = DriverManager.getConnection (
                                  url, "", "");
```

Create Prepared Statement with Parameter

A `PreparedStatement` object is then created using a SQL `select` statement that includes a parameter for the filter statement. This parameter is used to identify the list of customer table records that will be displayed in the HTML page. The value for this parameter is supplied by the CGI parameters passed to the program.

```
PreparedStatement stmt  = con.prepareStatement(
                   " select * from customers " +
                   " where lastname like ? " );
```

Parse CGI Arguments

The CGI parameters are passed to the program using a "+" to separate the arguments. These arguments must be parsed and the parameter values retrieved from the string passed to the program.

First the command line array is checked to determine whether or not any arguments have been passed to the program. If no arguments have been passed, the program will exit.

```
...
  // parse the CGI arguments
  if ( argv.length == 0 ) {
     System.out.println( "Invalid Parameters. Exiting ... " );
     System.exit( -1 );
  }

  StringTokenizer Params = new StringTokenizer(
                                 argv[0], delim );
  Vector vParams = new Vector();
  String s = null;

  while ( Params.hasMoreTokens() ) {

          s = Params.nextToken();
          vParams.addElement( s );
  }
...
```

Next, a `StringTokenizer` object is created using the array of strings passed on the command line and specifying the delimiter string (previously set to the "+" character) to be used to parse the string. A `Vector` object is also created to store the parameters passed on the command line. A `while` loop is then executed to retrieve each of the parameter values passed. As each of these values is retrieved, it is added to the `Vector` used to store the parameter values. (In this example, only one parameter value is passed.)

Set Parameters and Execute Query

The parameter values then are used as parameters for the query. This is accomplished by retrieving the parameter value from the `Vector` object used to store the values and using this string to set the first parameter in the `PreparedStatement` containing the query.

```
// Arg1 is the last name


stmt.setString( 1, vParams.elementAt( 0 ).toString() );
ResultSet rs = stmt.executeQuery();
```

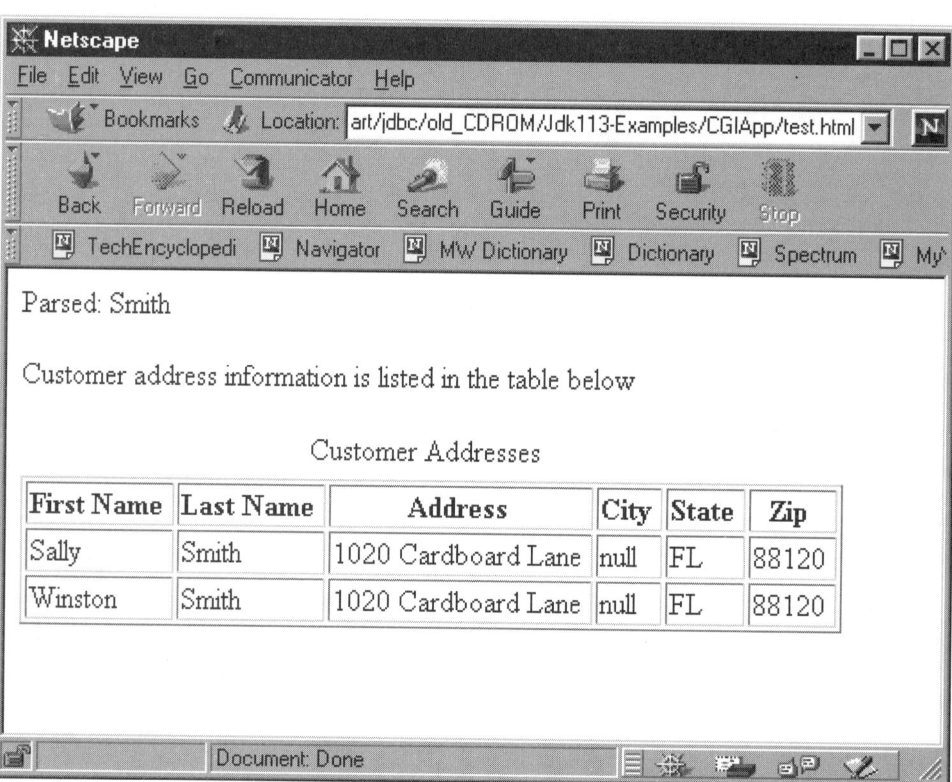

First Name	Last Name	Address	City	State	Zip
Sally	Smith	1020 Cardboard Lane	null	FL	88120
Winston	Smith	1020 Cardboard Lane	null	FL	88120

Figure 4.1: *Output of CGI demonstration application*

Retrieve Results and Display Formatted Output

The results of the query are then retrieved in a `ResultSet`. If no results have been retrieved, as indicated by the `boolean` value returned from the `next ResultSet` method call, then the program displays an error message and exits. If program execution continues, then values have been found and will be displayed using formatting commands for the HTML pages. These formatting commands display the page as an HTML table, as shown in Figure 4.1.

```
ResultSetMetaData rsmd = rs.getMetaData();

boolean more = rs.next();
if ( !more ) {
   System.out.println( "Error - no rows retrieved" );
   System.exit( -1 );
}

// HTML page header
System.out.println( "</ul>" );
System.out.println(
"<p> Customer address information is listed in the table below
</p>" );

// Table header
System.out.println( "<table border > " );
System.out.println( "<caption>Customer Addresses </caption> " );
System.out.println( "<th> First Name </th>" );
System.out.println( "<th> Last Name </th>" );
System.out.println( "<th> Address </th> " );
System.out.println( "<th> City </th> " );
System.out.println( "<th> State </th> " );
System.out.println( "<th> Zip </th> " );

// display the table rows
while ( more ) {
      System.out.println( "<tr> " );
      for ( n = 1; n <= rsmd.getColumnCount(); n++ )
            System.out.println( "<td > "  +
                             rs.getString( n ) +
```

```
                                  " </td> " );
        System.out.println( "</tr>" );
        more = rs.next();
   }
  System.out.println( "</table> " );

}
```

A `Statement` object is used to determine the number of columns in the retrieved `ResultSet`. Each column of the retrieved row is placed in the table, the result being a HTML table with rows of data for each row returned from the database.

The complete code for this example is displayed in Program 4.7.

Program 4.7 cgiapp.java

```
import java.sql.*;
import java.util.StringTokenizer;
import java.util.Vector;
import java.io.*;

class cgiApp {

     static String delim = "+";

public static void main( String argv[] ) {

   int n = 0;

  try {

     Class.forName ("sun.jdbc.odbc.JdbcOdbcDriver");
     String url = "jdbc:odbc:msaccessdb";
     Connection con = DriverManager.getConnection (
                                  url, "", "");

     PreparedStatement stmt  = con.prepareStatement(
                        " select * from customers " +
```

continued

```
                    " where lastname like ? " );


// parse the CGI arguments
if ( argv.length == 0 ) {
   System.out.println( "Invalid Parameters. Exiting ...
" );
   System.exit( -1 );
}

StringTokenizer Params = new StringTokenizer( argv[0],
 delim );
Vector vParams = new Vector();
String s = null;

while ( Params.hasMoreTokens() ) {

       s = Params.nextToken();
       vParams.addElement( s );
}

// Arg1 is the last name
s = vParams.elementAt(0).toString();

stmt.setString( 1, vParams.elementAt( 0 ).toString() );
ResultSet rs = stmt.executeQuery();

ResultSetMetaData rsmd = rs.getMetaData();

boolean more = rs.next();
if ( !more ) {
   System.out.println( "Error - no rows retrieved" );
   System.exit( -1 );
}

// HTML page header
System.out.println( "</ul>" );
```

continued

```
        System.out.println( "<p> Customer address information is
         listed in the table below </p>" );

        // Table header
        System.out.println( "<table border > " );
        System.out.println( "<caption>Customer Addresses
         </caption> " );
        System.out.println( "<th> First Name </th>" );
        System.out.println( "<th> Last Name </th>" );
        System.out.println( "<th> Address </th> " );
        System.out.println( "<th> City </th> " );
        System.out.println( "<th> State </th> " );
        System.out.println( "<th> Zip </th> " );

        while ( more ) {
              System.out.println( "<tr> " );
              for ( n = 1; n <= rsmd.getColumnCount(); n++ )
                   System.out.println( "<td > "  +
                                  rs.getString( n ) +
                                   " </td> " );
              System.out.println( "</tr>" );
              more = rs.next();
        }
        System.out.println( "</table> " );

    }

    catch ( java.lang.Exception ex ) {
        ex.printStackTrace();
    }
  }
}
```

Metadata Access

The JDBC interface provides access to a rich supply of information about the current database or a `ResultSet`. While many users never need to access this information, there is most likely some small subset that will be useful to most users. For instance, the

ResultSetMetaData class provides information on the number of columns retrieved in a ResultSet. It is very likely that generic routines reading a ResultSet will want to make use of this information rather than hard-coding the column count each time the routine is used.

The following example demonstrates the use of metadata methods for evaluating an unknown query at runtime. This example enables the user to enter a query and then processes the query, using metadata methods to determine the number and type of columns, and making a rudimentary attempt to format the data based on the data type. This program uses the following steps:

1. Retrieve query from the command line
2. Load driver and create connection
3. Create statement and execute the query
4. Retrieve the ResultSet and determine the number of columns
5. Execute formatting routine
6. Iterate results displaying formatted data

These steps are explained in more detail in the following sections.

Retrieve Query from the Command Line

The first step is to retrieve the query as a String from the command line. This is accomplished by setting the queryString string to the value of the first element of the argument string array (argv). If this value is null, the program displays an error message and aborts. This string is then used to execute the query.

```
// default query is NULL
String queryString = null;

// default data source name
String url   = "jdbc:odbc:msaccessdb";

// first argument is the query to execute
if ( argv.length > 0 )
   queryString = argv[0];
```

```
    // if no query, must abort
    if ( queryString == null ) {
        System.out.println(
            "Must enter a query as a  parameter. Aborting. " );
        System.exit(-1);
    }
```

Load Driver and Create Connection

As in the previous examples, the DriverManager must be loaded and the Connection object must be created. The url string is used to connect to a local Microsoft Access database using the database URL.

```
Class.forName ("sun.jdbc.odbc.JdbcOdbcDriver");
Connection con = DriverManager.getConnection (
                    url, "", "");
```

Create Statement and Execute the Query

The Statement object is then created and the query string received on the command line is executed. The results of the query execution are returned as a ResultSet. This ResultSet then is used to retrieve and process the results.

```
// Create statement
Statement stmt = con.createStatement( );

// Execute the query
ResultSet rs = stmt.executeQuery( queryString );
```

Retrieve the ResultSet and Determine the Number of Columns

A ResultSetMeta object is created from the ResultSet returned by the query statement execution. One of the more common uses of a ResultSetMetaData object is the retrieval of the number of columns returned by the ResultSet using the getColumnCount method as shown in the following code.

```
    // Determine the nature of the Results
    ResultSetMetaData md = rs.getMetaData();

    // display the results
    int numCols = md.getColumnCount();
```

Execute Formatting Routine

The ResultSetMetaData object is used to determine the nature of the data returned by the query. The formatOutputString routine is used to interpret and format the data. It receives three parameters: the ResultSetMetaData object, the ResultSet object, and the column index. The OutputString is the string that is returned by the method, and the colTypeNameString is the string used to store the data type name of the column data type:

```
  // Formatting routine
    static String formatOutputString( ResultSetMetaData rsmd,
                                      ResultSet   rs,
                                      int         colIndex ) {
    String OutputString = null;
    String colTypeNameString = null;

    try {

      int colType   = rsmd.getColumnType( colIndex );

      colTypeNameString = typeNameString( colType );
      if ( colTypeNameString.equals( "UNKNOWN" ) ||
        colTypeNameString.equals( "OTHER"  ) )
       colTypeNameString = rsmd.getColumnTypeName( colIndex );

      Object obj    = formattedValue( rs, rsmd, colIndex,
colType );
     if ( obj == null )
        return ( " ** NULL ** " );

     OutputString = rsmd.getColumnLabel( colIndex ) +
```

```
                        " Data Type is " +
                        colTypeNameString +
                        " ; value is " +  obj.toString();
    }
```

The getColumnType method of the ResultSetMetaData class is called to retrieve the column type of the ResultSet column being formatted (referenced by the colIndex parameter).

This method then calls the formattedValue method to format the data in the column based on the column data type. This method returns an object that is tested for a NULL value. If the object is NULL, then a string indicating a NULL value is returned. If the object is not null, a String is created with the column label as returned by the getColumnLabel method of the ResultMetaData object, the data type name as stored in the colTypeNameString variable, and the value of the object as returned by the Object class toString method. This String is returned by the method as shown in the return clause shown following the catch code block in the following code.

```
  catch ( SQLException ex ) {


            System.out.println ("\n*** SQLException
caught ***\n");


            while (ex != null) {
                System.out.println ("SQLState: " +
                        ex.getSQLState ());
                System.out.println ("Message:  " +
                        ex.getMessage ());
                System.out.println ("Vendor:   " +
                        ex.getErrorCode ());
                        ex = ex.getNextException ();
                System.out.println ("");
           }
       }

return( OutputString );

}
```

The `typeNameString` method evaluates the integer data type value returned by the `ResultSetMetaData getColType` method and simply maps the integer value to a character string name. This character string name then is displayed with the column data to indicate the column data type.

```
// return the type name as a string
static String typeNameString( int Type ) {

  switch ( Type ) {

case ( Types.BIGINT ):         return ( "BIGINT" );
case ( Types.BINARY ):         return ( "BINARY" );
case ( Types.BIT ):            return ( "BIT" );
case ( Types.CHAR ):           return ( "CHAR" );
case ( Types.INTEGER ):        return ( "INTEGER" );
case ( Types.DATE ):           return ( "DATE" );
case ( Types.DECIMAL ):        return ( "DECIMAL" );
case ( Types.FLOAT ):          return ( "FLOAT" );
case ( Types.LONGVARBINARY ): return ( "LONGVARBINARY" );
case ( Types.LONGVARCHAR ):    return ( "LONGVARCHAR" );
case ( Types.OTHER ):          return ( "OTHER" );

  }

return  ( "UNKNOWN" );

 }
```

The `formattedValue` method demonstrates the process of formatting column data based on data type. The method receives a `ResultSet` object, a `ResultSetMetaData` object, a column index, and a data type for the column. The method returns an `Object` reference.

The method evaluates the data type being passed into the method. Based on the data type, the correct `ResultSet` "get" method is called to retrieve the data. The correct data type object is identified as the return value for each "get" method, but when the object is returned from the method, it is cast as an `Object` reference. This allows the return value to be managed in a generic way in the calling method.

There is no specific effort to format the data in this example, though that could easily be managed in the appropriate `case` clause of the `switch` statement shown in the following code. In some cases, the method does map several data types to a single Java data type, but there is no effort made to drastically change the format of the specific data in the columns.

Each `case` clause in this `switch` statement returns an `Object` reference for the specific data type returned. Should control fall through the `switch` statement, a return statement returns the object reference for the `ResultSet` column (`getObject`).

```
  static Object formattedValue( ResultSet rs,
                                    ResultSetMetaData rsmd,
                                    int colIndex,
                                    int Type ) {

    Object generalObj = null;

         try {

    switch ( Type ) {

       case ( Types.BIGINT ):
          Long longObj = new Long( rs.getLong(colIndex ) );
              return ( (Object) longObj );
       case ( Types.BIT ):
           Boolean booleanObj = new Boolean( rs.getBoolean(
colIndex ) );
            return ( (Object) booleanObj );
       case ( Types.CHAR ):
          String stringObj = new String( rs.getString( colIndex ) );
            return ( (Object) stringObj );
       case ( Types.INTEGER ):
           Integer integerObj = new Integer( rs.getInt( colIndex )
);
           return ( (Object) integerObj );
       case ( Types.DATE ):
           Date dateObj = rs.getDate( colIndex );
           return ( (Object) dateObj );
       case ( Types.DECIMAL ):
```

```
        case ( Types.FLOAT ):
            Numeric numericObj = rs.getNumeric( colIndex,
rsmd.getScale( colIndex ) );
            return ( (Object) numericObj );

        case ( Types.BINARY ):
        case ( Types.LONGVARBINARY ) :
        case ( Types.LONGVARCHAR ) :
        case ( Types.OTHER ) :
            return ( rs.getObject( colIndex ) );

  }
  // get the object handle
  generalObj = rs.getObject( colIndex );
 }
```

Iterate Results Displaying Formatted Data

The `ResultSet` is iterated first by positioning the pointer before the first element using the `next` method, and then moving through the `ResultSet` using a `while` loop. For each row in the `ResultSet`, the row count is displayed and an inner loop displays the output of the `formatOutputString` method.

```
   // Display data, fetching until end of the result set
   boolean more = rs.next();
   int rowCount = 0;
   while (more) {

          rowCount++;
          System.out.println( "*** row " + rowCount + " *** " );

          // Loop through each column, getting the
          // column data and displaying

          for (n=1; n<=numCols; n++)
                // display formatted data
                System.out.println( formatOutputString(
md,rs, n ));
                System.out.println("");
```

```
                more = rs.next();
            }
    }
```

The complete code for this example is shown in Program 4.8.

Program 4.8 MetaDataExample1.Java

```
import java.net.URL;
import java.sql.*;

class MetaDataExample1 {

     public static void main( String argv[] ) {
       short n = 0;

       try {

         // default query is NULL
         String queryString = null;

         // default data source name
         String url   = "jdbc:odbc:msaccessdb";

         // first argument is the query to execute
         if ( argv.length > 0 )
            queryString = argv[0];

         // if no query, must abort
         if ( queryString == null ) {

            System.out.println(
                  "Must enter a query as a  parameter.
      Aborting. " );
            System.exit(-1);
         }

         Class.forName ("sun.jdbc.odbc.JdbcOdbcDriver");
```

continued

```
    Connection con = DriverManager.getConnection (
                          url, "", "");

    // Create statement
    Statement stmt = con.createStatement( );

    // Execute the query
    ResultSet rs = stmt.executeQuery( queryString );

    // Determine the nature of the Results
    ResultSetMetaData md = rs.getMetaData();

    // display the results
    int numCols = md.getColumnCount();

    System.out.println("");

    // Display data, fetching until end of the result set
    boolean more = rs.next();
    int rowCount = 0;
    while (more) {

      rowCount++;
     System.out.println( "*** row " + rowCount + " ***
  " );

           // Loop through each column, getting the
           // column data and displaying

           for (n=1; n<=numCols; n++)
                 // display formatted data
                  System.out.println(
  formatOutputString( md,rs, n ));
                 System.out.println("");
                 more = rs.next();
           }
}
```

continued

```
    catch ( SQLException ex ) {

                System.out.println (
                   "\n*** SQLException caught ***\n");

                while (ex != null) {
                  System.out.println ("SQLState: " +
                    ex.getSQLState ());
                  System.out.println ("Message:  " +
                    ex.getMessage ());
                  System.out.println ("Vendor:   " +
                    ex.getErrorCode ());
                  ex = ex.getNextException ();
                  System.out.println ("");
                }
        }
        catch (java.lang.Exception ex) {

                // Got some other type of exception.
    Dump it.

                ex.printStackTrace ();
        }
  }


   // Formatting routine
   static String formatOutputString( ResultSetMetaData rsmd,
                        ResultSet         rs,
                        int               colIndex ) {
     String OutputString = null;
     String colTypeNameString = null;

     try {

       int colType  = rsmd.getColumnType( colIndex );
```

continued

```
    colTypeNameString = typeNameString( colType );
    if ( colTypeNameString.equals( "UNKNOWN" ) ||
         colTypeNameString.equals( "OTHER"  ) )
         colTypeNameString = rsmd.getColumnTypeName(
  colIndex );



    Object obj    = formattedValue( rs, rsmd,
  colIndex, colType );
    if ( obj == null )
       return ( " ** NULL ** " );

    OutputString = rsmd.getColumnLabel( colIndex ) + " Data
  Type is " +
                 colTypeNameString +
                 " ; value is " +  obj.toString();



   }



 catch ( SQLException ex ) {

                     System.out.println ("\n*** SQLEx-
  ception caught ***\n");

             while (ex != null) {
                 System.out.println ("SQLState: " +
                   ex.getSQLState ());
                 System.out.println ("Message:  " +
                   ex.getMessage ());
                 System.out.println ("Vendor:   " +
                   ex.getErrorCode ());
                   ex = ex.getNextException ();
                 System.out.println ("");
```

continued

```
            }
        }

    return( OutputString );

    }


  // return the type name as a string

static String typeNameString( int Type ) {

  switch ( Type ) {
    case ( Types.BIGINT ):     return ( "BIGINT" );
    case ( Types.BINARY ):     return ( "BINARY" );
    case ( Types.BIT ):        return ( "BIT" );
    case ( Types.CHAR ):       return ( "CHAR" );
    case ( Types.INTEGER ):     return ( "INTEGER" );
    case ( Types.DATE ):       return ( "DATE" );
    case ( Types.DECIMAL ):    return ( "DECIMAL" );
    case ( Types.FLOAT ) :     return ( "FLOAT" );
    case ( Types.LONGVARBINARY ) : return (
       "LONGVARBINARY" );
    case ( Types.LONGVARCHAR ) : return (
       "LONGVARCHAR" );
    case ( Types.OTHER ) :     return ( "OTHER" );

    }


   return  ( "UNKNOWN" );

  }

  static Object formattedValue( ResultSet rs,
                          ResultSetMetaData rsmd,
```

continued

```
                         int colIndex,
                         int Type ) {

    Object generalObj = null;

        try {
    switch ( Type ) {
        case ( Types.BIGINT ):
          Long longObj = new Long( rs.getLong(colIndex ) );
             return ( (Object) longObj );
        case ( Types.BIT ):
           Boolean booleanObj = new Boolean(
      rs.getBoolean( colIndex ) );
           return ( (Object) booleanObj );
        case ( Types.CHAR ):
           String stringObj = new String( rs.getString(
      colIndex ) );
           return ( (Object) stringObj );
        case ( Types.INTEGER ):
          Integer integerObj = new Integer( rs.getInt(
      colIndex ) );
            return ( (Object) integerObj );
        case ( Types.DATE ):
            Date dateObj = rs.getDate( colIndex );
            return ( (Object) dateObj );
        case ( Types.DECIMAL ):
        case ( Types.FLOAT ):
          Numeric numericObj = rs.getNumeric( colIndex,
      rsmd.getScale( colIndex ) );
            return ( (Object) numericObj );

        case ( Types.BINARY ):
        case ( Types.LONGVARBINARY ) :
        case ( Types.LONGVARCHAR ) :
        case ( Types.OTHER ) :
            return ( rs.getObject( colIndex ) );
```

continued

```
      }
      // get the object handle
      generalObj = rs.getObject( colIndex );

    }
         catch ( SQLException ex ) {

System.out.println ("\n*** SQLException caught ***\n");

                        while (ex != null) {
                        System.out.println ("SQLState: " +
                          ex.getSQLState ());
                        System.out.println ("Message:  " +
                          ex.getMessage ());
                        System.out.println ("Vendor:   " +
                          ex.getErrorCode ());
                        ex = ex.getNextException ();
                        System.out.println ("");
                  }
           }


     // just return the object referernce
     return  ( generalObj );

    }
    }
```

Scrolling ResultSet Array

One of the limitations of the `ResultSet` is that *scroll* cursors are not supported. To overcome this limitation, the Java/JDBC programmer can make use of a small set of methods that provide this capability. These minor code changes provide the ability to move forward or backward through the data set, or to move to a specific row.

The following steps are taken in this program:

1. Declare `RSArray` object
2. Load `DriverManager` and `connection`
3. Create `Statement` and execute
4. Iterate `ResultSet` adding to `ResultSetArray` buffer
5. Display results

These steps are described in more detail in the following sections.

Declare RSArray Object

An `RSArray` object is declared to hold the `ResultSet` elements returned by the `Statement` object. This object contains the methods to store any `ResultSet` elements. The `RSArray` class contains a number of methods that will take any object reference passed (preferably a `ResultSet` object, but that is not required). These objects are stored in a `Vector` object; one for the `ResultSet` object pointer and the other for the columns. (The `RSArray` class is described later in this chapter.)

```
static RSArray rsBuff = new RSArray();
```

Load DriverManager and Connection

The `DriverManager` must be loaded and a `Connection` established. This code establishes a Microsoft Access database connection with a local database using the JDBC-ODBC bridge.

```
        Class.forName ("sun.jdbc.odbc.JdbcOdbcDriver");
String url = "jdbc:odbc:msaccessdb";
Connection con = DriverManager.getConnection ( url, "", "" );
```

Create Statement and Execute

Next, the `Statement` object is created and executed using a query that retrieves all columns and all rows for the `loadtest` table.

```
Statement stmt = con.createStatement();
ResultSet rs   = stmt.executeQuery( " select * from loadtest" );
```

Iterate ResultSet Adding to ResultSetArray Buffer

The ResultSet retrieved by executing the statement is then read in a serial fashion. Each row retrieved is added to the ResultSetArray object. At the end of the while loop, the number of records loaded (which is limited to 50 in this example) is stored in the rowsLoaded integer variable.

```
 while ( more && n++ < 50 ) {

        rsBuff.addElement( rs );

        more = rs.next();
}
int rowsLoaded = n;
```

Display Results

The results are then displayed in a serial fashion by using a RSArray method that displays a specific Vector element. A for loop is executed for the number of rows that have been loaded into the RSArray object. For each iteration of the loop, the BuffelementAt method returns a Vector data type for the element index value passed into the method. This Vector is the columns Vector for the row being displayed. By looping through the number of columns in the query ResultSet (as returned by the getColumnCount method of the ResultSetMetaData) all of the columns in the row will be displayed.

The Vector, named ColumnsVector, that has been returned by the RSArray elementAt method is then traversed. For each element in the Vector, the elementAt method returns an object, and the toString method converts the Object to a String for display.

```
System.out.println( "Processed " + n + " rows" );
// traverse the rs buffer vector ResultsBuffer
```

```
Vector columnsVector = null;
for ( x = 0; x < rowsLoaded-1; x++ ) {

    // get the row
    columnsVector = (Vector) rsBuff.ElementAt( x+1 );

    // display the row contents (columns)
    for ( n = 0; n < rs.getMetaData().getColumnCount(); n++ ) {

    System.out.println( "Row " + x +  " Column: " + n + " " +
                          columnsVector.elementAt( n
).toString() );
              }
            }
       }
```

Tip

Note that because the element is retrieved as an object, it is possible to determine the data type of the object by determining the name of the class. The code to perform this function would be as follows:

```
Object obj = columns.elementAt( x );
String s = obj.getClass().getName();
```

This code retrieves the `Object` reference for the specified element and then retrieves the class of the object and then calls the `getName` method to retrieve the name of the class. Using this class name, the data type of the object can be determined and then used accordingly.

The code for the entire application is presented in Program 4.9.

Program 4.9 RSArray1.java

```
import java.sql.*;
import java.io.*;
import java.util.Vector;

class rsArray1 {

     static RSArray rsBuff = new RSArray();
     public static void main( String argv[] ) {

       try {

          Class.forName ("jdbc.odbc.JdbcOdbcDriver");
          String url = "jdbc:odbc:msaccessdb";
          Connection con = DriverManager.getConnection (
       url, "", "" );

          Statement stmt = con.createStatement();
          ResultSet rs   = stmt.executeQuery( " select *
       from loadtest" );

          int n = 0;
          int x = 1;
          ResultSetMetaData rsmd = rs.getMetaData();

          boolean more = rs.next();
          int colCount = rsmd.getColumnCount();

          while ( more && n++ < 50 ) {

              rsBuff.addElement( rs );

              more = rs.next();

       }
```

continued

```
        int rowsLoaded = n;
        System.out.println( "Processed " + n + " rows" );
        // traverse the rs buffer vector ResultsBuffer

        Vector columnsVector = null;
        for ( x = 0; x < rowsLoaded-1; x++ ) {

            // get the row
            columnsVector = (Vector) rsBuff.ElementAt( x+1
      );

            // display the rows contents (columns)
            for ( n = 0; n <
      rs.getMetaData().getColumnCount(); n++ ) {

                System.out.println( "Row " + x +  "
      Column: " + n + " " +
                        columnsVector.elementAt( n
      ).toString() );
                }
            }
     }

     catch (java.lang.Exception ex) {

    // Print description of the exception.
    System.out.println( "** Error on data select. ** " );
    ex.printStackTrace ();

    }
  }
 }
```

The RSArray Class

The `RSArray` class as used in the previous example provides a means of moving forward and backward through the `ResultSet`. The `RSArray` class is composed of the following methods.

Class Definition

The `RSArray` class contains two `Vector` objects as instance variables. The `ResultsBuffer Vector` object is used to hold an array of `Vector` objects that contain the constituent columns of each of the rows. Instance variables are used to avoid having to instantiate new Vector objects each time the methods are called. The class definition for the `RSArray` class is as shown in the following code.

```
class RSArray {
   // instance variables
   int index = 0;

   // a vector of result sets
   Vector ResultsBuffer = new Vector();

   // a vector of rows (results columns and data values)
   Vector columns = new Vector();
```

A series of methods are used to manipulate the internal `Vector` objects. These methods are used to add elements to the `RSArray` object, retrieve an element at a specific position in the `Object`, or to retrieve the next or previous element in the array. These methods are:

- `AddElement`
- `ElementAt`
- `next`
- `previous`

These methods are described in more detail in the following sections.

AddElement

The `addElement` method takes a single `ResultSet` as its parameter. Each of the columns in this `ResultSet` are retrieved as an `Object` and added to the columns `Vector` object used to store the data in the `ResultSet` columns. A `for` loop is used to retrieve each of the columns in the `ResultSet` using the `getObject` method.

The object containing the columns is then cloned using the `Object` class method clone. This `cloned` object is then added to the

ResultsBuffer Vector object. The elements in the columns Vector then is cleared for the next iteration.

Java objects are passed by reference, so passing the original Object object would lead to problems. Cloning the object makes a new copy thus effectively passing the object by value.

```
addElement(
    void addElement( ResultSet rs ) {
    int x;

    try {

        // store the columns in a Vector
        for ( x = 1;
              x <= rs.getMetaData().getColumnCount();
              x++ )
            columns.addElement( (Object) rs.getObject( x ) );

        // store the columns Vector in the Results Vector
        ResultsBuffer.addElement( (Object) columns.clone() );
        columns.removeAllElements();

    }

    catch ( java.lang.Exception ex ) {

          ex.printStackTrace();
    }
  }
// ————————————————————
```

ElementAt Method

The ElementAt method is used to retrieve the Vector element at the index position passed into the method as a parameter. It returns the element at the index position as an Object by calling the elementAt method of the ResultBuffer. The result of the operation is returned as an Object reference.

```
Object ElementAt( int targetIndex ) {
 Vector returnVector = null;

 try {
   returnVector = (Vector) ResultsBuffer.elementAt( targetIndex-1 );
  }

 catch ( java.lang.Exception ex ) {
    ex.printStackTrace();
 }

return ( (Object) returnVector );

}
```

Next

The next method retrieves the next sequential element in the RSArray. It increments the internal index element and then attempts to retrieve the element at that position.

```
Object next() {
index++;

return ( ElementAt( index ) );

}
```

Previous

The previous method retrieves the previous method in the array. It first decrements the internal index and then attempts to retrieve the previous element in the RSArray.

The complete code for this program is presented in Program 4.10.

Program 4.10 RSArrayGen.java

```
import java.sql.*;
import java.io.*;
import java.util.Vector;

class RSArray {
   // instance variables
   int index = 0;

   // a vector of result sets
   Vector ResultsBuffer = new Vector();

   // a vector of rows (results columns and data values)
   Vector columns = new Vector();

       void addElement( ResultSet rs ) {
       int x;

       try {

           // store the columns in a Vector
           for ( x = 1;
               x <= rs.getMetaData().getColumnCount();
               x++ )
            columns.addElement( (Object) rs.getObject( x ) );

           // store the columns Vector in the Results
     Vector
           ResultsBuffer.addElement( (Object)
     columns.clone() );
           columns.removeAllElements();

        }

       catch ( java.lang.Exception ex ) {

            ex.printStackTrace();
```

continued

```
        }
      }

  // ─────────────────────────

  Object ElementAt( int targetIndex ) {

   Vector returnVector = null;

   try {
     returnVector = (Vector) ResultsBuffer.elementAt(
     targetIndex-1 );

   }

   catch ( java.lang.Exception ex ) {
      ex.printStackTrace();

   }
  return ( (Object) returnVector );

  }

 Object next() {
 index++;

 return ( ElementAt( index ) );

 }

 Object previous() {
 index—;

 return ( elementAt( index ) );

 }
}
```

Summary

This chapter has presented tutorials that demonstrated both the basics of JDBC and more advanced topics. The first example covered basic database access with JDBC and demonstrated the process of creating a connection to a database and retrieving data.

The process of retrieving and processing data with the JDBC `ResultSet`, a requirement for almost all JDBC applications, was demonstrated in several code examples. The important topics covered in the chapter are as follows:

- Database metadata reveals information about the nature of the database connection.
- `ResultSet` metadata reveals information about the nature of the results returned from the database.
- Using the `PreparedStatement` class to prepare a SQL statement provides performance gains and can simplify coding.
- To overcome the JDBC limitation of unidirectional cursors, results can be stored in a `Vector` object; this `Vector` object can then be used to access data randomly.

Coming Up

One of the primary uses of Java is to create applets. The following chapter provides an uncomplicated version of JDBC usage in an applet. This applet displays an applet window, retrieves data into a `ResultSet` vector, and then allows the user to browse the data moving both forward and backward through the data.

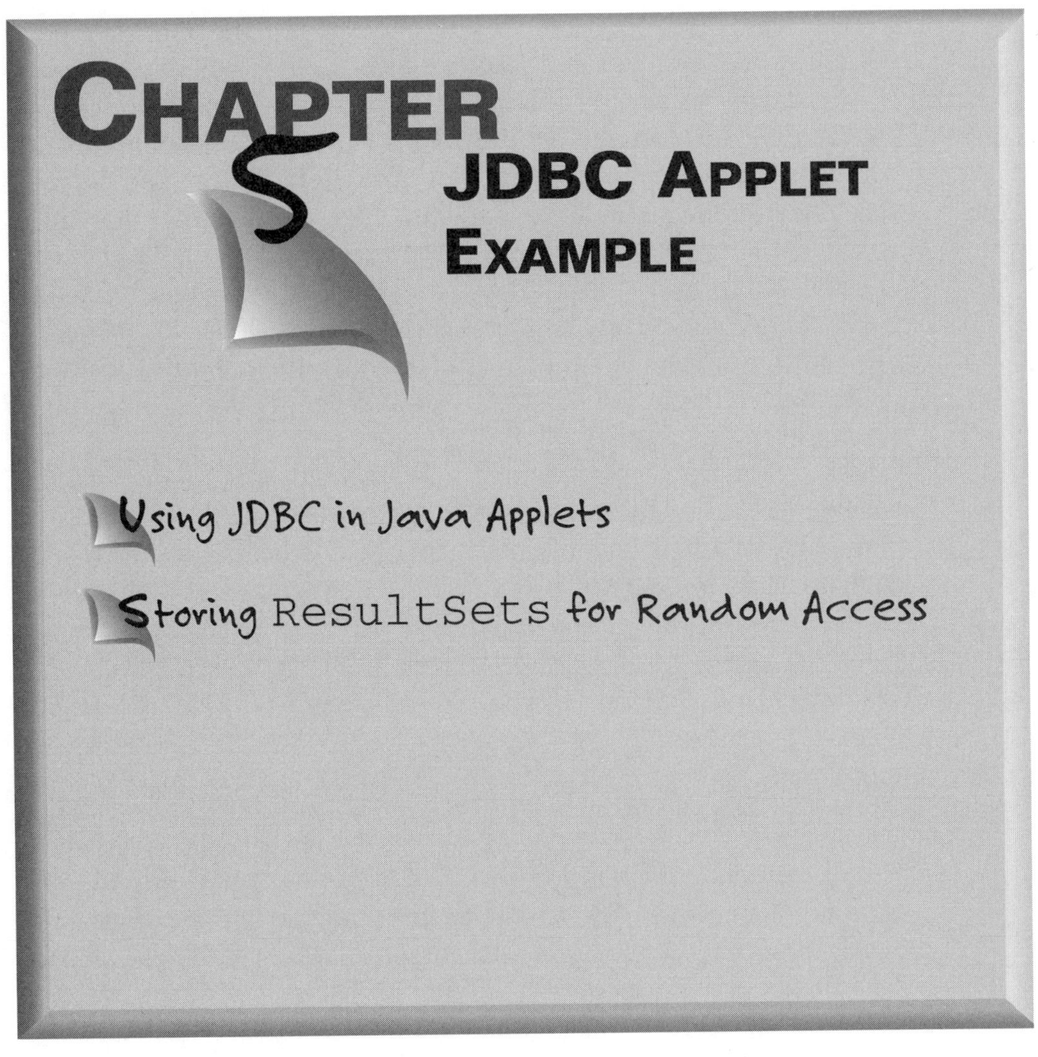

Currently the primary use of Java is the creation of applets that can be run within Web browsers. The use of JDBC in these applets is moderately different from the JDBC programming shown in the previous chapter. With applets, as with most GUI applications, users control the flow of the program. Database access is controlled via GUI controls. In these applications, JDBC calls are usually made as a result of button events triggered. JDBC calls are made in the button handler or in methods called from the button handlers.

Java applets currently have a security limitation that restricts their access to remote database sites. Java applets can only make connections, including database connections, to the site from which they were downloaded. This is not a problem if in fact the database server needed resides on the same machine as the server where the applet's HTML page resides. If this is not the case, then a three-tiered approach is needed; this would involve the applet communicating with a third-tier application on an accessible server that, in turn, would communicate with the database engine on another machine.

When an application allows a user to browse data, the user is usually allowed to move both forward and back in the data set. Because JDBC does not currently have this capability in the `ResultSet` class, this tutorial implements a concept shown in the previous chapter—the storage of query results in a `Vector` object to allow the data to be read in both directions.

This chapter presents a simple implementation of an applet using code generated by the Mojo Java development product. While some of the objects are named differently than would be the case with other development products or if the applet were written without a code generation tool, the implementation of the JDBC code would be the same.

Overview

This applet demonstrates a simple data browsing application for a list of names displaying a first name and last name field to the applet window. The applet user can press the get *data button* to retrieve all rows from the database. The button handler builds a query string, which is then executed and the results loaded into a `Vector` object. As the user progresses forward or back through the results using the buttons in the window, `Vector` elements (the result data) are retrieved from the `Vector` and displayed to the window. A button is also provided to allow the user to insert data into the database.

This code was generated using a Java development tool known as Mojo. Mojo contains a window painter and class browser combined in a flexible interface that allows for the insertion of pre-developed components. An evaluation version of Mojo version 2.0 is provided on the CD-ROM that accompanies this book.

The applet user controls the applet using the buttons on the window. These buttons are as follows.

- Insert data
- Get data
- Next row
- Previous row

The function of each of these buttons is explained in the following sections.

Insert Data

The *insert data* button retrieves data from the data fields. This data is then appended to a SQL `insert` statement and the statement is executed to insert the data into the database.

Get Data

The *get data* operation is executed to retrieve all data in the database table. A SQL statement is created to select data from the target table. This `select` statement is executed and the results returned into a `ResultSet`. The entire `ResultSet` is then stored in a `Vector` object. The data for the first row then is displayed to the window fields. An index variable is initialized; this variable will be used to track the current position in the "result" set.

Next Row

The *next row* operation is executed to retrieve the data in the next row and display the data to the window. This operation increments an internal index variable and retrieves the data at that index position in the `Vector` object being used to store the results. The information retrieved is displayed to the to the applet window.

Previous Row

The *previous row* operation retrieves the previous row of data and displays it to the window. This operation first decrements an internal index variable and then retrieves the data at that index position in the Vector object being used to store the results. The information retrieved is displayed to the window.

Applet Code

The JDBC applet code presented here is similar to most applets. Variables are declared, a window is displayed, buttons and controls are added to the window, and event handlers wait for user-initiated events. In this example, the code that interacts with the database is executed in the button handlers. A class is used to encapsulate the database activity and contains as instance variables the objects used to interact with the database. The following components comprise the JDBC applet example.

- Declarations
- Display applet window
- 'Get data' button handler
- 'Insert data' button handler
- 'Previous row' button handler
- 'Next row' button handler

Declarations

Two classes are declared to control the database interaction: a database results class (DBResults) and a database control class (DBControl). The database results class will be used to store the results of the database query, and the database control class will be used to encapsulate the objects used to control the database.

The database control class contains the objects that are used to interact with the database. The Connection, Statement, and ResultSet objects used by the applet are all instance variables in this class. These objects are initialized in the event handler for the 'get data' button.

A current position index variable and a Vector object are also components of this class; these variables combine to provide the functionality that enables the 'previous button' operation to work correctly. The current position variable is incremented and decremented in the button handlers. The value of this variable is used to retrieve the data from the `Vector` object containing the query results.

Display Applet Window

This section of code displays the applet window (see Figure 5.1). The applet window is described and any controls contained are added to the window.

Figure 5.1:

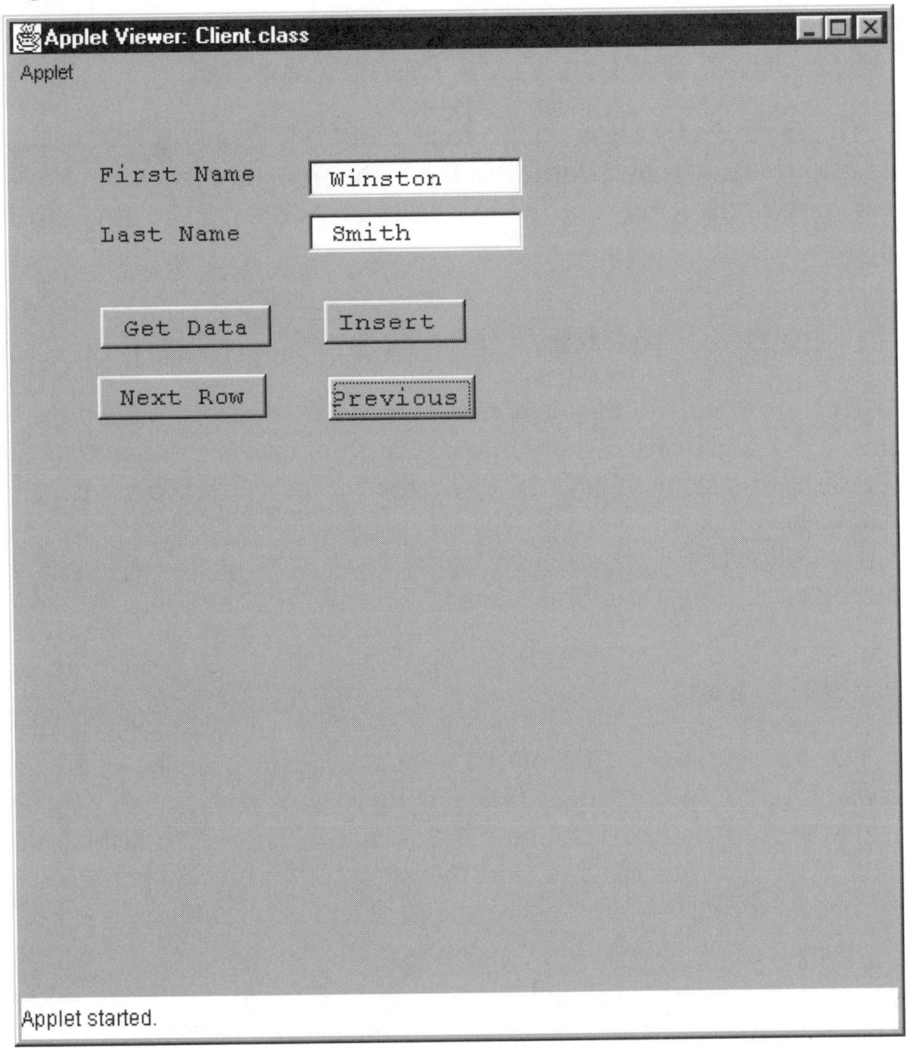

Applet Viewer: Client.class

Applet

First Name Winston

Last Name Smith

Get Data Insert

Next Row Previous

Applet started.

'Get Data' Button Click Event Handler

The button click event handler for the 'get data' button initializes the database control object and the JDBC objects contained in the class that are used to control the database.

'Previous Row' Button Click Event Handler

The 'previous row' button click event handler decrements the current position variable and retrieves the data from the `Vector` in the database control object. This data is then displayed to the applet window.

'Next Row' Button Click Event Handler

The 'next row' button click event handler increments the current position variable and retrieves the data from the `Vector` in the database control object. This data is then displayed to the applet window.

'Insert Data' Button Click Event Handler

The 'insert data' button click event handler retrieves the data from the applet window fields and uses them to build an insert statement. This insert statement is then executed to insert the data into the database.

The following sections describe these components of the applet in more detail.

Declarations

The declarations for the JDBC applet are shown in the following code snippet. The first declaration is for a class declared to contain two `Strings` that correspond to the data fields used to display the data. A `while` loop used to read the `ResultSet` instantiates a series of objects of the `DBResults` type. An object is instantiated for each `ResultSet` row within the `while` loop, data inserted into the objects for each `ResultSet` column, and the resulting object inserted into a

Vector. This vector then is used to display the data from the ResultSet in a random fashion controlled by the applet user.

```
// will store these objects in a vector
class DBResults extends Object {
      String TextField1;
      String TextField2;
}
```

The DBControl class contains declarations for objects to control database interaction. These objects control the database connection, the SQL statement, the ResultSet for the rows returned, and index variables for the current row position and the maximum number of rows that are currently stored. A Vector object is also declared to store the results of the query.

```
class DBControl {

    public static  Connection conn;
    public static  Statement  stmt;
    public static  ResultSet    rs;
    public static int       currpos;
    public static int       maxrows;
    public static  Vector ResultsStorage;

}
```

Display Applet Window

The main applet code which displays the applet window is shown in the following snippet. This code contains declarations for the AWT objects that are used to display the window. An init method, called when the applet is started, initializes the window and displays the screen to be used for data browsing.

```
// Main Applet
public class Client extends java.applet.Applet
{
   public Screen1_CLASS Screen1;
   // Task Object
```

```
    public Object taskdata;

    // access for screen flipping is provided here
    public CardLayout layoutManager;
    public void init()
    {
        layoutManager = new CardLayout();
        setLayout(layoutManager);

        // create an instance of the applet panels
        Screen1 = new Screen1_CLASS(this, this);
        // add the mail panel
        add("Screen1", Screen1);
    }
}
```

The screen class is declared by Mojo tool generated code to contain the labels for the text fields and the buttons used to provide user control. Each window object is declared to be a unique class for that window object.

Within the constructor for the `Screen1` class, the window objects are instantiated. This is followed by a series of method invocations to display the window and its controls.

```
class Screen1_CLASS extends Screen
{
    public Label1_CLASS Label1;
    public Label2_CLASS Label2;
    public TextField1_CLASS TextField1;
    public TextField2_CLASS TextField2;
    public GetData_CLASS GetData;
    public NextRow_CLASS NextRow;
    public InsertData_CLASS InsertData;
    public Previous_CLASS Previous;
    // Task Object
    public Object taskdata;
    public Client parent;

    Screen1_CLASS(Client app, Client aParent)
```

```
{
   applet = app;
   parent = aParent;

   // create instances of all subcomponents
   Label1 = new Label1_CLASS(applet, this);
   Label2 = new Label2_CLASS(applet, this);
   TextField1 = new TextField1_CLASS(applet, this);
   TextField2 = new TextField2_CLASS(applet, this);
   GetData = new GetData_CLASS(applet, this);
   NextRow = new NextRow_CLASS(applet, this);
   InsertData = new InsertData_CLASS(applet, this);
   Previous = new Previous_CLASS(applet, this);

   // add the buttons  to the panel
   setLayout(null);
   add(Previous);
   add(InsertData);
   add(NextRow);
   add(GetData);
   add(TextField2);
   add(TextField1);
   add(Label2);
   add(Label1);

   setFont(new Font("Courier",0,8));
   move(bounds().x, 0);
   move(0, bounds().y);
   resize(bounds().width, 500);
   resize(500, bounds().height);
   setForeground(Color.black);
   setBackground(Color.lightGray);
   setFont(new Font("Courier",
        getFont().getStyle(), getFont().getSize()));
   setFont(new Font(getFont().getName(),
        Font.PLAIN, getFont().getSize()));
   setFont(new Font(getFont().getName(),
        getFont().getStyle(), 15));
```

```
    }
    void initialize()
    {
    }
}
```

Button Class Declaration

Following is the the Java declaration for a class for the previous button control. This code demonstrates how a subclass of the `Button` class is declared with components to define the visual properties of the button. Declarations for the 'next', 'get data' and 'insert buttons' contains similar code.

```
class Previous_CLASS extends Button
{
   // A class that produces a labeled button component.

   // Task Object
   public Object taskdata;
    Client applet;
    public Screen1_CLASS parent;

   Previous_CLASS(Client app, Screen1_CLASS aParent)
   {
      applet = app;
      parent = aParent;

      // create instances of all subcomponents

      // add instances to the panel
      setFont(new Font("Courier",0,8));
      setLabel("Previous ");
      move(bounds().x, 160);
      move(180, bounds().y);
      resize(bounds().width, 24);
      resize(83, bounds().height);
      setForeground(Color.black);
      setBackground(Color.lightGray);
```

```
        setFont(new Font("Courier",
                 getFont().getStyle(), getFont().getSize()));
        setFont(new Font(getFont().getName(),
                 Font.PLAIN, getFont().getSize()));
        setFont(new Font(getFont().getName(),
                 getFont().getStyle(), 15));

    }
    void initialize()
    {
    }
```

Previous Button Click Handler

Following the calls made to format the display of the button, the Java AWT version of a button event handler is used to handle the "button click" event. Because this is the previous button, the current position index (`DBControl.currpos`) is decremented by 1 and tested. If the value is valid (>==1), then the current position is decremented and the resulting index variable value is used to retrieve the `DBResults` object at that element position. The data retrieved then is displayed to the fields in the window.

```
public boolean action(Event evt, Object what)
{
    // display the previous row
    if ( DBControl.currpos - 1 >= 1 ) {

        DBControl.currpos ;
        DBResults db = ( DBResults)
DBControl.ResultsStorage.elementAt( DBControl.currpos );

        parent.TextField1.setText( db.TextField1 );
        parent.TextField2.setText( db.TextField2 );

    }
    else {
        DBControl.currpos = 1;
    }
```

```
    return(true);
  }
  }
```

Insert Data Button Click Event

The 'insert' data button is declared as in the previous section. The handler for this button activate event is shown in the following code. A `String` first is prepared to insert the data into the database table. Values are retrieved from the text fields in the window; these string values are appended to the "insert" statement string that will be used to insert data into the table. Once the `String` is built, the `executeUpdate` method is used to insert the data into the database table.

```
public boolean action(Event evt, Object what)
{
 try {

 String InsertString = " insert into table1.txt values " + "(" +
                 " " + parent.TextField1.getText() + " " + "," +
                 " " + parent.TextField2.getText() + " " + ")";

 int Result = DBControl.stmt.executeUpdate( InsertString );

   }
```

NextRow Button Event

The 'next row' handler first increments the internal index variable and then tests the resulting value. If the value is less than or equal to the maximum number of rows stored in the `DBControl` object (the number of rows currently loaded), the method increments the current position index value and retrieves the `DBResults` object stored in the `Vector` at that position.

```
public boolean action(Event evt, Object what)
{

    if ( DBControl.currpos + 1 <= DBControl.maxrows ) {
```

```
        DBControl.currpos++;
        DBResults db = ( DBResults)
DBControl.ResultsStorage.elementAt( DBControl.currpos );

        // display the results
        parent.TextField1.setText( db.TextField1 );
        parent.TextField2.setText( db.TextField2 );

      }
      else {
        DBControl.currpos = DBControl.maxrows;
      }

   return(true);
}
}
```

Get Data Button Event

When the user presses the 'get data' button, the data from the database table is retrieved into the internal `Vector` object. The following code performs the operation of retrieving the data from the `ResultSet` and storing the data into the internal `Vector` object.

A database connection is first established and a query string is built to retrieve all of the data from the database table. The internal position index is initialized to a value of one and the query statement is executed, with the return value stored in a `ResultSet`. The `ResultSet` then is positioned to the first record using the `next` method and a `while` loop is started to retrieve the data.

```
...
public boolean action(Event evt, Object what)
{
    // local variables
    String url = "jdbc:odbc:textdb";
    DBResults db;
        try {
        // Load the jdbc-odbc bridge driver
        Class.forName ("sun.jdbc.odbc.JdbcOdbcDriver");
```

```
        // Attempt to connect to a driver.
        DBControl.conn = DriverManager.getConnection ( url, "", "" );
// get the data from the database
        DBControl.stmt = DBControl.conn.createStatement();
        String query = "select * from table1.txt";
        ResultSet rs = DBControl.stmt.executeQuery( query );
        DBControl.currpos = 1;
...
```

For each iteration of the `while` loop, data is retrieved from the `ResultSet` and stored in the `TextField` components of a `DBResults` object. This object then is added to the `ResultsStorage` `Vector`.

At the end of the loop, the number of rows that have been stored in the `ResultsStorage Vector` object is recorded in the `maxrows` instance variable. The current position is then set to the first row and the first row is displayed to the window. This is accomplished by retrieving the element at the current position using the `Vector` method `elementAt` to retrieve the `DBResults` object at the index position requested. The data in the `DBResults` object retrieved then is displayed to the window using the `setText` method for each of the text fields.

```
...
db = new DBResults();
while ( more ) {
              db = new DBResults();
              db.TextField1 = rs.getString( 1 );
              db.TextField2 = rs.getString( 2 );
              DBControl.ResultsStorage.addElement( db );
              DBControl.currpos++;
              more = rs.next();
        }


        // store the results
        boolean more = rs.next();
        DBControl.currpos = 1;
        DBControl.ResultsStorage = new Vector();
```

```
  while ( more ) {
        db = new DBResults();
        db.TextField1 = rs.getString( 1 );
        db.TextField2 = rs.getString( 2 );
        DBControl.ResultsStorage.addElement( db );
        DBControl.currpos++;
        more = rs.next();
  }
  DBControl.maxrows = DBControl.currpos - 1;

  // display the first row
  DBControl.currpos = 1;
  DBResults dbt =
   ( DBResults ) DBControl.ResultsStorage.elementAt(
                     DBControl.currpos );
  parent.TextField1.setText( dbt.TextField1 );
  parent.TextField2.setText( dbt.TextField2 );

 }
catch (SQLException ex) {

  // A SQLException was generated. Catch it and
  // display the error information. Note that there
  // could be multiple error objects chained
  // together

 System.out.println ("\n*** SQLException caught ***\n");

  while (ex != null) {
    System.out.println ("SQLState: " +
      ex.getSQLState ());
      System.out.println ("Message:  " +
           ex.getMessage ());
      System.out.println ("Vendor:   " +
           ex.getErrorCode ());
      ex = ex.getNextException ();
      System.out.println ("");
    }
```

```
        }

        catch (java.lang.Exception ex) {

        // Got some other type of exception. Dump it.
        ex.printStackTrace ();

      }

   return(true);
}


}
```

The complete applet application code is shown in Appendix B.

Call by reference

Note that objects in Java are passed by reference. A loop to store object references in a `Vector` must instantiate new objects for each iteration of the loop, otherwise the `Vector` would store a series of references to the same value. In the following code, an object is instantiated outside of the `for` loop. Within the `for` loop, the value of a member variable in this object is set and the object is stored in the Vector. This occurs with each iteration of the loop. Unfortunately, what is stored is not a new object but a reference to the same object. The output of the final `for` loop in this program is the value 10 for each row, the last value stored in object.

```
class testClass extends Object {
      int n;
}
...
   int n;
   Vector v = new Vector();
   testClass t = new testClass();

   for  ( n = 1;n < 11; n++ ) {
        t.n = n;
        v.addElement( (Object) t );
   }

   for ( n = 0; n < 10; n++ ) {
```

continued

```
        t = (testClass) v.elementAt( n );
        System.out.println( "element " + n + " t is  " +
t.n  );
    }
...
```

To avoid this problem, a new object must be instantiated on each iteration of the loop, as shown in the following code. In this example, a new object is instantiated, the value of the member variable is set, and the object is then added to the `Vector`. Because each `Vector` element is a reference to a unique object, the resulting output from this code fragment would be a series of values from 1 to 10.

```
...
     Vector h = new Vector();
     for  ( n = 1;n < 11; n++ ) {
          testClass z = new testClass();
          z.n = n;
          h.addElement( (Object) z );
     }

     for ( n = 0; n < 10; n++ ) {
          t = (testClass) h.elementAt( n );
          System.out.println( "element " + n + " t is  " +
t.n  );
     }
...
```

Summary

This chapter provided a demonstration of the process of inserting JDBC code into a Java applet. In this example, the JDBC objects were encapsulated in a class that made manipulation of the data easier. Because data browsing applications are common, the ability to traverse the result set moving forward and back is important; a process to support this functionality was demonstrated in this example. Other points covered in this chapter are as follows:

- Applets can only connect to the server from which they were downloaded.
- Button click events are a good location for JDBC calls.
- Scroll cursor functionality can be obtained by storing the result set in a `Vector` object.

CHAPTER 6
THREE-TIERED PROGRAMMING WITH JDBC
RMI Example: The Client
The Middle Tier
The Back End
Three-Tiered and Multitiered Programming with Java RMI
Using JDBC and RMI

The process of distributing and running portions of program code over multiple machines, sometimes referred to as *distributed software components*, is not new—it has been practiced for almost as long as computers have existed on networks. But this practice has been given new attention in the past few years, partly as a backlash against the 'fat client,' in which large amounts of binary code are placed on client platforms, and partly because of the requirements of browser-based programs, which because of their restricted network access must often use a remote *proxy* application to communicate with other network resources such as database servers. Regardless, the benefits of distributed software components are significant and the tools for developing such applications are improving at a rapid pace.

Three-tiered computing uses a client application that runs on one platform (the front end), a middle tier that can potentially run on another platform (the application server or remotely invoked component) and a remote application (the back end) that potentially runs on yet another platform. These three processes must communicate and process data in a way that is largely transparent to the user on the client. Software components such as the Distributed Component Object Model (DCOM) and the Common Object Request Broker (CORBA) represent one approach to three-tiered computing, but the use of an *application server* (a program using a specific communication protocol) on the middle tier is another valid approach (see Figure 6.1.)

Three-tiered computing is just the beginning. In practice, distributed software components can be invoked on multiple tiers, leading to what is termed *n-tiered* computing. With *n*-tiered computing, software components or application servers can reside on two or more servers. This allows applications to scale to large user and data processing loads by invoking additional middle-tier components (the application server or software components).

The following sections detail the elements of three-tiered or multi-tiered computing: the client, the middle tier and the back end. (Note that detailed coverage of RMI programming is beyond the scope of this text. There are a number of steps involved in programming, testing, and implementing RMI applications, which, though not prohibitive, nevertheless require some study before attempting. The Sun

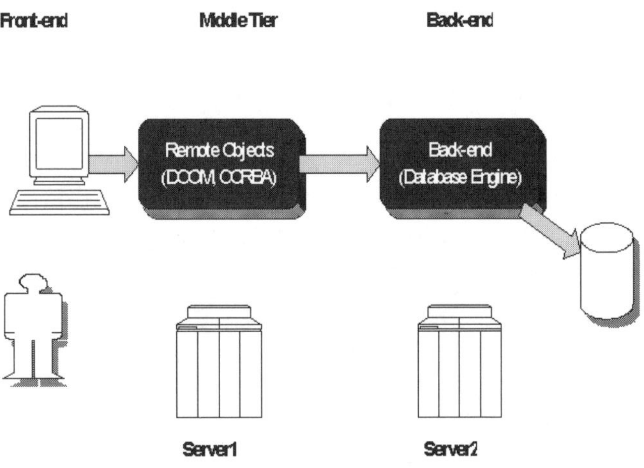

Figure 6.1: *Three-tiered Computing.*

documentation on RMI is recommended reading before attempting RMI development.)

RMI Example: The Client

The most common client applications today are PC-based applications that require access to processing that cannot easily be performed on the PC. This processing usually involves access to large amounts of data that must also be accessed by others, so a centralized database is required. And since this centralized database may require extensive processing, a hardware platform that can support this level of processing, such as a Unix machine or a mainframe, is necessary. The client application must therefore communicate with this server tier, preferably using a middle tier to buffer and process the data as needed.

But database applications are not the only applications that require a middle tier. Distributed software components using a middle tier can provide a significant benefit by allowing the logic and business rules of an enterprise to be consolidated in libraries using distributed software components (portions of software programs). These distributed components represent business logic that has been coded, tested, packaged, and then made available to the enterprise via a multitiered application. The client application invokes these software components transparently and performs processing on the middle tier.

The Middle Tier

The middle tier represents the portion of the application that performs some or all of the processing requested. This could be the *software component* being invoked, or the *application server* that is managing the requests from the client. The difference between the two approaches is in the means of access within the client application.

The *software component* is accessed in the program as a component portion of the software application—as a function or method. It is optionally passed values and optionally returns values back to the program. This approach is generally the more natural approach from a programming perspective.

An *application server* is accessed using a specific communication protocol. This approach requires more explicit programming to establish and communicate with the remote process. A network connection must be established and communication initiated and maintained using what is usually a proprietary protocol.

The middle tier will ultimately communicate with another application on the back end. This application is usually the centralized database running on a Unix server or mainframe, but it could be another process that is used to perform additional processing.

In many cases this middle tier is not used just to reduce the processing load for the client, but to provide access to network connections the client application can't reach. In this case the application acts as a *network proxy*, providing virtual network connections for the client platform. With this approach, the client machine still does not connect directly to restricted network addresses. The middle tier communicates with the restricted network address, performs the processing required, gathers and processes the information, and then returns the data.

The Back End

The back end represents the endpoint of the processing flow. This application receives requests from the middle tier, processes the requests, and then returns the results back to the middle tier. In many cases, this back end is a database server, but that is not a requirement. The back end could be another application running on a mainframe that provides access to mainframe flat files, or it could be simply another application that performs additional processing for the client.

Three-Tiered and Multitiered Programming with Java RMI

The Java language was designed with networks in mind and its developers were completely aware of the importance of distributed software components. Java developers released the RMI (Remote Method Invocation) specification soon after the initial release of the JDK. This specification, and the development library that soon followed, provided for the remote invocation of object methods. With RMI, a client application can instantiate an object that does not exist locally on the client machine but is instead a remote object. Once instantiated, the methods for the remote object can be invoked with few restrictions.

Using RMI to provide access to remote objects with Java provides a number of benefits. The RMI approach provides a natural interface and does not involve some of the complexity of other approaches such as CORBA. The coding of the client portion of the application is simple and straightforward and does not differ much from the use of local objects.

But there are issues with using RMI. RMI is *language dependent*, not *language-independent* like CORBA. RMI therefore only allows access to Java objects; objects created with other languages and code libraries developed in other languages are not directly available. This could be an impediment in MIS shops where a library of objects and code developed in other languages exist and are required by enterprise applications.

There are several protocol steps involved in invoking remote objects. One of the benefits of RMI is that these steps are managed by the API. The client program need only make one call to instantiate the remote object; it can then be used as any local object would, with a few minor restrictions.

Using RMI, data can be passed to and from remote methods. Data types can be any valid Java data type—including objects, as long as the objects implement the `Serializable` interface. Using the `Serializable` interface allows an object to be decomposed on the server, transmitted, and then reassembled on the client. Object serialization allows RMI to marshal and unmarshal parameters and does not truncate data types. Most Java classes in `java.lang` and `java.util` implement the `Serializable` interface.

Java RMI provides remote method invocation by creating a *stub* for the remote object on the client. This stub is generated by the RMI stub compiler (`rmic`) and provides information on the remote object and its members; it is required by Java to allow instantiation of the object locally.

Using JDBC and RMI

The RMI API can be especially useful to a JDBC application. Using RMI allows escape from the Java *security sandbox*, which restricts network access for an applet to the host machine from which it was downloaded. Using RMI, Java applets that would not otherwise be able to connect to a database on the network can use *proxy* objects on another server to provide communication with the database. These proxy objects can use JDBC to communicate with the database, gather the data results, and return the results to the client. (This approach is demonstrated in the RMI JDBC programming example discussed in this chapter; the complete example appears in Appendix C.)

Performance is a consideration whenever a network is involved. Regardless of the tool used to communicate with a remote database, the process of moving data over the network is expensive compared to retrieval of data from local memory. Each *package* of data (the data to be sent to the client) moved over the network incurs additional expense. For this reason, it is best to reduce the number of packets moved over the network. For example, if a number of rows must be retrieved from the database, then the rows should not be retrieved one at a time over the network through separate remote method invocations. A better approach is to buffer the rows being retrieved from the database and return the rows either all at once or in a small set of buffers, each with a sufficiently large number of rows.

Fortunately, Java provides a number of useful utility objects to store data. One that is particularly useful is the `Vector` object, which allows objects to be stored in a dynamic fashion. The `Vector` object can grow dynamically as elements are added to the `Vector`. It can be used to store objects of any type by casting the object being stored as the superclass `Object`. In the case of an RMI-based JDBC application, the `Vector` to be returned can be used to store the data returned by the `ResultSet`, potentially using a `Vector` to represent a row of data and then using another `Vector` to store a set of the 'row' `Vectors`.

Once the `Vector` has been loaded with the required data, it can be returned by the remote method. Since the `Vector` object implements the `Serializable` interface, it can be cleanly returned and managed by the client via RMI. The following example demonstrates this approach to using RMI with JDBC.

Three-tiered RMI Example

The example included here involves only three tiers—the client tier, the middle tier, and the back end (the database, not shown)—but the code could easily be extended to support additional tiers. The code is meant to demonstrate a client machine communicating with

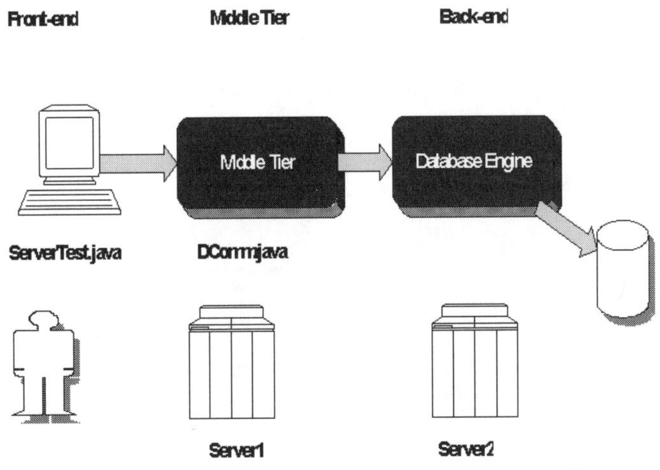

Figure 6.2: *Three-tiered RMI Example.*

an application running on a server, which in turn would communicate with a database server running on yet another machine. (See Figure 6.2.)

Still other deployment strategies are possible. A client could invoke methods running on another client that in turn could invoke methods on another client in what would be considered *peer-to-peer* communications. In fact, an application could instantiate a number of remote objects running on numerous different machines, using an *n*-tiered application with both peer-to-peer and client-server network communication.

The RMI/ JDBC Example

The code involved in creating a Java RMI application is relatively simple and straightforward. There are a number of compilation and deployment steps, which will not be examined in this chapter but are nevertheless not difficult.

In the sample application that follows, a client application requests data via a remote object. This application is simple and involves three Java source files as detailed in the following table.

Source File	Purpose
DBComm.java	Remote server
DBRemote.java	Interface implemented by the DBRemote class
ServerTest.java	Client application to test the remote method invocation

The `DBComm.java` code is the portion of the application that will run remotely. This will implement the remote method, receiving data from the client, executing JDBC code to retrieve data, placing the data in a buffer, and then returning the data to the client.

The `DBRemote.java` code contains the interface that is implemented by the `DBComm.java` code. This interface effectively provides the details on the class and methods to be implemented by `DBComm`.

The `ServerTest.java` code is a client application that will test the server. This program instantiates the remote `DBComm` object and then executes a member method of the object. The method invoked will pass a parameter to the remote object and then receive a buffer of data from the object.

The final pieces of the RMI code set are the skeletons and stubs for the classes to be executed using RMI. Any class invoked remotely requires a stub on the client platform. This stub provides details on the class and methods—details required in order to receive data (including objects) from the remote method. (These are created using the Java RMI compiler, `rmic`.)

The RMI Client Code

The client application will establish communication with the remote method server and then instantiate an object for the server class. Once the object has been instantiated, a method in the remote object will be invoked to retrieve, buffer, and then return data. The data returned will then be displayed.

The initiation of the communication between the client and server requires only two method invocations, the first to obtain the remote object and the second to invoke the method to retrieve the data (see below).

```
...
          Vector v = null;
          DBComm_Stub RemoteObj = (DBComm_Stub)
Naming.lookup(
                  "//jserve/JDBCServer" );
          System.out.println( "Retrieving Data." );
          v = RemoteObj.getData( "loadtest" );
...
```

In this client code fragment, the first call executes the `Naming.lookup` method to retrieve the object reference for the remote object. This object reference is cast as the stub class for the `DBComm` class, the class of the remote object. The class is found using the information passed in the Universal Resource Locator (URL), the string passed to the `lookup` method; in this case the string is `"//jserve/JDBCServer"` where `jserve` is the network name of the machine where the remote object resides and `JDBCServer` is the reference name for the remote object to retrieve.

In order for this call to succeed, the machine `jserve` must have the remote object registry running and listening on the correct network port (port 1099 by default, but alterable in the URL passed to the `Naming.lookup` function). The registry will look up the name passed and, if the object reference is found, will return the remote object specified by the name.

Once the object is successfully retrieved, the members of the object can be invoked and referenced as they would with any local object. In this case, the `getData` member is called passing the string `loadtest`, the name of the table to use for data retrieval. The `getData` method then retrieves the results of the query and places those results in a `Vector` object that is returned from the method. This `Vector` object can then be iterated through on the client to determine the results of the query, as shown in the following:

```
...
          System.out.println( "Processing results." );
          int n;

          // iterate through results
          for (n=0;n<50;n++)
```

```
            System.out.println( "row " + n + " - Value: " +
                                        v.elementAt( n ).toString() );
        }
         catch (Exception e) {

          System.out.println(
               "JDBCServer exception: " + e.getMessage() );
          e.printStackTrace();
         }
    }
```

For each element of data stored in the vector, the `Vector.elementAt` method is called to retrieve the `Object` stored at that element. The `Object.toString` method is then called to display the element as a string.

In practice, the client-side application would most likely be implemented as an applet using the same or similar calls shown here. These calls would be placed in event handlers or in separate methods to retrieve, process, and then format the data and display it to the applet window. Additionally, the data returned from the remote method would not necessarily be treated as string data. The data would be passed as an `Object` in the `Vector` buffer, so it could be retrieved and cast as the correct data type.

RMI Remote Method Programming (Server)

The code written for the RMI server contains the remote implementation of the object and method or methods to be invoked. The code for the middle tier requires specific declarations to indicate that it will be used as a remote object as shown in the following code.

```
...
public class DBComm extends  UnicastRemoteObject
         implements DBRemote {

     Vector v = new Vector();

     public DBComm() throws RemoteException {
          super();
```

```
    }
    public Vector getData( String pTableName ) {
...
```

The class definition for the server (or remote object) extends UnicastRemoteObject, specifying that the object will be exported (made available as a remote object) when the object is created. The DBComm class then implements the DBRemote interface, the class that contains the methods to invoke.

The final declaration in this example is the function signature for the DBComm class constructor. In this case, the constructor is specified to throw a RemoteException. This is required since the instantiation of a remote method could fail with a network connection error. These errors are better managed with this type of declaration.

The getData method executes the JDBC code to make the connection to the database and begin gathering data. The method receives a single parameter from the client application, which specifies the name of the table to query. The Class.forName method is first called to load the JDBC driver, in this case the JDBC-ODBC bridge. Once the JDBC driver is loaded, a connection is established using the getConection call, which will return a Connection object. The call to create the connection identifies the jdbcdsn data source name as the data source to use for the connection.

```
    public Vector getData( String pTableName ) {

      try {

            System.out.println( "Received query. Processing
... " );
            // get connected
            Class.forName ("sun.jdbc.odbc.JdbcOdbcDriver");
            Connection con = DriverManager.getConnection (
                                        "jdbc:odbc:jdbcdsn",
                                        "", "" );
```

The next section of the remote object code builds the query string to use to query the database. The query is built using the pTableName variable that was passed into the method as a parameter. A Statement object is instantiated using the createStatement method of the Connection object.

```
...
            // create the statement and execute the query
            String qs = "select * from " + pTableName;
            Statement stmt = con.createStatement( );
...
```

Now that the `Statement` object is created, the query can be executed using the `executeQuery` method. This method will execute the query and return a `ResultSet` object with the results. The first call to the `ResultSet` next method is used to position the cursor on the first tuple of the result set.

```
...
            ResultSet rs = stmt.executeQuery( qs );
            boolean more = rs.next();
...
```

Since the `ResultSet` will only return rows one at a time, returning single rows back to the client for the duration of the `ResultSet` would, as mentioned previously, incur excessive network overhead. It would be more efficient to load a buffer with a number of rows from the `ResultSet` and return the entire buffer to the client application in one network operation. The following code demonstrates the process of loading the `ResultSet` results into a buffer for return to the client application.

```
...
            Vector v;
            boolean more = rs.next();

            if ( more )
               System.out.println( "Loading results
... " );
            // load the results data into a Vector
            int n = 0;
            while ( ( more ) && ( n < 100 ) ) {
                v.addElement(  rs.getObject( 1 ) );
                more = rs.next();
                n++;
...
```

There is a size after which making the buffer larger will not improve performance. This size is usually around 1K but is dependent on the "network buffer size."

The first call to to the ResultSet method next positions the cursor and returns a boolean value that indicates that the call succeeded. If there had not been any rows in the cursor, the call would return 'false' and the remaining code to load the buffer would not have executed.

Once it has been determined that there are rows in the cursor, a while loop is executed to retrieve the rows from the ResultSet and load the rows into the buffer that will be returned to the client.

A Java language Vector object will be used to return the rows to the client. The Vector object will expand dynamically with successive calls to the addElement method. This example selects a single column from each row returned by the query and, using the getObject call, inserts the object reference into the Vector object. This example increments a counter and limits the size of the Vector object to be returned to 100 rows.

The remaining code in the server component catches any exceptions that may be thrown and reacts to them. The final step in the server code is to return the vector object containing the buffer of rows from the database.

```
...
catch (java.lang.Exception ex) {

     // Print description of the exception.
     System.out.println( "** Error on data select. ** " );
     ex.printStackTrace ();
  }
  return v ;
....
```

Remote Method Implementation: Main Program Block

The main program block of the remote method implementation is used to perform two main functions. First, it invokes a security manager to guarantee that classes that are loaded do not perform illegal operations. This secure layer is provided by invoking the `System.setSecurityManager` with an instantiation of the `RMISecurityManager` manager class. (Note that if the security manager is not loaded, then no class loading is allowed other than the classes in the local `CLASSPATH` environment variable.)

```
...
     public static void main ( String args[] ) {

        // create and install a security manager
        if ( System.getSecurityManager() == null ) {

           System.setSecurityManager( new RMISecurity-
Manager() );
        }
...
```

The next step is to register the name of the object on the RMI server. This call will bind the name of the server to the object for the remote method. This is accomplished by calling the constructor for the remote object, in this case `DBComm`, and passing the reference to this object to the `Naming.rebind` method. The `rebind` method will establish or bind the server name passed to the object passed as a parameter. If an error occurs, an exception is thrown. This assumes the RMI registry is running on the server.

```
        // Start the server
          try {

             DBComm obj = new DBComm();
             // Bind the object instance to the name
"JDBCServer"
             Naming.rebind( "//jserve/JDBCServer", obj
);
             System.out.println( "Server has been
bound." );
          }
          catch ( Exception e ) {
              System.out.println(
                   "JDBCServer error: " +
e.getMessage() );
```

```
                    e.printStackTrace();
            }
    }
}
```

Summary

This chapter detailed the benefits of multitiered programming, the process of running portions of an application on different machines. The Java answer to multitiered application development is the Remote Method Invocation (RMI) API. This API provides a natural, easy-to-use interface for the remote invocation of object methods.

Programming with RMI has additional benefits for JDBC application development. In order to provide a secure environment for code downloaded over the Internet, Java applets must run within a security sandbox, a restrictive environment that only allows network connections to the machine from which the applets were downloaded. Unfortunately, database applications must usually connect to additional machines to access the physical database.

Using RMI, a JDBC server can be developed to run as a middle tier in a three-tiered or multitiered application. This middle tier can run on the machine from which the applet was downloaded and, with less restrictive network security in place, can use JDBC to communicate with the database server as a *proxy* for the applet. The sample code in this chapter demonstrated just such an approach to three-tiered application development with JDBC.

Performance can be an issue for network applications. To manage performance, network I/O should be minimized. Network I/O can be reduced by increasing the amount of data transferred with each network access, effectively buffering the data to be returned. The Java language provides a number of objects that are useful for buffering data. One such object is the `Vector`, a storage facility that grows dynamically and allows random access of elements. The example in this chapter showed how a `Vector` can be used to accumulate database data and can then be returned to a client application via RMI.

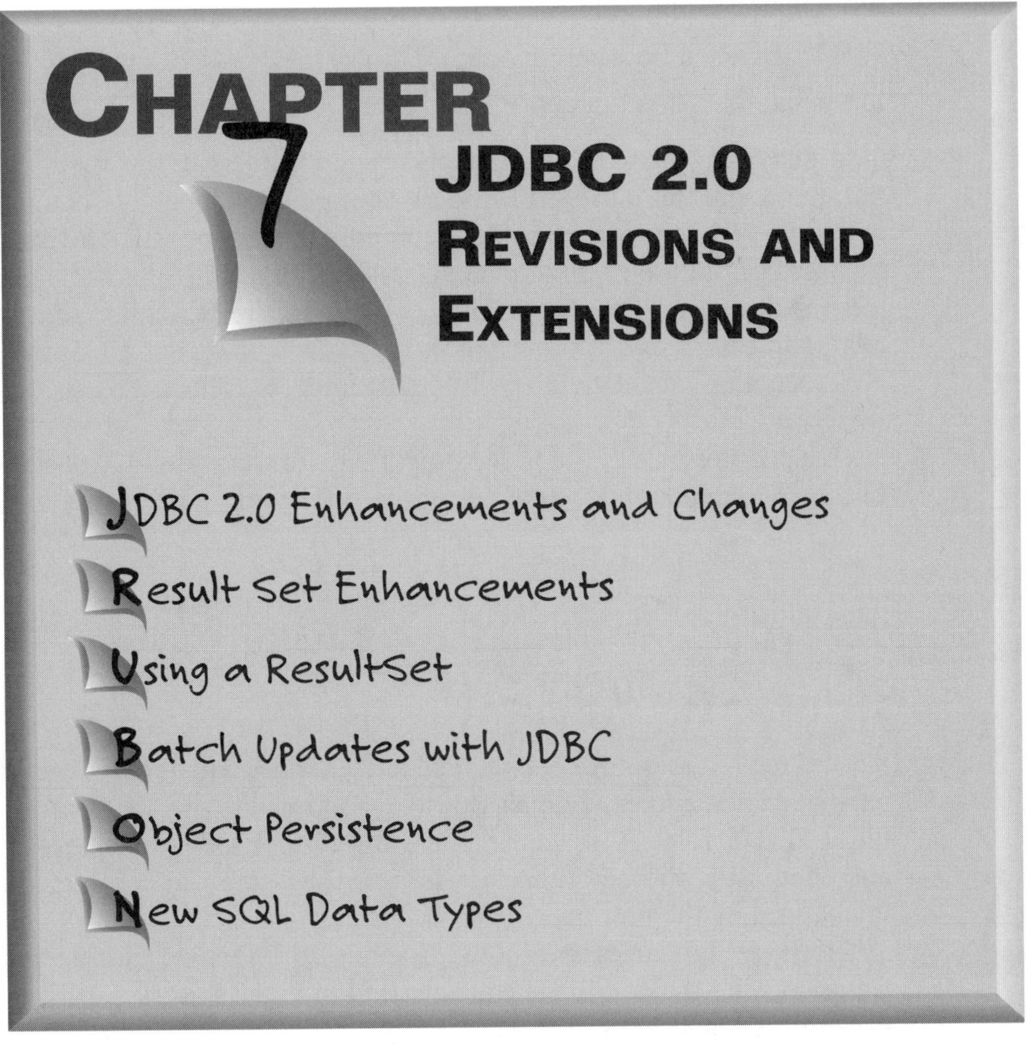

The JDBC 2.0 specification introduces a number of important features that expand the JDBC API into new directions. Features have been added to improve data retrieval and updates and to support extended data types, including the data types of the SQL-3 specification. Some of the more notable new features include:

- Batch updates
- Scrollable cursors
- Advanced data types
- Rowsets
- JNDI database naming

- Connection pooling
- Distributed transaction support
- Character stream support

In delivering these enhancements, the developers of the specification have split the JDBC API into two components: the *core* component and the *extensions*. The core component encompasses the basic functionality of the original package and many of the enhancements identified above. The extensions encompass functionality that is related to extensions in other pieces of the Java platform, such as the Java Naming and Directory Interface and the Java Transaction Service.

This chapter covers the new components of the JDBC 2.0 specification. Where possible, examples of the new syntax are provided.

JDBC 2.0 Enhancements and Changes

Several new classes have been added and changes and enhancements have been made to existing classes to accommodate the new features of JDBC 2.0. Table 7.1 lists the JDBC 2.0 core classes and interfaces and identifies whether the class is new, has changed, or remains unchanged by the new specification.

The Java Standard Extensions provides additional packages and classes for the JDBC API. The classes and interfaces of the JDBC 2.0 package are as follows:

- `javax.sql.ConnectionEvent`
- `javax.sql.ConnectionEventListener`
- `javax.sql.PoolDataSource`
- `javax.sql.CursorMovedEvent`
- `javax.sql.CursorMovedListener`
- `javax.sql.DataSource`
- `javax.sql.PooledConnection`
- `javax.sql.RowSet`
- `javax.sql.RowSetImpl`
- `javax.sql.RowSetMetaData`

Table 7.1: *JDBC 2.0 Classes*

Class/Interface	New	Original	Modified
java.sql.Array	X		
java.sql.BatchUpdateException	X		
java.sql.Blob	X		
java.sql.Date		X	X
java.sql.Driver		X	
java.sql.DriverManager		X	X
java.sql.DriverPropertyInfo		X	
java.sql.PreparedStatement		X	X
java.sql.Ref	X		
java.sql.ResultSet		X	X
java.sql.ResultSetMetaData		X	X
java.sql.SQLData	X		
java.sql.SQLException			X
java.sql.CallableStatement		X	X
java.sql.Clob	X		
java.sql.Connection		X	X
java.sql.DatabaseMetaData		X	X
java.sql.SQLException			X
java.sql.SQLInput	X		
java.sql.SQLOutput	X		
java.sql.SQLWarning			X
java.sql.Statement		X	X
java.sql.Struct	X		
java.sql.Time		X	X
java.sql.Timestamp		X	X
java.sql.Types		X	X
java.sql.DataTruncation		X	

- `javax.sql.RowSetMetaDataImpl`
- `javax.sql.RowSetUpdatedEvent`
- `javax.sql.RowSetUpdatedListener`
- `javax.sql.XAConnection`
- `javax.sql.XADataSource`

Result Set Enhancements

Applications often require the ability to move forward, backward, and sometimes randomly through the rows returned from a query. This type of cursor is known as a *scroll cursor* since users can scroll forward or backward through the results. The result set enhancements in JDBC 2.0 allow scroll cursors to be created and managed. The JDBC implementation of these cursors allows varying levels of update sensitivity to be applied to the cursors.

Batch Updates

Database updates with SQL can become tedious and require unnecessary processing cycles if implemented through a series of distinct update statements. The ability to group a series of updates into a single statement can reduce the amount of database I/O that must be performed to complete the updates. The batch update capability in JDBC 2.0 provides the ability to perform multiple updates in a single query request being sent to the database for execution.

Advanced Data Types

Most databases only support the simple data types offered by the SQL standard. The original version of JDBC supported these basic data types. But many databases today support more complex data types such as Blobs (Binary Large Objects), opaque datatypes, and object-relational data. The JDBC 2.0 specification will support data types through extensions to the original API combined with support for the SQL-3 standard.

Rowsets

SQL provides the ability to manipulate relational data through set logic. In the past this set logic has not always translated easily into the syntax of the programming languages that manipulated the data. This was because early structured programming languages did not have statements that manipulated sets. Their syntax is a "record-at-a-time" versus "set-at-a-time" manipulation of SQL.

Ultimately, relational database programmers were left with what has been termed an *impedance mismatch*. To integrate SQL with these languages, cursors were created to point to the retrieval set in the database, and each row from the set was retrieved one at a time.

Object-oriented languages are more adaptable to set manipulation with collections, lists, vectors, and other language facilities. In this vein, the JDBC 2.0 specification allows rows to be retrieved in sets known as *Rowsets*. As the name implies, these are sets of rows with methods available to manipulate these rows as a set.

JNDI Database Naming

Tracking and maintaining network names can be a trying experience. Large networks exacerbate this problem. With the JDBC 2.0 specification, the Java Naming and Directory Information Interface can be used to obtain a database connection in addition to the JDBC driver, thus allowing more direct, centralized administration of network names.

Connection Pooling

The creation of a database connection can be an expensive process, often requiring several seconds to establish. This overhead can be a problem in applications that must open and close a large number of database connections many times. Connection pooling in the JDBC 2.0 specification allows a single connection cache to span more than one JDBC driver. Connection pooling could improve performance for applications where connections must constantly be created and then destroyed.

Distributed Transaction Support

Distributed transactions have been available through the database in the previous versions of JDBC. JDBC 2.0 allows distributed transactions to be implemented through the Java Transaction Service.

Other Additions

Character stream support means that data can be retrieved from the database as a stream of Unicode characters. The `java.math.BigDecimal` class now provides methods for `BigDecimals` to be returned with full precision.

The following sections discuss several of the enhancements of the JDBC 2.0 specification in more detail. (To cover all of the features of the JDBC 2.0 specification is beyond the scope of this chapter.)

Result Set Enhancements

Some of the more important improvements in the JDBC 2.0 specification are the result set improvements, which provide for scrolling cursors, the ability to move forward and backward through a result set, and for updating through a result set. Together, these changes add significant functionality to the `ResultSet` class. Table 7.2 summarizes these capabilities.

Result set types distinguish the types of result sets that can be created: *forward-only*, *scroll-insensitive*, and *scroll-sensitive*. These designations identify scrolling support and whether or not changes made to the result set are visible.

Table 7.2: *New* `Result Set` *Features*

Type	Description
Scroll-sensitive	Scroll cursor sensitive to changes of underlying database
Scroll-insensitive	Scroll cursor not sensitive to changes of underlying database
Forward-only	Traditional cursor type; forward cursor movement only
Read-only concurrency	Cannot perform updates to cursor
Updatable concurrency	Can perform updates on the cursor
Performance hint	Specify the number of rows to pre-fetch

Result set concurrency identifies concurrency types: *read-only* and *updatable*. Read-only does not allow updates of the cursor contents. Updatable allows updates to the result set contents with varying levels of visibility to other users.

Performance changes allow two hints to be provided to the database engine for performance: the number of rows per fetch operation and the direction of the cursor.

ResultSet Scrolling

In JDBC 2.0, result sets provide several distinct scrolling capabilities. The original forward scrolling capability is still present and provides basic cursor functionality. This result set cursor allows only forward movement through the result set.

But the new scrollable result set cursor allows freedom of movement throughout the `ResultSet`. This movement can take the form of forward movement, backward movement, and movement to a specific row through relative or absolute positioning.

The JDBC 2.0 API distinguishes between three result-set types: forward-only, scroll-insensitive and scroll-sensitive. These cursors differ in the scrolling capabilities and the visibility of the changes made to their result set to other users.

A scroll-insensitive cursor is not sensitive to changes, meaning that changes made to the result set are not visible. This cursor provides a static view of the data returned.

A scroll-sensitive cursor is sensitive to change and provides a dynamic view of the data that has been retrieved. The changes made to the result set are visible to others.

Previous versions of the JDBC API did not support cursor movement through the result set, but it was possible to programmatically emulate this capability by pre-fetching and storing rows internally in the Java application. (In fact, this book demonstrates such a program in the Result Set Array example.) The advantage of having this capability supported in the driver is that the database engine may provide cursor scrolling capabilities more efficiently by buffering result set rows in the engine before returning data to the client.

Concurrency involves the ability of a database to manage more than one concurrent user in the database. The JDBC 2.0 specification identifies two modes of concurrency for the result set. They are *read-only* concurrency and *updatable* concurrency. The read-only concurrency level dictates that the result set does not allow updates. An *updatable* result set allows updates against the result set. Depending on how it is implemented, this can reduce concurrency since write locks must be held on the database records and could (depending on isolation mode and other factors) limit access to database records.

Using a ResultSet

The process of creating and using a `ResultSet` under JDBC 2.0 is similar to that of previous versions of JDBC; many of the methods used are the same. But certain methods have been overloaded and new methods added to support the new result set features. The following code provides an example of the creation of a new `ResultSet`.

```
...
Connection con = DriverManager.getConnection(
                    "jdbc:a_subprotocol:a_subname" );
Statement stmt = con.CreateStatement(
                    ResultSet.TYPE_SCROLL_SENSITIVE,
                    ResultSet.CONCUR_UPDATABLE );
stmt.setFetchSize( 100 );
ResultSet rs = stmt.executeQuery(
     "select * from current_sales " );
...
```

In this example, the `Connection` object is created using syntax identical to that of JDBC 1.0. But the subsequent creation of the `Statement` object uses the syntax of the overloaded `CreateStatement` method to pass parameters for a scroll-sensitive cursor (`TYPE_SCROLL_SENSITIVE`) with updatable concurrency (`CONCUR_UPDATABLE`). Note that this syntax defines `ResultSet` behavior but is applied to the creation of the `Statement` object, which is then used to create the `ResultSet`.

This code asserts that the database supports the `ResultSet` type being requested, but this may not always be the case. In practice, it may be better to determine beforehand whether or not the database supports the ResultSet features being requested. This would allow the code to gracefully support the existing capabilities of the database, rather than respond to a series of errors later in the code. Fortunately, the DatabaseMetaData class in JDBC 2.0 has been extended to provide additional information on the capabilities of the database engine, as the following code demonstrates.

```
...
DatabaseMetaData dmd;
Connection con;
...
if ( dmd.supportsResultSetType(
ResultSet.TYPE_SCROLL_SENSITIVE )
&&
     dmd.supportsResultSetType(
ResultSet.CONCUR_UPDATABLE ) ) {
      PreparedStatement stmt = con.prepareStatment(
            "select * from customers where sale_date >
? ",
            ResultSet.TYPE_SCROLL_SENSITVE,
            ResultSet.CONCUR_UPDATABLE );
      stmt.setFetchSize( 100 );
      stmt.setDate( "1/1/1998" );
      ResultSet rs = stmt.executeQuery();
...
```

In this example, a prepared statement (PreparedStatement) is created on the connection and a specific result set type is requested. But this statement object is only created if the conditional test succeeds. And the conditional test checks to determine whether or not the current database supports the ResultSet types that will be requested of the connection. This code tests for a scroll-sensitive cursor capability (TYPE_SCROLL_SENSITIVE) and an updatable concurrency (CONCUR_UPDATABLE) capability. A DatabaseMetaData.supportsResultSetConcurrency method is available to test the concurrency capabilities of the database on the connection.

Note that if the application asks the driver to create a statement for a ResultSet type that is not supported, then the driver signals a warning on the connection, not an error. The driver will then attempt to find a ResultSet that is similar to the result set that the application has requested and will return that ResultSet.

Updating with ResultSets

If a ResultSet is created as a ResultSet.CONCUR_UPDATABLE then it is updatable. With an updatable ResultSet, rows can be inserted, updated, and delated. Methods are available to make changes to the current row using a series of update<DataType> methods. Changes to the current row are not updated to the database until the updateRow method is called to update the database. The following provides an example of an updatable ResultSet.

```
...
ResultSet rs;
...
rs. rst();
rs.UpdateString( 1, "This String" );
rs.UpdateFloat( " rst_name", "Sam" );
rs.UpdateRow();
...
```

This example uses a series of calls to ResultSet methods to update the current result set row, which in this case is the first row in the result set (the call to ResultSet. rst moves the cursor to the first row).

ResultSet methods are also available to move to a specific row or a relative row using absolute or relative methods. A delete row method is also available to delete a row from a result set. Note that once the call is made to delete the row, the database is updated without the deleted row.

Inserting with ResultSets

Result set inserts allow rows to be added to the existing row updates. These rows are then updated (or inserted) into the database through the insertRow method. Columns that have not been specifically addressed in any of the update<DataType> statements must allow NULL values, since that is what the driver will attempt to insert into the column.

Visibility of Database Changes

The visibility of database changes depends in part on the isolation mode chosen. The *isolation mode* is set using the `setTransactionIsolation` call, as shown below.

```
...
Connection con;
...
con.setTransactionIsolation(
TRANSACTION_READ_COMMITTED );
...
```

This sample merely sets the isolation mode using the `setTransactionIsolation` method. The read commit isolation mode only allows other users to read changes that have been committed to the database.

The changes that others make to the database are not visible to the application when a scroll-insensitive cursor is used. The result set created by this cursor is static. If another user were to delete a row currently in a scroll-insensitive result set, the result set would not reflect this change.

A scroll-sensitive result set, however, is keenly aware of changes made in the database to rows in its result set. If another user were to make a change to a row in a scroll-sensitive result set, that changed row would be made visible to the scroll-sensitive cursor. Inserts and deletes, however, may not necessarily be visible. The `DatabaseMetaData` method `deletesAreDetected` will reveal whether or not the driver has the ability to detect deletes; it is called as follows:

```
...
DatabaseMetaData dmd;

   if ( dmd.deletesAreDetected(
ResultSet.TYPE_SCROLL_SENSITIVE ) )
       // we can detect deletes
...
```

If this call were to return false, that would indicate that deletes are not detected; the application would have to initiate logic that would take action to determine that a record being manipulated still exists in the database. This could be done by locking the record either directly or indirectly through a restrictive isolation mode; or the application could be coded to perform an insert if the record were not in the database, instead of an update as would be done if the record existed. Another alternative would be to refresh the current row in the ResultSet before taking a critical action; a ResultSet method refreshRow is available to perform this action.

Determining Cursor Capabilities

A number of DatabaseMetaData methods are available to provide information on the exact capabilities offered by the connected database engine. For example, the othersUpdatesAreVisible, othersDeletesAreVisible, and othersInsertsAreVisible methods provide information on the visibility of changes made by others. And likewise the methods ownUpdatesAreVisible, ownDeletesAreVisible, and ownInsertsAreVisible reveal information about whether or not changes made by the application itself are visible by the application. These methods are invoked with a parameter indicating the type of result set being used, as shown below.

```
...
DatabaseMetaData dmd;
  if ( dmd.ownUpdatesAreVisible(
ResultSet.TYPE_SCROLL_SENSITIVE ) )
     // result set scroll sensitive changes are
visible to myself
...
```

These concurrency capabilities rely heavily on the database engine, so it is not possible for the JDBC driver to guarantee a particular capability. In some cases, a driver may report that a capability exists, but a specific set of circumstances, such as the isolation mode in effect and the nature of the query driving the cursor, could void the capability. It is best to use calls to the metadata functions to determine the capabilities the driver believes are available and then perform tests to verify that the capabilities do perform as intended under specific circumstances.

Batch Updates with JDBC

Batch updates provide the potential for a significant performance improvement by allowing a series of SQL statements to be sent to the server and executed as a batch. This avoids the transaction overhead of sending each query to the server and waiting for the results of the query from the server—overhead that could be extremely high for a large number of SQL operations.

Batch update capability is implemented through the `Statement` class, allowing multiple queries to be attached to the statement and then executed through the `executeBatch` method. The following code sample demonstrates this capability.

```
...
Connection con;
...
con.setAutoCommit( false );
Statement stmt = con.createStatement();
stmt.addBatch( "delete from old_trans where tx_code =
10");
stmt.addBatch( "insert into old_trans select * from
todays_trans + " where tx_code = 11 ");
stmt.addBatch( "update stock set hprice = hprice *
1.1"  );
stmt.addBatch( "update customers set region  = 'z'  " +
                 " where region = h'  " );
// submit the batch for execution
int[] updateCounts = stmt.executeBatch();
...
```

In this example, the first step is to disable the autocommit mode using the `Connection.setAutoCommit` method. This will stop the JDBC driver from committing the batch as soon as it is executed. What is desired is to have the application decide whether or not to commit the entire batch based on the update counts (the number of rows touched by the update) returned from the execution of each statement. These update counts are placed in the `updateCounts` integer array and should be examined before the decision to commit or roll back is made.

Commands are executed in the order in which they have been added to the batch. The counts in the integer array returned by the `executeBatch` statement correspond to the position of the queries that were added to the batch. Should there be a decision not to execute the queries in the batch, the `Statement.clearBatch` method can be called to reset the batch and remove all updates that have been placed in the batch.

The batch update mechanism can also be used with prepared statements. A single statement is added to the `PreparedStatement` object. If different sets of values are applied to the query, then these values are applied as the distinct batch updates to be executed for the statement. The following provides an example of the `PreparedStatement` batch.

```
...
 con.setAutoCommit( false );
 PreparedStatement stmt = con.prepareStatement(
  "update inventory set lprice = lprice * 1.1 where
prodcode = ? " );
 stmt.setInt( 1, 1235 );
 stmt.addBatch();
 stmt.setInt( 1, 4321 );
 stmt.addBatch();
 stmt.setInt( 1, 5643 );
 stmt.addBatch();
 stmt.setInt( 1, 2344 );
 stmt.addBatch();
  int[] resultCount = stmt.executeBatch();
...
```

In this example, an update statement is prepared to perform a 10 percent price increase (`lprice * 1.1`) on a specific product code. A series of queries is then executed for a list of product codes.

An alternative method of performing this update would be to use the "in" subclause as in `"update product ... where prodcode in (1234,4555, ...)"`, but this would not generate the list of update counts that are returned using the batch update method.

Object Persistence: Storing Java Objects in the Database

The JDBC 2.0 API provides for the often-requested object-oriented programming feature of *object persistence*. Java objects can be stored in a database and then be retrieved at some later point in time. This is an important but often unavailable attribute of object-oriented programming.

The previous versions of the JDBC API supported the storage of Java objects in the database but did not provide any facility for metadata describing the Java objects. The JDBC 2.0 API extends the `DatabaseMetaData` class to provide additional information on Java objects. A new type code, `JAVA_OBJECT`, has been added. This type code has been added to `java.sql.Types` and is now returned by `DatabaseMetaData.getTypeInfo` and `DatabaseMetaData.getColumns`.

Note that this capability is dependent on the DBMS for support of Java object storage and SQL syntax to manage the objects. Without support in the underlying database, the JDBC driver will not be able to support this functionality. The JDBC syntax for storing and manipulating Java objects is shown below.

```
...
ResultSet rs = stmt.executeQuery (
    "select html_page from site_pages where page =
'main'" );
rs.next();
HTML_Page hpage = (HTML_Page) rs.getObject( 1 );
...
```

This example first executes a query that selects a single column, the `html_page` column. As the column name implies, this is a column that stores data that does not easily fit within the realm of the basic SQL data types. A `ResultSet` is created for the query and the `ResultSet.next` method is called to position the cursor on the first row. The `ResultSet.getObject` method is then called to retrieve the `html_page` column as a Java object. The JDBC driver must construct an instance of the object by deserializing a serialized object instance. It is then the job of the application to narrow this object reference to the `HTML_Page` object reference, the subclass of the `Object` class superclass.

The reverse of retrieval is the storage of the Java object. This works in a manner similar to object retrieval as shown below.

```
...
hpage.setPage( (HTML_Page) NewPageRef );
PreparedStatement stmt = con.prepareStatment(
          " insert into site_pages ( page_id,
html_page, page_code ) values " +
           " ( ?, ?, '012X' ) " );
stmt.setInt( 1, lPageID );
stmt.setObject( 1, hpage );
int rowsUpdated = stmt.executeUpdate( );
...
```

This example first sets the value of the object using a member method of that object. A statement is then prepared that allows parameters for the ID of the record and the Java object to be stored in the database. The `PreparedStatement.executeUpdate` method is then called to perform the update and store the object in the database.

Before being stored in the database, the database is usually provided information about a Java class. The Java object is a data type for the database, usually referred to as a *user-defined type* (UDT). To determine the UDTs in a database, the `DatabaseMetaData.getUDTs` method can be called, as shown below.

```
...
DatabaseMetaData dmd;
...
int[] types = {Types.JAVA_OBJECT};
ResultSet udtRS = dmd.getUDTs(
          "UDTcatalog-table", "UDTschema",  "%", types
);
...
```

The `ResultSet` in this example will be populated with the descriptions of all the Java types currently defined in the catalog named in the call. Each row returned from this query provides the following information.

Name	Data Type	Description
TYPE_CAT	String	the catalog of the type
TYPE_SCHEM	String	the schema of the type
TYPE_NAME	String	the database type name
JAVA_CLASS	String	Java class name
DATA_TYPE	short	data type as defined in java.sql.Types
REMARKS	String	comment on the type

New SQL Data Types

The SQL-3 specification identifies several new data types, including the Binary Large Object (Blob) and the Character Large Object (Clob). The capability to create new data types built on existing data types is also provided. The JDBC 2.0 API will try to support SQL-3 as much as possible. In this vein, it supports several new data types that closely mirror those of the SQL-3 specification. The new SQL-3 data types supported are shown in Table 7.3.

A REF (reference) represents a storage reference from the database server. It is persistent and can thus be stored and referenced at a later time. A LOCATOR is a transient reference and is generally used to manipulate a structure that is too large to store on the client, such as a

Table 7.3: *New SQL-3 Data Types*

Data Type	Description
BLOB	Binary Large Object
CLOB	Character Large Object
Structured types	created with SQL syntax based on a heterogenous set of existing data types (e.g., CREATE TYPE PLANE_POINT (X FLOAT, Y FLOAT))

continued

Data Type	Description
`Distinct types`	based on the representation of a built-in type (e.g., CREATE TYPE MONEY AS NUMERIC(10,2))
`Constructed types`	type based on an existing SQL data type
`base-type ARRAY[n]`	an array of *n* base-type elements
`Locator types`	a reference to a data element stored on the server
`LOCATOR(structured-type)`	locator to structured instance in server
`LOCATOR(array)`	locator to array in server
`LOCATOR(blob)`	locator to Binary Large Object in server
`LOCATOR(clob)`	locator to Character Large Object in server
`REF(structured-type)`	designates row containing a structured type instance

`Blob` with audio or visual data. The `LOCATOR` can be used to randomly retrieve the data it references. The following sections will discuss how to retrieve and manipulate these new data types using JDBC.

Distinct and Structured Data Types

A *distinct* type is a type that is derived from an existing data type and can thus be mapped to an underlying data type. A distinct data type can be created with SQL-3 syntax as follows:

```
create type sales_sum as numeric(10,2);
create table sales_info (
       ... regional_sales sales_sum,
           district_sales sales_sum ...
```

This example creates a distinct type named `sales_sum` based on a base SQL data type, `numeric`. This distinct type is then used in the creation of a table, thus specifying and enforcing the scale and precision of the sales totals to be stored in the database.

A *structured data* type is composed of a heterogeneous combination of data types (similar to a record). It can be created with the following SQL syntax:

```
   create type person_info (
      first_name char(15),
      last_name char(20),
      address1  char(25),
      address2  char(25),
      city        char(20),
      state       char(2),
      zip         char(8));
   create table customer of person_info ( OID ref(
residence ) values are system generated );
```

This example creates a structured data type for general information about people stored in the database, named `person_info`. This structured data type is then referenced in table-related statements as shown in the `'create table'` statement shown above.

Retrieving and Storing Large Objects: Blobs and Clobs

With JDBC 2.0, the JDBC API adds direct support for large objects. The data types for these large objects have been named the `Blob` and the `Clob`. These objects can be retrieved using calls to `ResultSet.getBlob()` and `ResultSet.getClob()` methods. The following provides an example of using these methods.

```
ResultSet rs;
...
Blob blob = rs.getBlob(1);
Clob clob = rs.getClob(2);
...
```

By default, `Blob` or `Clob` should be implemented using the `LOCATOR` reference. As mentioned previously, a `LOCATOR` reference is a transient reference, so the `Blob` and `Clob` objects retrieved using this reference will only be valid during a specified period of time, usually represented by the transaction in which they were created. It is up to the JDBC driver vendor to optionally alter this behavior. Programmers should check driver documentation to determine the actual behavior with their driver.

The `Blob` and `Clob` data types retain many of the features of the basic JDBC data types. A `Blob` or `Clob` data type can be passed as a parameter to a `PreparedStatement` object using the `setBlob` and `setClob` methods. The `setBinaryStream` and `SetObject` methods provide an alternative method of retrieving `Blob` data by allowing a data stream to be used to access the `Blob` data.

Retrieving Arrays

The ability to store and manipulate arrays in a relational database provides a long-sought level of functionality for the developer. Though they represent a certain level of denormalization (the first level of normalization, eliminate repeating groups, is violated), they nevertheless provide performance and convenience benefits.

The JDBC 2.0 specification provides for an SQL array data type that can be retrieved with a call to the `getArray` method of the `ResultSet` and `CallableStatement`. This call retrieves an array from the specified `ResultSet` column as shown below.

```
...
Resultset rs;
...
Array CustBalArray = rs.getArray( "cust_daily_balance" );
...
```

This code retrieves an array of customer daily balances (a time series) into an array named `CustBalArray`. The `Array` interface contains a number of methods that can be used to retrieve all or part of the data in the array, including methods to return the Array contents as a `ResultSet` using the `getResultSet` method, which can then be iterated through, or as a Java array using the `getArray` method. The following code provides an example of retrieving and iterating through the contents of a JDBC array.

```
...
ResultSet rs;
...
Array CustBalArray = rs.getArray( "cust_daily_balance" );
```

```
ResultSet CustBalRS = CustBalArray.getResultSet ();

ResultSetMetaData rsmd = CustBalRS.getMetaData();

 int n = 0;
 boolean more = CustBalRS.next();
 while ( more ) {
       for ( n = 1; n <= rsmd.getColumnCount(); n++ )
{
            System.out.println( "Element: " + n +
                                " value: " +
CustBalRS.getString( n ) );
            }
        more = CustBalRS.next();
  }
...
```

In this example, the CustBalRS array is retrieved from the cust_daily_balance column of the ResultSet. This array is then converted into a ResultSet to provide a convenient means of iterating through the data in the array. A ResultSetMetaData object is created to get the column count, and a for loop is initiated to iterate the results, the contents of the array.

Conversely, arrays can be stored back into the database using the same methods applied to other Java data types. The PreparedStatement.setArray method may be used to pass an array back to the database. And a Java programming language array can be passed as an object using the PreparedStatement.setObject method.

Note that a JDBC 2.0 array will be implemented as an SQL LOCATOR(array) by default and as such represents transient data. It will only exist during the current transaction. This default behavior can optionally be changed by the driver vendor.

Retrieving and Storing "refs"

A Ref (reference) references an instance of a structured type in the database. A Ref can be retrieved from the database using the getRef method for either the ResultSet or CallableStatement. The following provides an example of this call.

```
...
Ref ref = rs.getRef;
...
```

A Ref does not provide data—it only references data. A Ref refers to data in the database and can only be used to retrieve data from the database by using the reference in an SQL statement that requires an SQL reference.

By default, a Ref is only meaningful during the SQL session in which it was retrieved. This default behavior can optionally be overridden by a JDBC driver.

Retrieving and Storing Distinct Data Types

Distinct data types are retrieved using JDBC just as the underlying data type would be retrieved. Thus, to retrieve a sales_sum distinct type created for a numeric(10,2) data element as specified for a regional_sales column as shown previously, the following get<data type> call could be used.

```
...
   BigDecimal bd = rs.getBigDecimal( "regional_sales" );
...
```

Storing the data would merely require the use of the set<Data_Type> call to set the correct data type. For instance, to set the regional_sales column to a BigDecimal value, the following call could be used:

```
...
   rs.setBigDecimal( "regional_sales", new
BigDecimal( "1333333.33" ) );
...
```

Retrieving and Storing Structured Types

A structured type can be retrieved by calling the getObject method. The following represents a call to retrieve a structured type.

```
Struct CustStruct = (Struct) rs.getObject( 1 );
```

Conversely, a structured type may be stored in the database using a call to setObject. The java.util.map can be used to provide mapping between the structured and distinct types stored in the database and the Java classes in the application.

Using Stream I/O to Manipulate Structured Data Types

Structured data types can be retrieved and stored in the database using a stream I/O approach to data manipulation. The `SQLInput` interface is used to provide this functionality and contains the necessary methods. An `SQLData` object is used to hold the values to be retrieved or written using the stream methods. The following provides an example of data being retrieved using this interface.

```
...
SQLInput sqlin;
SQLData sqld;
...
sqld.str = sqlin.readString();
sqld.blob = sqlin.readBlob();
...
```

In this example, a `String` and a `Blob` are read using the stream mechanism. To write data out to the stream, the `SQLOutput` interface can be used. The following provides and example of using the `SQLOutput` interface to write structured data to the database.

```
SQLOutput sqlout;
...
sqlout.writeBlob( sqlout.blob );
...
```

Conclusion

The JDBC 2.0 specification added extremely useful programming features, such as scrollable cursors, batch updates, and extended data type support, and the JDBC database metadata has been extended to support these new features. The extended data type support allows JDBC to be used with the maturing object-relational technologies currently reaching the market, and this addition of scrollable cursors and batch updates improves the functionality and performance of JDBC applications.

PART TWO

JDBC Reference

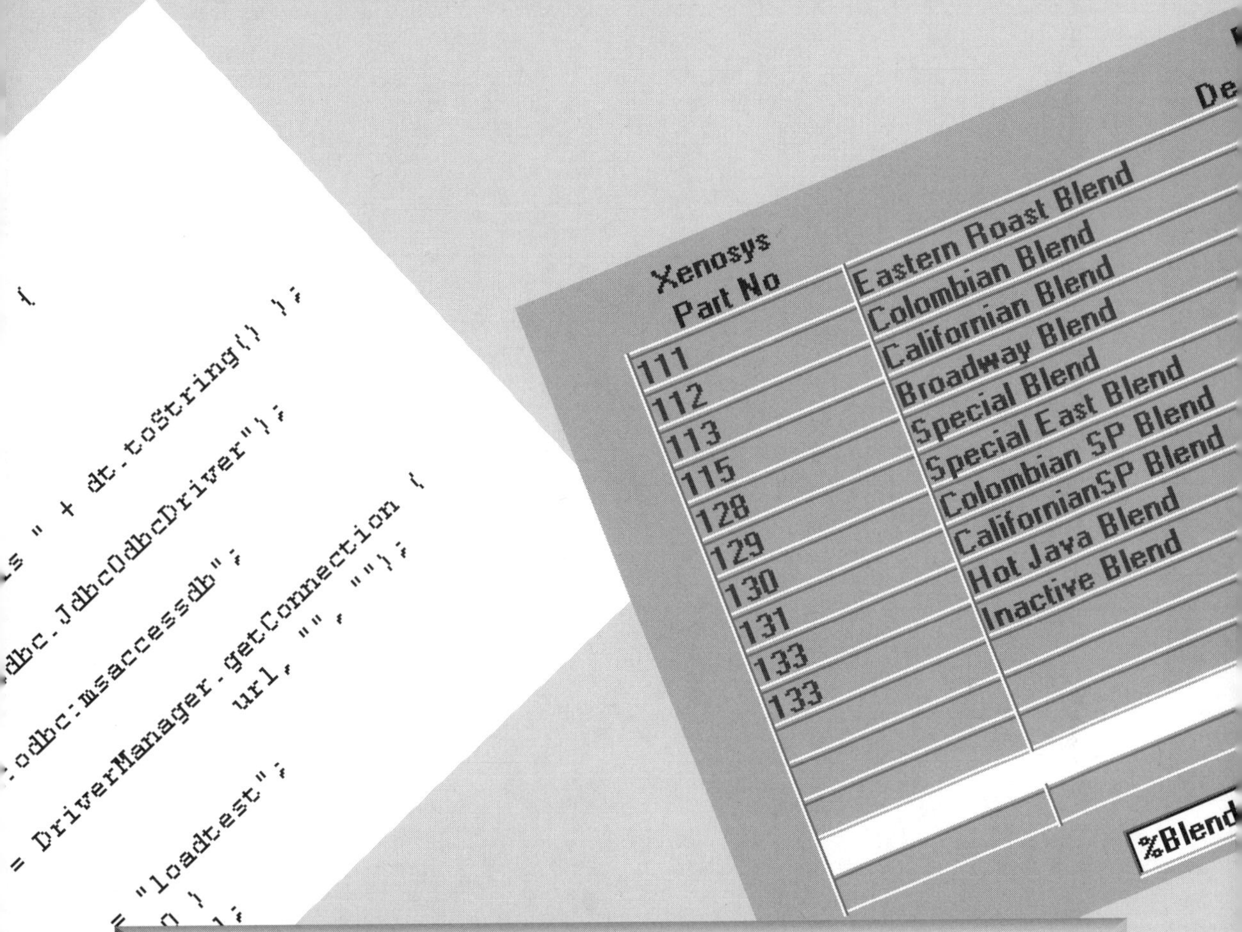

Chapter 8 JDBC Quick Reference

Chapter 9 JDBC Reference

Chapter 8 JDBC Quick Reference

JDBC Methods Summary

The following section lists the JDBC methods and fields in alphabetical order. A brief description of each method is provided. The next chapter will provide a detailed description of the method, its parameters, and examples of usage.

All JDBC Methods

Method (Parameter)	Interface	Purpose
BigDecimal abs()	BigDecimal	returns a BigDecimal whose value is the absolute value of the BigDecimal object, and whose scale is the scale of the BigDecimal object
BigInteger abs()	BigInteger	returns the absolute value of BigInteger object
boolean acceptsURL(String URLString)	Driver	will return true if driver can open a connection with a given URL
BigDecimal add(BigDecimal val)	BigDecimal	returns a BigDecimal whose value is the sum of the BigDecimal object and the BigDecimal val argument
BigInteger add(BigInteger val)	BigInteger	returns a BigInteger that represents the sum of the BigInteger object and the BigInteger supplied as an argument
boolean allProceduresAreCallable()	DatabaseMetaData	returns a true or false response on whether or not **all** of the procedures available can be called by the current user
boolean allTablesAreSelectable()	DatabaseMetaData	returns true or false response on whether or not the current user can execute a select on **all** of the tables available
BigInteger and(BigInteger val)	BigInteger	returns a BigInteger that represents the and operation of the BigInteger object and the BigInteger supplied as an argument
BigInteger andNot(BigInteger val)	BigInteger	returns a BigInteger that represents the and NOT operation of the BigInteger and the BigInteger supplied as an argument

Method (Parameter)	Interface	Purpose
BigDecimal BigDecimal(BigInteger unscaledVal, int scale)	BigDecimal	constructor for the BigDecimal class; takes as an argument a BigInteger unscaled value and an int scale and returns a BigDecimal
BigDecimal BigDecimal(BigInteger val)	BigDecimal	constructor for the BigDecimal class; takes a BigInteger argument and returns a BigDecimal value
BigDecimal BigDecimal(double val)	BigDecimal	constructor for the BigDecimal class; takes a double argument and returns a BigDecimal value
BigDecimal BigDecimal(String val)	BigDecimal	constructor for the BigDecimal class; takes a String argument containing a representation of a BigDecimal and returns a BigDecimal value
BigInteger BigInteger(byte[] val)	BigInteger	constructor for the BigInteger class; takes a byte array argument containing the two's-complement binary representation of a BigInteger and returns a BigInteger value
BigInteger BigInteger(int bitLength, int certainty, Random rnd)	BigInteger	constructor for the BigInteger class; constructs a randomly generated positive BigInteger with the specified bitLength
BigInteger BigInteger(int numBits, Random rnd)	BigInteger	constructor for the BigInteger class. Constructs a randomly generated BigInteger

Method (Parameter)	Interface	Purpose
BigInteger BigInteger(int signum, byte magnitude)	BigInteger	constructor for the BigInteger class; converts the sign-magnitude representation of a BigInteger into a BigInteger
BigInteger BigInteger(String val)	BigInteger	constructor for the BigInteger class; converts the decimal String representation of a BigInteger into a BigInteger
BigInteger BigInteger(String val, int radix)	BigInteger	constructor for the BigInteger class; converts a String representation of a BigInteger in the specified radix into a BigInteger
BigInteger abs()	BigInteger	returns the absolute value of BigInteger object
int bitCount()	BigInteger	returns the number of bits in the two's complement representation of the BigInteger that differ from the sign bit
int bitLength()	BigInteger	returns the number of bits in the minimal two's-complement representation of BigInteger, *excluding* a sign bit
void cancel()	Statement	executed by one thread to cancel a statement being executed by another thread
BigInteger clearBit(int n)	BigInteger	returns a BigInteger whose value is the BigInteger with the designated bit cleared
void clearParameters()	PreparedStatement	clears all parameter values in a paramaterized statement
void clearWarnings()	Connection	clears all warnings for the Connection instance
void clearWarnings()	ResultSet	clears all warnings in the ResultSet instance

Method (Parameter)	Interface	Purpose
void clearWarnings()	Statement	clears all warnings in the Statement instance
void close()	Connection	terminates the connection between the Connection instance and the database
void close()	ResultSet	terminates the connection between the ResultSet instance and the database
void close()	Statement	terminates the connection between the Statement instance and the database
void commit()	Connection	all changes since the previous commit/rollback or start of the transaction are made permanent in the database; any locks currently held by the Connection are released
int compareTo(BigDecimal val)	BigDecimal	compares the BigDecimal object with the BigDecimal argument
int compareTo(BigInteger val)	BigInteger	compares the BigInteger object with the BigInteger argument
int compareTo(Object o)	BigDecimal	compares the BigDecimal object with the specified Object argument
int compareTo(Object o)	BigInteger	compares the BigInteger object with the Object argument
Connection connect(String, Properties)	Driver	attempt to make a database connection to a given URL; returns a Connection object reference
Statement createStatement()	Connection	creates a SQL Statement object
boolean dataDefinitionCausesTransactionCommit()	DatabaseMetaData	returns true if a data definition language (DDL) statement forces a transaction commit

Method (Parameter)	Interface	Purpose
boolean dataDefinitionIgnoredInTransactions()	DatabaseMetaData	returns true if DDL statements are ignored in transactions
DataTruncation DataTruncation(int index, boolean parameter, boolean read, int dataSize, int transferSize)	DataTruncation	constructor for class; returns a DataTruncation object;
Date Date(int year, int month, int day)	Date	returns a Date object; constructor for the class Date
Void deregisterDriver(Driver driver)	DriverManager	eliminates a driver from the list maintained by the DriverManager
BigDecimal divide(BigDecimal val, int roundingMode)	BigDecimal	returns a BigDecimal whose value is the result of the division of the BigDecimal object by the BigDecimal argument
BigDecimal divide(BigDecimal val, int scale, int roundingMode)	BigDecimal	returns a BigDecimal whose value is the result of the division of the BigDecimal object by the BigDecimal argument
BigInteger divide(BigInteger val)	BigInteger	returns a BigInteger whose value represents the division of the BigInteger object with the BigInteger argument
BigInteger[] divideAndRemainder(BigInteger val)	BigInteger	returns an array of two BigIntegers containing the results of the division of the BigInteger object and the BigInteger argument followed by the remainder of the operation

Method (Parameter)	Interface	Purpose
boolean doesMaxRowSizeIncludeBlobs ()	DatabaseMetaData	returns true if the value returned by getMaxRowSize includes LONGVARCHAR and LONGVARBINARY blobs
double doubleValue()	BigDecimal	converts the BigDecimal object to a double
double doubleValue()	BigInteger	converts the BigInteger object to a double; returns a double
DriverManager DriverManager()	DriverManager	constructor for the class DriverManager
DriverPropertyInfo DriverPropertyInfo(String name, String value)	DriverPropertyInfo	constructor for class DriverPropertyInfo
boolean equals(Object x)	BigDecimal	performs an equality comparison with BigDecimal object the Object argument
boolean equals(Object x)	BigInteger	compares the BigInteger object with the specified Object for equality
boolean equals(Timestamp Timestamp)	Timestamp	returns true if the Timestamp equals that of the argument
boolean execute(String SQLString)	Statement	executes a SQL statement supplied in the parameter string
boolean execute()	PreparedStatement	executes the prepared SQL statement
ResultSet executeQuery(String SQLString)	Statement	executes a SQL query statement supplied in the parameter string
ResultSet executeQuery()	PreparedStatement	executes a prepared SQL query statement
int executeUpdate()	PreparedStatement	executes a prepared SQL insert, update or delete statement; returns the row count of the number of rows updated, if applicable

Method (Parameter)	Interface	Purpose
int executeUpdate(String)	Statement	executes a SQL insert, update, or delete statement supplied in the parameter string
int findColumn(String columnName)	ResultSet	returns the ResultSet column index identified by the column name supplied by the string parameter
BigInteger flipBit(int n)	BigInteger	returns a BigInteger whose value is equivalent to the BigInteger object with the designated bit flipped
float floatValue()	BigDecimal	converts BigDecimal object to a float
float floatValue()	BigInteger	converts the BigInteger object to a float. Returns a float
BigInteger gcd(BigInteger val)	BigInteger	returns the BigInteger whose value is the greatest common divisor of the absolute value of the BigInteger object and the BigInteger argument
InputStream getAsciiStream(int columnIndex)	ResultSet	returns the column value as a stream of ASCII characters for the column index supplied by the integer argument
InputStream getAsciiStream(String columnName)	ResultSet	returns the column value as a stream of ASCII characters for the column name supplied by the string argument
boolean getAutoClose()	Connection	returns the current auto-close state
boolean getAutoCommit()	Connection	returns the current auto-commit state

Method (Parameter)	Interface	Purpose
`ResultSet getBestRowIdentifier( String catalog, String schema, String table, int scope, boolean nullable)`	`DataBaseMetaData`	returns a description of a table's optimal set of columns that uniquely identifies a row
`InputStream getBinaryStream( String columnName )`	`ResultSet`	returns a column value as a binary stream based on the column name supplied by the string parameter
`InputStream getBinaryStream( int columnIndex)`	`ResultSet`	returns a column value as a binary stream based on the column index supplied by the integer parameter
`boolean getBoolean( int parameterIndex)`	`CallableStatement`	returns the value of a BIT parameter as a Java `boolean`
`boolean getBoolean( int columnIndex)`	`ResultSet`	returns the value of the column identified by the column index supplied by the integer parameter as a Java `boolean`
`boolean getBoolean( String columnName)`	`ResultSet`	returns a Java `boolean` value for the column identified by the column name in the string parameter
`byte getByte( int columnIndex)`	`CallableStatement`	returns the value of a TINYINT parameter as a Java `byte`
`byte getByte( int columnIndex)`	`ResultSet`	returns the value of the column identified by the column index
`byte getByte( String columnName)`	`ResultSet`	returns the value of the column identified by the column name supplied by the string parameter as a Java `byte`

Method (Parameter)	Interface	Purpose
`byte[] getBytes( int columnIndex)`	`ResultSet`	returns as a Java `byte[]` the value of the column identified by the column index supplied by the integer parameter
`byte[] getBytes( intcolumnIndex )`	`CallableStatement`	returns as a Java `byte[]` the value of the column identified by the column index supplied by the integer parameter
`byte[] getBytes( String columnName)`	`ResultSet`	returns as a Java `byte[]` the value of the column identified by the column name supplied by the `String` parameter
`String getCatalog()`	`Connection`	returns the `Connection`'s current catalog name
`String getCatalogName( int columnIndex)`	`ResultSetMetaData`	returns the column's table's catalog name
`ResultSet getCatalogs()`	`DatbaseMetaData`	returns the catalog names available in the database
`String getCatalogSeparator()`	`DatabaseMetaData`	returns the separator between catalog and table name
`String getCatalogTerm()`	`DatabaseMetaData`	returns the database vendor's preferred term for catalog
`int getColumnCount()`	`ResultSetMetaData`	returns the number of columns in the `ResultSet`
`int getColumnDisplaySize( int ColumnIndex)`	`ResultSetMetaData`	returns the column's maximum width in characters for the column referenced by the column index for the integer parameter
`String getColumnLabel( int columnIndex )`	`ResultSetMetaData`	returns the column label for the column referenced by the column index supplied by the integer parameter

Method (Parameter)	Interface	Purpose
`String getColumnName( int columnIndex )`	`ResultSetMetaData`	returns the column name for the column referenced by the column index supplied by the integer parameter
`ResultSet getColumnPrivileges( String, String, String, String )`	`DatabaseMetaData`	returns a description of the access rights for a table's columns
`ResultSet getColumns( String catalog, String schemaPattern, String tableNamePattern, String columnNamePattern)`	`DatabaseMetaData`	returns a description of the table columns available in a catalog
`int getColumnType( int columnIndex )`	`ResultSetMetaData`	returns the column SQL type for the column referenced by the integer parameter
`String getColumnTypeName( int columnIndex )`	`ResultSetMetaData`	returns the column data type in the data source's specific type name for the column referenced by the integer parameter
`Connection getConnection( String url)`	`DriverManager`	attempts to establish a connection to a database URL contained in the `String` parameter.
`getConnection( String url, Properties info )`	`DriverManager`	attempts to establish a connection to a database URL; returns a connection object
`Connection getConnection( String url, String user, String password )`	`DriverManager`	attempts to establish a connection to a database URL; returns a `Connection` object
`ResultSet getCrossReference( String primaryCatalog, String primarySchema, String primaryTable, String foreignCatalog, String foreignSchema, String foreignTable)`	`DatabaseMetaData`	returns a description of the foreign key columns in the foreign key table that reference the primary key columns of the primary key table

Method (Parameter)	Interface	Purpose
`String GetCursorName()`	`ResultSet`	returns the name of the SQL cursor used by this `ResultSet`
`String getDatabaseProductName()`	`DatabaseMetaData`	returns the product name of the current database
`String getDatabaseProductVersion()`	`DataBaseMetaData`	returns the version of the database product
`int getDataSize()`	`DataTruncation`	returns the number of bytes that should have been transferred
`Date getDate( int columnIndex)`	`ResultSet`	returns the value of the column referenced by the integer parameter as a `java.sql.Date` object
`Date getDate( int columnIndex )`	`CallableStatement`	returns the value of the SQL DATE parameter as a `java.sql.Date` object
`Date getDate( String columnName)`	`ResultSet`	returns the value of the column referenced by the column name as a `java.sql.Date` object
`int getDefaultTransactionIsolation()`	`DatabaseMetaData`	returns the database's default transaction isolation level
`double getDouble( int parameterIndex)`	`CallableStatement`	returns the value of the SQL DOUBLE parameter as a Java `double`
`double getDouble( int columnIndex)`	`ResultSet`	returns the value of the column referenced by the integer parameter as a Java `double`
`double getDouble( String columnName)`	`ResultSet`	returns the value of the column in the current row as a Java `double`
`Driver getDriver( String URL )`	`DriverManager`	attempts to find a driver that can interpret the URL passed in the string parameter; if successful, returns a `Driver` object reference

Method (Parameter)	Interface	Purpose
`int getDriverMajorVersion()`	`DatabaseMetaData`	returns the major version number for the JDBC driver
`int getDriverMinorVersion()`	`DatabaseMetaData`	returns the minor version of the JDBC driver
`String getDriverName()`	`DatabaseMetaData`	returns the name of the JDBC driver
`Enumeration getDrivers()`	`DriverManager`	returns a list of all the currently loaded JDBC drivers that can be accessed
`String getDriverVersion()`	`DatabaseMetaData`	returns the version of the JDBC driver
`int getErrorCode()`	`SQLException`	returns the vendor specific exception code
`ResultSet getExportedKeys( String catalog, String schema, String table)`	`DatabaseMetaData`	returns a description of foreign key columns that reference a table's primary key columns
`String getExtraNameCharacters ()`	`DatabaseMetaData`	returns all the characters that can be used as SQL identifiers in addition to alpha-numeric characters
`float getFloat( int columnIndex )`	`ResultSet`	returns the value as a Java `float` for a column referenced by the `int` parameter
`float getFloat( int columnIndex )`	`CallableStatement`	returns the value of a FLOAT parameter as a Java `float`
`float getFloat( String columnName )`	`ResultSet`	returns the value as a Java float for a column referenced by the `String` parameter
`String getIdentifierQuoteString ()`	`DatabaseMetaData`	returns the string used to quote SQL identifiers; returns a space if identifier quoting is not supported

Method (Parameter)	Interface	Purpose
`ResultSet getImportedKeys( String catalog, String schema, String table)`	DatabaseMetaData	returns a description of the primary key columns that are referenced as foreign keys
`int getIndex()`	`DataTruncation`	returns the index of the column or parameter that was truncated
`ResultSet getIndexInfo( String catalog, String schema, String table, boolean unique, boolean approximate)`	`DatabaseMetaData`	returns a description of a table's indices and statistics
`int getInt( int columnIndex )`	`CallableStatement`	returns the integer value of the column referenced by the integer parameter
`int getInt( int columnIndex )`	`ResultSet`	returns as an integer the value of the column referenced by the integer parameter
`int getInt( String columnName)`	`ResultSet`	returns an integer for the value of the column referenced by the column name contained in the `String` parameter
`int getLoginTimeout()`	`DriverManager`	returns the maximum time in seconds that drivers can wait when attempting to login to a database
`PrintStream getLogStream()`	`DriverManager`	returns the logging/tracing `PrintStream` that is used by the `DriverManager`
`long getLong( int columnIndex )`	`CallableStatement`	returns as a Java `long` integer the value of the BIGINT (`integer`) parameter
`long getLong( int columnIndex )`	`ResultSet`	returns as a Java `long` integer the value of the column referenced by the integer parameter

Method (Parameter)	Interface	Purpose
`long getLong( String columnName )`	`ResultSet`	returns as a `long` integer the value of the column referenced by the column name in the `String` parameter
`int getLowestSetBit()`	`BigInteger`	returns the index of the rightmost (lowest-order) one bit in the `BigInteger` object (the number of zero bits to the right of the rightmost one bit)
`int getMajorVersion()`	`Driver`	returns the driver's major version number
`int getMaxBinaryLiteralLength ()`	`DatabaseMetaData`	returns the number of hex characters that can be placed in a binary literal
`int getMaxCatalogNameLength ()`	`DatabaseMetaData`	returns the maximum length of a catalog name
`int getMaxCharLiteralLength ()`	`DatabaseMetaData`	returns the maximum length for a character literal
`int getMaxColumnNameLength ()`	`DatabaseMetaData`	returns the limit on column name length
`int getMaxColumnsInGroupBy ()`	`DatabaseMetaData`	returns the maximum number of columns allowed in a SQL GROUP BY clause
`int getMaxColumnsInIndex()`	`DatabaseMetaData`	returns the maximum number of columns allowed in an index
`int getMaxColumnsInOrderBy ()`	`DatabaseMetaData`	returns the maximum number of columns that can appear in a SQL ORDER BY clause
`int getMaxColumnsInSelect ()`	`DatabaseMetaData`	returns the maximum number of columns allowed in a SQL SELECT statement

Method (Parameter)	Interface	Purpose
`int getMaxColumnsInTable()`	`DatabaseMetaData`	returns the maximum number of columns in a table
`int getMaxConnections()`	`DatabaseMetaData`	returns the maximum number of database connections allowed
`int getMaxCursorNameLength()`	`DatabaseMetaData`	returns the maximum cursor name length
`int getMaxCursorNameLength()`	`DatabaseMetaData`	returns the maximum cursor name length
`int getMaxFieldSize()`	`Statement`	returns the maximum amount of data returned for any column value for BINARY, VARBINARY, LONGVARBINARY, CHAR, VARCHAR, and LONGVARCHAR columns only
`int getMaxIndexLength()`	`DataBaseMetaData`	returns the maximum length of an index in bytes
`int getMaxProcedureNameLength()`	`DatabaseMetaData`	returns the maximum length of a procedure name
`int getMaxRows()`	`Statement`	returns the maximum number of rows that a `ResultSet` can contain
`int getMaxRowSize()`	`DatabaseMetaData`	returns the maximum length of a single row
`int getMaxSchemaNameLength()`	`DatabaseMetaData`	returns the maximum length allowed for a schema name
`int getMaxStatementLength()`	`DatabaseMetaData`	returns the maximum length of a SQL statement
`int getMaxStatements()`	`DatabaseMetaData`	returns the active statements that can be open at the same time
`int getMaxTableNameLength()`	`DatabaseMetaData`	returns the maximum length of a table name

Method (Parameter)	Interface	Purpose
int getMaxTablesInSelect()	DatabaseMetaData	returns the maximum number of tables allowed in a SQL SELECT statement
int getMaxUserNameLength()	DatabaseMetaData	returns the maximum length of a user name
DatabaseMetaData getMetaData()	Connection	returns a DataBaseMetaData object containing information about the database connection
ResultSetMetaData getMetaData()	ResultSet	returns a ResultSetMeta data object containing information on the number, types and properties of a ResultSet's columns
int getMinorVersion()	Driver	returns the driver's minor version number
boolean getMoreResults()	Statement	positions to a Statement's next result
int getNanos()	Timestamp	returns the Timestamp's nanos value
SQLExcepion getNextException()	SQLException	returns the next exception in the chain of exceptions
SQLWarning getNextWarning()	SQLWarning	returns the next warning in the chain
Numeric getNumeric(int columnIndex, int scale)	CallableStatement	returns the value of the SQL NUMERIC parameter as a Java Numeric object
Numeric getNumeric(int parameterIndex, int Scale)	ResultSet	returns the value of the column referenced by the integer parameter as a Java Numeric object
Numeric getNumeric(String columnName, int scale)	ResultSet	returns the column referenced by the column name in the String parameter as a Java Numeric object
String getNumericFunctions()	DatabaseMetaData	returns a comma separated list of math functions

Method (Parameter)	Interface	Purpose
Object getObject(int columnIndex)	ResultSet	returns the value of the column referenced by the integer parameter as a Java Object
Object getObject(int parameterIndex)	CallableStatement	returns the value of the parameter as a Java object
Object getObject(String columnName)	ResultSet	returns the value of the column referenced by the name in the String parameter as a Java object
boolean getParameter()	DataTruncation	returns TRUE if the value is a parameter, FALSE if it is a column value
int getPrecision(int columnnIndex)	ResultSetMetaData	returns a column's precision (number of decimal digits)
ResultSet getPrimaryKeys(String catalog, String schema, String table)	DatabaseMetaData	returns a description of the table's primary key columns
ResultSet getProcedureColumns(String catalog,String schemaPattern,String ProcedureNamePattern, String columnNamePattern)	DatabaseMetaData	returns a description of a catalog's stored procedure parameters and result columns
ResultSet getProcedures(String catalog, String schemaPattern, String procedureNamePattern)	DatabaseMetaData	returns a description of the stored procedures available
String getProcedureTerm()	DatabaseMetaData	returns the database vendor's preferred term for 'procedure'
DriverPropertyInfo[] getPropertyInfo(String url, Properties info)	Driver	returns the property information for a database

Method (Parameter)	Interface	Purpose
`int getQueryTimeout()`	`Statement`	returns the time the driver will wait for a `Statement` to execute before aborting the statement
`boolean getRead()`	`DataTruncation`	returns true if the value was truncated when read from the database; false if the data was truncated on a write
`ResultSet getResultSet()`	`Statement`	returns a `ResultSet` for the executed SQL statement
`int getScale( int columnIndex )`	`ResultSetMetaData`	returns a column's scale (digits to the right of the decimal point)
`long getScaled()`	`Numeric`	returns the value multiplied by 10** scale
`String getSchemaName( int columnIndex )`	`ResultSetMetaData`	returns the column's table's schema name
`ResultSet getSchemas()`	`DatabaseMetaData`	returns the schema names available
`String getSchemaTerm()`	`DatabaseMetaData`	returns the vendor's preferred term for 'schema'
`String getSearchStringEscape()`	`DatabaseMetaData`	returns the escape patterns used by the database
`short getShort( int columnIndex)`	`ResultSet`	returns the value of the column referenced by the integer parameter as a Java `short`
`short getShort( int ParameterIndex)`	`CallableStatement`	returns the value of the SMALLINT parameter as a Java `short`
`short getShort( String columnName)`	`ResultSet`	returns the value of the column referenced by the column name in the string parameter as a Java `short`

Method (Parameter)	Interface	Purpose
`String getSQLKeywords()`	`DatabaseMetaData`	returns a comma separated list of all SQL keywords used by the database that are not SQL-92 keywords
`String getSQLState()`	`SQLException`	returns the SQLState
`String getString( int columnIndex )`	`ResultSet`	returns the value of the column referenced by the integer parameter as a Java `String`
`String getString( String columnName )`	`ResultSet`	returns the value of the column referenced by the column name in the `String` parameter as a Java `String`
`String getString( int columnName )`	`CallableStatement`	returns the value of the parameter referenced by the integer argument as a Java `String`
`String getStringFunctions()`	`DatabaseMetaData`	returns a comma separated list of string functions
`String getSystemFunctions()`	`DatabaseMetaData`	returns a comma separated list of system functions
`String getTableName( int columnIndex )`	`ResultSetMetaData`	returns the table name for a column referenced by the integer parameter
`ResultSet getTablePrivileges( String catalog, String schemaPattern,String tableNamePattern)`	`DatabaseMetaData`	returns a description of access rights for each table available
`ResultSet getTables( String catalog,String schemaPattern,String tableNamePattern, String types[])`	`DatabaseMetaData`	returns a description of tables available in the catalog
`ResultSet getTableTypes()`	`DatabaseMetaData`	returns a list of the table types available in this database

Method (Parameter)	Interface	Purpose
`int getTime( int ColumnIndex )`	`ResultSet`	returns the value of the column referenced by the integer parameter as a `Time` object
`int getTime( int parameterIndex )`	`CallableStatement`	returns the value of a SQL TIME parameter as a `Time` object
`int getTime( String ColumnName )`	`ResultSet`	returns the value of the column referenced by the column name in the `String` parameter as a `Time` object
`String getTimeDateFunctions()`	`DatabaseMetaData`	returns a comma separated list of time and date functions
`Timestamp getTimestamp( int columnIndex )`	`ResultSet`	returns the value of the column referenced by the integer parameter as a `Timestamp` object
`Timestamp getTimestamp( int parameterIndex )`	`CallableStatement`	returns the value of the SQL TIMESTAMP parameter as a `Timestamp` object
`Timestamp getTimestamp( String columnName )`	`ResultSet`	returns the value of the column referenced by the column name in the `String` parameter as a `Timestamp` object
`int getTransactionIsolation ()`	`Connection`	return the connection's current isolation mode from `java.sql.Connection`
`int getTransferSize()`	`DataTruncation`	returns the number of bytes actually transferred (after the truncation)
`ResultSet getTypeInfo()`	`DatabaseMetaData`	returns a description of all the standard SQL types supported by this database
`InputStream getUnicodeStream( int columnIndex )`	`ResultSet`	returns a column value that can be retrieved as a stream of Unicode characters

Method (Parameter)	Interface	Purpose
InputStream getUnicodeStream(String columnName)	ResultSet	returns a value referenced by the column name in the string parameter as a stream of Unicode characters
int getUpdateCount()	Statement	returns the current update result as an integer value
String getURL()	DatabaseMetaData	returns the URL for this database
String getUserName()	DatabaseMetaData	returns the name of the user running database session as perceived by the database
ResultSet getVersionColumns(String catalog, String schema,String table)	DatabaseMetaData	returns a description of a table's columns that are automatically updated when any value in a row is updated
SQLWarning getWarnings()	Connection	the first warning reported on calls through this connection
SQLWarning getWarnings()	ResultSet	the first warning reported on calls to this ResultSet
SQLWarning getWarnings()	Statement	returns the first warning reported by the execution of this Statement
int hashCode()	BigDecimal	returns the hash code for BigDecimal object
int hashCode()	BigInteger	returns the hash code for the BigInteger object
int intValue()	BigDecimal	converts the BigDecimal object to an int
int intValue()	BigInteger	converts the BigInteger object to an int; returns an int
boolean isAutoIncrement(int)	ResultSetMetaData	returns TRUE if the column is automatically numbered
boolean isCaseSensitive(int columnIndex)	ResultSetMetaData	returns TRUE if the column is case sensitive

Method (Parameter)	Interface	Purpose
`boolean isCatalogAtStart()`	`DatabaseMetaData`	returns true if the catalog names appears at the start of the table name (if false, assert it appears at the end)
`boolean isClosed()`	`Connection`	returns true if a connection is closed
`boolean isCurrency( int )`	`ResultSetMetaData`	returns true if the column referenced by the integer parameter is a CURRENCY value
`boolean isDefinitelyWritable( int columnIndex)`	`ResultSetMetaData`	returns true if a write will succeed to the column
`boolean isNullable( int )`	`ResultSetMetaData`	returns true if a NULL can be entered in this column
`boolean isProbablePrime( int certainty)`	`BigInteger`	returns true if this `BigInteger` is probably prime, false if it's definitely composite
`boolean isReadOnly( int )`	`ResultSetMetaData`	returns true if the column referenced by the integer parameter is not writable
`boolean isReadOnly()`	`Connection`	returns true if a connection is read-only
`boolean isReadOnly()`	`DatabaseMetaData`	returns true if the database is in read-only mode
`boolean isSearchable( int )`	`ResultSetMetaData`	returns true if the column can be used in a SQL where clause
`boolean isSigned( int columnIndex)`	`ResultSetMetaData`	returns true if the column is a signed number
`boolean isWritable( int columnIndex)`	`ResultSetMetaData`	returns true if a write can be made on the column referenced by the integer parameter
`boolean jdbcCompliant()`	`Driver`	returns true if the `Driver` is a JDBC Compliant (tm) driver

Method (Parameter)	Interface	Purpose
`boolean lessThan( Numeric NumericValue)`	`Numeric`	returns true if the `Numeric` value is less-than the `Numeric` argument
`long longValue()`	`BigDecimal`	converts `BigDecimal` object to a `long`
`long longValue()`	`BigInteger`	converts the `BigInteger` object to a long; returns a long
`BigDecimal max(BigDecimal val)`	`BigDecimal`	returns the maximum of the `BigDecimal` object and `BigDecimal val` argument
`BigInteger max(BigInteger val)`	`BigInteger`	returns the maximum of the `BigInteger` object and `BigInteger` argument
`BigDecimal min(BigDecimal val)`	`BigDecimal`	returns a `BigDecimal` value that represents the minimum of the `BigDecimal` object and the `BigDecimal` argument
`BigInteger min(BigInteger val)`	`BigInteger`	returns the minimum of the `BigInteger` object and the `BigInteger` argument
`BigInteger mod(BigInteger m)`	`BigInteger`	returns a `BigInteger` whose value is the modulus of the `BigInteger` object and the `BigInteger` argument
`BigInteger modInverse( BigInteger m)`	`BigInteger`	returns a `BigInteger` whose value is the inverse modulus of the `BigInteger` object and the `BigInteger` argument
`BigInteger modPow( BigInteger exponent, BigInteger m)`	`BigInteger`	returns a `BigInteger` whose value is ($this^{exponent}$ mod m) where m and the exponent are arguments to the method

Method (Parameter)	Interface	Purpose
BigDecimal movePointLeft(int n)	BigDecimal	Returns a BigDecimal value that is equivalent to the BigDecimal object with the decimal point moved the specified number of positions to the left.
BigDecimal movePointRight(int n)	BigDecimal	returns the BigDecimal value that represents the BigDecimal object with the decimal point moved the specified number of positions to the right
BigDecimal multiply(BigDecimal val)	BigDecimal	returns a BigDecimal value that represents the product of the BigDecimal object and the specified BigDecimal argument
BigInteger multiply(BigInteger val)	BigInteger	returns a BigInteger whose value is the product of the BigInteger object and the BigInteger argument
Numeric multiply(Numeric NumericValue)	Numeric	returns the product of the Numeric and the Numeric argument
String nativeSQL(String SQLString)	Connection	returns the native form of the SQL statement that would have been sent
BigDecimal negate()	BigDecimal	returns a BigDecimal whose value is the negation of the BigDecimal object value and whose scale is the current scale
BigInteger negate()	BigInteger	returns a BigInteger whose value is the negation of the value of the BigInteger object
BigInteger not()	BigInteger	returns a BigInteger whose value is the result of a NOT operation on the BigInteger object

Method (Parameter)	Interface	Purpose
boolean next()	ResultSet	moves to the next element in the ResultSet; returns false if no more rows
NullData NullData()	NullData	constructor for the NullData class
boolean nullPlusNonNullIsNull()	DatabaseMetaData	returns true if concatenations between NULL and non-NULL values generates a NULL; a JDBC compliant driver will return true
boolean nullsAreSortedAtEnd()	DatabaseMetaData	returns true if NULL values are sorted at the end of the sort order
boolean nullsAreSortedAtStart()	DatabaseMetaData	returns true if NULL values are sorted at the start of the sort order
boolean nullsAreSortedHigh()	DatabaseMetaData	returns true if NULL values are sorted high in the sort order
boolean nullsAreSortedLow()	DatabaseMetaData	returns true if NULL values are sorted low in the sort order
BigInteger or(BigInteger val)	BigInteger	returns a BigInteger whose value is the result of an OR operation of the BigInteger argument and the BigInteger object
CallableStatement prepareCall(String sqlStmt)	Connection	returns a CallableStatement object for the stored procedure call contained in the String parameter
PreparedStatement prepareStatement(String sqlStmt)	Connection	returns a PreparedStatement object using the SQL statement in the String parameter; the SQL statement may contain placeholders ('?')
void println(String)	DriverManager	prints a message to the current JDBC log stream

Method (Parameter)	Interface	Purpose
BigInteger pow(int exponent)	BigInteger	returns a BigInteger whose value is the BigInteger object raised to the power specified in the integer argument
void registerDriver(Driver driver)	DriverManager	registers the Driver with the DriverManager
void registerOutParameter(int parameterIndex, int SQLType, int scale)	CallableStatement	registers Numeric or Decimal stored procedure OUT parameters
void registerOutParameter(int parameterIndex, int SQLType)	CallableStatement	registers a stored procedure OUT parameter
boolean relationNames()	DatabaseMetaData	returns true if relation names are supported
BigInteger remainder(BigInteger val)	BigInteger	returns a BigInteger whose value is the remainder of the division of the BigInteger object and the BigInteger argument
void rollback()	Connection	rollback the current transaction; drops all changes made since the previous commit/rollback and releases any database locks currently held by the connection
int scale()	BigDecimal	returns the scale of the BigDecimal object
void setAsciiStream(int parameterIndex, InputStream inputStreamValue,int length)	PreparedStatement	assigns an input parameter to an ASCII Stream

Method (Parameter)	Interface	Purpose
`void setAutoCommit( boolean booleanValue)`	`Connection`	sets auto-commit mode based on the `boolean` parameter supplied. If argument is true, auto-commit mode will be set on; if argument is false, auto-commit mode will be set off
`void setBinaryStream( int parameterIndex, InputStream inputStreamValue, int length )`	`PreparedStatement`	set a LONGVARBINARY parameter input to a Java `InputStream`
`BigInteger setBit(int n)`	`BigInteger`	returns a BigInteger whose value is equivalent to `BigInteger` object with the designated bit set
`void setBoolean( int parameterIndex , boolean booleanValue)`	`PreparedStatement`	sets the parameter referenced by the integer argument to a Java `boolean` value
`void setByte( int parameterIndex, byte byteValue )`	`PreparedStatement`	sets the parameter referenced by the `integer` parameter to a Java `byte` value supplied
`void setBytes( int parameterIndex, byte[] bytesValue)`	`PreparedStatement`	sets the parameter referenced by the `integer` argument to the Java array of `byte` values supplied
`void setCatalog( String catalogName )`	`Connection`	select a specific database catalog
`void setCursorName( String cursorName )`	`Statement`	set the SQL cursor name that will be used to execute the `Statement`
`void setDate( int parameterIndex, Date DateValue)`	`PreparedStatement`	set a parameter referenced by the integer argument to a Java `Date`
`void setDouble( int parameterIndex, double doubleValue)`	`PreparedStatement`	sets the parameter referenced by the integer argument to the Java `double` argument

Method (Parameter)	Interface	Purpose
void setEscapeProcessing(boolean booleanValue)	Statement	sets escape processing on or off based on the boolean argument
void setFloat(int parameterIndex, float floatValue)	PreparedStatement	sets the parameter referenced by the integer argument to a Java float
void setInt(int parameterIndex, int intValue)	PreparedStatement	sets the parameter referenced by the integer argument to a Java int value
void setLoginTimeout(int timeoutSeconds)	DriverManager	sets the maximum timeout in seconds that drivers will wait when trying to connect to a database
void setLogStream(PrintStream outputPrintStream)	DriverManager	sets the logging/tracing PrintStream used by the DriverManager
void setLong(int parameterIndex, long longValue)	PreparedStatement	sets the parameter referenced by the integer argument to a Java long value
void setMaxFieldSize(int fieldSizeValue)	Statement	sets the field size limit in bytes that can be returned for any column value of type BINARY, VARBINARY, LONGVARBINARY, CHAR, VARCHAR, and LONGVARCHAR
void setMaxRows(int maxValue)	Statement	sets the number of rows limit that a ResultSet can contain
void setNanos(int nanoValue)	Timestamp	sets the Timestamp's nanos value
void setNextException(SQLException exceptionValue)	SQLException	adds an SQLException to the end of the exception chain
void setNextWarning(SQLWarning sqlwarningValue)	SQLWarning	adds an SQLWarning to the end of the warning chain

Method (Parameter)	Interface	Purpose
void setNull(int parameterIndex, int SQLType)	PreparedStatement	sets the value of the parameter referenced by the integer argument to a SQL NULL; sqlType from java.sql.Types
void setNumeric(int parameterIndex, Numeric NumericValue)	PreparedStatement	sets the value of the parameter referenced by the integer parameter to the Numeric value
setObject(int parameterIndex, Object objectValue, int SQLType,int scale)	PreparedStatement	sets the value of a parameter to that of the Object parameter; sqlType from java.sql.Types
void setObject(int parameterIndex, Object ObjectValue, int SQLType)	PreparedStatement	sets the value of the parameter referenced by the first integer parameter assuming a scale of zero; sqlType from java.sql.Types
void setObject(int parameterIndex, Object ObjectValue)	PreparedStatement	sets the value of a parameter to that of the object argument
void setQueryTimeout(int timeoutSeconds)	Statement	sets the query timeout limit—the number of seconds the driver will wait for a Statement to execute
void setReadOnly(boolean)	Connection	sets the connection's read-only mode based on the value of the boolean argument
BigDecimal setScale(int scale)	BigDecimal	returns a BigDecimal whose scale is set to the value specified in the scale argument, and whose value is equal to that of the BigDecimal object

Method (Parameter)	Interface	Purpose
`BigDecimal setScale(int scale, int roundingMode)`	`BigDecimal`	returns a `BigDecimal` whose scale is specified by the `scale` argument, and whose unscaled value is determined by multiplying or dividing this `BigDecimal` unscaled value by the appropriate power of ten to maintain its overall value
`void setShort( int parameterIndex, short shortValue )`	`PreparedStatement`	sets the parameter referenced by the integer argument to the value of the Java `short` parameter
`setString( int parameterIndex, String StringValue)`	`PreparedStatement`	sets the value of the parameter referenced by the integer argument to the Java `String` value
`void setTime( int paramterIndex, Time TimeValue )`	`PreparedStatement`	sets the parameter referenced by the integer argument to the value of the `Time` argument
`void setTimestamp( int parameterIndex, Timestamp TimestampValue )`	`PreparedStatement`	sets the parameter referenced by the integer argument to the `Timestamp` value
`void setTransactionIsolation( int transLevel )`	`Connection`	sets the transaction isolation mode based on the integer parameter; `transLevel` from `java.sql.Connection`
`void setUnicodeStream( int parameterIndex, InputStream InputStreamValue, int length )`	`PreparedStatement`	sets the input parameter to a Unicode input stream
`BigInteger shiftLeft(int n)`	`BigInteger`	returns a `BigInteger` whose value is the result of the *shift left* operation of the `BigInteger` object

Method (Parameter)	Interface	Purpose
`BigInteger shiftRight(int n)`	`BigInteger`	returns a `BigInteger` whose value is the result of a *right shift* operation of the `BigInteger` argument
`int signum()`	`BigInteger`	returns the result of the `signum` function on `BigInteger` object
`SQLException SQLException( String reason )`	`SQLException`	constructor for the `SQLException` class
`SQLException SQLException( String reason, String SQLState, int vendorCode )`	`SQLException`	constructor for the `SQLException` class
`SQLException SQLException( String reason, String SQLState )`	`SQLException`	constructor for the `SQLException` class
`SQLException SQLException()`	`SQLException`	constructor for the `SQLException` class
`SQLWarning SQLWarning( String reason)`	`SQLWarning`	constructor for the `SQLWarning` class
`SQLWarning SQLWarning( String reason, String SQLState, int vendorCode )`	`SQLWarning`	constructor for the `SQLWarning` class
`SQLWarning SQLWarning( String reason, String SQLState)`	`SQLWarning`	constructor for the `SQLWarning` class
`SQLWarning SQLWarning()`	`SQLWarning`	constructor for the `SQLWarning` class
`boolean storesLowerCaseIdentifiers()`	`DatabaseMetaData`	returns true if the database stores mixed case unquoted SQL identifiers in lower case
`boolean storesLowerCaseQuotedIdentifiers()`	`DatabaseMetaData`	returns true if the database stores mixed case SQL identifiers in lower case

Method (Parameter)	Interface	Purpose
`boolean storesMixedCaseIdentifiers ()`	`DatabaseMetaData`	returns true if the database stores mixed case unquoted SQL identifiers in mixed case.
`boolean storesMixedCaseQuotedIdentifiers()`	`DatabaseMetaData`	returns true if the database stores mixed case quoted SQL identifiers
`boolean storesUpperCaseIdentifiers()`	`DatabaseMetaData`	returns true if the database stores mixed case unquoted SQL in upper case
`boolean storesUpperCaseQuotedIdentifiers()`	`DatabaseMetaData`	returns true if the database stores mixed case quoted SQL in upper case.
`BigDecimal subtract( BigDecimal val)`	`BigDecimal`	returns a `BigDecimal` value equal to the `BigDecimal` object less the `BigDecimal` argument; the scale is the maximum of the scale of `BigDecimal` object or the scale of the argument
`BigInteger subtract( BigInteger val)`	`BigInteger`	returns a `BigInteger` whose value is the result of a subtraction operation between the `BigInteger` object and the `BigInteger` argument
`boolean supportsAlterTableWithAddColumn()`	`DatabaseMetaData`	returns true if the alter table statement is supported with the 'add column' clause
`boolean supportsAlterTableWithDropColumn()`	`DatabaseMetaData`	returns true if the database supports the '`alter table`' statement with the '`drop column`' clause
`boolean supportsANSI92EntryLevelSQL()`	`DatabaseMetaData`	returns true if the ANSI-92 entry level grammar is supported
`boolean supportsANSI92FullSQL()`	`DatabaseMetaData`	returns true if the SQL ANSI-92 grammar is supported in full

Method (Parameter)	Interface	Purpose
boolean supportsANSI92IntermediateSQL()	DatabaseMetaData	returns true if the ANSI-92 intermediate grammar is supported
boolean supportsCatalogsInDataManipulation()	DatabaseMetaData	returns true if the catalog name can be used in a data manipulation statement
boolean supportsCatalogsInIndexDefinitions()	DatabaseMetaData	returns true if a catalog name can be used in an index definition statement
boolean supportsCatalogsInPrivilegeDefinitions()	DatabaseMetaData	returns true if a catalog name can be used in a privilege definition statement
boolean supportsCatalogsInProcedureCalls()	DatabaseMetaData	returns true if a catalog name can be used in a procedure call statement
boolean supportsCatalogsInTableDefinitions()	DatabaseMetaData	returns true if a catalog name can be used in a table create
boolean supportsColumnAliasing()	DatabaseMetaData	returns true if column aliasing can be used
boolean supportsConvert()	DatabaseMetaData	returns true if the CONVERT function for data conversion between SQL types is supported
boolean supportsCoreSQLGrammar()	DatabaseMetaData	returns true if the ODBC core SQL grammar is supported
boolean supportsCorrelatedSubqueries()	DatabaseMetaData	returns true if correlated subqueries are supported
boolean supportsDataDefinitionAndDataManipulationTransactions()	DatabaseMetaData	returns true if both data definition and data manipulation statements in the same transaction
boolean supportsDataDefinitionAndDataManipulationTransactions()	DataBaseMetaData	returns true if both data manipulation and data definition statements can appear in the same transaction

Method (Parameter)	Interface	Purpose
boolean supportsDataManipulationTransactionsOnly()	DatabaseMetaData	returns true if only data manipulation statements can be executed within a transaction
boolean supportsDifferentTableCorrelationNames()	DatabaseMetaData	returns true if table correlation names are supported and they are restricted to be different from the names of the tables
boolean supportsExpressionsInOrder	DatabasMetaDaata	returns true if expressions are supported in the order by clause
boolean supportsExtendedSQLGrammar()	DatabaseMetaData	returns true if the ODBC extended SQL grammar is supported
boolean supportsFullOuterJoins()	DatabaseMetaData	returns true if full nested outer joins are supported
boolean supportsGroupBy()	DatabaseMetaData	returns TRUE if some form of the 'group by' clause can be used
boolean supportsGroupByBeyondSelect()	DatabaseMetaData	returns true if a 'group by' clause can add columns not in the select (list) provided it specifies all columns in the select
boolean supportsMixedCaseIdentifiers()	DatabaseMetaData	returns true if the database supports mixed case SQL identifiers
boolean supportsMixedCaseQuotedIdentifiers()	DatabaseMetaData	returns true if the database supports mixed case quoted SQL identifiers
boolean supportsMultipleResultSets()	DatabaseMetaData	returns true if multiple ResultSets from a single execute are supported
boolean supportsMultipleTransactions()	DatabaseMetaData	returns true if multiple transactions on separate connections can be active at the same time
boolean supportsNonNullableColumns()	DatabaseMetaData	returns true if columns can be defined as not storing NULL values

Method (Parameter)	Interface	Purpose
boolean supportsOpenCursorsAcrossCommit()	DatabaseMetaData	returns true if cursors remain open after transaction is committed
boolean supportsOpenCursorsAcrossRollback()	DatabaseMetaData	returns true if cursors remain open after a transaction rollback
boolean supportsOpenStatementsAcrossCommit()	DatabaseMetaData	returns true if statements remain open after a transaction commit
boolean supportsOpenStatementsAcrossRollback()	DatabaseMetaData	returns true if statements remain open after a transaction rollback
boolean supportsOrderByUnrelated()	DatabaseMetaData	returns true if the `order by` clause can use columns not in the `select` list
boolean supportsOuterJoins()	DatabaseMetaData	returns true if outer joins are supported
boolean supportsPositionedDelete()	DatabaseMetaData	returns true if a positioned SQL `delete` is supported
boolean supportsPositionedUpdate()	DatabaseMetaData	returns true if a positioned SQL `update` is allowed
boolean supportsSchemasInDataManipulation()	DatabaseMetaData	returns true if a schema name can be used in a DML statement
boolean supportsSchemasInIndexDefinitions()	DatabaseMetaData	returns true if a schema name can be used in an index definition statement
boolean supportsSchemasInPrivilegeDefinitions()	DatabaseMetaData	returns true if a schema name can be used in a database privilege statement
boolean supportsSchemasInProcedureCalls()	DatabaseMetaData	returns true if a schema name can be used in a stored procedure call statement
boolean supportsSchemasInTableDefinitions()	DatabaseMetaData	returns true if a schema name can be used in a table definition statement

Method (Parameter)	Interface	Purpose
boolean supportsSelectForUpdate()	DatabaseMetaData	returns true if the SQL 'select .. for update' statement is supported
boolean supportsStoredProcedures()	DatabaseMetaData	returns true if stored procedure calls are allowed using escape syntax
boolean supportsSubqueriesInComparisons()	DatabaseMetaData	returns true if subqueries are allowed in comparison expressions
boolean supportsSubqueriesInExists()	DatabaseMetaData	returns true if subqueries are allowed in SQL 'exists' clause
boolean supportsSubqueriesInIns()	DatabaseMetaData	returns true if subqueries are allowed in SQL 'in' clauses
boolean supportsSubqueriesInQuantifieds()	DatabaseMetaData	returns true if subqueries are allowed in quantified expressions
boolean supportsTableCorrelationNames()	DatabaseMetaData	returns true if table correlation names are supported
boolean supportsTransactionIsolationLevel(int)	DatabaseMetaData	returns true if the database supports the transaction isolation level represented by the integer parameter
boolean supportsTransactions()	DatabaseMetaData	returns true if transactions are supported in this database
boolean supportsUnion()	DatabaseMetaData	returns true if the SQL 'union' statement is supported
boolean supportsUnionAll()	DatabaseMetaData	returns true if the SQL 'union all' statement is supported
boolean testBit(int n)	BigInteger	returns true if the designated bit is set
Time Time(int hour,int minute, int second)	Time	constructor for the Time class; returns a Time object

Method (Parameter)	Interface	Purpose
Timestamp Timestamp(int year,int month, int date,int hour, int minute,int second, int nano)	Timestamp	constructor for the Timestamp class; returns a Timestamp object
byte[] toByteArray()	BigInteger	returns a byte array containing the two's-complement representation of the BigInteger object
BigInteger toBigInteger()	BigDecimal	converts the BigDecimal object to a BigInteger object; returns a BigInteger object
String toString()	BigDecimal	returns a string representation of the BigDecimal; returns a String object
String toString()	BigInteger	returns the String representation of the BigInteger object
String toString()	Date	returns a Date formatted as a string in the format 'yyyy-mm-dd'
String toString()	Time	returns a Time formatted as a string in the format 'hh:mm:ss'
String toString()	Timestamp	returns a Timestamp formatted as a string in the format 'yyyy-mm-dd hh:mm:ss.f'
String toString(int radix)	BigInteger	returns the String representation of BigInteger in the given radix
Types Types()	Types	constructor for Types class; returns a Types object
BigInteger unscaledValue()	BigDecimal	returns a BigInteger whose value is the unscaled value of the BigDecimal object
boolean usesLocalFilePerTable()	DatabaseMetaData	returns true if the database uses a local file for each table

Method (Parameter)	Interface	Purpose
`boolean usesLocalFiles()`	`DatabaseMetaData`	returns true if the database stores tables in a local file
`static BigDecimal valueOf(long val)`	`BigDecimal`	parameters are provided for a `long` value; returns a `BigDecimal` value for the long integer parameter
`static BigInteger valueOf(long val)`	`BigInteger`	returns a `BigInteger` whose value is equal to that of the `long` argument
`static BigDecimal valueOf( long unscaledVal, int scale)`	`BigDecimal`	parameters are provided for a `long` unscaled value and an `int` scale; returns a `BigDecimal` value based on the parameters
`Timestamp valueOf ( String TimestampValue )`	`Timestamp`	returns a `Timestamp` value based on the formatted `String` parameter
`Date valueOf( String stringDate )`	`Date`	returns a `Date` value based on the formatted `String` parameter
`Time valueOf( String stringTime )`	`Time`	returns a `Time` value based on the formatted `String` parameter
`wasNull()`	`CallableStatement`	returns true if the last value read was a NULL value
`boolean wasNull()`	`ResultSet`	returns true or false based on whether or not the last value read was a NULL
`BigInteger xor(BigInteger val)`	`BigInteger`	returns a `BigInteger` whose value is the result of an XOR operation of the `BigInteger` object and the `BigInteger` argument

Class Variables

Variable	Interface/Class	Description
`bestRowNotPseudo`	`DatabaseMetaData`	indicates that the *best row* is NOT a pseudo column
`bestRowPseudo`	`DatabaseMetaData`	indicates that the best row is a pseudo column
`bestRowSession`	`DatabaseMetaData`	indicates the best row scope is valid for the current session
`bestRowTemporary`	`DatabaseMetaData`	indicates the best row scope is temporary
`bestRowTransaction`	`DatabaseMetaData`	indicates the best row scope is only valid for the remainder of the current transaction
`bestRowUnknown`	`DatabaseMetaData`	indicates that it is not known whether or not the best row is a pseudo-column
`BIGINT`	`Types`	indicates the column contains a SQL `BIGINT` value
`BINARY`	`Types`	indicates the column contains a SQL `BINARY` type
`BIT`	`Types`	indicates the column contains a SQL `BIT` value
`CHAR`	`Types`	indicates the column contains a SQL `CHAR` value
`choices`	`DriverPropertyInfo`	indicates there may be an array of possible values
`columnNoNulls`	`ResultSetMetaData`	indicates that the column does not allow NULL values
`columnNoNulls`	`DatabaseMetaData`	the column might not allow NULL values
`ColumnNullable`	`DatabaseMetaData`	column allows NULL values
`columnNullable`	`ResultSetMetaData`	indicates that the column or parameter allows NULL values

Variable	Interface/Class	Description
columnNullableUnknown	ResultSetMetaData	indicates that it is not known whether or not the column allows NULL values
columnNullableUnknown	DatabaseMetaData	indicates that it is not known whether or not the column allows NULL values
DATE	Types	indicates the column or parameter contains a SQL DATE type
DECIMAL	Types	indicates the column or parameter contains a SQL DECIMAL value
description	DriverPropertyInfo	contains brief description of the property
DOUBLE	Types	indicates the column or parameter contains a SQL DOUBLE type
FLOAT	Types	indicates the column contains a SQL FLOAT type
importedKeyCascade	DatabaseMetaData	indicates the for update, an imported key is changed to agree with a primary key update; for delete, delete rows that import a deleted key
importedKeyRestrict	DatabaseMetaData	indicates the updates of a primary key are not allowed if the primary key has been imported
importedKeySetNull	DatabaseMetaData	indicates that the imported key will be changed to NULL if its primary key has been updated or deleted
index	NullData	indicates the index of the column or parameter that was NULL
INTEGER	Types	indicates the column or parameter contains an INTEGER value

Variable	Interface/Class	Description
LONGVARBINARY	Types	indicates the column or parameter contains a LONGVARBINARY value
LONGVARCHAR	Types	indicates the column or parameter contains a LONGVARCHAR value
name	DriverPropertyInfo	indicates the name of the property
NULL	Types	indicates a NULL data type
NUMERIC	Types	indicates that the column or parameter contains a SQL NUMERIC data value
OTHER	Types	indicates that the SQL type is a database-specific data type and will be mapped to a Java object
parameter	NullData	set to true if the NULL value was a parameter
procedureColumnIn	DatabaseMetaData	indicates the column type is an IN parameter
procedureColumnInOut	DatabaseMetaData	indicates the column type is an INOUT parameter
procedureColumnOut	DatabaseMetaData	indicates the column type is an OUT parameter
procedureColumnResult	DatabaseMetaData	indicates that the column type is a result column in a ResultSet
procedureColumnReturn	DatabaseMetaData	indicates the column type is a procedure return value
procedureColumnUnknown	DatabaseMetaData	indicates the column type is unknown
procedureNoNulls	DatabaseMetaData	the procedure does not allow NULLs
procedureNoResult	DatabaseMetaData	indicates the procedure does not return a result
procedureNullable	DatabaseMetaData	indicates that NULL values are allowed

Variable	Interface/Class	Description
procedureNullableUnknown	DatabaseMetaData	indicates the procedure may or may not be able to manage NULLs
procedureResultUnknown	DatabaseMetaData	indicates the procedure may return a result
procedureReturnsResult	DatabaseMetaData	indicates the procedure returns a result
REAL	Types	indicates the column or parameter contains a SQL SMALLINT value
required	DriverPropertyInfo	indicates a value must be supplied for this property
SMALLINT	Types	indicates the column or parameter contains a SQL SMALLINT value
tableIndexClustered	DatabaseMetaData	identifies a clustered index
tableIndexHashed	DatabaseMetaData	indicates a hashed index on the table
tableIndexOther	DatabaseMetaData	indicates some form of index other than hashed
tableIndexStatistic	DatabaseMetaData	indicates that statistics are returned in conjunction with a table's index description
TIME	Types	indicates the column or parameter contains a SQL TIME value
TIMESTAMP	Types	indicates the column or parameter contains a SQL TIMESTAMP value
TINYINT	Types	indicates the column or parameter contains a SQL TINYINT value
TRANSACTION_NONE	Connection	indicates that transactions are not supported on this database
TRANSACTION_READ_COMMITTED	Connection	indicates that only reads on the current row are repeatable

Variable	Interface/Class	Description
TRANSACTION_READ_UNCOMMITTED	Connection	indicates that 'dirty reads' are performed, i.e., a user can read an updated row that has not been committed
TRANSACTION_REPEATABLE_READ	Connection	indicates that reads on all rows are repeatable
TRANSACTION_SERIALIZABLE	Connection	indicates that all rows of a transaction are repeatable
typeNoNulls	DatabaseMetaData	indicates that this type does not allow NULL values
typeNullable	DatabaseMetaData	indicates that this type allows NULL values
typeNullableUnknown	DatabaseMetaData	indicates that it is not known whether or not this type can store NULL values
typePredBasic	DatabaseMetaData	indicates that this data type can be used in basic search clauses except for 'WHERE .. LIKE' clauses.
typePredChar	DatabaseMetaData	indicates that the type information is searchable only with 'WHERE … LIKE' clauses
typePredNone	DatabaseMetaData	indicates that there is no search support for this data type
typeSearchable	DatabaseMetaData	indicates the type information is searchable in SQL WHERE clauses
value	DriverPropertyInfo	specifies the current value of the property
VARBINARY	Types	indicates the column or parameter contains an SQL VARBINARY value
VARCHAR	Types	indicates the column or parameter contains an SQL VARCHAR value

Variable	Interface/Class	Description
`versionColumnNotPseudo`	`DatabaseMetaData`	indicates that the version column IS NOT a pseudo-column
`versionColumnPseudo`	`DatabaseMetaData`	indicates that the version column IS a pseudo-column
`versionColumnUnknown`	`DatabaseMetaData`	indicates that it is not known whether or not the version columns are pseudo-columns

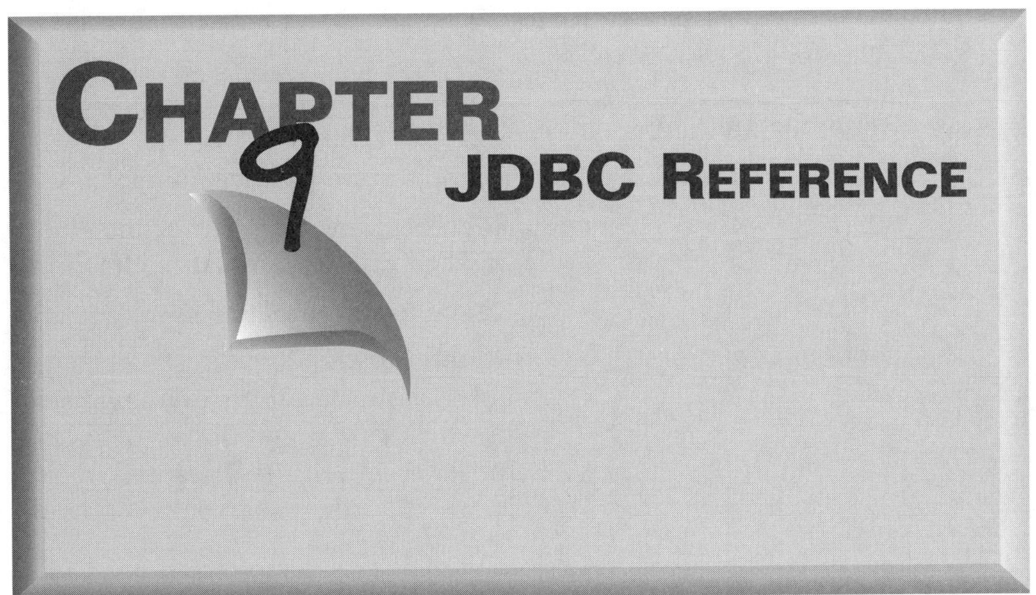

Interface BigDecimal

Declaration: `public class BigDecimal`

```
extends Number
implements Comparable
```

The `BigDecimal` class provides decimal numbers for use in Java applications, specifically in JDBC applications that need a data type to correspond to the SQL numeric or decimal number. Using an internal representation, the precision and scale of the `BigDecimal` are not platform- or database-specific.

The `BigDecimal` class provides methods for basic arithmetic, scale manipulation, comparison, hashing, and format conversion. Methods also provide the capability to control rounding and convert the `BigDecimal` into native Java data types.

Instance Variables

The `BigDecimal` class provides a number of static instance variables that are used to control the rounding behavior. These integers are passed to various `BigDecimal` methods to dictate rounding behavior if rounding must be done. All variables are declared as 'static int'. The following table identifies these instance variables.

Rounding Method	Description
ROUND_CEILING	Round toward positive infinity
ROUND_DOWN	Round toward zero. Never increments the digit prior to a discarded fraction
ROUND_FLOOR	Round toward negative infinity
ROUND_HALF_DOWN	Round toward "nearest neighbor" unless both neighbors are equidistant, in which case round down. Behaves as for ROUND_UP if the discarded fraction is >= .5; otherwise, behaves as for ROUND_DOWN
ROUND_HALF_EVEN	Round towards the "nearest neighbor" unless both neighbors are equidistant, in which case, round towards the even neighbor
ROUND_HALF_UP	Rounding mode to round toward "nearest neighbor" unless both neighbors are equidistant, in which case round up. Behaves as for ROUND_UP if the discarded fraction is >= .5; otherwise, behaves as for ROUND_DOWN
ROUND_UNNECESSARY	Rounding mode to assert that the requested operation has an exact result and rounding is necessary
ROUND_UP	Rounding mode to round away from zero. Always increments the digit prior to a non-zero discarded fraction

BigDecimal Methods

BigDecimal

Declaration: `public BigDecimal(String val)`

This constructor uses a `String` parameter containing the representation of a decimal to create a `BigDecimal`. The string consists of an optional minus sign followed by a sequence of zero or more decimal digits, optionally followed by a fraction. The fraction consists of a decimal point followed by zero or more decimal digits.

```
...
   BigDecimal bd = new BigDecimal( "123.456" );
   System.out.println( "BigDecimal with scale of 3 - " +
                        bd.toString() );
...
```

Parameters:

val—a String containing the representation of BigDecimal

BigDecimal

Declaration: public BigDecimal(double val)

This constructor creates a BigDecimal using the double value supplied as a parameter. The scale is the smallest value that allows the double value to be represented as an integer.

Note that because of the nature of the native Java double, certain numbers are not represented as would be expected. The use of this constructor could therefore be unpredictable. The constructor BigDecimal(String val) is perfectly predictable and is recommended.

```
...
  double dblval = 1.334;
  BigDecimal bd = new BigDecimal( dblval );
  System.out.println( "BigDecimal value is " + db.toString()
);
...
```

Parameters

val—double value to be converted to BigDecimal

BigDecimal

Declaration: public BigDecimal(BigInteger val)

This constructor creates a BigDecimal based on the BigInteger parameter supplied. The scale of the BigDecimal is zero.

Parameters

val—a BigInteger value to be converted to BigDecimal

BigDecimal

Declaration: `public BigDecimal(BigInteger unscaledVal, int scale)`

This constructor creates a `BigDecimal` based on two parameters: a `BigInteger` unscaled value and an integer scale. It returns a `BigDecimal`.

Parameters

`unscaledVal`—a `long` integer with the unscaled value of the `BigDecimal`

`scale`—scale of the `BigDecimal`

Returns

A `BigDecimal` value

valueOf

Declaration: `public static BigDecimal valueOf(long unscaledVal, int scale)`

This method takes two parameters, a `long` integer unscaled value and an integer specifying the scale, and creates a `BigDecimal`.

```
...
   bd1 = BigDecimal.valueOf( (long ) 5543,3 );
   bd2 = BigDecimal.valueOf( (long ) 1234,3 );
   if ( bd1.compareTo( bd2 ) > 0  )
      System.out.println( "bd1 is greater than bd2." );
...
```

Parameters

`unscaledVal`—unscaled `long` integer with the value of the `BigDecimal`

`scale`—integer scale of the `BigDecimal`

Returns

A `BigDecimal` value

valueOf

Declaration: `public static BigDecimal valueOf(long val)`

This method creates a `BigDecimal` from a `long` value provided as a parameter. The scale of the `BigDecimal` is zero.

Parameters

val—value of the BigDecimal

Returns

A BigDecimal whose value is val

add

Declaration: public BigDecimal add(BigDecimal val)

This method performs addition on the BigDecimal object and the BigDecimal parameter supplied. The scale of the result is the maximum scale of the two operands.

```
...
   BigDecimal bd = new BigDecimal( "133.33" );
  bd = bd.add( new BigDecimal( "333.333" ) );
  System.out.println( "new BigDecimal value is " +
                     bd.toString() );
...
```

Parameters

val—BigDecimal value to be added

Returns

A BigDecimal result

subtract

Declaration: public BigDecimal subtract(BigDecimal val)

This method subtracts the value of the BigDecimal object from the value of the BigDecimal parameter. The scale of the result is the maximum scale of the two operands.

Parameters

val—value to be subtracted from the BigDecimal

Returns

A BigDecimal result

multiply

Declaration: `public BigDecimal multiply(BigDecimal val)`

This method performs multiplication on the `BigDecimal` object and the `BigDecimal` parameter provided. The scale of the result is the total scale of the two operands.

Parameters

`val`—value to be multiplied by the `BigDecimal`

Returns

A `BigDecimal` result

divide

Declaration: `public BigDecimal divide(BigDecimal val, int scale, int roundingMode)`

This method performs a multiplication operation on the `BigDecimal` object and the `BigDecimal` parameter provided. The scale is specified by the integer parameter provided. An additional parameter allows a rounding mode to be specified.

```
...
  bd = bd.divide( new BigDecimal( "23.33" ),
                      10,
                      BigDecimal.ROUND_HALF_UP );
...
```

Parameters

`val`—`BigDecimal` value to be divided

`scale`—integer scale of the quotient to be returned

`roundingMode`—rounding mode to apply

Returns

A `BigDecimal` result

divide

Declaration: `public BigDecimal divide(BigDecimal val, int roundingMode)`

This method divides the `BigDecimal` object by the `BigDecimal` parameter. A parameter is used to dictate a rounding mode for the result of the operation. The scale of the result is the scale of the `BigDecimal` object.

Parameters

`val`—`BigDecimal` value to be divided

`roundingMode`—integer rounding mode to apply

Returns

A `BigDecimal` result

abs

Declaration: `public BigDecimal abs()`

This method returns the absolute value of the `BigDecimal` object. The scale of the result is the scale of the object.

```
...
  System.out.println( "The absolute value is " +
                          bd.abs().toString()  );
...
```

Returns

A `BigDecimal` result

negate

Declaration: `public BigDecimal negate()`

This method returns a `BigDecimal` that is the negation of the `BigDecimal` value. The scale of the result is the scale of the `BigDecimal` object.

Returns

A `BigDecimal` result

signum

Declaration: `public int signum()`

This method returns the `signum` of the `BigDecimal`. It returns a –1 if the value is negative, 0 if the value is zero, or 1 if the value is positive.

Returns

An integer result

scale

Declaration: `public int scale()`

This method returns the scale of the `BigDecimal`, the number of digits to the right of the decimal point.

```
...
   BigDecimal bd;
   System.out.println( "The scale is " +    bd.scale() );
...
```

Returns

An integer result

unscaledValue

Declaration: `public BigInteger unscaledValue()`

This method returns a `BigInteger` whose value represents the unscaled value of the `BigDecimal` object.

Returns

A `BigInteger` result

setScale

Declaration: `public BigDecimal setScale(int scale, int roundingMode)`

This method returns a `BigDecimal` with the specified scale. The scale is dictated by an integer argument. An additional argument indicates a rounding mode to apply if rounding is required.

Parameters

`scale`—integer scale

`roundingMode`—integer rounding mode

Returns

A `BigDecimal` with the specified scale

setScale

Declaration: `public BigDecimal setScale(int scale)`

This method returns a `BigDecimal` with the specified scale. The scale is specified as an integer argument. This call returns the same result as the `setScale` method with the rounding mode argument, but it eliminates this argument since in many cases it is not needed.

Parameters

`scale`—an integer specifying the scale of the `BigDecimal` result

Returns

A `BigDecimal` with the specified scale

movePointLeft

Declaration: `public BigDecimal movePointLeft(int n)`

The `movePointLeft` method returns a `BigDecimal` with the decimal point moved a specified number of spaces to the left. An integer argument specifies the number of decimal places to move. The results of this call are dependent on whether the scale specified is positive or negative. If the scale is positive, the call will move the decimal point to the left. If the scale is negative, the call will move the decimal point to the right.

Parameters

`n`—an integer specifying the number of spaces to move the decimal point

Returns

A `BigDecimal` result

movePointRight

Declaration: `public BigDecimal movePointRight(int n)`

This method returns a `BigDecimal` with the decimal point moved the specified number of spaces to the right. An integer argument specifies the number of spaces to move. If the specified scale is negative, the decimal point is moved to the right.

Parameters

`n`—an integer specifying the number of spaces to move the decimal point

Returns

A `BigDecimal` result

compareTo

Declaration: `public int compareTo(BigDecimal val)`

This method returns the comparison between the `BigDecimal` object value and the `BigDecimal` argument value. If the two `BigDecimals` are equal in value but different in scale, this method will still report them as equal.

This method returns –1 if the BigDecimal object is greater than the argument, 0 if they are equal, and –1 if the BigDecimal object is less than the argument.

The suggested syntax for performing these comparisons is

```
(x.compareTo(y) <op> 0),
```

where <op> is one of the six comparison operators.

Parameters

val—the BigDecimal value for comparison

Returns

An integer result

compareTo

Declaration: `public int compareTo(Object o)`

This method performs a comparison between the BigDecimal object and the Object argument. This method returns 1 if the BigDecimal object is greater than the argument, 0 if they are equal, and –1 if the BigDecimal object is less than the argument. Note that the Object argument must be a BigDecimal object, or the method will throw an exception.

The suggested idiom for performing these comparisons is

```
(x.compareTo(y) <op> 0),
```

where <op> is one of the six comparison operators.

```
...
   bd1 = BigDecimal.valueOf( (long ) 5543 );
   bd2 = BigDecimal.valueOf( (long ) 1234 );
   if ( bd1.compareTo( bd2 ) > 0  )
      System.out.println( "bd1 is greater than bd2." );
...
```

Parameters

o—the object for comparison

Returns

An integer result

equals

Declaration: `public boolean equals(Object x)`

This method performs an equality comparison between the `BigDecimal` object and the `Object` argument. If the `Object` argument is equal to the `BigDecimal` object, the method returns a boolean true. If they are not equal, the method returns a boolean false. The `BigDecimal` object and the `Object` are only equal if they are equal in both value and scale.

Parameters

`o`—object for comparison

Returns

A boolean value of true if the two objects are equal

min

Declaration: `public BigDecimal min(BigDecimal val)`

This method returns the minimum of the `BigDecimal` argument and the `BigDecimal` object.

Parameters

`val`—`BigDecimal` value for comparison

Returns

The `BigDecimal` result

max

Declaration: `public BigDecimal max(BigDecimal val)`

This method compares the `BigDecimal` object and the `BigDecimal` argument and returns the `BigDecimal` with the higher value.

Parameters

`val`—`BigDecimal` value for comparison

Returns

The `BigDecimal` with the larger value

hashCode

Declaration: `public int hashCode()`

This method returns the hash code for the `BigDecimal` object. (Note that `BigDecimals` that are numerically equal but differ in scale will not have the same hash code.)

Returns

Integer hash code

Overrides

Integer result

toString

Declaration: `public String toString()`

This method returns the `String` representation of the `BigDecimal` value. A leading minus sign indicates the sign of the number, and the number of digits to the right of the decimal point is used to indicate the scale.

Returns

A `String` representation of this `BigDecimal`

Overrides

`toString` in class `Object`

toBigInteger

Declaration: `public BigInteger toBigInteger()`

This method returns a `BigInteger` object for the `BigDecimal` object. Any fractional part of the `BigDecimal` object will be discarded in the conversion process.

Returns

The `BigInteger` result

intValue

Declaration: `public int intValue()`

This method returns an integer representation of the `BigDecimal` object. Any fractional part of the `BigDecimal` will be discarded. If the resulting integer (`BigInteger`) is too large to fit in an `int` data element, then only the low-order 32 bits are returned.

Returns

An `int` result

Overrides

`intValue` in class `Number`

longValue

Declaration: `public long longValue()`

The `longValue` method returns a `long` integer for the `BigDecimal` value. If the resulting integer (`BigInteger`) value is too large to fit in a `long` data variable, only the low-order 64 bits are returned.

Returns

A `long` integer result

Overrides

`longValue` in class `Number`

floatValue

Declaration: `public float floatValue()`

This method converts the value of the `BigDecimal` object to a native Java float. If the `BigDecimal` is too large to fit into a float, it will be converted as appropriate.

Returns

A `float` result

Overrides

`floatValue` in class `Number`

doubleValue

Declaration: `public double doubleValue()`

This method returns a `double` value representation for the `BigDecimal` object value. If the `BigDecimal` is too great to fit into a `double`, it will be converted as needed.

Returns

A `double` value representation

Overrides

`doubleValue` in class `Number`

Interface BigInteger

Declaration: `public class BigInteger extends Number`

The `BigInteger` class provides for the creation of arbitrary-precision integers. Methods provide for basic operations and behave basically like the operations on primitive Java integer types. In addition to these basic operations, this class also provides operations for greatest common denominator (GCD) calculation, modular arithmetic, primality testing, prime generation, bit manipulation, and other miscellaneous operations.

This class mirrors the operations and behavior of primitive integers with one major exception: overflow is not possible, since `BigInteger`s are made as large as necessary to accommodate the results of an operation. Bitwise, binary, and comparison operations are also provided in this class.

Instance Variables

The `BigInteger` class contains two static members that indicate specific values for a `BigInteger`. They are as follows.

ZERO

Declaration: `public static final BigInteger ZERO`

The `BigInteger` constant for the value 0.

ONE

Declaration: `public static final BigInteger ONE`

The `BigInteger` constant for the value 1.

BigInteger Methods

BigInteger

Declaration: `public BigInteger(byte[] val)`

This constructor converts the contents of a byte array containing a two's-complement representation of an integer into a `BigInteger` object. The input array is assumed to be a big-endian representation of an integer number.

Parameters

`val`—big-endian two's-complement binary representation of a `BigInteger`

BigInteger

Declaration: `public BigInteger(int signum, byte[] magnitude)`

This constructor function instantiates a `BigInteger` object based on the sign-magnitude representation of an integer number. The `signum` argument is –1 for negative, 0 for zero, and 1 for positive. The magnitude argument is a byte array in big-endian byte order.

Parameters

`signum`—`signum` of the number

`magnitude`—byte-array big-endian binary representation of the magnitude of the number

BigInteger

Declaration: `public BigInteger(String val,int radix)`

This constructor function instantiates a `BigInteger` object based on the `String` value argument passed to the method. The `String` value contains an image of the integer with an optional sign in the leftmost position, followed by a sequence of one or more digits in the specified radix. The radix must be in the range of `Character.MIN_RADIX (2)` to `Character.MAX_RADIX (36)`, inclusive.

```
...
    bi = new BigInteger( "12334", 10 );
    System.out.println( "BigInteger is " + bi.toString() );
...
```

Parameters

`val`—`String` representation of the `BigInteger` to create

`radix`—radix to be used in interpreting `val`

BigInteger

Declaration: `public BigInteger(String val)`

This constructor converts a decimal string representation of a `BigInteger` into a `BigInteger` using a `String` argument. The string contains an optional minus sign followed by a sequence of one or more decimal digits. The string should not contain any extraneous characters.

```
...
    bi = new BigInteger( "12334" );
    System.out.println( "BigInteger is " + bi.toString() );
...
```

Parameters

val—decimal string representation of BigInteger

Declaration: `public BigInteger(int numBits, Random rnd)`

This constructor creates a randomly generated positive BigInteger. The uniformity of the randomness is provided in part by the number of random bits provided in the Random argument.

An integer parameter provides the maximum number of bits to be used to generate the new BigInteger, and a Random parameter dictates the source of the randomness.

Parameters

numBits—maximum bit length of the new BigInteger

rnd—source of randomness

BigInteger

Declaration: `public BigInteger(int bitLength, int certainty, Random rnd)`

This constructor creates a randomly generated positive BigInteger, which may be prime. An integer parameter defines the maximum bit length of the new BigInteger, and another integer parameter indicates the level of certainty that should be pursued to generate a prime integer. And a final parameter specifies the source of the random bits from which to select candidates for the new BigInteger.

Parameters

bitlength—integer specifying the bit length

certainty—integer specifying the measure of uncertainty

rnd—Random object providing a source of random bits

BigInteger

Declaration: `public static BigInteger valueOf(long val)`

The valueOf method returns a BigInteger value for the specified Java long integer.

Parameters

val—value of the BigInteger to return

Returns

A BigInteger value

add

Declaration: `public BigInteger add(BigInteger val)`

This method returns a `BigInteger` whose value is the sum of the `BigInteger` object and the `BigInteger` parameter provided.

Parameters

`val`—value to be added

Returns

A `BigInteger` value representing the sum

subtract

Declaration: `public BigInteger subtract(BigInteger val)`

This method returns a `BigInteger` whose value is the result of a subtraction operation: the `BigInteger` object less the `BigInteger` parameter.

```
...
  bi = bi.subtract( new BigInteger( "239333" ) );
...
```

Parameters

`val`—`BigInteger` value to be subtracted

Returns

A `BigInteger` value representing the result of the operation

multiply

Declaration: `public BigInteger multiply(BigInteger val)`

This method returns the `BigInteger` product of the `BigInteger` parameter provided and the `BigInteger` object.

Parameters

`val`—value to be multiplied by the `BigInteger`

Returns

A `BigInteger` value representing the product

divide

Declaration: `public BigInteger divide(BigInteger val)`

This method returns a `BigInteger` that represents the result of a division operation of the `BigInteger` object by the `BigInteger` parameter.

Parameters

`val`—value by which this `BigInteger` is to be divided

Returns

A `BigInteger` value representing the quotient

remainder

Declaration: `public BigInteger remainder(BigInteger val)`

This method returns the remainder of the division operation between the `BigInteger` object and the `BigInteger` parameter.

Parameters

`val`—value by which this `BigInteger` is to be divided, and the remainder computed

Returns

A `BigInteger` value representing the remainder

divideAndRemainder

Declaration: `public BigInteger[] divideAndRemainder(BigInteger val)`

This method returns an array of two `BigInteger`s containing both the quotient and the remainder of the division operation between the `BigInteger` object and its argument.

Parameters

`val`—value by which this `BigInteger` is to be divided, and the remainder computed.

Returns

`BigInteger` results of the operation

pow

Declaration: `public BigInteger pow(int exponent)`

This method returns a `BigInteger` that represents the `BigInteger` object raised to the power of 10 specified by the integer exponent.

Parameters

`exponent`—exponent to which this `BigInteger` is to be raised

Returns

The `BigInteger` result of the operation

gcd

Declaration: `public BigInteger gcd(BigInteger val)`

This method returns a `BigInteger` that represents the greatest common denominator (GCD) between the absolute value of the `BigInteger` object and the `BigInteger` argument. If both the object and the argument are zero, then the method returns a 0.

Parameters

`val`—value with which the GCD is to be computed

Returns

A `BigInteger` result representing the GCD

abs

Declaration: `public BigInteger abs()`

This method returns a `BigInteger` representing the absolute value of the `BigInteger` object.

Returns

A `BigInteger` result

negate

Declaration: `public BigInteger negate()`

This method returns a `BigInteger` that represents the negation of the value of the `BigInteger` object.

Returns

A `BigInteger` value

signum

Declaration: `public int signum()`

This method returns the results of the `signum` function for the value of the `BigInteger` object. This method will return –1, 0, or 1 as the value of this `BigInteger` is negative, zero, or positive.

Returns

An integer result

mod

Declaration: `public BigInteger mod(BigInteger m)`

The mod method returns the remainder of the division operation between the `BigInteger` object and the `BigInteger` argument.

Parameters

`m`—the modulus

Returns

A `BigInteger` that represents 'this mod m'

modPow

Declaration: `public BigInteger modPow(BigInteger exponent, BigInteger m)`

This method returns a `BigInteger` that represents the `BigInteger` object raised to the specified power of 10 and then a modulus between the `BigInteger` object (raised to the power of 10) and the integer argument.

Parameters

`exponent`—the exponent

`m`—the modulus

Returns

`BigInteger` value

modInverse

Declaration: `public BigInteger modInverse(BigInteger m)`

This method returns a BigInteger whose value represents the 'mod Inverse' operation on the BigInteger. A single BigInteger parameter is provided for the modulus.

Parameters

m—a BigInteger representing the modulus

Returns

The BigInteger result of the operation

shiftLeft

Declaration: `public BigInteger shiftLeft(int n)`

This method returns a BigInteger whose value represents the BigInteger object left-shifted the number of spaces specified in the int argument.

Parameters

n—an integer representing the shift distance in bits

Returns

A BigInteger result

shiftRight

Declaration: `public BigInteger shiftRight(int n)`

This method returns a BigInteger whose value represents the BigInteger object right-shifted the number of times specified in the int argument.

Parameters

n—an integer representing the shift distance in bits

Returns

A BigInteger result

and

Declaration: `public BigInteger and(BigInteger val)`

This method returns a BigInteger whose value is the result of a binary *and* operation between the BigInteger object and the BigInteger argument. (This method returns a negative BigInteger if and only if this and val are both negative.)

Parameters

val—a BigInteger value

Returns

A BigInteger result

or

Declaration: public BigInteger or(BigInteger val)

This method returns a BigInteger whose value is the result of a binary *or* operation between the BigInteger object and the BigInteger argument.

Parameters

val—a BigInteger value to be used in the binary operation

Returns

A BigInteger, the result of the binary operation

xor

Declaration: public BigInteger xor(BigInteger val)

This method returns a BigInteger whose value is the result of a binary *exclusive-or* (xor) operation between the BigInteger object and the BigInteger operand.

Parameters

val—BigInteger value to be used in the binary operation

Returns

The BigInteger result of the binary operation

not

Declaration: public BigInteger not()

This method returns a BigInteger whose value is the result of a binary *not* operation on the BigInteger object value. (This method returns a negative value if and only if this BigInteger is non-negative.)

Returns

The BigInteger result of the binary *not* operation

andNot

Declaration: `public BigInteger andNot(BigInteger val)`

This method returns a `BigInteger` whose value represents the binary *and* `not` operation on the `BigInteger` object and the `BigInteger` argument. This method returns a negative `BigInteger` if the object is negative and the `BigInteger` argument `val` is positive. This method is the equivalent to

```
and(val.not())
```

Parameters

`val`—a `BigInteger` value to be operated on

Returns

A `BigInteger` representing the result of the operation

testBit

Declaration: `public boolean testBit(int n)`

This method returns true if the designated bit specified by the integer parameter is set.

Parameters

`n`—integer index of the bit to test

Returns

Boolean true if the designated bit is set

setBit

Description: `public BigInteger setBit(int n)`

This method returns a `BigInteger` whose value is that of the `BigInteger` object with the bit designated by the `int` parameter set.

```
...
   bi1 = new BigInteger( "0" );
   bi1 = bi1.setBit( 5 );
   bi1 = bi1.setBit( 1 );
   bi1 = bi1.setBit( 4 );
...
```

```
    // test bit flag
    if ( bi1.testBit( 5 ) )
        // perform action based on flag setting
...
```

Parameters

n—integer providing the index of the bit to be set

Returns

A `BigInteger` value with the specified bit set

clearBit

Declaration: `public BigInteger clearBit(int n)`

This method returns a `BigInteger` whose value is equivalent to the `BigInteger` object with the bit designated by the `int` argument cleared.

```
...
  bi1 = bi1.clearBit( 5 ) ;
...
  // test bit flag
   if ( bi1.testBit( 5 ) )
       // perform action based on flag setting

...
```

Parameters

n—integer with the index value of the bit to be cleared

Returns

A `BigInteger` value with the specified bit cleared

flipBit

Declaration: `public BigInteger flipBit(int n)`

This method returns a `BigInteger` whose value is equivalent to the `BigInteger` object with the bit designated by the integer parameter flipped.

Parameters

n—integer value with the index of the bit to be flipped

Returns

A BigInteger value with the specified bit flipped

getLowestSetBit

Declaration: `public int getLowestSetBit()`

This method returns an integer with the index of the rightmost (lowest-order) one bit in BigInteger (this is effectively the number of zero bits to the right of the rightmost one bit). The method returns –1 if this BigInteger contains no one bits.

Returns

An integer value containing the result

bitLength

Declaration: `public int bitLength()`

This method returns the number of bits in the minimal two's-complement representation of the BigInteger, *excluding* the sign bit.

Returns

An integer value representing the number of bits

bitCount

Declaration: `public int bitCount()`

This method returns the number of bits in the two's-complement representation of the BigInteger that differ from its sign bit.

Returns

An integer representing the number of bits

isProbablePrime

Declaration: `public boolean isProbablePrime(int certainty)`

This method returns true if this BigInteger is probably prime, false if it's not. An integer value argument is passed into the method to indicate the level of certainty to use for the test. Execution time for the method increases as the level of certainty increases.

Parameters

certainty—integer representing the level of certainty

Returns

A boolean value

compareTo

Declaration: `public int compareTo(BigInteger val)`

This method compares the `BigInteger` with the `BigInteger` argument. It returns a value indicating whether the `BigInteger` is greater than, less than, or equal to the compared object. A –1 indicates the value is less than, a 0 indicates the value is equal to, and a 1 indicates the value is greater than the value of the `BigInteger` object.

```
...
   if ( bi1.compareTo( bi2 ) > 0 )
      System.out.println( "bi1 is greater than bi2 " );
...
```

Parameters

`val`—a `BigInteger` to which this `BigInteger` is to be compared

Returns

An integer result of the comparison

compareTo

Declaration: `public int compareTo(Object o)`

This method compares the `BigInteger` object with the `Object` passed as an argument. If the `Object` is a `BigInteger`, this method will perform as with `compareTo(BigInteger)`. Note that this method will only process `Objects` that reference `BigIntegers`; otherwise, a `ClassCastException` is thrown.

This method returns a –1 if the `BigInteger` is less than the `Object`, 0 if they are equal, and 1 or more if the `BigInteger` is greater than the reference provided by the `Object`.

Parameters

`o`—`Object` to which this `BigInteger` is to be compared

Returns

An integer value with the result of the comparison

equals

Declaration: `public boolean equals(Object o)`

This method compares the `BigInteger` with the `Object` argument for numeric equality. It returns true if the `Object` is equal to the `BigInteger`, false if it is not.

Parameters

`o`—an `Object` for comparison

Returns

A boolean value of true

min

Declaration: `public BigInteger min(BigInteger val)`

This method returns the minimum of the `BigInteger` object and the `BigInteger` argument. It returns the `BigInteger` with the lower value.

Parameters

`val`—a `BigInteger` value for comparison

Returns

The `BigInteger` with the lower value

max

Declaration: `public BigInteger max(BigInteger val)`

This method returns the maximum of the `BigInteger` object and the `BigInteger` argument. It returns the `BigInteger` with the higher value.

Parameters

`val`—a `BigInteger` value for comparison

Returns

The `BigInteger` with the higher value

hashCode

Declaration: `public int hashCode()`

This method returns the hash code for the `BigInteger` object.

```
...
    bi1 = new BigInteger( "12345" );
    bi2 = new BigInteger( "12345" );
    if ( bi1.hashCode() == bi2.hashCode() )
         System.out.println( "bi1 and bi2 have the same
value." );
...
```

Returns

Integer hash code for the `BigInteger`

Overrides

The `hashCode` method in class `Object`

toString

Declaration: `public String toString(int radix)`

This method returns the `String` representation of the `BigInteger` object in the given radix. If the radix is outside the range from `Character.MIN_RADIX (2)` to `Character.MAX_RADIX (36)` inclusive, it will default to 10. A minus sign is prepended to the string if it is needed.

```
...
   bi1 = new BigInteger( "23443" );
   System.out.println( "bi1 is " + bi1.toString() );
...
```

Parameters

`radix`—an integer representing the radix of the `String` representation

Returns

A `String` representation of the `BigInteger`

toString

Declaration: `public String toString()`

This method returns the decimal `String` representation of the `BigInteger` object in the form of a `String` object.

Returns

A decimal `String` representation of the `BigInteger`

Overrides

The `toString` method in class `Object`

toByteArray

Declaration: `public byte[] toByteArray()`

This method returns a byte array containing the two's-complement representation of the `BigInteger`. The byte array will be in big endian byte-order with the most significant byte in the zeroth or first element. The resulting representation will contain the minimum number of bytes needed to represent the integer number, including a sign bit.

Returns

A byte array containing the `BigInteger` representation

intValue

Declaration: `public int intValue()`

This method converts the `BigInteger` object to an `int`. If the `BigInteger` is too big, only the lower-order 32 bits are returned, which can lead to a loss of precision.

Returns

Integer representation of the `BigInteger`

Overrides:

`intValue` in class `Number`

longValue

Declaration: `public long longValue()`

This method converts the `BigInteger` object to a `long` integer. If the `BigInteger` value is too big, only the lower-order 32 bits are returned, which can lead to a loss of precision.

Returns

This `BigInteger` converted to a `long`

Overrides:

The `longValue` method in class `Number`

floatValue

Declaration: `public float floatValue()`

The method converts the `BigInteger` object to a native Java `float`. If the `BigInteger` is too large to be represented, it will be converted to infinity or negative infinity, as appropriate.

Returns

A `float` value equivalent to the `BigInteger` value

Overrides

The `floatValue` method in class `Number`

doubleValue

Declaration: `public double doubleValue()`

This method converts the `BigInteger` object to a `double` value. If the `BigInteger` is too large to be represented as a `double`, it will be converted to infinity or negative infinity, as appropriate.

Returns

`double` value equivalent to the `BigInteger` value

Overrides

The `doubleValue` method in class `Number`

Interface java.sql.CallableStatement

Declaration: `public interface` **`CallableStatement`**

`extends Object`

`extends PreparedStatement`

The `CallableStatement` object is used to execute SQL stored procedures. The JDBC specification provides a standard way to call stored procedures for all databases.

Stored procedures are called via an escape syntax using a '{' character as the escape clause start and a '}' character as an escape clause end.

There are two forms of parameter inclusion for stored procedures: one form allows inclusion of a result parameter and the other form does not. If result parameters are used they must be registered as OUT parameters using the appropriate `CallableStatement` method. Parameters are numbered sequentially from left to right starting with the number 1.

```
import java.sql.*;
import java.io.*;
    class SProc2 {
             public static void main( String argv[] ) {
           try {
              Class.forName("jdbc.odbc.JdbcOdbcDriver");
              String url = "jdbc:odbc:informix5";

              Connection con = DriverManager.getConnection (
                                          url, "", "");
              System.out.println(
                  "Database connection made." );
              String qs = " { call p1(?) }";
              String outSQL = con.nativeSQL( qs );
              System.out.println(
                   "Native SQL is " + outSQL );
              CallableStatement sproc = con.prepareCall(
                                                  qs );
              System.out.println(
                 "Stored procedure has been prepared." );

              sproc.setInt( 1, 1 );

              ResultSet rs = sproc.executeQuery();
```

```
                boolean more = rs.next();

                while ( more ) {

                        System.out.println(
                            "Parm1: "  + rs.getInt( 1 ) +
                            " Parm2: " + rs.getInt( 2 ) );
                        more = rs.next();
                }

            }

            catch (java.lang.Exception ex) {

            // Print description of the exception.
            System.out.println(
                  "** Error on data select. ** " );
            ex.printStackTrace ();
           }
        }
    }
```

In this example, the stored procedure `p1` is called via a `CallableStatement` object. The `setint` method is used to set the value of the stored procedure parameter. The `executeQuery` method is then used to execute the stored procedure. This method returns a `ResultSet`. This `ResultSet` is then used as any other `ResultSet` would be used; the results are read sequentially and the `getInt` method is used to retrieve the values returned by the stored procedure.

Parameters are either IN parameters or OUT parameters. The IN parameters are set using methods inherited from `PreparedStatement`. The OUT parameters type can be registered using methods supplied in `CallableStatement`.

A `CallableStatement` may return a `ResultSet` or multiple `ResultSets`. Methods exist to manage multiple `ResultSets`.

See Also: `prepareCall`, `ResultSet`

CallableStatement Methods

getBoolean

Declaration: `public abstract boolean getBoolean(int parameterIndex) throws SQLException`

This method returns the value of a SQL BIT parameter as a Java `boolean`.

```
....
Connection con = DriverManager.getConnection (
url, " ", " ");
CallableStatement stmt = con.prepareCall( stmtString );
...
boolean colValue = stmt.getBoolean( 3 );
...
```

Parameters

`parameterIndex`—numbered sequentially, left to right starting with 1

Returns

A Java `boolean`.

getByte

Declaration: `Public abstract byte getByte(int parameterIndex) throws SQLException`

Returns the value of a SQL TINYINT parameter as a Java byte.

```
...
Connection con = DriverManager.getConnection (
url, " ", " ");
CallableStatement stmt = con.prepareCall( stmtString );
...
byte colValue = stmt.getByte( 4 );
...
```

Parameters

`parameterIndex`—numbered sequentially, left to right starting with 1

Returns

A Java `byte`. If the value is SQL null, the result is 0.

getBytes

Declaration: `public abstract byte[] getBytes(int parameterIndex) throws SQLException`

Returns the value of a SQL BINARY or VARBINARY as a Java `byte[];`

```
...

Connection con = DriverManager.getConnection (
url, " ", " ");
CallableStatement stmt = con.prepareCall( stmtString );
...
byte[] bytesVal[] = stmt.getBytes( 3 );

...
```

Parameters

`parameterIndex`—numbered sequentially, left to right starting with 1

Returns

A byte array; if the value is SQL NULL the result is null

getDate

Declaration: `public abstract Date getDate(int parameterIndex) throws SQLException`

Returns the value of a SQL DATE parameter as a Java `Date` object.

```
...

Connection con = DriverManager.getConnection (
url, " ", " ");
CallableStatement stmt = con.prepareCall( stmtString );
...
Date dateVal = stmt.getDate( 3 );

...
```

Parameters

`parameterIndex`—numbered sequentially, left to right starting with 1

Returns

Returns a `Date` object or a NULL if the result is SQL NULL.

getDouble

Declaration: `public abstract double getDouble(int parameterIndex) throws SQLException`

Returns the value of a DOUBLE as a Java `double`.

```
...

Connection con = DriverManager.getConnection (
url, " ", " ");
CallableStatement stmt = con.prepareCall( stmtString );
...
double colValue = stmtProc.getDouble( 6 );


...
```

Parameters

`parameterIndex`—numbered sequentially, left to right starting with 1

Returns

A Java `double`. If the result is SQL NULL, then it returns 0.

getFloat

Declaration: `public abstract float getFloat(int parameterIndex) throws SQLException`

Returns the value of a SQL FLOAT parameter as a Java `float`.

```
...
Connection con = DriverManager.getConnection (
url, " ", " ");
CallableStatement stmt = con.prepareCall( stmtString );
...
float colValue = stmt.getFloat( 3 );


...
```

Parameters

`parameterIndex`—numbered sequentially, left to right starting with 1

Returns

A Java `float`. If the value is SQL NULL, then it returns 0.

getInt

Declaration: `public abstract int getInt(int parameterIndex) throws SQLException`

Returns the value of a SQL INTEGER as a Java `int`.

```
...

Connection con = DriverManager.getConnection (
url, " ", " ");
CallableStatement stmt = con.prepareCall( stmtString );
...
int colValue = stmt.getInt( 3 );

...
```

Parameters

`parameterIndex`—numbered sequentially, left to right starting with 1

Returns

A Java `int`. If the result is SQL NULL, returns a 0.

getLong

Declaration: `public abstract long getLong(int parameterIndex) throws SQLException`

Returns the value of a SQL BIGINT parameter as a Java `long`.

```
...

Connection con = DriverManager.getConnection (
url, " ", " ");
CallableStatement stmt = con.prepareCall( stmtString );

...

long colValue = stmt.getlong( 3 );

...
```

Parameters

`parameterIndex`—numbered sequentially, left to right starting with 1

Returns

A Java `long`; if the value is SQL NULL then the return value is 0.

getNumeric

Declaration: `public abstract Numeric getNumeric(int parameterIndex, int scale) throws SQLException`

Returns the value of a SQL NUMERIC parameter as a `Numeric` object.

```
...

Connection con = DriverManager.getConnection (
url, " ", " ");
CallableStatement stmt = con.prepareCall( stmtString );
...
Numeric colValue = stmtProc.getNumeric( 8, 8 );

...
```

Parameters

`parameterIndex`—numbered sequentially, left to right starting with 1

`scale`—a value greater than or equal to zero representing the desired number of digits to the right of the decimal point

Returns

A Java `Numeric` object. If the value is SQL NULL, then the value is NULL.

getObject

Declaration: `public abstract Object getObject(int parameterIndex) throws SQLException`

This method returns a Java object for the value of the parameter. The object type corresponds to the SQL type that was registered for this parameter using `registerOutParameter`.

This method can be used to read database specific abstract data types by specifying a target Sql Type of `java.sql.types.OTHER`; this allows the driver to return a specific database Java type.

```
...

Connection con = DriverManager.getConnection (
url, " ", " ");
```

```
CallableStatement stmt = con.prepareCall( stmtString );
...
Object objValue = stmtProc.getObject( 13 );

...
```

Parameters

parameterIndex—numbered sequentially, left to right starting with 1

Returns

Returns a `java.lang.Object` holding the OUT parameter value.

See Also: Types

getShort

Declaration: `public abstract short getShort(int parameterIndex) throws SQLException`

This method returns the value of a SQL SMALLINT as a Java `short`.

```
...

Connection con = DriverManager.getConnection (
url, " ", " ");
CallableStatement stmt = con.prepareCall( stmtString );
...
short colValue = stmt.getShort( 3 );

...
```

Parameters

parameterIndex—numbered sequentially, left to right starting with 1

Returns

A Java `short`. If the value is SQL NULL then the result is 0

getString

Declaration: `public abstract String getString(int parameterIndex) throws SQLException`

This method retrieves the value of a SQL CHAR, VARCHAR, or LONG-VARCHAR parameter.

```
...

Connection con = DriverManager.getConnection (
url, " ", " ");
CallableStatement stmt = con.prepareCall( stmtString );
...
String strVal = stmt.getString( 1 );

...
```

Parameters

parameterIndex—numbered sequentially, left to right starting with 1

Returns

A Java `String` object.

getTime

Declaration: `public abstract Time getTime(int parameterIndex) throws SQLException`

Get the value of a SQL TIME parameter as a `java.sql.Time` object.

```
...
Connection con = DriverManager.getConnection (
url, " ", " ");
CallableStatement stmt = con.prepareCall( stmtString );
...
Time colValue = stmtProc.getTime( 4 );
...
```

Parameters

parameterIndex—numbered sequentially, left to right starting with 1

Returns

A Java `Time` object or a NULL if the value is SQL NULL.

getTimestamp

Declaration: `public abstract Timestamp getTimestamp(int parameterIndex) throws SQLException`

Returns a `Timestamp` value for the parameter specified.

```
...

Connection con = DriverManager.getConnection (
url, " ", " ");
CallableStatement stmt = con.prepareCall( stmtString );
...
Timestamp retValue = stmtProc.getTimestamp( 11 );
...
```

Parameters

`parameterIndex`—numbered sequentially, left to right starting with 1

Returns

Returns a `Timestamp` object or a NULL if the result is SQL NULL.

registerOutParameter

Declaration: `public abstract void registerOutParameter(int parameterIndex, int sqlType) throws SQLException`

The `registerOutParameter` method is used to set the Type of each OUT parameter. (When reading the value of these parameters, the appropriate method must be used.)

```
...

Connection con = DriverManager.getConnection (
url, " ", " ");

CallableStatement stmt = con.prepareCall( SPString );

stmt.registerOutParameter( 1, Types.Float );
stmt.registerOutParameter( 2, Types.Date );
stmt.registerOutParameter( 3, Types.Char );

ResultSet rs = stmt.executeQuery();
...
```

Parameters

`parameterIndex`—numbered sequentially, left to right starting with 1 sqlType—the Type of the parameter as defined in java.sql.Types. If a scale is required for a Numeric or Decimal, the appropriate version of RegisterOutParameter must be used to allow a scale argument to be passed to the method.

See Also: Type

registerOutParameter

Declaration: public abstract void registerOutParameter(int parameterIndex,int sqlType, int scale) throws SQLException

This is a version of registerOutParameter that allows a scale parameter to be passed. This scale parameter is needed for Decimal and Numeric data values.

```
...

Connection con = DriverManager.getConnection (
url, " ", " ");
CallableStatement stmt = con.prepareCall( stmtString );
stmt.registerOutParameter( 1, Types.Integer );
stmt.registerOutParameter( 2, Types.Decimal, 8 );

...
```

Parameters

parameterIndex—numbered sequentially, left to right starting with 1

sqlType—should use either java.sql.Type.NUMERIC or java.sql.Type.DECIMAL

scale—a value greater than or equal to zero representing the desired number of digits to the right of the decimal point

See Also: Numeric, Type

wasNull

Declaration: public abstract boolean wasNull() throws SQLException

This method reports whether the last OUT parameter retrieved has a value of NULL or not. The appropriate getXXX method must first be called to read the parameter value.

```
...
Connection con = DriverManager.getConnection (
url, " ", " ");

CallableStatement stmt = con.prepareCall( stmtString );
...

String Stringval = null;
while ( more ) {
    Stringval = stmt.getString( 1 );
    if ( stmt.wasNull() )
        continue;
    else
       System.out.println( "Col1: + Stringval );
...
```

Returns

A boolean value of true if the last parameter read was SQL NULL

Interface java.sql.Connection

Declaration: `public interface` **`Connection`** `extends Object`

A database connection is required before database activity can begin. The database connection can only be obtained after the appropriate driver has been loaded and is represented in JDBC through the `Connection` object. The `Connection` object is returned by the `DriverManager` class as follows.

```
import java.sql.*;
import java.io.*;

...

 Class.forName ("jdbc.odbc.JdbcOdbcDriver");
 String url = "jdbc:odbc:msaccessdb";
 Connection con = DriverManager.getConnection (
                                           url, "", "");

 String qs = "select * from loadtest";
 PreparedStatement prepStmt = con.prepareStatement( qs );

...
```

In this example, the `Class` method `forName` is used to load the JDBC-ODBC driver. Once the driver has been loaded, the `DriverManager` method `getConnection` is used to instantiate the `Connection` object.

The `Connection` object provides methods to create a `Statement`, `PreparedStatement` or `CallableStatetment` object. In this example, a `PreparedStatement` object is created which is then used to execute SQL statements against the database. Results are returned with the `ResultSet` object created via the `PreparedStatement` object.

Information about the `Connection` is available using the `DatabaseMetaData` object created using the `getMetaData` method. This information includes a description of the database tables, supported SQL grammar, stored procedures, transaction modes and other pertinent information.

The `Connection` class contains methods to set the transaction mode of the database; a series of constants are used to indicate the transaction mode.

Transaction behavior is both database and database-vendor-specific. Calls are available to discover transaction capabilities and set transaction modes when they are available.

By default, a `Connection` will commit changes immediately after execution. This behavior can be changed using the `setAutoCommit` method.

See Also: `getConnection`, `Statement`, `ResultSet`, `DatabaseMetaData`

Instance Variables

The following instance variables are used to set and test the transaction mode of the database connection. They are defined in the `Connection` class and represent *constant* values to be used with several of the methods in this class (they cannot be modified because they are declared with the Java keyword `final`).

Isolation Level	Description
TRANSACTION_NONE	The database does not support transactions
TRANSACTION_READ_COMMITTED	Only committed rows are read and only reads on the current row are repeatable
TRANSACTION_READ_UNCOMMITTED	Uncommitted rows will be read (dirty reads)
TRANSACTION_REPEATABLE_READ	Only committed rows are read and reads on all rows of a result are repeatable
TRANSACTION_SERIALIZABLE	Only committed rows are read and reads on all rows of a transaction are repeatable

TRANSACTION_NONE

Declaration: `public final static int TRANSACTION_NONE`

Method Returned by: `getTransactionIsolation`

As a return value from the `getTransactionIsolation` method. This value indicates that database transactions are not supported by this database.

```
import java.sql.*;
import java.io.*;

...
```

```
Connection con = DriverManager.getConnection (
                                          url, "", "");

// need transacation support
if ( con.getTransactionIsolation() = = Connection.TRANSACTION_NONE )
    return; // can't continue without transactions
...
```

TRANSACTION_READ_UNCOMMITTED

Declaration: `public final static int TRANSACTION_READ_UNCOMMITTED`

Method Returned by: `getTransactionIsolation`

As a return value from the `getTransactionIsolation` method, this indicates that database transactions are supported by this database and that the database is currently operating in a READ_UNCOMMITTED or DIRTY_READ isolation mode.

```
import java.sql.*;
import java.io.*;

...

Connection con = DriverManager.getConnection (
                                          url, "", "");

// need dirty read transaction mode
if ( con.getTransactionIsolation() ==
Connection.TRANSACTION_READ_UNCOMMITTED )

    // need committed read isolation mode
    con.setTransactionIsolation(
Connection.TRANSACTION_READ_COMMITTED);
...
```

TRANSACTION_READ_COMMITTED

Declaration: `public final static int TRANSACTION_READ_COMMITTED`

Method Returned by: `getTransactionIsolation`

If this value is returned from the `getTransactionIsolation` method it indicates the database supports transactions and the database is currently in a READ COMMITTED isolation mode. Only committed rows are read and only reads on the current row are repeatable.

```
import java.sql.*;
import java.io.*;

...

Connection con = DriverManager.getConnection (
                                        url, "", "");

// need READ COMMITTED transaction support
if ( con.getTransactionIsolation() !=
     Connection.TRANSACTION_READ_COMMITTED )
     con.setTransactionIsolation(
               Connection.TRANSACTION_READ_COMMITTED );
...
```

TRANSACTION_REPEATABLE_READ

Declaration: `public final static int TRANSACTION_REPEATABLE_READ`

Method Returned by: `getTransactionIsolation`

As a return value from the `getTransactionIsolation` method, this value indicates that transactions are supported by the database and the database connection is currently in REPEATABLE READ isolation mode.

```
import java.sql.*;
import java.io.*;

...

Connection con = DriverManager.getConnection (
                                        url, "", "");

// need REPEATABLE READ transaction support
if ( con.getTransactionIsolation() !=
      Connection.TRANSACTION_REPEATABLE_READ )
  con.setTransactionIsolation(
               Connection.TRANSACTION_REPEATABLE_READ );
...
```

TRANSACTION_SERIALIZABLE

Declaration: `public final static int TRANSACTION_SERIALIZABLE`

Method Returned by: `getTransactionIsolation`

When this value is returned by the `getTransactionIsolation` method it indicates that the database supports transactions and the database connection is currently in a REPEATABLE READ isolation mode where all transactions are *serializable*. In this mode, reads on multiple rows in a selected set are repeatable.

```
import java.sql.*;
import java.io.*;

...

Connection con = DriverManager.getConnection (
                                              url, "", "");

// need SERIALIZABLE  transaction support
if ( con.getTransactionIsolation() !=
     Connection.TRANSACTION_SERIALIZABLE )
   con.setTransactionIsolation(
                Connection.TRANSACTION_SERIALIZABLE );
...
```

Connection Methods

A variety of `Connection` methods exist to control the database connection. Methods exist to test and set the transaction isolation mode of the connection, to set auto-commit modes, and to create objects to manage the various flavors of SQL statements.

clearWarnings

Declaration: `public abstract void clearWarnings() throws SQLException`

This method will clear all warnings for this connection.

```
import java.sql.*;
import java.io.*;
...
```

```
        Connection con = DriverManager.getConnection (
                                                url, "", "");
...
        SQLWarning warn = con.clearWarnings();
...
```

In this example, a `Connection` object is created to provide a database connection. The `clearWarnings` call is then made to clear all warnings from the current connection.

close

Declaration: `public abstract void close() throws SQLException`

This method will close the current database connection and release all resources associated with the database connection. (A `Connection` is implicitly closed when the object has no more references and it is garbage collected.)

```
import java.sql.*;
import java.io.*;
...
        Connection con = DriverManager.getConnection (
                                            url, "", "");
....
       con.commit();
       con.close();
...
```

commit

Declaration: `public abstract void commit() throws SQLException`

This method takes all current database activity and commits it to the database. By default, each SQL statement represents a transaction; this is the default auto-commit mode.

```
import java.sql.*;
import java.io.*;

...
            Connection con = DriverManager.getConnection (
```

```
                                            url, "", "");

          con.setAutoCommit( false );
          con.commit();
          Statement stmt = con.createStatement();

          int result =
            stmt.executeUpdate(
            "create table transtest( col1 int,  col2 int, "
col3 char(10) )" );


          result =
            stmt.executeUpdate(
                  "create index idx1 on transtest( col1 ) " );


          con.commit();

...
```

This example first executes the `setAutoCommit` method and is called to turn auto-commit mode off and allow multiple statements to be grouped together as transactions to be completed. A series of DDL statements are executed and then the `commit` method is called to commit the transaction to the database.

See Also: `setAutoCommit`

createStatement

Declaration: `public abstract Statement createStatement() throws SQLException`

This method creates the `Statement` object that is then used to execute SQL statements against the database. The method returns a `Statement` object as shown.

```
import java.sql.*;
import java.io.*;

...
      Class.forName ("jdbc.odbc.JdbcOdbcDriver");
      Connection con = DriverManager.getConnection (  url,
```

```
                                              "", "");
      Statement  stmt = con.createStatement();
...
```

As shown in this example, the `forName` method of the class object loads the JDBC-ODBC driver of class `DriverManager`. The method `getConnection` then returns a `Connection` object that is then used to create a `Statement` object via the `createStatement` method.

Return Values

Returns a new `Statement` object.

isClosed

Declaration: `public abstract boolean isClosed() throws SQLException`

This method returns a boolean true if a `Connection` is closed, or a boolean false if a `Connection` is open.

```
import java.sql.*;
import java.io.*;

...
  Connection con = DriverManager.getConnection (
                                          url, "", "");

...


 if ( con.isClosed() )
     System.out.println( "Connection is closed."  );

...
```

Returns

`A boolean value`

isReadOnly

Declaration: `public abstract boolean isReadOnly() throws SQLException`

This method returns a boolean true if the database is in read-only mode, or a boolean false if the database is not in read-only mode.

```
import java.sql.*;
import java.io.*;

...

      Connection con = DriverManager.getConnection (
                                     url, "", "");

      if ( con.isReadOnly() )
          System.out.println(
               "Database is read-only. Updates will fail."  );
...
```

Returns

A `boolean` value

getAutoCommit

Declaration: `public abstract boolean getAutoCommit() throws SQLException`

This method returns the current auto-commit state for this `Connection`. If it returns a boolean TRUE, the database connection is in auto-commit mode; if it returns a boolean FALSE, the database connection is NOT in auto-commit mode.

```
import java.sql.*;
import java.io.*;

...
      // turn auto commit on if not already set
      if ( con.getAutoCommit() == false )
          con.setAutoCommit( true );
...
```

Returns

A `boolean` value indicating the current state of auto-commit mode.

See Also: `setAutoCommit`

getCatalog

Declaration: `public abstract String getCatalog() throws SQLException`

This method will return the connection's current catalog name.

```
import java.sql.*;
import java.io.*;

...
        Connection con = DriverManager.getConnection( url, "", "" );
        String catalogName = con.getCatalog();
...
```

Returns

A Java `String` corresponding to the current catalog name

getMetaData

Declaration: `public abstract DatabaseMetaData getMetaData() throws SQLException`

This method returns a `DatabaseMetaData` object that contains information about the database connection.

```
import java.sql.*;
import java.io.*;

...
       Connection con = DriverManager.getConnection (
                                                url, "", "");

      DatabaseMetaData   dmd = con.getMetaData();
      System.out.println( "Database Product: " +
                         dmd.getDatabaseVendor()
                          + " Version: " +
                          dmd.getDatabaseVersion() );
...
```

Returns

A `DatabaseMetaData` object

getTransactionIsolation

Declaration: `public abstract int getTransactionIsolation() throws SQLException`

This method returns the connection's current isolation level as an integer. Valid values and their meanings are listed below.

```
import java.sql.*;
import java.io.*;

...

Connection con = DriverManager.getConnection (
                                    url, "", "");

if ( con.getTransactionIsolation() == Connection.TRANSACTION_NONE )
     System.out.println( "Database does not support transactions. "
);
...
```

This code demonstrates the use of the `getTransactionIsolation` method. The method is called and the return value is evaluated against the values listed in the following table.

Isolation Level	Description
TRANSACTION_NONE	The database does not support transactions
TRANSACTION_READ_COMMITTED	Only committed rows are read and only reads on the current row are repeatable
TRANSACTION_READ_UNCOMMITTED	Uncommitted rows will be read (dirty reads)
TRANSACTION_REPEATABLE_READ	Only committed rows are read and reads on all rows of a result are repeatable
TRANSACTION_SERIALIZABLE	Only committed rows are read and reads on all rows of a transaction are repeatable

Returns

An integer corresponding to the current transaction isolation level

getWarnings

Declaration: `public abstract SQLWarning getWarnings() throws SQLException`

This method returns the first warning for this `Connection`. This warning is returned in the form of a `SQLWarning` object. All other warnings can be found by examining the *chain* (a series of `SQLWarning` objects) attached to this initial warning.

```
import java.sql.*;
import java.io.*;

...
      Connection con = DriverManager.getConnection (
                                                url, "", "");
...
              //  multiple warnings are chained together
              //  loop through all warnings

              SQLWarning warn = con.getWarnings();

          if (warn != null) {
            System.out.println ("\n *** Warning ***\n");
            while (warn != null) {
              System.out.println ("SQLState: " +
                    warn.getSQLState ());
              System.out.println ("Message:  " +
                    warn.getMessage ());
              System.out.println ("Vendor:   " +
                    warn.getErrorCode ());
              System.out.println ("");
              warn = warn.getNextWarning ();
            }
              }

...
```

In this example, a SQLWarning object is returned from a call to the getWarnings method. Warnings are chained together. The call to getWarnings returns the first in the chain. Within the while loop, a call to the SQLWarning getNextWarning method returns the next SQLWarning object in the chain.

Returns

A SQLWarning object corresponding to the initial SQL warning for this connection.

nativeSQL

Declaration: public abstract String nativeSQL(String sql) throws SQLException

This method takes the JDBC SQL grammar and converts it into the form that the driver will send to the database. It returns a String containing the SQL in the native form.

```
import java.sql.*;
import java.io.*;
...
      String sqlString = " {call storedProc( 1,2,3) }";

      String nSQL = con.nativeSQL( sqlString );
      System.out.println( "The native SQL is " + nSQL );
...
```

This code demonstrates the nativeSQL method by first creating a String containing the SQL statement to parse. This SQL statement is passed to the nativeSQL method of the Connection class and returned in a String as the native form of the SQL statement.

Parameters

sql—a SQL statement that may contain one or more '?' parameter placeholders

Returns

A Java String containing the native SQL form of the statement

prepareCall

Declaration: public abstract CallableStatement prepareCall(String sql) throws SQLException

This method creates a CallableStatement object used for executing stored procedures. The CallableStatement object has methods for establishing IN and OUT parameters for the stored procedure and methods for executing the stored procedure.

```
import java.sql.*;
import java.io.*;


...
      Class.forName ("jdbc.odbc.JdbcOdbcDriver");
      Connection con = DriverManager.getConnection (
url, " ", " ");

      String  sqlProcedure =
       " {call getRecProc( 1, 1, 3 )}";

      CallableStatement stmtProcedure =
                    con.prepareCall( sqlProcedure );
...
```

This example demonstrates the creation of a CallableStatement object. First a Connection object is created. A string containing the stored procedure to execute is then passed to the PrepareCall method of the Connection class; the return value of this method is a CallableStatement. object.

Parameters

sql—a SQL statement containing the stored procedure statement

Returns

A new CallableStatement object containing the pre-compiled SQL stored procedure statement

prepareStatement

Declaration: public abstract PreparedStatement prepareStatement(String sql) throws SQLException

This method creates a PreparedStatement object that is used to execute an SQL statement. Unlike the Statement object, the PreparedStatement object allows the SQL statement to be sent to the database for parsing and optimization before execution as shown in the following code.

```
import java.sql.*;
import java.io.*;

...
      Class.forName ("jdbc.odbc.JdbcOdbcDriver");
      Connection con = DriverManager.getConnection (
url, "", "");

      String sql = "select * from table1 where col1 = ?
";
      PreparedStatement   prepStmt = con.PrepareStatement( sql );

            int n = 1;
            prepStmt.setInt( 1, n );
            ResultSet rs = prepStmt.executeQuery();

            boolean more = rs.next();
            for (; n < 2000 && more ; n++ ) {

          processResult( rs );
                prepStmt.setInt( 1, n );


                rs.close();
                rs       = prepStmt.executeQuery();
                more = rs.next();

           }
...
```

In this example, a `Connection` object is created by the `Driver`, which is then used to create a `PreparedStatement` object. Note that the creation of the `PreparedStatement` object requires a SQL statement string be passed into the method. The `setInt PreparedStatement` member function is used to set the first parameter. Next, a `for` loop is started and within the `for` loop the integer value for the column is set before the `PreparedStatement` is executed. The cursor is closed via the `ResultSet close` method before the next iteration of the `executeQuery` method call.

The next iteration of the `executeQuery` method retrieves additional rows and returns a `ResultSet` stored with the reference of the previously used `ResultsSet`.

For SQL statements that are executed multiple times, using *prepared* statements will improve performance.

Parameters

`sql`—a Java String that contains the SQL statement to be sent to the database and prepared for execution

Returns

A `PreparedStatement` object containing the pre-compiled SQL statement

rollback

Declaration: `public abstract void rollback() throws SQLException`

The `rollback` method rejects all database changes made since the last database commit. These changes are then lost to the database. A rollback will release any locks currently held by the `Connection`.

```
import java.sql.*;
import java.io.*;

...
     Connection con = DriverManager.getConnection (
                                            url, "", "");
...

catch ( SQLException ex ){
      System.out.println( "Error ... rolling back work."  );
      con.rollback();
}

...
```

A common location for the `rollback` method to be executed would be in a `catch` code block as shown in this example. This code block is executed in the event an exception is generated while executing a JDBC method.

See Also: `setAutoCommit`

setAutoCommit

Declaration: `public abstract void setAutoCommit(boolean autoCommit) throws SQLException`

This method sets the auto-commit mode of the database connection. If a connection is in auto-commit, all SQL statements are executed as individual transactions; changes made by an executed statement are immediately committed to the database. This is the default behavior of a JDBC connection and can be changed by the `setAutoCommit` method. A boolean value of TRUE enables auto-commit mode and a boolean value of FALSE disables auto-commit mode.

```
import java.sql.*;
import java.io.*;

...

      try {
        con.setAutoCommit( false );
        Statement stmt = con.createStatement();

    // begin transaction
        con.commit();
        int result = 0;
        result = stmt.executeUpdate( sqlUpdate1 );
        result = stmt.executeUpdate( sqlUpdate2 );
        result = stmt.executeUpdate( sqlUpdate3 );

       // no exception thrown, so OK to commit()
        con.commit();
      }
      catch ( SQLException ex) {
        System.out.println( "Failure on update. Rolling
back" );
        con.rollback();
      }

...
```

In this example, the auto-commit mode is set to false, effectively turning the auto-commit behavior off. A series of update statements is then executed. After the updates are completed, the database transaction is committed using the `commit` method.

In the event there is an error with one of the updates, the `catch` code block would be executed. This code block would simply print an error statement and then execute a database rollback using the `Connection` class `rollback` method.

Parameters

autoCommit—a Java boolean value that indicates the auto-commit setting to be made for this Connection

setCatalog

Declaration: `public abstract void setCatalog(String catalog) throws SQLException`

This method allows a specific catalog to be set for this connection. If the driver does not support catalogs, it will silently ignore this call.

```
import java.sql.*;
import java.io.*;
...
        Connection con = DriverManager.getConnection (
                                                    url, "", "");
        con.setCatalog( "catalog1" );
...
```

setReadOnly

Declaration: `public abstract void setReadOnly(boolean readOnly) throws SQLException`

This method can set a database connection into read-only mode, or set the connection to read-write mode. This method cannot be executed in the middle of a transaction. Passing a boolean parameter of `true` enables read-only mode and passing a boolean parameter of `false` disables read-only mode.

```
import java.sql.*;
import java.io.*;

...
        Connection con = DriverManager.getConnection (
                                              url, "", "");
                // just view the database
        con.setReadOnly( true );

...
```

Parameters

readOnly—a boolean value

setTransactionIsolation

Declaration: `public abstract void setTransactionIsolation(int level) throws SQLException`

This method will set a connection's current transaction isolation level. The isolation levels passed are one of the following from `java.sql.Connection`.

Isolation Level	Description
TRANSACTION_READ_COMMITTED	Only committed rows are read and only reads on the current row are repeatable
TRANSACTION_READ_UNCOMMITTED	Uncommitted rows will be read (dirty reads)
TRANSACTION_REPEATABLE_READ	Only committed rows are read and reads on all rows of a result are repeatable
TRANSACTION_SERIALIZABLE	Only committed rows are read and reads on all rows of a transaction are repeatable

Note that this method cannot be called within a transaction.

```
import java.sql.*;
import java.io.*;

...
      Connection con = DriverManager.getConnection (
                                                url, "", "");

      con.setTransactionIsolation(
Connection.TRANSACTION_REPEATABLE_READ );
      con.commit(); // begin work

...
```

In this example, a database connection is created and the isolation mode for the database is set to *repeatable read*.

Parameters

`level`—an integer corresponding to the isolation level of the database

See Also: `supportsTransactionIsolationLevel`

The java.sql.DatabaseMetaData Interface

Declaration: `public interface DatabaseMetaData extends Object`

The `DatabaseMetaData` interface provides methods to access a wealth of information on the current database connection. These methods reveal information on transaction isolation modes, the nature and type of SQL syntax supported, the name of the database vendor, the version number of the database driver, and other database-specific information.

The goal in designing the JDBC API was to provide simple methods with few parameters; this was attempted even if it meant creating a large number of methods with very similar functions. The impact of this design goal is seen here in this interface. The large number of methods represent a welcome alternative to complex methods with numerous parameters.

Instance Variables

bestRowNotPseudo

Declaration: `public final static int bestRowNotPseudo`

Method Returned by: `getBestRowIdentifier`

This value is returned in a `ResultSet` column by the `getBestRowIdentifier` method. If the PSEUDO_COLUMN column contains this value, it indicates that the best row is **not** a pseudo-column.

bestRowPseudo

Declaration: `public final static int bestRowPseudo`

Method Returned by: `getBestRowIdentifier`

This value is returned in a `ResultSet` column by the `getBestRowIdentifier` method. If the PSEUDO_COLUMN column contains this value, it indicates that the best row **is** a pseudo-row.

bestRowSession

Declaration: `public final static int bestRowSession`

Method Returned by: `getBestRowIdentifier`

This value is returned in a `ResultSet` column by the `getBestRowIdentifier` method. If the PSEUDO_COLUMN column contains this value, it indicates that the best row is valid for the remainder of the current session.

bestRowTemporary

Declaration: `public final static int bestRowTemporary`

Method Returned by: `getBestRowIdentifier`

This value is returned in a `ResultSet` column by the `getBestRowIdentifier` method. If the PSEUDO_COLUMN column contains this value, it indicates that the best row is temporary and only valid during the use of the row.

bestRowTransaction

Declaration: `public final static int bestRowTransaction`

Method Returned by: `getBestRowIdentifier`

This value is returned in a `ResultSet` column by the `getBestRowIdentifier` method. If the PSEUDO_COLUMN column contains this value, it indicates that the best row is temporary and only valid during the remainder of the current transaction.

bestRowUnknown

Declaration: `public final static int bestRowUnknown`

Method Returned by: `getBestRowIdentifier`

This value is returned in a `ResultSet` column by the `getBestRowIdentifier` method. If the PSEUDO_COLUMN column contains this value, it indicates that the best row may or may not be a pseudo-column.

columnNoNulls

Declaration: `public final static int columnNoNulls`

Method Returned by: `getColumns`

This value is returned in a `ResultSet` column by the `getColumns` method. If the NULLABLE column contains this value, it indicates that the database table column referenced does **not** allow NULL values.

columnNullable

Declaration: `public final static int columnNullable`

Method Returned by: `getColumns`

This value is returned in a `ResultSet` column by the `getColumns` method. If the NULLABLE column contains this value, then the database table column referenced **does** allow NULL values.

columnNullableUnknown

Declaration: `public final static int columnNullableUnknown`

Method Returned by: `getColumns`

This value is returned in a `ResultSet` column by the `getColumns` method. If the NULLABLE column is set to this value, it indicates that the column referenced may or may not allow NULL values.

importedKeyCascade

Declaration: `public final static int importedKeyCascade`

Method Returned by: `getImportedKeys`

This value is returned by the `getImportedKeys` method in a `ResultSet` column. If the UPDATE_RULE column is set to this value, it indicates that for update, the imported key is changed to agree with the primary key; for delete, rows that import a deleted key are deleted.

importedKeyRestrict

Declaration: `public final static int importedKeyRestrict`

Method Returned by: `getImportedKeys`

This value is returned by the `getImportedKeys` method in a `ResultSet` column. If this value is returned in the UPDATE_RULE column then the update or delete of an imported primary key is not allowed.

importedKeySetNull

Declaration: `public final static int importedKeySetNull`

Method Returned by: `getImportedKeys`

This value is returned by the `getImportedKeys` method in a `ResultSet` column.

If the UPDATE_RULE column is set to this value, it indicates that an imported key is set to NULL if its primary key has been updated or deleted.

procedureColumnIn

Declaration: `public final static int ProcedureColumnIn`

Method Returned by: `getProcedureColumns`

This value is returned in a `ResultSet` column by the `getProcedureColumns` method. If the COLUMN_TYPE column is set to this value, it indicates that the column referenced by the `ResultSet` row represents an IN parameter.

procedureColumnInOut

Declaration: `public final static int ProcedureColumnInOut`

Method Returned by: `getProcedureColumns`

This value is returned in a `ResultSet` column by the `getProcedureColumns` method. If the COLUMN_TYPE column is set to this value, it indicates that the column referenced by the `ResultSet` row represents an IN-OUT parameter.

procedureColumnOut

Declaration: `public final static int ProcedureColumnOut`

Method Returned by: `getProcedureColumns`

This value is returned in a `ResultSet` column by the `getProcedureColumns` method. If the COLUMN_TYPE column is set to this value, it indicates that the column referenced by the `ResultSet` row represents an OUT parameter.

procedureColumnResult

Declaration: `public final static int ProcedureColumnResult`

Method Returned by: `getProcedureColumns`

This value is returned in a `ResultSet` column by the `getProcedureColumns` method. If the COLUMN_TYPE column is set to this value, it indicates that the column referenced by the `ResultSet` row represents a result column parameter.

procedureColumnReturn

Declaration: `public final static int ProcedureColumnReturn`

Method Returned by: `getProcedureColumns`

This value is returned in a `ResultSet` column by the `getProcedureColumns` method. If the COLUMN_TYPE column is set to this value, it indicates that the column referenced by the `ResultSet` row represents a return value.

procedureColumnUnknown

Declaration: `public final static int ProcedureColumnReturn`

Method Returned by: `getProcedureColumns`

This value is returned in a `ResultSet` column by the `getProcedureColumns` method. If the COLUMN_TYPE column is set to this value, it indicates that the column referenced by the `ResultSet` row represents a an unknown column.

procedureNoNulls

Declaration: `public final static int procedureNoNulls`

Method Returned by: `getProcedureColumns`

This value is returned in a `ResultSet` column by the `getProcedureColumns` method. If the NULLABLE column is set to this value, then the procedure referenced does **not** allow NULL values.

procedureNoResult

Declaration: `public final static int procedureNoResult`

Method Returned by: `getProcedureColumns`

This value is returned in a `ResultSet` column by the `getProcedureColumns` method. If this value is returned in the NULLABLE column, it indicates that the stored procedure does not return results

procedureNullable

Declaration: `public final static int procedureNullable`

Method Returned by: `getProcedureColumns`

This value is returned in a `ResultSet` column by the `getProcedureColumns` method. If this value is returned in the NULLABLE column, it indicates that the stored procedure allows NULL values.

procedureNullableUnknown

Declaration: `public final static int procedureNullableUnknown`

Method Returned by: `getProcedureColumns`

This value is returned in a `ResultSet` column by the `getProcedureColumns` method. If this value is returned in the NULLABLE column, it indicates that it is not known whether or not the stored procedure allows NULL values.

procedureResultUnknown

Declaration: `public final static int procedureNullableUnknown`

Method Returned by: `getProcedures`

This value is returned in a `ResultSet` column by the `getProcedures` method. If this value is returned in the PROCEDURE_TYPE column, it indicates that it is not known whether or not the procedure returns a result.

procedureReturnsResult

Declaration: `public final static int procedureReturnsResult`

Method Returned by: `getProcedures`

This value is returned in a `ResultSet` column by the `getProcedures` method. If this value is returned in the PROCEDURE_TYPE column it indicates that the procedure returns a result.

tableIndexClustered

Declaration: `public final static int tableIndexClustered`

Method Returned by: `getIndexInfo`

This value is returned in a `ResultSet` column by the `getIndexInfo` method. If this value is returned in the TYPE column, it identifies the index as a clustered index.

tableIndexHashed

Declaration: `public final static int tableIndexHashed`

Method Returned by: `getIndexInfo`

This value is returned in a `ResultSet` column by the `getIndexInfo` method. If this value is returned in the TYPE column, it identifies the index as a hashed index.

tableIndexOther

Declaration: `public final static int tableIndexOther`

Method Returned by: `getIndexInfo`

This value is returned in a `ResultSet` column by the `getIndexInfo` method. If this value is returned in the TYPE column, it identifies the index as some other form of index, specifically not hashed or clustered.

tableIndexStatistic

Declaration: `public final static int tableIndexStatistic`

Method Returned by: `getIndexInfo`

This value is returned in a `ResultSet` column by the `getIndexInfo` method. If this value is returned in the TYPE column, it identifies table statistics that are returned in conjunction with a table's index descriptions.

typeNoNulls

Declaration: `public final static int typeNoNulls`

Method Returned by: `getTypeInfo`

This value is returned in a `ResultSet` column by the `getTypeInfo` method. If this value is returned in the NULLABLE column, it indicates that this data type does not allow NULL values.

typeNullable

Declaration: `public final static int typeNullable`

Method Returned by: `getTypeInfo`

This value is returned in a `ResultSet` column by the `getTypeInfo` method. If this value is returned in the NULLABLE column, it indicates that this data type does allow NULL values.

typeNullableUnknown

Declaration: public final static int typeNullableUnknow

Method Returned by: getTypeInfo

This value is returned in a `ResultSet` column by the `getTypeInfo` method. If this value is returned in the NULLABLE column, it indicates that it is not known whether or not this data type allows NULL values.

typePredBasic

Declaration: `public final static int typePredBasic`

Method Returned by: `getTypeInfo`

This value is returned in a ResultSet column by the getTypeInfo method. If this value is returned in the SEARCHABLE column, it indicates that this data type is searchable except for 'WHERE .. LIKE.'

typePredChar

Declaration: public final static int typePredChar

Method Returned by: getTypeInfo

This value is returned in a ResultSet column by the getTypeInfo method. If this value is returned int the SEARCHABLE column, it indicates that this data type is searchable only with 'WHERE .. LIKE'.

typePredNone

Declaration: public final static int typePredNone

Method Returned by: getTypeInfo

This value is returned in a ResultSet column by the getTypeInfo method. If this value is returned in the SEARCHABLE column, it indicates that there is no support for WHERE clause searches with this data type.

typeSearchable

Declaration: public final static int typeSearchable

Method Returned by: getTypeInfo

This value is returned in a ResultSet column by the getTypeInfo method. If this value is returned in the SEARCHABLE column, it indicates that there is support for WHERE clause searches with this data type.

versionColumnNotPseudo

Declaration: public final static int versionColumnNotPseudo

Method Returned by: getVersionColumns

This value is returned in a ResultSet column by the getVersionColumns method. If this value is returned in the PSEUDO_COLUMN column, it indicates that this version column is not a pseudo-column.

versionColumnPseudo

Declaration: public final static int versionColumnPseudo

Method Returned by: getVersionColumns

This value is returned in a `ResultSet` column by the `getVersionColumns` method. If this value is returned in the PSEUDO_COLUMN column, it indicates that this version column is a pseudo-column.

versionColumnUnknown

Declaration: `public final static int versionColumnUnknown`

Method Returned by: `getVersionColumns`

This value is returned in a `ResultSet` column by the `getVersionColumns` method. If this value is returned in the PSEUDO_COLUMN column, it indicates that it is not known whether or not the version column is a pseudo-column.

DatabaseMetaData Methods

allProceduresAreCallable

Declaration: `public abstract boolean allProceduresAreCallable() throws SQLException`

This method returns a `boolean` true if the current user can call **all** stored procedures available in the database, or false if the user cannot.

```
...
Connection con = DriverManager.getConnection (
                                         url, "", "");
DatabaseMetaData dmd = con.getMetaData();
if ( dmd.allProceduresAreCallable() ) {
     CallableStatement stmtProc =
           con.prepCall( "{ call getSalesCount(?) }" );
...
```

Returns

A Java `boolean`

allTablesAreSelectable

Declaration: `public abstract boolean allTablesAreSelectable() throws SQLException`

This method returns a boolean true if all of the tables available can be read by the current user (SQL `select`), or false if the current user cannot.

```
...
Connection con = DriverManager.getConnection (
                                    url, "", "");
DatabaseMetaData dmd = con.getMetaData();
if ( dmd.allTablesAreSelectable() ) {
   Statement stmt = con.createStatement( );
...
```

Returns

A Java `boolean` value

dataDefinitionCausesTransactionCommit

Declaration: `public abstract boolean dataDefinitionCausesTransactionCommit() throws SQLException`

This method returns `boolean` true if a SQL DDL statement within a transaction forces a database commit. If this is the case, then each DDL is a singleton transaction and is committed to the database upon completion.

```
...
Connection con = DriverManager.GetConnection( url, "", "" );
DatabaseMetaData dmd = con.getMetaData();

Statement stmt = con.createStatement();

if ( dmd.dataDefinitionCausesTransactionCommit() )

     // execute DDL outside transaction since single transaction
     int resultCount = stmt.executeUpdate(
       " create table table1 ( col1 smallint, col2 smallint ) " );
     resultCount = stmt.executeUpdate(
       " create index idx1 on table1 ( col1 ) " );

     // begin work
     con.commit();
     resultCount = stmt.executeUpdate(
         " insert into table1 values ( 1, 1 ) " );
     resultCount = stmt.executeUpdate(
         " insert into table1 values ( 2, 2 ) " );
     resultCount = stmt.executeUpdate(
```

```
            " update table1 set col2 = 1 " );
      // commit the DML statements
      con.commit();

}
```

Returns

A Java boolean

dataDefinitionIgnoredInTransactions

Declaration: public abstract boolean dataDefinitionIgnoredInTransactions() throws SQLException

This method returns a boolean true if a SQL DDL statement within a transaction is ignored.

```
...
Connection con = DriverManager.GetConnection( url, "", "" );
DatabaseMetaData dmd = con.getMetaData();
if ( dmd.dataDefinitionIgnoredInTransactions() )
     System.out.println( "DDL ignored in transactions." );
...
```

Returns

A Java boolean

doesMaxRowSizeIncludeBlobs

Declaration: public abstract boolean doesMaxRowSizeIncludeBlobs() throws SQLException

This method determines whether or not the maximum row size as returned by the getMaxRowSize method includes LONGVARCHAR and LONGVARBINARY Blobs (binary large objects). If it does, a boolean true is returned by the method.

```
...
Connection con = DriverManager.GetConnection( url, "", "" );
DatabaseMetaData dmd = con.getMetaData();

if ( dmd.doesMaxRowSizeIncludeBlobs() )
    System.out.println( "Max RowSize includes blobs."  );
```

. . .

Returns

A `boolean` value

getBestRowIdentifier

Declaration: `public abstract  ResultSet getBestRowIdentifier( String catalog, String schema, String table, int scope, boolean nullable) throws SQLException`

This method provides a description of the optimal set of columns that uniquely identifies a row; this row is known as a *best row*. Parameters are provided to the method to identify the catalog, schema, table, scope, and NULL value characteristics of the best row.

The values are returned in a `ResultSet` ordered by SCOPE. The columns returned provide information about the best row, as shown in the following table.

Return Values for getBestRowIdentifier

Number	Type	Column Name	Description
1	short	SCOPE	actual scope of result
2	String	COLUMN_NAME	column name
3	short	DATA_TYPE	SQL data type from `java.sql.Types`
4	String	TYPE_NAME	Data source dependent type name
5	int	COLUMN_SIZE	precision
6	int	BUFFER_LENGTH	not currently used
7	short	DECIMAL_DIGITS	scale
8	short	PSEUDO_COLUMN	identifies this column as a pseudo column

. . .

```
Connection con = DriverManager.GetConnection( url, "", "" );
DatabaseMetaData dmd = con.getMetaData();
Statement stmt = con.createStatement();

ResultSet rs = dmd.getBestRowIdentifier( "",
                                          "",
                                          "orders",
                                          0,
                                          true );
boolean more = rs.next();

while ( more ) {
System.out.println( "Column Name: " +
                    rs.getString( 2 ) +
                    " - Data Type: " +
                    rs.getShort( 3 )   );

more = rs.next();
}
...
```

Parameters

`catalog`—a catalog name; "" retrieves those without a catalog
`schema`—a schema name; "" retrieves those without a schema
`table`—a table name
`scope`—the scope of interest; use same values as SCOPE
`nullable`—include columns that are nullable?

Returns

`ResultSet` each row is a column description

getCatalogs

Declaration: `public abstract ResultSet getCatalogs() throws SQLException`

This method determines the catalogs available in the current database. It returns the catalog names in a `ResultSet`. The `ResultSet` is composed of a single column as shown in the following table. The `ResultSet` is ordered by table schema name.

Number	Type	Column Name	Description
1	String	TABLE_CAT	the table schema name

```
...
Connection con = DriverManager.GetConnection( url, "", "" );
DatabaseMetaData dmd = con.getMetaData();
Statement stmt = con.createStatement();
ResultSet rs = dmd.getCatalogs() throws SQLException
boolean more = rs.next();

while ( more ) {
      System.out.println( "Catalog name: " +
                              rs.getString( 1 ) );
      more = rs.next();
}

...
```

Returns

A `ResultSet` for each catalog in the database.

getCatalogSeparator

Declaration: `public abstract String getCatalogSeparator() throws SQLException`

This method returns a string containing the separator between the catalog name and the table name.

```
...
Connection con = DriverManager.GetConnection( url, "", "" );
DatabaseMetaData dmd = con.getMetaData();
System.out.println( " Catalog separator is " +
                      dmd.getCatalogSeparator() );
...
```

Returns

A Java `String`

getCatalogTerm

Declaration: `public abstract String getCatalogTerm() throws SQLException`

This method returns a string containing the database vendor's preferred name for 'catalog'.

```
...
Connection con = DriverManager.GetConnection( url, "", "" );
DatabaseMetaData dmd = con.getMetaData();

System.out.println( " Vendor's term for catalog is " +
                    dmd.getCatalogTerm() );

...
```

Returns

A Java `String`

getColumns

Declaration: `public abstract ResultSet getColumns(String catalog, String schemaPattern, String tableNamePattern, String columnNamePattern) throws SQLException`

This method returns a description of table columns available in a database. Parameters are passed into the method for a catalog name, a schema name, a table name, and a column name. Only column descriptions matching the parameters passed into the method will be retrieved.

The information retrieved is returned in a `ResultSet` ordered by TABLE_SCHEM, TABLE_NAME and ORDINAL_POSITION. The columns retrieved in the `ResultSet` are described in the following table.

Column Information Returned by getColumns

Number	Type	Column Name	Description
1	String	TABLE_CAT	table catalog name (may be null)
2	String	TABLE_SCHEM	table schema name (may be null)
3	String	TABLE_NAME	table name
4	String	COLUMN_NAME	column name

continued

Number	Type	Column Name	Description
5	short	DATA_TYPE	the SQL data type from java.sql.Types
6	String	TYPE_NAME	the data source dependent type name
7	int	COLUMN_SIZE	the column size. For char or date types this is the maximum number of characters, for numeric or decimal types this is precision
8		BUFFER_LENGTH	currently not used.
9	int	DECIMAL_DIGITS	the number of fractional digits
10	int	NUM_PREC_RADIX	radix (typically either 10 or 2)
11	int	NULLABLE	indicates whether or not NULL values are allowed
12	String	REMARKS	description of the column (may be null)
13	String	COLUMN_DEF	default value for the column (may be null)
14	int	SQL_DATA_TYPE	currently unused
15	int	SQL_DATETIME_SUB	currently unused
16	int	CHAR_OCTET_LENGTH	for char types this is the maximum number of bytes in the column
17	int	ORDINAL_POSITION	the ordinal position of the column in table (starting at 1)
18	String	IS_NULLABLE	indicates whether or not the column allows NULL values; possible values for this column are shown in the NULLABLE value table shown below

The NULLABLE column can take on several data values. Essentially, the column either allows NULL values, does not allow NULL values, or it is not known if the column allows NULL values. The Java Strings which indicate these possibilities are shown in the following table.

NULLABLE Value	Description
NO	the column does **not** allow NULL values
YES	the column **does** allow NULL values
NULL	a NULL value indicates that it is not known whether or not the column allows NULL values

A variety of data types can be stored in the column. The data types are defined in `java.sql.Types`; their names and the corresponding Java data types are shown in the following table.

JDBC SQL Data Types

SQL Type	Java Type	Description
CHAR	`String`	fixed length character string
VARCHAR	`String`	variable length character string
LONGVARCHAR	`String`	variable length character string—large (sometimes stores Blob data)
NUMERIC	`java.sql.Numeric`	numeric data type of variable precision
DECIMAL	`java.sql.Numeric`	numeric data type of variable precision and scale
BIT	`boolean`	data type with only two possible values
TINYINT	`byte`	8-bit signed integer data type
SMALLINT	`short`	16-bit signed integer data type
INTEGER	`int`	32-bit signed integer data type
BIGINT	`long`	32-bit signed integer data type
REAL	`float`	floating point number

continued

SQL Type	Java Type	Description
FLOAT	`double`	double precision floating point number
DOUBLE	`double`	double precision floating point number
BINARY	`byte[]`	fixed length binary data
VARBINARY	`byte[]`	variable length binary data
LONGVARBINARY	`byte[]`	variable length binary data
DATE	`java.sql.Date`	date data
TIME	`java.sql.Time`	time data
TIMESTAMP	`java.sql.Timestamp`	date and time data

```
...
Connection con = DriverManager.GetConnection( url, "", "" );
DatabaseMetaData dmd = con.getMetaData();
Statement stmt = con.createStatement();

ResultSet rs = dmd.getColumns( "",
                               "",
                               "orders"
                               ""      ) throws SQLException
boolean more = rs.next();
while ( more ) {
      System.out.println( "Table type: " +
                             rs.getString( "TABLE_TYPE" )
);
      more = rs.next();
}
...
```

Parameters

`catalog`—a catalog name; “” retrieves those without a catalog

`schemaPattern`—a schema name pattern; “” retrieves those without a schema

`tableNamePattern`—a table name pattern

columnNamePattern—a column name pattern

Returns

A ResultSet is returned for each column description

See Also: getSearchStringEscape

getColumnPrivileges

Declaration: public abstract ResultSet getColumnPrivileges(String catalog, String schema, String table, String columnNamePattern) throws SQLException

This method retrieves the access rights for a table column. Parameters are passed into the function for catalog name, schema name, table name, and column name. Only data matching the parameters passed into the method are retrieved. The results are returned in a ResultSet ordered by the COLUMN_NAME and PRIVILEGE columns.

Return Values for getColumnPrivileges

Number	Type	Column Name	Description
1	String	TABLE_CAT	table catalog name (may be null)
2	String	TABLE_SCHEM	table schema name (may be null)
3	String	TABLE_NAME	table name
4	String	COLUMN_NAME	column name
5	String	GRANTOR	grantor of access (may be null)
6	String	GRANTEE	grantee of access
7	String	PRIVILEGE	type of access (SELECT, INSERT, UPDATE, REFERENCES, ...)
8	String	IS_GRANTABLE	indicates whether or not this user (the grantee) can grant this privilege can be granted to someone else; value is "YES" if grantee is permitted to grant to others; value is "NO" if not; NULL value if unknown

```
...
Connection con = DriverManager.GetConnection( url, "", "" );
DatabaseMetaData dmd = con.getMetaData();
Statement stmt = con.createStatement();

ResultSet rs = dmd.getColumnPrivileges( "",
                                        "",
                                        "orders"
                                        ""      ) throws SQLException
boolean more = rs.next();
System.out.println( "Column Name: " +
                    rs.getString( "COLUMN_NAME" ) +
                    "—privilege: " +
                    rs.getString( "PRIVILEGE" ) +
                    "—grantor Name: " +
                    rs.getString( "GRANTOR" ) );
        more = rs.next();
}
```

Parameters

`catalog`—a Java `String` representing the catalog name; a “” retrieves privileges without a catalog

`schema`—a Java `String` representing the schema name; “” retrieves privileges without a schema

`table`—a Java `String` representing the table name

`columnNamePattern`—a Java `String` representing the column name

Returns

A `ResultSet` row for each column privilege

See Also: `getSearchStringEscape`

getCrossReference

Declaration: `public abstract ResultSet getCrossReference(String primaryCatalog String primarySchema, String primaryTable, String foreignCatalog, String foreignSchema, String foreignTable) throws SQLException`

This method determines the foreign key columns in the foreign key table that reference the primary key columns of the primary key table (describe how one table imports another table's primary key.) Parameters are passed into the method for primary and foreign key catalog, primary and foreign key schema and primary and foreign key table. Results are returned in a `ResultSet` ordered by the FKTABLE_CAT, FKTABLE_SCHEM, FKTABLE_NAME, and KEY_SEQ columns.

Return Values for getCrossReference

Number	Type	Column Name	Description
1	String	PKTABLE_CAT	primary key table catalog name (may be a NULL value)
2	String	PKTABLE_SCHEM	primary key table schema name (may be a NULL value)
3	String	PKTABLE_NAME	primary key table name
4	String	PKCOLUMN_NAME	primary key column name
5	String	FKTABLE_CAT	foreign key table catalog being exported (may be a NULL value)
6	String	FKTABLE_SCHEM	foreign key table schema being exported (may be a NULL value)
7	String	FKTABLE_NAME	foreign key table name being exported
8	String	FKCOLUMN_NAME	foreign key column name being exported
9	short	KEY_SEQ	sequence number within foreign key
10	short	UPDATE_RULE	indicates what happens to a foreign key when a primary is updated; values from `java.sql.DatabaseMetaData`
11	short	DELETE_RULE	indicates what happens to a foreign key when primary is deleted; values from `java.sql.DatabaseMetaData`

continued

Number	Type	Column Name	Description
12	String	FK_NAME	foreign key identifier (may be a NULL value)
13	String	PK_NAME	primary key identifier (may be a NULL value)

The UPDATE_RULE column indicates what will happen to the foreign key when the primary key is updated (in the foreign key table). This column contains a Java short value whose meaning can be determined by comparison with member variables of `java.sql.DatabaseMetaData` as shown in the following table.

UPDATE_RULE Value	Description
importedKeyCascade	change imported key to agree with corresponding primary key update
importedKeyRestrict	do not allow update of primary key if it has been imported
importedKeySetNull	change imported key to NULL if its corresponding primary key has been updated

The DELETE_RULE column indicates what will happen to the foreign key when the primary key is deleted (in the foreign key table). This column contains a Java `short` value whose meaning can be determined by comparison with member variables of `java.sql.DatabaseMetaData` as shown in the following table.

DELETE_RULE Value	Description
importedKeyCascade	delete rows that import a deleted key
importedKeyRestrict	do not allow delete of primary key if it has been imported
importedKeySetNull	change imported key to NULL if its corresponding primary key has been deleted

```
...
Connection con = DriverManager.GetConnection( url, "", "" );
DatabaseMetaData dmd = con.getMetaData();
Statement stmt = con.createStatement();
ResultSet rs =      dmd.getCrossReference("",
```

```
                                        "",
                                        "orders",
                                        "",
                                        "",
                                        "items" )
                        boolean more = rs.next();
System.out.println( "Cross reference key components. " );
while ( more ) {
      System.out.println( "PK Column: " +
                          rs.getString( 4 ) +
                          "—FK Table: " +
                          rs.getString( 7 ) );

      more = rs.next();
}
...
```

Parameters

`PrimaryCatalog`– a Java `String` containing the catalog name; an “” retrieves cross reference information without a catalog

`PrimarySchema`—a Java `String` containing the schema name pattern; an “” retrieves cross reference information without a schema

`PrimaryTable`—a Java `String` containing table name

`ForeignCatalog`—a Java `String` containing the catalog name; an “” retrieves cross reference information without a catalog

`ForeignSchema`—a Java `String` containing the schema name pattern; an “” retrieves cross reference information without a schema

`ForeignTable`—a Java `String` containing the table name

Returns

A `ResultSet` for each that contains a cross reference description

See Also: `getImportedKeys`

getDatabaseProductName

Declaration: `public abstract String getDatabaseProductName() throws SQLException`

This method returns a Java `String` containing the name of the database product.

```
...
Connection con = DriverManager.getConnection (
```

```
                                         url, "", "");
DatabaseMetaData dmd = con.getMetaData();

System.out.println( "Database Product: " +
                      dmd.getDatabaseProductName() );
...
```

Returns

A Java `String`

getDatabaseProductVersion

Declaration: `public abstract String getDatabaseProductVersion() throws SQLException`

This method returns a Java `String` containing the version of the current database.

```
...
Connection con = DriverManager.getConnection (
                                         url, "", "");
DatabaseMetaData dmd = con.getMetaData();
System.out.println( "Database Product Version: " +
                      dmd.getDatabaseProductVersion() );
...
```

Returns

A Java `string`

getDefaultTransactionIsolation

Declaration: `public abstract int getDefaultTransactionIsolation() throws SQLException`

This method determines the default transaction level for a database. The default transaction level is returned as an integer and is represented by one of the values from the `java.sql.Connection` class shown in the following table.

Isolation Level	Description
TRANSACTION_NONE	The database does not support transactions
TRANSACTION_READ_COMMITTED	Only committed rows are read and only reads on the current row are repeatable

continued

TRANSACTION_READ_UNCOMMITTED	Uncommitted rows will be read (dirty reads)
TRANSACTION_REPEATABLE_READ	Only committed rows are read and reads on all rows of a result are repeatable
TRANSACTION_SERIALIZABLE	Only committed rows are read and reads on all rows of a transaction are repeatable

```
...
Connection con = DriverManager.GetConnection( url, "", "" );
DatabaseMetaData dmd = con.getMetaData();
if ( dmd.getDefaultTransactionIsolation() ==
      Connection.TRANSACTION_READ_UNCOMMITTED )
      con.setTransactionIsolation(
                  Connection.TRANSACTION_REPEATABLE_READ );
...
```

Returns

An `int` value

See Also: `Connection`

getDriverMajorVersion

Declaration: `public abstract int getDriverMajorVersion()`

This method returns an integer representing the major version number for the JDBC driver.

```
...
Connection con = DriverManager.getConnection (
                                    url, "", "");
DatabaseMetaData dmd = con.getMetaData();

System.out.println( "Driver Major Version: +
                  dmd.getDriverMajorVersion() );

...
```

Returns

A Java `int`

getDriverMinorVersion

Declaration: `public abstract int getDriverMinorVersion()`

This method returns an integer corresponding to the JDBC driver's minor version number.

```
...
Connection con = DriverManager.getConnection (
                                     url, "", "");
DatabaseMetaData dmd = con.getMetaData();
System.out.println( "Driver Minor Version: +
                      dmd.getDriverDriverMinorVersion() );
...
```

Returns

A Java `int`

getDriverName

Declaration: `public abstract String getDriverName() throws SQLException`

This method returns a Java `String` containing the name of the current JDBC driver.

```
...
Connection con = DriverManager.getConnection (
                                     url, "", "");
DatabaseMetaData dmd = con.getMetaData();
System.out.println( "Database Driver Name: " +
                      dmd.getDriverName() );
...
```

Returns

A Java `String`

See also: `getDriverVersion`

getDriverVersion

Declaration: `public abstract String getDriverVersion() throws SQLException`

This method returns a Java `String` containing the version of the current JDBC driver.

```
...
Connection con = DriverManager.getConnection (
                                        url, "", "");
DatabaseMetaData dmd = con.getMetaData();
System.out.println( "Driver Version: " +
                        dmd.getDriverVersion() );
...
```

Returns

A Java `String`

getExportedKeys

Declaration: `public abstract ResultSet getExportedKeys(String catalog, String schema, String table) throws SQLException`

This method determines the exported keys of a table (foreign key columns that reference a table's primary key columns). Parameters are passed into the method for catalog, schema, and table name. Results are returned in a `ResultSet` ordered by the FKTABLE_CAT, FKTABLE_SCHEM, FKTABLE_NAME, and KEY_SEQ columns.

Return Values for getExportedKeys

Number	Type	Column Name	Description
1	String	PKTABLE_CAT	primary key table catalog (may be a NULL value)
2	String	PKTABLE_SCHEM	primary key table schema (may be a NULL value)
3	String	PKTABLE_NAME	primary key table name
4	String	PKCOLUMN_NAME	primary key column name
5	String	FKTABLE_CAT	foreign key table catalog being exported (may be NULL value)

continued

6	String	FKTABLE_SCHEM	foreign key table schema being exported (may be a NULL value)
7	String	FKTABLE_NAME	foreign key table name being exported
8	String	FKCOLUMN_NAME	foreign key column name being exported
9	short	KEY_SEQ	sequence number within foreign key
10	short	UPDATE_RULE	indicates what will happen to foreign key when primary is updated; value from `java.sql.DatabaseMetaData`
11	short	DELETE_RULE	indicates what will happen to the foreign key when primary is deleted; value from `java.sql.DatabaseMetaData`
12	String	FK_NAME	foreign key name (may be a NULL value)
13	String	PK_NAME	primary key name (may be a NULL value)

The UPDATE_RULE column indicates what will happen to the foreign key when the primary key is updated (in the foreign key table). This column contains a Java `short` value whose meaning can be determined by comparison with member variables of `java.sql.DatabaseMetaData` as shown in the following table.

UPDATE_RULE Value	Description
`importedKeyCascade`	change imported key to agree with corresponding primary key update
`importedKeyRestrict`	do not allow update of primary key if it has been imported
`importedKeySetNull`	change imported key to NULL if its corresponding primary key has been updated

The DELETE_RULE column indicates what will happen to the foreign key when the primary key is deleted (in the foreign key table). This column contains a Java `short` value whose meaning can be determined by comparison with member variables of `java.sql.DatabaseMetaData` as shown in the following table.

DELETE_RULE Value	Description
`importedKeyCascade`	delete rows that import a deleted key
`importedKeyRestrict`	do not allow delete of primary key if it has been imported
`importedKeySetNull`	change imported key to NULL if its corresponding primary key has been deleted

```
...
Connection con = DriverManager.GetConnection( url, "", "" );
DatabaseMetaData dmd = con.getMetaData();
Statement stmt = con.createStatement();

ResultSet rs = dmd.getExported Keys("",
                                   "",
                                   "orders")
boolean more = rs.next();
System.out.println( "Exported key components. " );
while ( more ) {
      System.out.println( "PK Column" +
                          rs.getString( 4 ) +
                          "—FK Table: " +
                          rs.getString( 7 ) );

       more = rs.next();
}
...
```

Parameters

`catalog`—a Java `String` containing the catalog name; a "" retrieves data without a catalog

`schema`—a Java `String` containing the schema name; a "" retrieves data without a schema `table`—a Java `String` containing the table name

Returns

A `ResultSet` for each row with a foreign key column description that matches the parameter criteria

See Also: `getImportedKeys`

getExtraNameCharacters

Declaration: `public abstract String getExtraNameCharacters() throws SQLException`

This method returns all special characters that can be used in unquoted character names (characters beyond 'a-z' and '0-9').

```
...
Connection con = DriverManager.getConnection (
                                        url, "", "");
DatabaseMetaData dmd = con.getMetaData();
String extraNameCharacters = dmd.getExtraNameCharacters();
System.out.println( "Special name characters: " +
                        extraNameCharacters );

...
```

Returns

A Java `String`

getIdentifierQuoteString

Declaration: `public abstract String getIdentifierQuoteString() throws SQLException`

This method returns a Java `String` representing the string used to quote SQL identifiers. It will return a " " (space character) if identifier quoting isn't supported. (A JDBC compliant driver will always return a double quote character.)

```
...
Connection con = DriverManager.getConnection (
                                        url, "", "");
DatabaseMetaData dmd = con.getMetaData();
String QuoteString = dmd.getIdentifierQuoteString();
if ( QuoteString != " " )
```

```
    String tableName = QuoteString +
                       "ThisTable" +
                        QuoteString;
...
```

Returns

A Java `String`

getImportedKeys

Declaration: `public abstract ResultSet getImportedKeys(String catalog, String schema, String table)  throws SQLException`

This method determines the imported keys for a table (the primary key columns that are referenced by a table's foreign key columns). Parameters are supplied for catalog, schema and table names. Results are returned in a `ResultSet` and ordered by the PKTABLE_CAT, PKTABLE_SCHEM, PKTABLE_NAME, and KEY_SEQ columns.

Return Values for getImportedKeys

Number	Type	Column Name	Description
1	String	PKTABLE_CAT	primary key table catalog that is being imported (may be a NULL value)
2	String	PKTABLE_SCHEM	primary key table schema that is being imported (may be a NULL value)
3	String	PKTABLE_NAME	primary key table name that is being imported
4	String	PKCOLUMN_NAME	primary key column name that is being imported
5	String	FKTABLE_CAT	foreign key table catalog (may be a NULL value)
6	String	FKTABLE_SCHEM	foreign key table schema (may be a NULL value)
7	String	FKTABLE_NAME	foreign key table name
8	String	FKCOLUMN_NAME	foreign key column name

continued

Number	Type	Column Name	Description
9	String	KEY_SEQ	sequence number within foreign key
10	short	UPDATE_RULE	indicates what will happen to foreign key when the primary key is updated; value from java.sql.DatabaseMetaData
11	short	DELETE_RULE	indicates what will happen to the foreign key when primary is deleted; value from java.sql.DatabaseMetaData
12	String	FK_NAME	foreign key name (may be a NULL value)
13	String	PK_NAME	primary key name (may be a NULL value)

The UPDATE_RULE column indicates what will happen to the foreign key when the primary key is updated (in the foreign key table). This column contains a Java `short` value whose meaning can be determined by comparison with member variables of `java.sql.DatabaseMetaData` as shown in the following table.

UPDATE_RULE Value	Description
importedKeyCascade	change imported key to agree with corresponding primary key update
importedKeyRestrict	do not allow update of primary key if it has been imported
importedKeySetNull	change imported key to NULL if its corresponding primary key has been updated

The DELETE_RULE column indicates what will happen to the foreign key when the primary key is deleted (in the foreign key table). This column contains a Java `short` value whose meaning can be determined by comparison with member variables of `java.sql.DatabaseMetaData` as shown in the following table.

DELETE_RULE Value	Description
importedKeyCascade	delete rows that import a deleted key
importedKeyRestrict	do not allow delete of primary key if it has been imported
importedKeySetNull	change imported key to NULL if its primary key has been deleted

```
...
Connection con = DriverManager.GetConnection( url, "", ""
);
DatabaseMetaData dmd = con.getMetaData();
Statement stmt = con.createStatement();
ResultSet rs =      dmd.getImportedKeys("",
                                          "",
                                           "orders")
boolean more = rs.next();
System.out.println(
   "Imported key components. " );
while ( more ) {
       System.out.println( "Column Name: " +
                                rs.getString( 4 ) +
                                "—Foreign Key Table: " +
                                rs.getString( 7 ) );

     more = rs.next();
}
...
```

Parameters

catalog—a Java String containing the catalog name; a "" retrieves those without a catalog

schema—a Java String containing the schema name; a "" retrieves those without a schema

table—a Java String containing the table name

Returns

A ResultSet for each row imported key column description retrieved

See Also: getExportedKeys

getIndexInfo

Declaration: `public abstract ResultSet getIndexInfo(String catalog, String schema, String table, boolean unique, boolean approximate)  throws SQLException`

This method retrieves basic information and statistics about a table's indices. Parameters are passed into the method for catalog, schema, and table name, and whether or not unique indices should be selected and whether or not approximate or out of data values are to be returned.

Results are returned in a `ResultSet` and are ordered by the NON_UNIQUE, TYPE, INDEX_NAME, and ORDINAL_POSITION columns.

Return Values for getIndexInfo

Number	Type	Column Name	Description
1	`String`	`TABLE_CAT`	table catalog name (may be a NULL value)
2	`String`	`TABLE_SCHEM`	table schema name (may be a NULL value)
3	`String`	`TABLE_NAME`	table name
4	`boolean`	`NON_UNIQUE`	TRUE if index values can be non-unique (allows duplicates); false when TYPE is `tableIndexStatistic`
5	`String`	`INDEX_QUALIFIER`	index catalog (may be a NULL value); NULL when TYPE is `tableIndexStatistic`
6	`String`	`INDEX_NAME`	index name; NULL when TYPE is `tableIndexStatistic`
7	`short`	`TYPE`	index type; a value from `java.sql.DatabaseMetaData`

continued

Number	Type	Column Name	Description
8	short	ORDINAL_POSITION	column sequence number within index; zero when TYPE is `tableIndexStatistic`
9	String	COLUMN_NAME	column name; NULL when TYPE is `tableIndexStatistic`
10	String	ASC_OR_DESC	column sort sequence where "A" = ascending and "D" = descending
11	int	CARDINALITY	when TYPE is `tableIndexStatistic` then this is the number of rows in the table; otherwise it is the number of unique values in the index
12	int	PAGES	when TYPE is `tableIndexStatistic` then this is the number of pages used for the table, otherwise it is the number of pages used for the current index
13	String	FILTER_CONDITION	filter condition for the index, if any (may be a NULL value)

The TYPE column indicates the index type. The index type is defined using a series of values from `java.sql.DatabaseMetaData`; these values are listed in the following table.

TYPE Value	Description
`tableIndexStatistic`	identifies table statistics that are returned in conjunction with a table's index descriptions
`tableIndexClustered`	identifies a clustered index
`tableIndexHashed`	identifies a hashed index
`tableIndexOther`	identifies some other type of index

```
...
Connection con = DriverManager.GetConnection( url, "", "" );
DatabaseMetaData dmd = con.getMetaData();
Statement stmt = con.createStatement();
ResultSet rs =       dmd.getIndexInfo( "",
                                       "",
                                       "orders",
                                       true,
                                       false );

boolean more = rs.next();
System.out.println( "Index information ... " );
while ( more ) {
            System.out.println( Index Name: " +
                    rs.getString( "INDEX_NAME" ) +
                    "—Column Name: " +
                    rs.getString( "COLUMN_NAME" ) +
                    "—Type: " +

            rs.getShort( "TYPE" ) +
                      "—Ordinal Position: " +
            rs.getShort( "ORDINAL_POSITION" ) +
                      "—ASC_OR_DESC: " +
            rs.getString( "ASC_OR_DESC" ) +
                       "—Cardinality: " +
            rs.getInt( "CARDINALITY" ) );

      more = rs.next();
}
...
```

Parameters

`catalog`—a Java `String` containing the catalog name; “” retrieves those without a catalog

`schema`—a Java `String` containing the schema name; “” retrieves those without a schema

`table`—a Java `String` containing the table name

`unique`—a Java `boolean` reflecting uniqueness of indices to retrieve; when true, only unique indices are retrieved; when false indices are retrieved regardless of uniqueness `approximate`—when true, retrieve approximate or out of data values; when false, results are requested to be accurate

Returns

A `ResultSet` for each index column description

getIndexInfo

Declaration: `public abstract ResultSet getIndexInfo(String catalog, String schema, String table, boolean unique, boolean approximate) throws SQLException`

This method retrieves information about a table's indices. Parameters are passed into the method for catalog, schema, and table name, and whether or not unique indices should be selected and whether or not approximate or out-of-data values are to be returned. Results are returned in a `ResultSet` ordered by the NON_UNIQUE, TYPE, INDEX_NAME, and ORDINAL_POSITION columns.

Return Values for getIndexInfo

Number	Type	Column Name	Description
1	`String`	TABLE_CAT	table catalog name (may be a NULL value)
2	`String`	TABLE_SCHEM	table schema name (may be a NULL value)
3	`String`	TABLE_NAME	table name
4	`boolean`	NON_UNIQUE	TRUE if index values can be non-unique (allows duplicates); false when TYPE is `tableIndexStatistic`
5	`String`	INDEX_QUALIFIER	index catalog (may be a NULL value); NULL when TYPE is `tableIndexStatistic`
6	`String`	INDEX_NAME	index name; NULL when TYPE is `tableIndexStatistic`
7	`String`	TYPE	index type; a value from `java.sql.DatabaseMeta Data`

continued

Number	Type	Column Name	Description
8	short	ORDINAL_POSITION	column sequence number within index; zero when TYPE is tableIndexStatistic
9	String	COLUMN_NAME	column name; NULL when TYPE is tableIndexStatistic
10	String	ASC_OR_DESC	column sort sequence where "A" = ascending and "D" = descending
11	int	CARDINALITY	when TYPE is tableIndexStatistic then this is the number of rows in the table; otherwise it is the number of unique values in the index
12	int	PAGES	when TYPE is tableIndexStatistic then this is the number of pages used for the table, otherwise it is the number of pages used for the current index
13	String	FILTER_CONDITION	filter condition for the index, if any (may be a NULL value)

The TYPE column indicates the index type. The index type is defined using a series of values from `java.sql.DatabaseMetaData`; these values are listed in the following table.

TYPE Value	Description
tableIndexStatistic	identifies table statistics that are returned in conjunction with a table's index descriptions
tableIndexClustered	identifies a clustered index
tableIndexHashed	identifies a hashed index
tableIndexOther	identifies some other type of index

```
    Connection con = DriverManager.getConnection (
                              url, "", "");

    Statement stmt1 = con.createStatement();

    DatabaseMetaData dmd = con.getMetaData();

    ResultSet IndexInfoRS =
             dmd.getIndexInfo( "",
                               "",
                               "customer",
                               false,
                               false);

    boolean more = IndexInfoRS.next();

    System.out.println(
         "Index information [table name—index name]: " );
    while ( more )
          System.out.println(
               IndexInfoRS.getString( 3 ) +
               "—" + IndexInfoRS.getString( 6 )   +
               "," );
...
```

Parameters

`catalog`—a Java `String` containing the catalog name; “” retrieves those without a catalog

`schema`—a Java `String` containing the schema name; “” retrieves those without a schema

`table`—a Java `String` containing the table name

`unique`—a Java `boolean` reflecting uniqueness of indices to retrieve; when true, only unique indices are retrieved; when false indices are retrieved regardless of uniqueness

`approximate`—when true, retrieve approximate or out of data values; when false, results are requested to be accurate

Returns

A `ResultSet` for each index column description

getMaxBinaryLiteralLength

Declaration: `public abstract int getMaxBinaryLiteralLength() throws SQLException`

This method returns an integer which indicates the number of characters that can be included in an inline binary literal.

```
...
     Connection con = DriverManager.getConnection (
                          url, "", "");


    Statement stmt1 = con.createStatement();
    DatabaseMetaData dmd = con.getMetaData();

    System.out.println( "Maximum binary literal length is " +
                         dmd.getMaxBinaryLiteralLength() );
...
```

Returns

A Java `int`

getMaxCatalogNameLength

Declaration: `public abstract int getMaxCatalogNameLength() throws SQLException`

This method determines the maximum length of a catalog name. The maximum length is returned as an integer value.

```
...
     Connection con = DriverManager.getConnection (
                          url, "", "");

    Statement stmt1 = con.createStatement();
    DatabaseMetaData dmd = con.getMetaData();
    System.out.println(
               "Maximum catalog name length: " +
               dmd.getMaxCatalogNameLength() );
...
```

Returns

A Java `int`

getMaxCharLiteralLength

Declaration: `public abstract int getMaxCharLiteralLength() throws SQLException`

This method determines the maximum length for a character literal as supported by the database. The value is returned as a Java `integer`.

```
...
     Connection con = DriverManager.getConnection (
                          url, "", "");

    Statement stmt1 = con.createStatement();

    DatabaseMetaData dmd = con.getMetaData();

    System.out.println(
               "Maximum Character literal length is " +
               dmd.getMaxCharLiteralLength() );
...
```

Returns

An `int`

getMaxColumnNameLength

Declaration: `public abstract int getMaxColumnNameLength() throws SQLException`

This method determines the maximum length of a column name in the database. The value is returned as an integer.

```
...
     Connection con = DriverManager.getConnection (
                          url, "", "");

    Statement stmt1 = con.createStatement();
    DatabaseMetaData dmd = con.getMetaData();
    System.out.println(
               "Maximum column name length is " +
               dmd.getMaxColumnNameLength() );
...
```

Returns

A Java `int`

getMaxColumnsInGroupBy

Declaration: `public abstract int getMaxColumnsInGroupBy() throws SQLException`

This method determines the maximum number of columns that can be placed in a SQL 'group by' clause. The value is returned as an integer.

```
...
     Connection con = DriverManager.getConnection (
                          url, "", "");

    Statement stmt1 = con.createStatement();

    DatabaseMetaData dmd = con.getMetaData();

   System.out.println(
              "Maximum columns in 'group by' clause: " +
              dmd.getMaxColumnsInGroupBy() );
...
```

Returns

A Java `int`

getMaxColumnsInIndex

Declaration: `public abstract int getMaxColumnsInIndex() throws SQLException`

This method determines the maximum number of columns allowed in a table index. The value is returned as an integer.

```
...
     Connection con = DriverManager.getConnection (
                          url, "", "");

    Statement stmt1 = con.createStatement();

    DatabaseMetaData dmd = con.getMetaData();
```

```
    System.out.println(
                "Maximum columns in index is " +
                dmd.getMaxColumnsInIndex() );
...
```

Returns

A Java `int`

getMaxColumnsInOrderBy

Declaration: `public abstract int getMaxColumnsInOrderBy() throws SQLException`

This method determines the maximum number of columns the database will support in a SQL '`order by`' clause. The value is returned as an integer.

```
...
     Connection con = DriverManager.getConnection (
                         url, "", "");

    Statement stmt1 = con.createStatement();

    DatabaseMetaData dmd = con.getMetaData();

    System.out.println(
                "Maximum columns in 'order by' clause: " +
                dmd.getMaxColumnsInOrderBy() );

...
```

Returns

A Java `int`

getMaxColumnsInSelect

Declaration: `public abstract int getMaxColumnsInSelect() throws SQLException`

This method determines the maximum number of columns the database will allow in a SQL 'select' list. The value is returned as an integer.

```
...
```

```
     Connection con = DriverManager.getConnection (
                        url, "", "");

    Statement stmt1 = con.createStatement();
    DatabaseMetaData dmd = con.getMetaData();

    System.out.println(
              "Maximum columns in 'select' list: " +
              dmd.getMaxColumnsInSelect() );
...
```

Returns

A Java `int`

getMaxColumnsInTable

Declaration: `public abstract int getMaxColumnsInTable() throws SQLException`

This method determines the maximum number of columns the database will allow in a table. The value is returned as an integer.

```
...
     Connection con = DriverManager.getConnection (
                        url, "", "");

    Statement stmt1 = con.createStatement();
    DatabaseMetaData dmd = con.getMetaData();
    System.out.println(
              "Maximum columns in a table: " +
              dmd.getMaxColumnsInTable() );
...
```

Returns

A Java `int`

getMaxConnections

Declaration: `public abstract int getMaxConnections() throws SQLException`

This method determines how many concurrent active connections can be made to the current database. It returns an integer value representing the number of concurrent active connections allowed by the database.

```
...
     Connection con = DriverManager.getConnection (
                          url, "", "");

    Statement stmt1 = con.createStatement();
    DatabaseMetaData dmd = con.getMetaData();
    System.out.println(
              "Maximum number of connections: " +
              dmd.getMaxConnections() );

...
```

Returns

An `int`

getMaxCursorNameLength

Declaration: `public abstract int getMaxCursorNameLength() throws SQLException`

This method determines the maximum cursor name length allowed by the database. The value is returned as an integer.

```
...
     Connection con = DriverManager.getConnection (
                          url, "", "");
    Statement stmt1 = con.createStatement();
    DatabaseMetaData dmd = con.getMetaData();

   System.out.println(
              "Maximum cursor name length: " +
              dmd.getMaxCursorNameLength() );

...
```

Returns

A Java `int`

getMaxIndexLength

Declaration: `public abstract int getMaxIndexLength() throws SQLException`

This method determines the maximum length of an index allowed by the database. The maximum length allowed is returned as an integer.

```
...
     Connection con = DriverManager.getConnection (
                      url, "", "");
    Statement stmt1 = con.createStatement();
    DatabaseMetaData dmd = con.getMetaData();

    System.out.println(
              "Maximum index length is " +
              dmd.getMaxIndexLength() );
...
```

Returns

A Java `int`

getMaxProcedureNameLength

Declaration: `public abstract int getMaxProcedureNameLength() throws SQLException`

This method determines the maximum length allowed for a procedure name. The maximum length is returned as an integer value.

```
...
     Connection con = DriverManager.getConnection (
                      url, "", "");
    Statement stmt1 = con.createStatement();
    DatabaseMetaData dmd = con.getMetaData();

    System.out.println(
              "Maximum procedure name length: " +
              dmd.getMaxProcedureNameLength() );
...
```

Returns

A Java `int`

getMaxRowSize

Declaration: `public abstract int getMaxRowSize() throws SQLException`

This method determines the maximum length of a single row. The maximum length is returned as an integer value.

```
...
     Connection con = DriverManager.getConnection (
                          url, "", "");
    Statement stmt1 = con.createStatement();
    DatabaseMetaData dmd = con.getMetaData();

    System.out.println(
               "Maximum row size: " +
               dmd.getMaxRowSize() );
...
```

Return

A Java `int`

getMaxSchemaNameLength

Declaration: `public abstract int getMaxSchemaNameLength() throws SQLException`

This method determines the maximum length allowed for a schema name. The maximum length is returned as an integer value.

```
...
     Connection con = DriverManager.getConnection (
                          url, "", "");
    Statement stmt1 = con.createStatement();
    DatabaseMetaData dmd = con.getMetaData();

    System.out.println(
               "Maximum schema name length is " +
               dmd.getMaxSchemaNameLength() );
...
```

Returns

A Java `int`

getMaxStatementLength

Declaration: `public abstract int getMaxStatementLength() throws SQLException`

This method determines the maximum length in bytes for a SQL statement. The maximum length is returned as an integer value.

```
...
     Connection con = DriverManager.getConnection (
                        url, "", "");
    Statement stmt1 = con.createStatement();
    DatabaseMetaData dmd = con.getMetaData();

    System.out.println(
              "Maximum statement length is " +
              dmd.getMaxStatementLength() );
...
```

Returns

A Java `int`

getMaxStatements

Declaration: `public abstract int getMaxStatements() throws SQLException`

This method determines how many active concurrent statements can be open with the database. The number of active statements is returned as an integer value.

```
...
     Connection con = DriverManager.getConnection (
                        url, "", "");
    Statement stmt1 = con.createStatement();
    DatabaseMetaData dmd = con.getMetaData();

   System.out.println(
     "Maximum number of concurrent open statements: " +
     dmd.getMaxStatements() );
...
```

Returns

A Java `int`

getMaxTableNameLength

Declaration: `public abstract int getMaxTableNameLength() throws SQLException`

This method determines the maximum allowable length of a table name in the database. The maximum length is returned as an integer.

```
...
     Connection con = DriverManager.getConnection (
                         url, "", "");

    Statement stmt1 = con.createStatement();

    DatabaseMetaData dmd = con.getMetaData();

   System.out.println(
               "Maximum table name length: " +
               dmd.getMaxTableNameLength() );
...
```

Returns

A Java `int`

getMaxTablesInSelect

Declaration: `public abstract int getMaxTablesInSelect() throws SQLException`

This method determines the maximum number of tables that can be referenced in a SQL 'select' statement. The maximum number is returned as an integer value.

```
...
     Connection con = DriverManager.getConnection (
                         url, "", "");
    Statement stmt1 = con.createStatement();
    DatabaseMetaData dmd = con.getMetaData();

    System.out.println(
 "Maximum number of tables in a 'select' statement: " +
               dmd.getMaxTablesInSelect() );
...
```

Returns

A Java `int`

getMaxUserNameLength

Declaration: `public abstract int getMaxUserNameLength() throws SQLException`

This method determines the maximum length of a user name allowed by the database. The maximum length is returned as an integer value.

```
...
     Connection con = DriverManager.getConnection (
                         url, "", "");
    Statement stmt1 = con.createStatement();
    DatabaseMetaData dmd = con.getMetaData();

    System.out.println(
               "Maximum user name length: " +
               dmd.getMaxUserNameLength() );

...
```

Returns

A Java `int`

getNumericFunctions

Declaration: `public abstract String getNumericFunctions() throws SQLException`

This method returns a Java `String` containing a comma separated list of math functions supported by this database.

```
...
Connection con = DriverManager.getConnection (
                                         url, "", "");
DatabaseMetaData dmd = con.getMetaData();

String mathFunctions = dmd.getNumericFunctions();
System.out.println( "Math functions: " + mathFunctions );
  ...
```

Returns

A Java `String`

getPrimaryKeys

Declaration: `public abstract ResultSet getPrimaryKeys(String catalog, String schema, String table) throws SQLException`

This method retrieves a description of a table's primary key columns. Parameters provide the method with a catalog name, a schema name and a table name.

Results are returned in a `ResultSet` which provides a number of columns with information about the primary keys. The results are ordered by the COLUMN_NAME column.

Return Values for getPrimaryKeys

Number	Type	Column Name	Description
1	String	TABLE_CAT	table catalog name (may be null)
2	String	TABLE_SCHEM	table schema name (may be null)
3	String	TABLE_NAME	table name
4	String	COLUMN_NAME	column name
5	short	KEY_SEQ	sequence number within primary key
6	String	PK_NAME	primary key name (may be null)

```
...
Connection con = DriverManager.GetConnection( url, "", "" );
DatabaseMetaData dmd = con.getMetaData();
Statement stmt = con.createStatement();

ResultSet rs = dmd.getPrimaryKeys("",
                                  "",
                                  "orders");

boolean more = rs.next();
```

```
System.out.println( "Primary key components. " );
while ( more ) {
      System.out.println( "Key seq: " +
                          rs.getShort( 5 ) +
                          "—Column Name: " +
                          rs.getString( 6 ) );
      more = rs.next();
}
...
```

Parameters

catalog—a Java String corresponding to a catalog name; a value of "" would retrieve descriptions for those primary keys without catalogs

schema—a Java String corresponding to a schema name; a value of "" would retrieve those without a schema

table—a table name

Returns

A ResultSet for each primary key column description

getProcedures

Declaration: `public abstract ResultSet getProcedures(String catalog, String schemaPattern, String procedureNamePattern) throws SQLException`

This method returns a detailed description of a stored procedure from the database. Parameters for the catalog name, the schema pattern, and the procedure name are passed into the method. The information about the procedure is returned as elements of a ResultSet. Only the procedures matching the schema and procedure name will be returned.

The return results are ordered by the PROCEDURE_SCHEM, and PROCEDURE_NAME columns of the ResultSet. Each row of the returned ResultSet has the following columns.

Stored Procedure Meta Data

Number	Type	Column Name	Description
1	String	PROCEDURE_CAT	procedure catalog (could be NULL)
2	String	PROCEDURE_SCHEM	procedure schema (may be null)

continued

Number	Type	Column Name	Description
3	String	PROCEDURE_NAME	procedure name
4		future use	
5		future use	
6		future use	
7	String	REMARKS	information about the procedure
8	short	PROCEDURE_TYPE	type of procedure (Possible values listed below)

The PROCEDURE_TYPE column can take on several values as defined in `java.sql.DatabaseMetaData`. These values and their meanings are listed in the following table.

Procedure Type Values

Value	Description
procedureResultUnknown	is not known whether or not the procedure will return a result
procedureNoResult	the procedure does **not** return a result
procedureReturnsResult	the procedure **does** return a result

```
...
Connection con = DriverManager.GetConnection( url, "", "" );
DatabaseMetaData dmd = con.getMetaData();
Statement stmt = con.createStatement();

ResultSet rs = dmd.getProcedures( "catalog1",
                                  "orders ",
                                  "getOrderResults" );
boolean more = rs.next();
while ( more ) {
      System.out.println( "Procedure Name: " +
                          rs.getString( "PROCEDURE_NAME" ) +
                           "—Type: " +
                          rs.getShort( "PROCEDURE_TYPE" );
```

```
    more = rs.next();
}
```

Parameters

catalog—a Java String representing the catalog name; use two quotes ("") if there is no catalog name

schemaPattern— a Java String representing a schema name pattern; use two quotes ("") if there is no schema

procedureNamePattern—a Java String representing the procedure name

Returns

A ResultSet for each procedure description

See Also: getSearchStringEscape

getProcedureColumns

Declaration: public abstract ResultSet getProcedureColumns(String catalog, String schemaPattern, String procedureNamePattern, String columnNamePattern) throws SQLException

This method retrieves a description of the stored procedure parameters and result columns. A series of string parameters are passed into the method for the catalog, the schema, the procedure name and the procedure column.

The return values are returned as a ResultSet and is ordered by the PROCEDURE_SCHEM and the PROCEDURE_NAME columns in the ResultSet. The columns returned are described in the following table below.

ResultSet Columns Returned by getProcedureColumns

Number	Type	Column Name	Description
1	String	PROCEDURE_CAT	the procedure catalog (may be NULL)
2	String	PROCEDURE_SCHEM	procedure schema (may be NULL)
3	String	PROCEDURE_NAME	procedure name
4	String	COLUMN_NAME	result column or parameter name

continued

Number	Type	Column Name	Description
5	short	COLUMN_TYPE	type of result column or parameter (java.sql.DatabaseMeta)
6	short	DATA_TYPE	SQLtype of column (from java.sql.Types)
7	String	TYPE_NAME	SQL type name
8	int	PRECISION	precision of result column or parameter
9	int	LENGTH	length of data in bytes
10	short	SCALE	scale of result column or parameter
11	short	RADIX	radix of result column or parameter
12	short	NULLABLE	indicates whether or not the column can contain NULL values (java.sql.DatabaseMetaData)
13	String	REMARKS	describes the result column or parameter

The COLUMN_TYPE column can be one of the following values from the java.sql.DataBaseMetaData class.

COLUMN_TYPE Values

COLUMN_TYPE	Description
procedureColumnUnknown	column has an unknown column type
ProcedureColumnIn	column is an IN parameter
ProcedureColumnInOut	column is a INOUT parameter
ProcedureColumnOut	column is an OUT parameter
ProcedureColumnReturn	column is a procedure return value
ProceureColumnResult	column is a result column

The DATA_TYPE column references the SQL data type of the result column or parameter. It can be one of the following values from the `java.sql.Types` class. The SQL data types supported by JDBC and their corresponding Java data types are listed in the following table.

JDBC SQL Data Types

SQL type	Java Type	Description
CHAR	`String`	fixed length character string
VARCHAR	`String`	variable length character string
LONGVARCHAR	`String`	variable length character string—large (sometimes stores blob data)
NUMERIC	`java.sql.Numeric`	numeric data type of variable precision
DECIMAL	`java.sql.Numeric`	numeric data type of variable precision and scale
BIT	`boolean`	data type with only two possible values
TINYINT	`byte`	8-bit signed integer data type
SMALLINT	`short`	16-bit signed integer data type
INTEGER	`int`	32-bit signed integer data type
BIGINT	`long`	32-bit signed integer data type
REAL	`float`	floating point number
FLOAT	`double`	double precision floating point number
DOUBLE	`double`	double precision floating point number
BINARY	`byte[]`	fixed length binary data
VARBINARY	`byte[]`	variable length binary data
LONGVARBINARY	`byte[]`	variable length binary data
DATE	`java.sql.Date`	date data
TIME	`java.sql.Time`	time data
TIMESTAMP	`java.sql.Timestamp`	date and time data

The NULLABLE column represents the conditions under which the result column or parameter may or may not contain a NULL value. It can have one of the following values from `java.sql.DataBaseMetaData`.

NULLABLE Column Values

NULLABLE Column Value	Description
`procedureNoNulls`	the stored procedure does not allow NULL values
`procedureNullable`	the store procedure does allow NULL values
`procedureNullableUnknown`	whether or not the stored procedure allows NULL values is not known

Note that not all databases will return column descriptions for a stored procedure. Also, the database may add additional columns beyond the REMARKS column.

```
...
Connection con = DriverManager.GetConnection( url, "", "" );
DatabaseMetaData dmd = con.getMetaData();
Statement stmt = con.createStatement();
ResultSet rs = dmd.getProcedures( "catalog1",
                                  "orders ",
                                  "getOrderResults",
                                   "" );

boolean     more     = rs.next();
while ( more ) {
            // get information about the procedure columns
            System.out.println( " Column name: " +
                                rs.getString( "COLUMN_NAME" ) +
                                "-data type: " +
                                rs.getInt( "DATA_TYPE" ) );
            more = rsCols.next();
      }
```

```
        // get the next row
        more = rs.next();
}
```

Parameters

`catalog`—a catalog name; "" retrieves those without a catalog

`schemaPattern`—a schema name pattern; "" retrieves those without a schema

`procedureNamePattern`—a procedure name pattern

`columnNamePattern`—a column name pattern

Returns

A `ResultSet` row is returned for each stored procedure parameter or result column

See Also: `getSearchStringEscape`

getProcedureTerm

Declaration: `public abstract String getProcedureTerm() throws SQLException`

This method returns a string containing the database vendor's preferred term for 'procedure'.

```
...
Connection con = DriverManager.GetConnection( url, "", "" );
DatabaseMetaData dmd = con.getMetaData();

System.out.println( " Vendor's term for procedure  is " +
                     dmd.getProcedureTerm() );
...
```

Returns

A Java `String`

getSchemas

Declaration: `public abstract ResultSet getSchemas() throws SQLException`

This method returns a list of schemas available in this database. The schema names are returned in the form of a `ResultSet` containing the schemas available.

Number	Type	Column Name	Description
1	String	TABLE_SCHEM	the table schema name

```
...

Connection con = DriverManager.GetConnection( url, "", "" );
DatabaseMetaData dmd = con.getMetaData();
Statement stmt = con.createStatement();

ResultSet rs = getSchemas() throws SQLException
boolean more = rs.next();

while ( more ) {
      System.out.println( "Schema name: " +
                              rs.getString( "TABLE_SCHEM" ) );
      more = rs.next();
}
...
```

Returns

A ResultSet for each schema found

getSchemaTerm

Declaration: `public abstract String getSchemaTerm() throws SQLException`

This method returns a string with the database's preferred term for 'schema'.

```
...
Connection con = DriverManager.GetConnection( url, "", "" );
DatabaseMetaData dmd = con.getMetaData();
System.out.println( " Schema term is " +
dmd.getSchemaTerm() );
...
```

Returns

A Java `String`

getSearchStringEscape

Declaration: `public abstract String getSearchStringEscape() throws SQLException`

This method returns a Java `String` containing the string that can be used to escape special characters in SQL statements.

```
...
Connection con = DriverManager.getConnection (
                                    url, "", "");
DatabaseMetaData dmd = con.getMetaData();

String searchEscape = dmd.getSearchStringEscape();
String sqlQuery = "select * from table1 where col1 matches " +
                    searchEscape + "*";
 ...
```

Returns

A Java `String`

getSQLKeywords

Declaration: `public abstract String getSQLKeywords() throws SQLException`

This method returns a Java `String` containing a comma separated list of all the databases SQL keywords that are **not** SQL92 keywords.

```
...
Connection con = DriverManager.getConnection (
                                    url, "", "");
DatabaseMetaData dmd = con.getMetaData();
String sqlKeywords = dmd.getSQLKeywords();
System.out.println( "Non-SQL92 Keywords: " + sqlKeywords );
...
```

Returns

A Java `String`

getStringFunctions

Declaration: `public abstract String getStringFunctions() throws SQLException`

This method returns a Java `String` containing a comma separated list of string functions supported by the database.

```
...
Connection con = DriverManager.getConnection (
                                             url, "", "");
DatabaseMetaData dmd = con.getMetaData();

String stringFunctions = dmd.getStringFunctions();
System.out.println( "String Functions: " + stringFunctions
);
...
```

Returns

A Java `String`

getSystemFunctions

Declaration: `public abstract String getSystemFunctions() throws SQLException`

This method returns a Java `String` containing a comma separated list of system functions.

```
...
Connection con = DriverManager.getConnection (
                                             url, "", "");
DatabaseMetaData dmd = con.getMetaData();
String systemFunctions = dmd.getSystemFunctions();
System.out.println( "System Functions: " + systemFunctions
);
...
```

Returns

A Java `String`

getTables

Declaration: `public abstract ResultSet getTables(String catalog, String schemaPattern, String tableNamePattern, String types[]) throws SQLException`

This method returns a description of the tables in the current database. Parameters are passed to the method for the catalog name (this can be passed as a blank if this does not apply), a schema name (this can also be left blank if it does not apply), the name of the table, and an array of table types (a NULL value returns all types). Only table descriptions that match the parameters passed are returned. The `ResultSet` is ordered by the TABLE_TYPE, TABLE_SCHEM and TABLE_NAME columns.

The description of the tables is returned in a `ResultSet`; a `ResultSet` row is returned for each table to be described. The columns in the `ResultSet` contain information on the table catalog, the table schema, the table name, the type of table, and a short description of the table.

Number	Type	Column Name	Description
1	String	TABLE_CAT	the table catalog (may be a NULL value)
2	String	TABLE_SCHEM	the table schema (may be a NULL value)
3	String	TABLE_NAME	the table name
4	String	TABLE_TYPE	the table type as listed below
5	String	REMARKS	a description of the table

The TABLE_NAME column can contain a number of different values. Possible values are "TABLE", "VIEW", "SYSTEM TABLE", "GLOBAL TEMPORARY", "LOCAL TEMPORARY", "ALIAS", and "SYNONYM".

Note that some databases may not return all information for all tables.

```
...
// determine whether or not the table exists
DatabaseMetaData dmd = con.getMetaData();

         ResultSet tablesRS =  dmd.getTables(
                                             null,
                                             null,
                                             "transtest",
                                             null);

           more = tablesRS.next();

           if ( more )
              System.out.println(
```

```
            "transtest table exists. It will not be created." );
            else
              {
               Statement stmt = con.createStatement();
               int result =
                       stmt.executeUpdate(
"create table transtest( col1 int, col2 int, col3 char(10) )"_);
```

Parameters

`catalog`—a Java `String` corresponding to the catalog name ("" if there is no catalog)

`schemaPattern`—a Java `String` corresponding to the schema name ("" if there is no schema name)

`tableNamePattern`—a Java `String` corresponding to the table name

`types`—An array of Java `String`s corresponding to a list of table types to retrieve; a NULL value returns all types

Returns

A `ResultSet` for each table to be described

See Also: `getSearchStringEscape`

getTablePrivileges

Declaration: `public abstract ResultSet getTablePrivileges(String catalog, String schemaPattern, String tableNamePattern) throws SQLException`

This method determines the access rights for each table in the catalog. Parameters are passed into the method for catalog name, schema name, and table name. Only privileges that match the schema name and table name are returned.

Information is returned in a `ResultSet` ordered by TABLE_SCHEM, TABLE_NAME, and PRIVILEGE. The columns returned in the `ResultSet` are detailed in the following table.

Return Values for getTablePrivileges

Number	Type	Column Name	Description
1	String	TABLE_CAT	table catalog name (may be null)
2	String	TABLE_SCHEM	table schema name (may be null)

continued

3	String	TABLE_NAME	table name
4	String	COLUMN_NAME	column name
5	String	GRANTOR	grantor of access (may be null)
6	String	GRANTEE	grantee of access
7	String	PRIVILEGE	name of access (SELECT, INSERT, UPDATE, REFERENCES, ...)
8	String	IS_GRANTABLE	indicates whether or not this user (the grantee) can grant this privilege can be granted to someone else; value is "YES" if grantee is permitted to grant to others; value is "NO" if not; NULL value if unknown

```
...
Connection con = DriverManager.GetConnection( url, "", "" );
DatabaseMetaData dmd = con.getMetaData();
Statement stmt = con.createStatement();
ResultSet rs = dmd.getTablePrivileges(
                            "",
                            "",
                            "orders" )
boolean more = rs.next();
System.out.println( "Table Name: " +
                    rs.getString( 3 ) +
                    "—privilege: " +
                    rs.getString( 7 ) +
                    "—grantor Name: " +
                    rs.getString( 5 );
}
```

Parameters

catalog—a Java String representing a catalog name; "" retrieves those without a catalog

schemaPattern—a Java String representing a schema name; "" retrieves those without a schema

tableNamePattern—a table name

Returns

A `ResultSet` is returned for each table privilege description selected

See Also: `getSearchStringEscape`

getTableTypes

Declaration: `public abstract ResultSet getTableTypes() throws SQLException`

This method retrieves the table types available in the current database. The table types are returned in a `ResultSet` containing a single column for the table types. The `ResultSet` is ordered by table type.

Number	Type	Column Name	Description
1	String	TABLE_TYPE	the table type

Possible table type names are "TABLE", "VIEW", "SYSTEM TABLE", "GLOBAL TEMPORARY", "LOCAL TEMPORARY", "ALIAS", and "SYNONYM".

```
...
Connection con = DriverManager.GetConnection( url, "", "" );
DatabaseMetaData dmd = con.getMetaData();
Statement stmt = con.createStatement();

ResultSet rs = getTableTypes() throws SQLException
boolean more = rs.next();

while ( more ) {
      System.out.println( "Table type: " +
                              rs.getString( 1 ) );
      more = rs.next();
}
```

Returns

A `ResultSet` is returned for each table type found in the database.

getTimeDateFunctions

Declaration: `public abstract String getTimeDateFunctions() throws SQLException`

This method returns a Java String containing a comma separated list of time and date functions.

```
...
Connection con = DriverManager.getConnection (
                                    url, "", "");
DatabaseMetaData dmd = con.getMetaData();

String timeDateFunctions = dmd.getTimeDateFunctions();
System.out.println( "Time and Date Functions: " +
                       timeDateFunctions );
...
```

Returns

A Java String

getTypeInfo

Declaration: public abstract ResultSet getTypeInfo() throws SQLException

This method returns a description of all SQL types supported by this database. The results are returned in a ResultSet ordered by the DATA_TYPE column and then by how closely the data type maps to the corresponding JDBC SQL type.

Return Values for getTypeInfo

Number	Type	Column Name	Description
1	String	TYPE_NAME	data type name
2	short	DATA_TYPE	SQL data type; value from java.sql.Types
3	int	PRECISION	maximum precision for data type
4	String	LITERAL_PREFIX	prefix used to quote a literal (may be a NULL value)
5	String	LITERAL_SUFFIX	suffix used to quote a literal (may be a NULL value)
6	String	CREATE_PARAMS	parameters used in creating the type (may be a NULL value)

continued

Number	Type	Column Name	Description
7	short	NULLABLE	indicates whether or not you can use a NULL value for this type; value from java.sql.DatabaseMetaData
8	boolean	CASE_SENSITIVE	indicates whether or not the data type is case sensitive; boolean true if case sensitive
9	short	SEARCHABLE	indicates conditions under which this data type can be used in a where clause; values from java.sql.DatabaseMetaData
10	boolean	UNSIGNED_ATTRIBUTE	indicates whether or not the data type is unsigned; boolean true if unsigned
11	boolean	FIXED_PREC_SCALE	indicates whether or not the data type can be a money value (fixed precision); boolean true if it can be a money value
12	boolean	AUTO_INCREMENT	indicates whether or not the data type can be used for an auto-increment value; boolean true if it can be used for an auto-increment value
13	String	LOCAL_TYPE_NAME	localized version of data type name (may be a NULL value)
14	short	MINIMUM_SCALE	minimum scale supported
15	short	MAXIMUM_SCALE	maximum scale supported
16	int	SQL_DATA_TYPE	currently unused
17	int	SQL_DATETIME_SUB	currently unused
18	int	NUM_PREC_RADIX	radix—usually 2 or 10

The value in the DATA_TYPE column indicates the JDBC SQL data type of the database data type. This is a Java `short` value that would correspond to one of the following values from `java.sql.DatabaseMetaData`.

JDBC SQL Data Types

SQL Type	Java Type	Description
CHAR	`String`	fixed length character string
VARCHAR	`String`	variable length character string
LONGVARCHAR	`String`	variable length character string—large (sometimes stores blob data)
NUMERIC	`java.sql.Numeric`	numeric data type of variable precision
DECIMAL	`java.sql.Numeric`	numeric data type of variable precision and scale
BIT	`boolean`	data type with only two possible values
TINYINT	`byte`	8-bit signed integer data type
SMALLINT	`short`	16-bit signed integer data type
INTEGER	`int`	32-bit signed integer data type
BIGINT	`long`	32-bit signed integer data type
REAL	`float`	floating point number
FLOAT	`double`	double precision floating point number
DOUBLE	`double`	double precision floating point number
BINARY	`byte[]`	fixed length binary data
VARBINARY	`byte[]`	variable length binary data
LONGVARBINARY	`byte[]`	variable length binary data
DATE	`java.sql.Date`	date data

continued

SQL Type	Java Type	Description
TIME	`java.sql.Time`	time data
TIMESTAMP	`java.sql.Timestamp`	date and time data

The NULLABLE column indicates whether or not the data type can be set to a NULL value. The value in this column is from `java.sql.DatabaseMetaData` and would be one of the values listed in the following table.

NULLABLE Value	Description
`typeNoNulls`	data type does **not** allow NULL values
`typeNullable`	data type allows NULL values
`typeNullableUnknown`	it is not known whether or not this data type supports NULL values

The SEARCHABLE column indicates the conditions under which the corresponding data type can be used for searches. The values in the this column are from `java.sql.DatabaseMetaData` and are listed in the following table.

SEARCHABLE Value	Description
`typePredNone`	there is no support for searches with this data type
`typePredChar`	there is support only for searches in the SQL 'like' clause
`typePredBasic`	there is support for searching in every clause with the exception of the 'like' clause
`typeSearchable`	There is support for searches with this data type in all 'where' clause components

```
...
Connection con = DriverManager.GetConnection( url, "", "" );
DatabaseMetaData dmd = con.getMetaData();
Statement stmt = con.createStatement();

ResultSet rs =       dmd.getTypeInfo()
```

```
boolean more = rs.next();
System.out.println(
   "Data types supported ...   " );
while ( more ) {
    System.out.println( "Data Type Name: " +
                         rs.getString( 1 ) +
                         "," ) );

    more = rs.next();
...
```

Returns

A ResultSet each row with a SQL type description

getURL

Declaration: `public abstract String getURL() throws SQLException`

This method returns a Java String containing the URL for this database.

```
...
Connection con = DriverManager.getConnection (
                                          url, "", "");
DatabaseMetaData dmd = con.getMetaData();
String URLString = dmd.getURL();
...
```

Returns

A Java String containing the URL

getUserName

Declaration: `public abstract String getUserName() throws SQLException`

This method returns the user name as known to the current database.

```
...
Connection con = DriverManager.getConnection (
                                          url, "", "");
DatabaseMetaData dmd = con.getMetaData();
String UserName = dmd.getUserName();
```

...

Returns

A Java `String` containing the user name

getVersionColumns

Declaration: `public abstract ResultSet getVersionColumns(String catalog, String schema, String table) throws SQLException`

This method retrieves information about the version columns for a table. Parameters are passed into the method for the catalog name, the schema name, and the table name. Results are returned as a `ResultSet` with a series of columns containing information about the version columns. The `ResultSet` is unordered.

Return Values for getVersionColumns

Number	Type	Column Name	Description
1	short	SCOPE	not currently used
2	String	COLUMN_NAME	column name
3	short	DATA_TYPE	SQL data type from `java.sql.Types`
4	String	TYPE_NAME	Data source dependent type name
5	int	COLUMN_SIZE	precision
6	int	BUFFER_LENGTH	length of column value in bytes
7	short	DECIMAL_DIGITS	scale
8	short	PSEUDO_COLUMN	indicates whether or not this is a pseudo-column using values defined in `java.sql.DatabaseMetaData`

The PSEUDO_COLUMN column in the `ResultSet` references a series of values defined in the `java.sql.DatabaseMetaData` class. These values are used to indicate whether or not the column is a pseudo-column or whether or not this can be determined.

PSEUDO_COLUMN Value	Description
versionColumnUnknown	it is not known whether or not the column is a pseudo column
versionColumnNotPseudo	the column is **not** a pseudo column
versionColumnPseudo	the column is a pseudo column

```
...
Connection con = DriverManager.GetConnection( url, "", "" );
DatabaseMetaData dmd = con.getMetaData();
Statement stmt = con.createStatement();
ResultSet rs = dmd.getVersionColumns( "",
                                     "",
                                     "orders" );
boolean more = rs.next();
System.out.println( "Version columns  values ... " );

while ( more ) {
System.out.println( "Column Name: " +
                     rs.getString( 2 ) +
                     "—Data Type: " +
                     rs.getShort( 3 ) ) ;



more = rs.next();
}
```

Parameters

catalog—a Java String representing a catalog name; a value of "" would retrieve data for version columns without a catalog

schema—a Java String representing a schema name; a value of "" would retrieve data for version columns without schemas

table—a Java String representing a table name

Returns

A ResultSet for each row with a version column description

isCatalogAtStart

Declaration: `public abstract boolean isCatalogAtStart() throws SQLException`

This method returns a `boolean` true if the catalog name appears at the **start** of a qualified table name.

```
...

Connection con = DriverManager.GetConnection( url, "", "" );
DatabaseMetaData dmd = con.getMetaData();

if ( dmd.isCatalogAtStart() )
       System.out.println(
               "Catalog name is at start of table name."  );
...
```

Returns

A Java `boolean`

isReadOnly

Declaration: `public abstract boolean isReadOnly() throws SQLException`

This method returns a `boolean` true if the database is in read-only mode, and a `boolean` false if the database is not in read-only mode.

```
...
Connection con = DriverManager.getConnection (
                                         url, "", "");
DatabaseMetaData dmd = con.getMetaData();

if ( dmd.isReadOnly() )
    System.out.println( "Database is read-only."  );
...
```

Returns

A Java `boolean`

nullPlusNonNullIsNull

Declaration: `public abstract boolean nullPlusNonNullIsNull() throws SQLException`

This method returns a boolean true if concatenations between NULL and non-NULL values are allowed. (A JDBC compliant driver always returns true.)

```
...
Connection con = DriverManager.getConnection (
                                    url, "", "");
DatabaseMetaData dmd = con.getMetaData();

if ( dmd.nullPlusNonNullIsNull() )
   System.out.println( "NULL concatenation allowed."  );
...
```

Returns

A Java boolean

nullsAreSortedAtEnd

Declaration: public abstract boolean nullsAreSortedAtEnd() throws SQLException

This method returns a boolean value of true if NULL values are sorted at the end of the result set regardless of the sort order.

```
...
Connection con = DriverManager.getConnection (
                                    url, "", "");
DatabaseMetaData dmd = con.getMetaData();

if ( dmd.nullsAreSortedAtEnd() )
    Statement stmt = con.createStatement();
    ResultSet rs = stmt.executeQuery( "select * " +
                  " from customers order by purchases" );
...
```

Returns

A Java boolean

nullsAreSortedAtStart

Declaration: public abstract boolean nullsAreSortedAtStart() throws SQLException

This method returns a boolean value of true if NULL values are sorted at the start of the return results regardless of the sort.

```
...
Connection con = DriverManager.getConnection (
                                          url, "", "");
DatabaseMetaData dmd = con.getMetaData();
if ( dmd.nullsAreSortedAtStart() )
      Statement stmt = con.createStatement();
      ResultSet rs = stmt.executeQuery( "select * " +
                     " from customers order by purchases" );
...
```

Returns

A Java boolean

nullsAreSortedHigh

Declaration: `public abstract boolean nullsAreSortedHigh() throws SQLException`

This method returns a boolean value of true if NULL values are sorted high by the current database.

```
...
Connection con = DriverManager.getConnection (
                                          url, "", "");
DatabaseMetaData dmd = con.getMetaData();
if ( dmd.nullsAreSortedHigh() ) {
     Statement stmt = con.createStatement();
     ResultSet rs = stmt.executeQuery( "select * " +
                    " from customers order by purchases" );
...
```

Returns

A Java boolean

nullsAreSortedLow

Declaration: `public abstract boolean nullsAreSortedLow() throws SQLException`

This method returns a boolean value of true if NULL values are sorted low by the database.

```
...
Connection con = DriverManager.getConnection (
                                            url, "", "");
DatabaseMetaData dmd = con.getMetaData();
if ( dmd.nullsAreSortedLow() ) {
     Statement stmt = con.createStatement();
     ResultSet rs = stmt.executeQuery( "select * " +
                      " from customers order by purchases" );
...
```

Returns

A Java boolean

storesLowerCaseIdentifiers

Declaration: public abstract boolean storesLowerCaseIdentifiers() throws SQLException

This method returns a boolean true if mixed case unquoted SQL identifiers are stored in lower case.

```
...

Connection con = DriverManager.getConnection (
                                            url, "", "");
DatabaseMetaData dmd = con.getMetaData();

if ( dmd.storesLowerCaseIdentifiers() ) {
     System.out.println( "Stores lower case identifiers."  );
     String tableName = "ThisTable";
...
```

Returns

A Java boolean

storesLowerCaseQuotedIdentifiers

Declaration: `public abstract boolean storesLowerCaseQuotedIdentifiers() throws SQLException`

This method returns a boolean true if the database stores lower case quoted SQL identifiers in lower case. (A JDBC compliant driver will always return false.)

```
...
Connection con = DriverManager.getConnection (
                                         url, "", "");
DatabaseMetaData dmd = con.getMetaData();

if ( dmd.storesLowerCaseQuotedIdentifiers() )
    System.out.println(
         "Stores lower case quoted identifiers."  );
...
```

Returns

A Java `boolean`

storesMixedCaseIdentifiers

Declaration: `public abstract boolean storesMixedCaseIdentifiers() throws SQLException`

This method returns a `boolean` true if mixed case unquoted SQL identifiers are stored in the database in mixed case, i.e., the case of the identifier is not shifted.

```
...
Connection con = DriverManager.getConnection (
                                         url, "", "");
DatabaseMetaData dmd = con.getMetaData();

if ( dmd.storesMixedCaseIdentifiers() ) {
    System.out.println( "Supports mixed case identifiers."  );
    String sqlString =
                        "create ThisTable (col1 integer, "
+
```

```
                        " col2 integer) " ;
...
```

Returns

A Java boolean

storesMixedCaseQuotedIdentifiers

Declaration: public abstract boolean storesMixedCaseQuotedIdentifiers() throws SQLException

This method returns a boolean true if the database stores mixed case quoted SQL identifiers in mixed case. (A JDBC compliant driver will always return false.)

```
...
Connection con = DriverManager.getConnection (
                                    url, "", "");
DatabaseMetaData dmd = con.getMetaData();

if ( dmd.supportsMixedCaseQuotedIdentifiers() )
    System.out.println(
 "Stores mixed case quoted identifiers in mixed case." );
...
```

Returns

A Java boolean

storesUpperCaseIdentifiers

Declaration: public abstract boolean storesUpperCaseIdentifiers() throws SQLException

This method returns a boolean true if the database stores mixed case unquoted SQL identifiers in upper case.

```
...

Connection con = DriverManager.getConnection (
                                    url, "", "");
DatabaseMetaData dmd = con.getMetaData();
```

```
if ( dmd.storesUpperCaseIdentifiers() ) {
    System.out.println( "Stores upper case identifiers."  );
    String tableName = "ThisTable";
...
```

Returns

A Java `boolean`

storesUpperCaseQuotedIdentifiers

Declaration: `public abstract boolean storesUpperCaseQuotedIdentifiers() throws SQLException`

This method returns a `boolean` true if the database stores mixed case quoted SQL identifiers in upper case. (A JDBC compliant driver will always return TRUE.)

```
...
Connection con = DriverManager.getConnection (
                                        url, "", "");
DatabaseMetaData dmd = con.getMetaData();

if ( dmd.supportsUpperCaseQuotedIdentifiers() )
    System.out.println(
         "Supports upper case quoted identifiers."  );
...
```

Returns

A Java `boolean`

supportsAlterTableWithAddColumn

Declaration: `public abstract boolean supportsAlterTableWithAddColumn() throws SQLException`

This method returns a `boolean` true if the SQL 'alter table' statement with the 'add column' clause is supported by the current database.

```
...

Connection con = DriverManager.getConnection (
                                        url, "", "");
```

```
DatabaseMetaData dmd = con.getMetaData();

if ( dmd.supportsAlterTableWithAddColumn() )
     String sqlAlter =
    "alter table customer add (city char(20) ) ";
...
```

Returns

A Java boolean

supportsAlterTableWithDropColumn

Declaration: public abstract boolean supportsAlterTableWithDropColumn() throws SQLException

This method returns a boolean true if the SQL 'alter table' statement is supported with the 'drop column' clause.

```
...

Connection con = DriverManager.getConnection (
                                        url, "", "");
DatabaseMetaData dmd = con.getMetaData();

if ( dmd.supportsAlterTableWithDropColumn() )
     String sqlAlter = "alter table customer drop  ( state
) ";
...
```

Returns

A Java boolean

supportsANSI92EntryLevelSQL

Declaration: public abstract boolean supportsANSI92EntryLevelSQL() throws SQLException

This method returns a boolean true if the ANSI-92 entry level SQL grammar is supported. (All JDBC compliant drivers must return true.)

```
...
```

```
Connection con = DriverManager.GetConnection( url, "", "" );
DatabaseMetaData dmd = con.getMetaData();

if ( dmd.supportsANSI92EntryLevelSQL() )
   System.out.println( "Supports ANSI 92 Entry Level SQL grammar."  );
...
```

Returns

A Java boolean

supportsANSI92FullSQL

Declaration: `public abstract boolean supportsANSI92FullSQL() throws SQLException`

This method returns a boolean true if the database supports ANSI-92 full SQL grammar is supported.

```
...

Connection con = DriverManager.GetConnection( url, "", "" );
DatabaseMetaData dmd = con.getMetaData();

if ( dmd.supportsANSI92FullSQL() )
   System.out.println( "Supports ANSI 92 Full Level."  );
...
```

Returns

A Java boolean

supportsANSI92IntermediateSQL

Declaration: `public abstract boolean supportsANSI92IntermediateSQL() throws SQLException`

This method returns a boolean true if the ANSI-92 intermediate SQL grammar supported.

```
...
Connection con = DriverManager.GetConnection( url, "", "" );
DatabaseMetaData dmd = con.getMetaData();
```

```
if ( dmd.supportsANSI92IntermediateSQL() )
   System.out.println(
         "Supports ANSI 92 Intermediate Level SQL Grammar."  );
...
```

Returns

A Java `boolean`

supportsCatalogsInDataManipulation

Declaration: `public abstract boolean supportsCatalogsInDataManipulation() throws SQLException`

Returns a `boolean` true if the catalog name can be used in a data manipulation statement.

```
...

Connection con = DriverManager.GetConnection( url, "", "" );
DatabaseMetaData dmd = con.getMetaData();

if ( dmd.supportsCatalogsinDataManipulation() )
    System.out.println(
 "Supports catalogs in data manipulation statements." );
...
```

Returns

A Java `boolean`

supportsCatalogsInIndexDefinitions

Declaration: `public abstract boolean supportsCatalogsInIndexDefinitions() throws SQLException`

This method returns a `boolean` value of true if a catalog name can be used in an index definition statement.

```
...

Connection con = DriverManager.GetConnection( url, "", "" );
DatabaseMetaData dmd = con.getMetaData();
```

```
if ( dmd.supportsCatalogsinIndexDefinition() )
    System.out.println(
 "Supports catalogs in index definition statements." );
...
```

Returns

A Java boolean

supportsCatalogsInPrivilegeDefinitions

Declaration: public abstract boolean supportsCatalogsInPrivilegeDefinitions() throws SQLException

This call returns a boolean true if a catalog name can be used in a privilege definition statement.

```
...
Connection con = DriverManager.GetConnection( url, "", "" );
DatabaseMetaData dmd = con.getMetaData();

if ( dmd.supportsCatalogsinPrivilegeDefinitions() )
    System.out.println(
 "Supports catalogs in privilege definition statements." );
...
```

Returns

A Java boolean

supportsCatalogsInProcedureCalls

Declaration: public abstract boolean supportsCatalogsInProcedureCalls() throws SQLException

This method returns a boolean true if a catalog name can be used in a procedure call statement.

```
...

Connection con = DriverManager.GetConnection( url, "", "" );
DatabaseMetaData dmd = con.getMetaData();
```

```
if ( dmd.supportsCatalogsInProcedureCalls() )
    System.out.println(
                "Supports catalogs in procedure calls." );
...
```

Returns

A Java boolean

supportsCatalogsInTableDefinitions

Declaration:public abstract boolean supportsCatalogsInTableDefinitions() throws SQLException

This method returns boolean value of true if the catalog name can be used in a table definition statement.

```
...

Connection con = DriverManager.GetConnection( url, "", "" );
DatabaseMetaData dmd = con.getMetaData();

if ( dmd.supportsCatalogsinTableDefinition() )

    System.out.println(
  "Supports catalogs in table definition statements." );
...
```

Returns

A Java boolean

supportsColumnAliasing

Declaration: public abstract boolean supportsColumnAliasing() throws SQLException

This method returns a boolean true if column aliasing is supported. With column aliasing, the SQL 'as' clause can be used to provide names for computed columns and provide alias names for normal columns. (A JDBC compliant driver always returns true.)

```
...
```

```
Connection con = DriverManager.getConnection (
                                          url, "", "");
DatabaseMetaData dmd = con.getMetaData();

if ( dmd.supportsColumnAliasing() )
     String sqlSelect =
      "select order_num, (tax/amount) as tax_rate from orders ";

...
```

Returns

A Java boolean

supportsConvert

Declaration: public abstract boolean supportsConvert() throws SQLException

This method returns true if the convert function is available to convert between SQL types.

```
...

Connection con = DriverManager.getConnection (
                                          url, "", "");
DatabaseMetaData dmd = con.getMetaData();

if ( dmd.supportsConvert() )
     System.out.println( "Supports convert function."  );
...
```

Return

A Java boolean

supportsConvert

Declaration: public abstract boolean supportsConvert(int fromType, int toType) throws SQLException

This method is passed two integers representing supported SQL data types. It returns true if the SQL convert function can convert the two types. The types are from java.sql.Types.

```
...

Connection con = DriverManager.getConnection (
                                    url, "", "");
DatabaseMetaData dmd = con.getMetaData();

if ( dmd.supportsConvert( Types.BIGINT, Types.DECIMAL ) )
...
```

Parameters

`fromType`—an integer representing the type to convert from

`toType`—an integer representing the type to convert to

Returns

A Java `boolean`

See Also: `Types`

supportsCoreSQLGrammar

Declaration: `public abstract boolean supportsCoreSQLGrammar() throws SQLException`

This method returns true if the ODBC core SQL grammar is supported.

```
...

Connection con = DriverManager.GetConnection( url, "", "" );
DatabaseMetaData dmd = con.getMetaData();

if ( dmd.supportsCoreSQLGrammar() )
   System.out.println( "Supports Core SQL Grammar."  );
...
```

Returns

A Java `boolean`

supportsCorrelatedSubqueries

Declaration: `public abstract boolean supportsCorrelatedSubqueries() throws SQLException`

This method will return a `boolean` true if correlated subqueries are supported. (A JDBC compliant driver will always return true.)

```
...

Connection con = DriverManager.GetConnection( url, "", "" );
DatabaseMetaData dmd = con.getMetaData();

if ( dmd.supportsCorrelatedSubqueries() )
    // get list of orders for a sales rep within the sales period
    String SQLQuery =
           "select * from orders " +
           " where district_code in ( " +
           " select district_code from districts " +
           " where sales_rep = 42 and " +
           " orders.order_date <= district.period_close_date
)" ;
...
```

Returns

A Java `boolean`

supportsDataDefinitionAndDataManipulationTransactions

Declaration: `public abstract boolean supportsDataDefinitionAndDataManipulationTransactions() throws SQLException`

This method determines whether or not data definition (SQL DDL) and data manipulation (SQL DDL) statements are supported in the same transaction. If both are supported, the method returns a `boolean` true.

```
...

Connection con = DriverManager.GetConnection( url, "", "" );
DatabaseMetaData dmd = con.getMetaData();
```

```
if (
dmd.supportsDataDefinitionandDataManipulationTransactions() ) {
      // begin work
      con.commit();
      Statement stmt = con.createStatement();
      int resultCount = stmt.executeUpdate(
           " create table table1 ( col1 smallint, col2 smallint ) "
);
      resultCount = stmt.executeUpdate(
           " create index idx1 on table1 ( col1 ) " );
      resultCount = stmt.executeUpdate(
           " insert into table1 values ( 1, 1 ) " );
      resultCount = stmt.executeUpdate(
           " insert into table1 values ( 2, 2 ) " );
      resultCount = stmt.executeUpdate(
           " update table1 set col2 = 1 " );

      // commit the transaction
      con.commit();
}
...
```

Returns

A Java `boolean` value

supportsDataManipulationTransactionsOnly

Declaration: `public abstract boolean supportsDataManipulationTransactionsOnly() throws SQLException`

This method returns a `boolean` true if only data manipulation statements (SQL DML) are supported within a transaction.

```
...

Connection con = DriverManager.GetConnection( url, "", "" );
DatabaseMetaData dmd = con.getMetaData();
```

```
Statement stmt = con.createStatement();

if ( dmd.supportsDataManipulationTransactionsOnly() ) {

      // execute DDL outside transaction
      int resultCount = stmt.executeUpdate(
           " create table table1 ( col1 smallint, col2 smallint ) "
);
      resultCount = stmt.executeUpdate(
           " create index idx1 on table1 ( col1 ) " );

      // begin work
      con.commit();
      resultCount = stmt.executeUpdate(
           " insert into table1 values ( 1, 1 ) " );
      resultCount = stmt.executeUpdate(
           " insert into table1 values ( 2, 2 ) " );
      resultCount = stmt.executeUpdate(
           " update table1 set col2 = 1 " );
      // commit the transaction
      con.commit();

}
...
```

Returns

A Java boolean

supportsDifferentTableCorrelationNames

Declaration: `public abstract boolean supportsDifferentTableCorrelationNames() throws SQLException`

This method returns true if table correlation names are supported and restricted to be different from the names of the tables. (A JDBC compliant driver always returns true.)

```
...

Connection con = DriverManager.getConnection (
```

```
                    url, "", "");
DatabaseMetaData dmd = con.getMetaData();

if ( dmd.supportsDifferentTableCorrelationNames() )
   System.out.println(
        "Supports different table correlation names."  );
...
```

Returns

A Java `boolean`

supportsExpressionsInOrderBy

Declaration: `public abstract boolean supportsExpressionsInOrderBy() throws SQLException`

This method returns true if expressions in an SQL '`order by`' clause are supported.

```
...

Connection con = DriverManager.getConnection (
                                    url, "", "");
DatabaseMetaData dmd = con.getMetaData();

if ( dmd.supportsExpressionInOrderBy() )
   String sqlQuery =
    "select * from orders order by (tax/amount) ";
...
```

Returns

A Java `boolean`

supportsExtendedSQLGrammar

Declaration: `public abstract boolean supportsExtendedSQLGrammar() throws SQLException`

This method returns true if the ODBC extended SQL grammar is supported.

```
...

Connection con = DriverManager.GetConnection( url, "", "" );
DatabaseMetaData dmd = con.getMetaData();

if ( dmd.supportsExtendedSQLGrammar() )
   System.out.println( "Supports ODBC Extended SQL Grammar."  );

...
```

Returns

A Java boolean

supportsFullOuterJoins

Declaration: public abstract boolean supportsFullOuterJoins() throws SQLException

Returns a boolean true if full nested outer joins supported.

```
...

Connection con = DriverManager.GetConnection( url, "", "" );
DatabaseMetaData dmd = con.getMetaData();

if ( dmd.supportsFullOuterJoins() )
    System.out.println(
         "Full nested outer joins are supported. " );


...
```

Returns

A Java boolean

supportsFullOuterJoins

Declaration: public abstract boolean supportsFullOuterJoins() throws SQLException

Returns a boolean if full nested outer joins supported.

```
...

Connection con = DriverManager.GetConnection( url, "", "" );
DatabaseMetaData dmd = con.getMetaData();

if ( dmd.supportsFullOuterJoins() )



String SQLQuery =
        "select orders.*, line_items.*, district.* " +
        " from orders, outer ( outer line_items, district ) " +
        " where orders.order_num = line_items.order_num ";

...
```

Returns

A Java boolean

supportsGroupBy

Declaration: public abstract boolean supportsGroupBy() throws SQLException

This method returns a boolean true if some form of the SQL 'group by' clause is supported.

```
...

Connection con = DriverManager.getConnection (
                                    url, "", "");
DatabaseMetaData dmd = con.getMetaData();

if ( dmd.supportsGroupBy() )
    String sqlQuery =
        "select state, count(*) from orders group by state ";
...
```

Returns

A Java boolean

supportsGroupByUnrelated

Declaration: `public abstract boolean supportsGroupByUnrelated() throws SQLException`

This method returns true if the SQL 'group by' clause can use columns that are not in the 'select' list.

```
...
Connection con = DriverManager.getConnection (
                                         url, "", "");
DatabaseMetaData dmd = con.getMetaData();

if ( dmd.supportsGroupByUnrelated() )
    String sqlQuery =
         "select state, count(*) from orders group by zip ";
...
```

Returns

A Java `boolean`

supportsGroupByBeyondSelect

Declaration: `public abstract boolean supportsGroupByBeyondSelect() throws SQLException`

This method returns a `boolean` true if a 'group by' clause can list columns not listed in the 'select' list provided it lists all of the existing columns in the 'select' list.

```
...

Connection con = DriverManager.getConnection (
                                         url, "", "");
DatabaseMetaData dmd = con.getMetaData();

if ( dmd.supportsGroupByBeyondSelect() )
    String sqlQuery =
         "select state, county, count(*) " +
         " from orders " +
         " group by state,county, zip_code ";
...
```

Returns

A Java `boolean`

supportsIntegrityEnhancementFacility

Declaration: `public abstract boolean supportsIntegrityEnhancementFacility() throws SQLException`

Returns a `boolean` true if the database supports the SQL Integrity Enhancement Facility.

```
...

Connection con = DriverManager.GetConnection( url, "", "" );
DatabaseMetaData dmd = con.getMetaData();

if ( dmd.supportsIntegrityEnhancementFacility() )
    System.out.println(
        "Supports Integrity Enhancement Facility."  );
...
```

Returns

A Java `boolean`

supportsLimitedOuterJoins

Declaration: `public abstract boolean supportsLimitedOuterJoins() throws SQLException`

Returns a `boolean` true if there is limited support for outer joins.

```
...

Connection con = DriverManager.GetConnection( url, "", "" );
DatabaseMetaData dmd = con.getMetaData();

if ( dmd.supportsLimitedOuterJoins() )

    String SQLQuery =
      "select orders.*, line_items.* " +
```

```
        " from orders, outer line_items " +
        " where orders.order_num = line_items.order_num ";
...
```

Returns

A Java boolean

supportsMinimumSQLGrammar

Declaration: `public abstract boolean supportsMinimumSQLGrammar() throws SQLException`

This method returns true if the database supports ODBC minimum SQL grammar.

```
...

Connection con = DriverManager.GetConnection( url, "", "" );
DatabaseMetaData dmd = con.getMetaData();

if ( dmd.supportsMinimumSQLGrammar() )
   System.out.println( "Supports Minimum SQL Grammar."  );
...
```

Returns

A Java boolean

supportsMixedCaseIdentifiers

Declaration: `public abstract boolean supportsMixedCaseIdentifiers() throws SQLException`

This method returns a boolean true if the database supports mixed case unquoted SQL identifiers.

```
...

Connection con = DriverManager.getConnection (
                                        url, "", "");
DatabaseMetaData dmd = con.getMetaData();
```

```
if ( dmd.supportsMixedCaseIdentifiers() ) {
     System.out.println( "Supports mixed case identifiers."  );
     String tableName = "ThisTable";
...
```

Returns

A Java boolean

supportsMixedCaseQuotedIdentifiers

Declaration: `public abstract boolean supportsMixedCaseQuotedIdentifiers() throws SQLException`

This method returns a boolean true if the database supports mixed case quoted SQL identifiers. (A JDBC compliant driver should always return TRUE.)

```
...

Connection con = DriverManager.getConnection (
                                        url, "", "");
DatabaseMetaData dmd = con.getMetaData();
if ( dmd.supportsMixedCaseQuotedIdentifiers() )
     System.out.println( "Supports mixed case quoted identifiers."  );
...
```

Returns

A Java boolean

supportsMultipleResultSets

Declaration: `public abstract boolean supportsMultipleResultSets() throws SQLException`

This method returns a boolean true if the database supports multiple ResultSets from a single SQL execution.

```
...

Connection con = DriverManager.GetConnection( url, "", "" );
DatabaseMetaData dmd = con.getMetaData();
```

```
if ( dmd.supportsMultipleResultSets() )
    System.out.println( "Supports multiple result sets." );
...
```

Returns

A Java `boolean`

supportsMultipleTransactions

Declaration: `public abstract boolean supportsMultipleTransactions() throws SQLException`

This method returns a boolean true if the database supports multiple transactions open at the same time on different connections.

```
...

Connection con1 = DriverManager.GetConnection( url, "", "" );
Connection con2 = DriverManager.GetConnection( url, "", "" );

DatabaseMetaData dmd = con1.getMetaData();

if ( dmd.supportsMultipleTransactions() ) {

    // begin multiple transactions
    con1.commit();
    con2.commit();

...
```

Returns

A Java `boolean`

supportsNonNullableColumns

Declaration: `public abstract boolean supportsNonNullableColumns() throws SQLException`

Returns a `boolean` true if the database allows columns to be defined as not allowing NULL values. (A JDBC compliant driver will always return true.)

```
...

Connection con = DriverManager.GetConnection( url, "", "" );
DatabaseMetaData dmd = con.getMetaData();

if ( dmd.supportsNonNullableColumns() )
   String sqlQuery =
      " create table fixed_price ( price_key char(5) not null, " +
                                  price_amount decimal(12,2) ); ";

...
```

Returns

A Java `boolean`

supportsOpenCursorsAcrossCommit

Declaration: `public abstract boolean supportsOpenCursorsAcrossCommit() throws SQLException`

This method determines whether or not database cursors will remain open across commits. This would allow a `ResultSet` or `PreparedStatement` to remain open after a transaction commit.

```
...
Connection con = DriverManager.GetConnection( url, "", "" );
DatabaseMetaData dmd = con.getMetaData();

if ( (dmd.supportsOpenCursorsAcrossCommit()) == false )
   System.out.println( " Cursor must be re-opened after commit." );
...
```

Returns

A Java `boolean`

supportsOpenCursorsAcrossRollback

Declaration: `public abstract boolean supportsOpenCursorsAcrossRollback() throws SQLException`

This method will determine whether or not the database supports the ability for cursors to remain open after a transaction rollback.

```
...
     Connection con = DriverManager.getConnection (
                         url, "", "");

    Statement stmt1 = con.createStatement();
    DatabaseMetaData dmd = con.getMetaData();

    if (dmd.supportsOpenCursorsAcrossRollback() ) {
        System.out.println(
           " Supports open cursors across rollback." );
...
```

Returns

A Java `boolean`

supportsOpenStatementsAcrossCommit

Declaration: `public abstract boolean supportsOpenStatementsAcrossCommit() throws SQLException`

This method determines whether or not the database supports statements (`Statement`, `PreparedStatement`, and `CallableStatement` objects) remaining open across database commits and rollbacks. If this behavior is supported by the database, then the method returns a `boolean` true.

```
...

Connection con = DriverManager.GetConnection( url, "", "" );
DatabaseMetaData dmd = con.getMetaData();

if ( dmd.supportsOpenCursorsAcrossCommit() )
   System.out.println(
      "Open cursors supported across commit operations. " );
...
```

Returns

A Java `boolean`

supportsOpenStatementsAcrossRollback

Declaration: `public abstract boolean supportsOpenStatementsAcrossRollback() throws SQLException`

This method determines whether or not the database supports statements (`Statement`, `PreparedStatement`, and `CallableStatement` objects) remaining open across database commits and rollbacks. If this behavior is supported by the database, then the method returns a `boolean` true.

```
...
Connection con = DriverManager.GetConnection( url, "", "" );
DatabaseMetaData dmd = con.getMetaData();

if ( dmd.supportsOpenStatementsAcrossRollback() )
   System.out.println(
     "Open cursors supported across rollback operations. " );
...
```

Returns

A Java boolean

supportsOrderByUnrelated

Declaration: `public abstract boolean supportsOrderByUnrelated() throws SQLException`

This method returns a boolean true if an SQL '`order by`' clause can use columns that are not contained in the '`select`' list.

```
...
Connection con = DriverManager.getConnection (
                                    url, "", "");
DatabaseMetaData dmd = con.getMetaData();

if ( dmd.supportsOrderByUnrelated() )
   String sqlQuery =
  "select order_num, order_date from orders order by state ";
...
```

Returns

A Java `boolean`

supportsOuterJoins

Declaration: `public abstract boolean supportsOuterJoins() throws SQLException`

This method returns a `boolean` true if outer joins are supported by the current database.

```
...

Connection con = DriverManager.GetConnection( url, "", "" );
DatabaseMetaData dmd = con.getMetaData();

if ( dmd.supportsOuterJoins() )
   String SQLQuery = " select orders.*, items.* " +
                         " from orders, outer items " +
         " where orders.order_num = items.order_num";
...
```

Returns

A Java boolean

supportsPositionedDelete

Declaration: `public abstract boolean supportsPositionedDelete() throws SQLException`

This method returns a boolean true if a positioned delete is supported by the database. A positioned delete allows a delete operation to be performed at the current cursor position as demonstrated in the following code fragment.

```
...
     Connection con = DriverManager.getConnection (
                          url, "", "");

    Statement stmt1 = con.createStatement();

  // need a database that supports positioned deletes
     DatabaseMetaData dmd = con.getMetaData();
     if ( dmd.supportsPositionedDelete() == false ) {
          System.out.println(
```

```
"Positioned delete is not supported by this database."  );
            System.exit( -1 );
     }

     ResultSet rs = stmt1.executeQuery( "select " +
             " * from customer where cust_no = 5" +
             " for update " );
     rs.next(); // look at the first row (cust_no=5)

     // get the cursor name
     String cursName = rs.getCursorName();

     // create delete statement
     Statement stmt2 = con.createStatement();

     // use positioned delete
     int result = stmt2.executeUpdate(
                "delete from loadtest " +
                " where current of " + cursName );
...
```

Returns

A Java boolean

supportsPositionedUpdate

Declaration: public abstract boolean supportsPositionedUpdate() throws SQLException

This method returns a boolean true if a positioned update is supported by the database. The following code sample demonstrates the use of positioned update with JDBC.

```
...
   import java.sql.*;
   import java.io.*;


   class PosUpd {
```

```
public static void main( String argv[] ) {

  try {

     Class.forName ("jdbc.odbc.JdbcOdbcDriver");

      Connection con = DriverManager.getConnection (
                       url,
                       " ",
                       " ");

     Statement stmt1 = con.createStatement();

    // need a database that supports positioned updates
    DatabaseMetaData dmd = con.getMetaData();
    if ( dmd.supportsPositionedUpdate() == false ) {
       System.out.println(
"Positioned update is not supported." );
         System.exit( -1 );
     }

     ResultSet rs = stmt1.executeQuery(
            "select " +
            " * from loadtest where col1 = 5" +
            " for update " );
     // look at the first row (col1 = 5)
     rs.next();
     String cursName = rs.getCursorName();
     System.out.println(
          "cursor name is " + cursName );

     // update stmt2 at col1 = 5
     Statement stmt2 = con.createStatement();
     int result = stmt2.executeUpdate(
         "update loadtest set col2 = '1000' " +
         " where current of " + cursName );
```

```
            rs = stmt1.executeQuery(
                "select * from loadtest " +
                " where col1 = 5 " );

            rs.next();
            System.out.println( "col1 = " +
                                  rs.getInt( 1 ) +
                                 " col2 = " +
                                 rs.getInt( 2 ) );

        }

        catch (java.lang.Exception ex) {

       // Print description of the exception.
       System.out.println(
            "** Error on data select. ** " );
       ex.printStackTrace ();
            }
    }
}
```

Returns

A Java boolean

supportsSchemasInDataManipulation

Declaration: public abstract boolean supportsSchemasInDataManipulation() throws SQLException

Returns a boolean true if the schema name can be used in a data manipulation statement.

```
...
Connection con = DriverManager.GetConnection( url, "", "" );
DatabaseMetaData dmd = con.getMetaData();
if (dmd.supportsSchemasInDataManipulation() )
     System.out.println(
         "Schema name can be used in a DML statement." );
...
```

Returns

A Java boolean

supportsSchemasInIndexDefinitions

Declaration: public abstract boolean supportsSchemasInIndexDefinitions() throws SQLException

Returns a boolean true if the schema name can be used in an index definition statement.

```
...
Connection con = DriverManager.GetConnection( url, "", "" );
DatabaseMetaData dmd = con.getMetaData();
if (dmd.supportsSchemasInIndexDefinitions() )
    System.out.println(
  "Schema name can be used in an index definition statement." );
...
```

Returns

A Java boolean

supportsSchemasInPrivilegeDefinitions

Declaration: public abstract boolean supportsSchemasInPrivilegeDefinitions() throws SQLException

Returns a boolean true if the schema name can be used in a privilege definition statement.

```
...
Connection con = DriverManager.GetConnection( url, "", "" );
DatabaseMetaData dmd = con.getMetaData();
if (dmd.supportsSchemasInPrivilegeDefinitions() )
    System.out.println(
        "Schema name can be used in privilege " +
        " definition statements." );
...
```

Returns

A Java boolean

supportsSchemasInProcedureCalls

Declaration: `public abstract boolean supportsSchemasInProcedureCalls() throws SQLException`

This method returns a `boolean` true if a schema name can be used in a procedure call state.

```
...

Connection con = DriverManager.GetConnection( url, "", "" );
DatabaseMetaData dmd = con.getMetaData();

if ( dmd.supportsSchemasInProcedureCalls() )
     System.out.println(
            "Supports schemas in procedure calls." );
...
```

Returns

A Java `boolean`

supportsSchemasInTableDefinitions

Declaration: `public abstract boolean supportsSchemasInTableDefinitions() throws SQLException`

This method returns a `boolean` true if a schema name can be used in a table definition statement.

```
...

Connection con = DriverManager.GetConnection( url, "", "" );
DatabaseMetaData dmd = con.getMetaData();

if ( dmd.supportsSchemasInTableDefinitions() )
     System.out.println(
          "Supports schemas in table definitions." );
...
```

Returns

A Java `boolean`

supportsSelectForUpdate

Declaration: `public abstract boolean supportsSelectForUpdate() throws SQLException`

This method returns a `boolean` true if 'select ... for update' is supported by this database.

```
...
     Connection con = DriverManager.getConnection (
                          url, "", "");

    Statement stmt1 = con.createStatement();

  // need a database that supports positioned deletes
     DatabaseMetaData dmd = con.getMetaData();
     if ( dmd.supportsSelectForUpdate() == false ) {
          System.out.println(
  "Select for update operations are not supported "  +
   " by this database."  );
          System.exit( -1 );
     }
     else
          String sqlStmt = "select * from customer " +
                           " where cust_no = 5 " +
                           " for update "
...
```

Returns

A Java `boolean`

supportsStoredProcedures

Declaration: `public abstract boolean supportsStoredProcedures() throws SQLException`

This method returns a `boolean` true if stored procedure calls are supported using the JDBC stored procedure escape syntax.

```
...

Connection con = DriverManager.GetConnection( url, "", "" );
DatabaseMetaData dmd = con.getMetaData();
```

```
if ( dmd.supportsStoredProcedures() )
   String SQLStmt =
        " { call storedProc1( ?,?,? ) } ";
   CallableStatement stmt = con.prepareCall( SQLStmt );
...
```

Returns

A Java boolean

supportsSubqueriesInComparisons

Declaration: public abstract boolean supportsSubqueriesInComparisons() throws SQLException

This method returns a boolean true if subqueries in comparison expressions are supported by the database. (A JDBC compliant driver will always returns true.)

```
...

Connection con = DriverManager.GetConnection( url, "", "" );
DatabaseMetaData dmd = con.getMetaData();

if ( dmd.supportsSubqueriesInComparisons() )
   // get list of most recent orders
   String SQLQuery =
        "select * from orders " +
        " where order_date = ( " +
        " select max(order_date) from orders ) " ;
...
```

Returns

A Java boolean

supportsSubqueriesInExists

Declaration: public abstract boolean supportsSubqueriesInExists() throws SQLException

This method returns a boolean true if subqueries in 'exists' clauses are supported. (A JDBC compliant driver will always return true.)

```
...

Connection con = DriverManager.GetConnection( url, "", "" );
DatabaseMetaData dmd = con.getMetaData();

if ( dmd.supportsSubqueriesInExists() )
   // get list of stock that has never been ordered
   String SQLQuery =
        "select item_number from line_items, orders " +
        " where orders.order_num = line_items.order_num and " +
        " not exists( select * from stock_items " +
        " where line_items.stock_num = stock_items.stock_num " +
        " and stock_items.purchase_date > orders.order_date ) " ;
...
```

Returns

A Java `boolean`

supportsSubqueriesInIns

Declaration: `public abstract boolean supportsSubqueriesInIns() throws SQLException`

This method returns a `boolean` true if subqueries in 'in' clauses are supported. (A JDBC compliant driver will always return true.)

```
...

Connection con = DriverManager.GetConnection( url, "", "" );
DatabaseMetaData dmd = con.getMetaData();

if ( dmd.supportsSubqueriesInIns() )
   // get list of orders for a sales rep
   String SQLQuery =
        "select * from orders " +
        " where district_code in ( " +
        " select district_code from districts " +
        " where sales_rep = 42 ) " ;
...
```

Returns

A Java boolean

supportsSubqueriesInQuantifieds

Declaration: public abstract boolean supportsSubqueriesInQuantifieds() throws SQLException

This method returns a boolean true if subqueries in quantified expressions are supported. (A JDBC compliant driver will always return true.)

```
...

Connection con = DriverManager.GetConnection( url, "", "" );
DatabaseMetaData dmd = con.getMetaData();

if ( dmd.supportsSubqueriesInQuantifieds() )
   // get list of orders for a sales rep
   String SQLQuery =
         "select * from orders " +
         " where district_code in ( " +
" select district_code from districts where sales_rep = 42 ) " ;
...
```

Returns

A Java boolean

supportsTableCorrelationNames

Declaration: public abstract boolean supportsTableCorrelationNames() throws SQLException

This method returns true if table correlation names are supported. (A JDBC compliant driver always returns true.)

```
...

Connection con = DriverManager.getConnection (
                                    url, "", "");
DatabaseMetaData dmd = con.getMetaData();

if ( dmd.supportsTableCorrelationNames() )
```

```
   System.out.println( "Supports table correlation names."
);
...
```

Returns

A Java boolean

supportsTransactions

Declaration: `public abstract boolean supportsTransactions() throws SQLException`

This method determines whether or not transactions are supported by the database. If transactions are supported, a boolean true is returned. (If transactions are not supported, then a database commit will fail silently and the isolation level is set to TRANSACTION_NONE.)

```
...

Connection con = DriverManager.GetConnection( url, "", "" );
DatabaseMetaData dmd = con.getMetaData();

if ( dmd.supportsTransactions() )
   con.setTransactionIsolation(
        Connection.TRANSACTION_REPEATABLE_READ );
...
```

Returns

A Java boolean

supportsTransactionIsolationLevel

Declaration: `public abstract boolean supportsTransactionIsolationLevel(int level) throws SQLException`

This method determines whether or not the database supports a specific transaction level. The transaction isolation (from java.sql.Connection) is passed to the method as a parameter. If the method returns a boolean true, then the transaction isolation mode is supported by the database.

```
...

Connection con = DriverManager.GetConnection( url, "", "" );
```

```
DatabaseMetaData dmd = con.getMetaData();

// does the database support repeatable read isolation ?
if ( dmd.supportsTransactionIsolationLevel(
      Connection.TRANSACTION_REPEATABLE_READ ) )
   con.setTransactionIsolation(
      Connection.TRANSACTION_REPEATABLE_READ );
...
```

Parameters

An `int` value corresponding to the isolation level as defined in `java.sql.Connection`

Returns

A Java `boolean`

See Also: `Connection`

supportsUnion

Declaration: `public abstract boolean supportsUnion() throws SQLException`

Returns a `boolean` true if the SQL 'union' operation is supported.

```
...

Connection con = DriverManager.GetConnection( url, "", "" );
DatabaseMetaData dmd = con.getMetaData();

if ( dmd.supportsUnion() )

   String SQLQuery =
         " select order_num, order_date, amount from orders " +
         " where order_date > = '1/1/1991' and order_date < '1/1/1995' " +
         " union " +
         " select order_num, order_date, amount from orders " +
         " where order_date > = '1/1/1995' and order_date < '1/1/1996' ";
...
```

Returns

A Java `boolean`

supportsUnionAll

Declaration: `public abstract boolean supportsUnionAll() throws SQLException`

This method will return a `boolean` true if the SQL 'union all' operation is supported.

```
...

Connection con = DriverManager.GetConnection( url, "", "" );
DatabaseMetaData dmd = con.getMetaData();

if ( dmd.supportsUnionAll() )

   String SQLQuery =
        " select order_num, order_date, amount from orders " +
       " where order_date >= '1/1/1991' and order_date < '1/1/1995' " +
        " union all " +
        " select order_num, order_date, amount from orders " +
        " where order_date >= '1/1/1995' and order_date < '1/1/1996' ";
...
```

Returns

A Java `boolean`

usesLocalFiles

Declaration: `public abstract boolean usesLocalFiles() throws SQLException`

This method returns a `boolean` true if the database stores tables as a local file.

```
...

Connection con = DriverManager.getConnection (
                                          url, "", "");
DatabaseMetaData dmd = con.getMetaData();
```

```
if ( dmd.usesLocalFiles() )
     System.out.println( "Database uses local files."  );

...
```

Returns

A Java boolean

usesLocalFilePerTable

Declaration: public abstract boolean usesLocalFilePerTable() throws SQLException

This method returns a boolean value of true if the database use a local file for each table.

```
...

Connection con = DriverManager.getConnection (
                                        url, "", "");
DatabaseMetaData dmd = con.getMetaData();


if ( dmd.usesLocalFilePerTable()  )
     System.out.println( "Uses local file per table."  );


...
```

Returns

A Java boolean

Class java.sql.DataTruncation

Declaration: `public class DataTruncation extends SQLWarning`

If a value is unexpectedly truncated with JDBC, a `DataTruncation` warning is thrown on read operations. On write operations, a `DataTruncation` exception is thrown. The `SQLstate` for `DataTruncation` is set to "01004".

DataTruncation

Declaration: `public DataTruncation(int index,` boolean parameter, boolean read, int dataSize, int transferSize)

This is the constructor for the `DataTruncation` class. Five parameters are passed representing the index offset in the parameters where the truncation occurred, a `boolean` to indicate whether or not the error occurred in a parameter or column, a `boolean` that indicates whether the truncation occurred during a read or write operation, the size of the data transferred if the operation had succeeded, and the number of bytes actually transferred.

DataTruncation Methods

getDataSize

Declaration: `public int getDataSize()`

This method returns an integer representing the number of bytes that would have been transferred if the operation had succeeded. This number may be approximate if data conversions were being performed during the operation. The return value would be –1 if the size is unknown.

```
import java.net.URL;
import java.sql.*;
import java.lang.Runtime;

...

catch ( DataTruncation warn ) {

       int x = warn.getDataSize();
       if ( x != -1 )
          System.out.println(
               "Should have received " + x + " bytes." );
       else
```

```
            System.out.println(
 "Size of truncated data transfer is unknown." );
}
```

Returns

An `int` value

getIndex

Declaration: `public int getIndex()`

This method returns the index (ordinal position) of the parameter that was truncated. This could return a value of –1 if the parameter index is unknown. If the parameter is unknown, then the `getParameter` and `getRead` return values of this interface should be ignored.

```
...
catch ( DataTruncation warn ) {
...
System.out.println(
      "The parameter at index position " +
        warn.getIndex() + " was truncated" );
...
```

Returns

An `int`

getParameter

Declaration: `public boolean getParameter()`

This method returns a `boolean` value representing the type of value that triggered the error. This method returns true if the value was a parameter; false if the value was a column value.

```
import java.net.URL;
import java.sql.*;
import java.lang.Runtime;

...

catch ( DataTruncation warn ) {
```

```
        if ( warn.getParameter() )
            System.out.println( "Parameter has been truncated."  );
        else
            System.out.println( "Column has been truncated."  );
...
```

Returns

A Java `boolean`

getRead

Declaration: `public boolean getRead()`

This method returns a `boolean` value that indicates how the data truncation occurred. The method returns true if the operation occurred during a read operation; false if the data was truncated on a write operation.

```
import java.net.URL;
import java.sql.*;
import java.lang.Runtime;

...
catch ( DataTruncation warn ) {
        if ( warn.getRead() )
            System.out.println(
                "Data truncated on a read operation."  );
        else
            System.out.println(
                "Data truncated on a write operation."  );

}
```

Returns

A Java `boolean`

getTransferSize

Declaration: `public int getTransferSize()`

This method returns an integer representing the number of bytes actually transferred during the operation. A '–1' indicates the size is unknown.

```
import java.net.URL;
import java.sql.*;
import java.lang.Runtime;

...

catch ( DataTruncation warn ) {

        int x = warn.getTransferSize();
        if ( x != -1 )
           System.out.println( "Received " + x + " bytes." );
        else
           System.out.println(
                   "Received an unknown number of bytes." );
}
```

Returns

An `int`

Interface java.sql.Date

Declaration: `public class **Date** extends Date`

The `Date` class provides the capability to manipulate SQL DATE fields.

Date

Declaration: `public Date(int year, int month, int day)`

This method constructs a `Date` object from the three integer parameters passed.

```
import java.net.URL;
import java.sql.*;
import java.sql.Date;
...

Date dt = new Date( 1988, 8, 17);

...
```

Parameters

`year`—a positive integer value

`month`—an integer value in the range 0 to 11

`day`—an integer value in the range 1 to 31

toString

Declaration: `public String toString()`

This method returns a `Date` formatted as a `String`. The date is formatted as "yyyy-mm-dd".

```
import java.net.URL;
import java.sql.*;
import java.sql.Date;
...

Date dt1 = new Date( 1991, 6, 6 );
System.out.println( "Date is " + dt1.toString() );

...
```

Returns

A Java String

ValueOf

Declaration: `public static Date valueOf( String s )`

This method converts a formatted string to a Date value. A String parameter is passed into the method containing a formatted string representation of a date. The date format string should be formatted as 'yyyy-mm-dd'.

```
import java.net.URL;
import java.sql.*;
import java.sql.Date;
...

Date dt1 = Date.valueOf( "1996-10-23" );

...
```

Parameters

A Java String

Returns

A Java Date

Interface java.sql.Driver

Declaration: `public interface **Driver** extends Object`

The `Driver` class contains the method to establish a connection with a given database. Various methods exist to determine the nature of the driver.

```
...

// Load the jdbc-odbc bridge driver
Class.forName ("jdbc.odbc.JdbcOdbcDriver");

// get a Driver object
Driver dr = DriverManager.getDriver ( url );

...
```

See Also: `DriverManager, Connection`

Driver Methods

acceptsURL

Declaration: `public abstract boolean acceptsURL(String url) throws SQLException`

This method determines whether or not the driver can make a connection to the given URL. The driver will return a `boolean` true if the driver can understand the subprotocol specified in the URL and a false is returned if it cannot.

```
...

// Load the jdbc-odbc bridge driver
Class.forName ("jdbc.odbc.JdbcOdbcDriver");

// get a Driver
Driver dr = DriverManager.getDriver ( url );

if ( dr.acceptsURL( url )
   // can continue processing

...
```

Parameters

`url`—A `String` containing the URL

Returns

A Java `boolean`

connect

Declaration: `public abstract Connection connect(String url, Properties info) throws SQLException`

The `connect` method attempts to make a database connection to a given URL and returns a `Connection` object. A NULL will be returned if the driver cannot connect to a particular URL. An `SQLException` will be raised if the driver can connect to the URL but cannot connect to the database.

Parameters are passed for the URL and the `Properties` of the driver. The `Properties` argument can be used to pass a 'user' and 'password' for the database, or provide other information for the connection.

```
...

// Load the jdbc-odbc bridge driver
Class.forName ("jdbc.odbc.JdbcOdbcDriver");

// get a Driver
Driver dr = DriverManager.getDriver ( url );

Connection con = dr.connect( url, info );

...
```

Parameters

`url`—A Java `String` containing the URL

`info`—A `Property` object—a list of arbitrary string tag/value pairs as connection arguments; normally at least a "user" and "password" property should be included

Returns

A `Connection` object for the connection to the URL

getPropertyInfo

Declaration: `public abstract DriverPropertyInfo[] getPropertyInfo(String url, Properties info) throws SQLException`

This method returns information on the current driver in the form of a `DriverPropertyInfo` object. Because additional values may become necessary, `DriverPropertyInfo` is an array.

```
...

// Load the jdbc-odbc bridge driver
Class.forName ("jdbc.odbc.JdbcOdbcDriver");

// get a Driver
Driver dr = DriverManager.getDriver ( url );

DriverPropertyInfo[] drp = dr.getPropertyInfo( url, info );

...
```

Parameters

url—A Java String containing the URL

info—A Properties object containing a list of tag/value pairs

Returns

An array of DriverPropertyInfo objects describing possible properties.

getMajorVersion

Declaration: public abstract int getMajorVersion()

This method returns an integer representing the major version number of the driver.

```
...

// Load the jdbc-odbc bridge driver
Class.forName ("jdbc.odbc.JdbcOdbcDriver");

// get a Driver
Driver dr = DriverManager.getDriver ( url );

System.out.println( "Major version number: " +
                    dr.getMajorVersion() );

...
```

Returns

An int

getMinorVersion

Declaration: `public abstract int getMinorVersion()`

This method returns an integer representing the minor version number of the driver.

```
...

// Load the jdbc-odbc bridge driver
Class.forName ("jdbc.odbc.JdbcOdbcDriver");

// get a Driver
Driver dr = DriverManager.getDriver ( url );

System.out.println( "Minor version number: " +
                    dr.getMinorVersion() );
...
```

Returns

An `int`

jdbcCompliant

Declaration: `public abstract boolean jdbcCompliant()`

This method will return true if the database driver is JDBC compliant. JDBC compliance requires full support for the JDBC API and full support for the SQL 92 Entry Level standard. If the database driver does not support this level, a value of false is returned.

```
...

// Load the jdbc-odbc bridge driver
Class.forName ("jdbc.odbc.JdbcOdbcDriver");

// get a Driver
Driver dr = DriverManager.getDriver ( url );
if ( dr.jdbcCompliant() )
    System.out.println( "Database is JDBC compliant."  )
else
    System.out.println( "Database is NOT JDBC compliant."  )
...
```

Returns

A Java `boolean`

Interface java.sql.DriverManager

Declaration: `public class DriverManager extends Object`

When invoked, the `DriverManager` will use the JDBC driver's property to determine a list of drivers to load and then attempt to load each of these drivers in turn.

The `DriverManager` uses the universal resource locator (URL) mechanism to identify a database resource to use. The format for the URL parameter is

```
jdbc:subprotocol:subname
```

where *subprotocol* indicates the access method used in addition to JDBC and the *subname* is a name that has significance for the *subprotocol* being used. The *subprotocol* identifies a particular type of database connectivity mechanism that may be supported by one or more drivers. The contents and syntax of the *subname* depend on the *subprotocol*. The following syntax has been recommended for the *subname*

```
//hostname:port/subname
```

See Also: `Driver, Connection`

DriverManager

```
public DriverManager()
```

DriverManager Methods

deregisterDriver

Declaration: `public static void deregisterDriver(Driver driver) throws SQLException`

This method will deregister a specific driver from the `DriverManager`'s list of drivers. Applets can only deregister `Drivers` from their own classloader. A single parameter is supplied for the `Driver` object which references the driver to deregister.

```
...

import java.sql.*;
import java.io.*;

...
```

```
Class.forName ("jdbc.odbc.JdbcOdbcDriver");
String url = "jdbc:odbc:msaccessdb";

Driver drv = DriverManager.getDriver( url );
DriverManager.deregisterDriver( drv );

...
```

Parameters

`driver`–the JDBC Driver to deregister

getConnection

Declaration: `public static synchronized Connection getConnection(String url, Properties info) throws SQLException`

This method attempts to connect to a given database URL. The `DriverManager` will select an appropriate driver from the set of registered JDBC drivers.

Parameters are passed for the URL (universal resource locator), and information on the `Properties` for the connection. If the connection is successful, then a `Connection` object is returned by the method.

```
...

import java.sql.*;
import java.io.*;
import java.util.Date;

...
     Class.forName ("jdbc.odbc.JdbcOdbcDriver");
     String url = "jdbc:odbc:msaccessdb";
     Properties info = new Properties();
     p.put( "user", "sam");
     p.put( "password", "x12345" );
 ...
     Connection con = DriverManager.getConnection ( url, info );
     Statement stmt = con.createStatement();
...
```

Parameters

url—A Java String containing database URL of the form jdbc:*subprotocol*:*subname*

info—a Properites object containing a list of arbitrary string tag/value pairs as connection arguments; normally at least a "user" and "password" property should be included.

Returns

A Connection object connected to the URL

getConnection

Declaration: public static synchronized Connection getConnection(String url, String user, String password) throws SQLException

This method overloads the getConnection method. It attempts to connect to a given URL supplied with parameters for URL, user name and password. The URL is supplied in the form

jdbc:subprotocol:subname

```
...

import java.sql.*;
import java.io.*;
import java.util.Date;

...
    Class.forName ("jdbc.odbc.JdbcOdbcDriver");

    String url = "jdbc:odbc:msaccessdb";
    String userName = "fred';
    String passWord = "xxaa42";

    Connection con = DriverManager.getConnection ( url,
                                                   userName,
                                                   passWord );

    Statement stmt = con.createStatement();
...
```

Parameters

url—a Java String containing the database URL
user—a Java String containing the user's name
password—a Java String containing the user's password

Returns

A Connection object with a connection to the designated URL

getConnection

Declaration: public static synchronized Connection getConnection(String url) throws SQLException

This method attempts to establish a connection to the given database URL. The appropriate driver will be selected from the list of registered drivers. It receives a single String parameter containing the URL in the form

jdbc:subprotocol:subname

The method returns a Connection object with a connection to the designated URL.

```
...

import java.sql.*;
import java.io.*;

...
     Class.forName ("jdbc.odbc.JdbcOdbcDriver");
     String url = "jdbc:odbc:msaccessdb";
     Connection con = DriverManager.getConnection ( url );
     Statement stmt = con.createStatement();
...
```

Parameters

url—A Java String containing the database URL

Returns

A Connection object with a connection to the designated URL.

getDriver

Declaration: public static Driver getDriver(String url) throws SQLException

This method locates a driver that can process the URL. A single `String` parameter is used to supply the URL. The URL must be in the format

```
jdbc:subprotocol:subname
```

The method returns a `Driver` object that can process the URL.

```
...

import java.sql.*;
import java.io.*;
import java.sql.Date;

...
      Class.forName ("jdbc.odbc.JdbcOdbcDriver");
      String url = "jdbc:odbc:msaccessdb";

      Driver drv = DriverManager.getDriver( url );

...
```

Parameters

`url`—A Java `String` containing the database URL

Returns

A `Driver` object that can connect to the URL

getDrivers

Declaration: `public static Enumeration getDrivers()`

This method returns an enumeration of all the currently loaded JDBC drivers the user can access. The enumerated list will contain the `Driver`'s currently loaded by the caller's class loader. (Note: The class name of a driver can be found using `d.getClass().getName()`)

```
...

import java.sql.*;
import java.io.*;
import java.util.*;

...
```

```
Class.forName ("jdbc.odbc.JdbcOdbcDriver");
String url = "jdbc:odbc:msaccessdb";
Enumeration en = DriverManager.getDrivers();

System.out.println( "Drivers loaded: " );
while ( en.hasMoreElements() )
      System.out.println( en.nextElement() +
                                "—" );

...
```

Returns

An `Enumeration` object

getLoginTimeout

Declaration: `public static int getLoginTimeout()`

This method returns the maximum time in seconds that drivers will wait when attempting to login to a database. It returns an integer with the time-out value.

```
...

import java.sql.*;
import java.io.*;

...
   Class.forName ("jdbc.odbc.JdbcOdbcDriver");

   String url = "jdbc:odbc:msaccessdb";
   String userName = "fred';
   String passWord = "xxxxxx42";

   Connection con = DriverManager.getConnection ( url,
                                                  userName,
                                                  passWord );

   System.out.println( "Login timeout is " +
                  DriverManager.getLoginTimeout( ) );
```

```
...
```

Returns

An `int`

getLogStream

Declaration: `public static PrintStream getLogStream()`

This method retrieves the logging/tracing `PrintStream` being used by the `DriverManager` and all loaded JDBC drivers. A `PrintStream` object is returned by the method; if logging/tracing is disabled, the method returns a NULL.

```
...

import java.sql.*;
import java.io.*;

...
     Class.forName ("jdbc.odbc.JdbcOdbcDriver");

     String url = "jdbc:odbc:msaccessdb";
     String userName = "fred';
     String passWord = "freddie42";

     Connection con = DriverManager.getConnection ( url,
                                                    userName,
                                                    passWord );

     PrintStream errorLogPS = DriverManager.getLogStream( );
```

Returns

A `PrintStream` object

println

Declaration: `public static synchronized void println(String message)`

This method prints a message to the JDBC logging/tracing `Printstream`. A single `String` parameter is used to supply the message.

```
...

import java.sql.*;
import java.io.*;
import java.util.Date;

...
      Class.forName ("jdbc.odbc.JdbcOdbcDriver");

      String url = "jdbc:odbc:msaccessdb";
      String userName = "fred';
      String passWord = "xxxxxx42";

      Connection con = DriverManager.getConnection ( url,
                                                     userName,
                                                     passWord );

      DriverManager.println( "An error has occurred …" );

...
```

Parameters

message—a String containing a log or tracing message

registerDriver

Declaration: public static synchronized void registerDriver(Driver driver) throws SQLException

This method registers the loaded driver with the DriverManager. A Driver object is supplied as a parameter.

```
...

import java.sql.*;
import java.io.*;
import java.util.Date;

...
```

```
    Class.forName ("jdbc.odbc.JdbcOdbcDriver");
    String url = "jdbc:odbc:msaccessdb";

    Driver drv = DriverManager.getDriver( url );
    DriverManager.registerDriver( drv );

...
```

Parameters

driver—the JDBC Driver

setLoginTimeout

Declaration: `public static void setLoginTimeout(int seconds)`

This method sets the maximum time in seconds that drivers can wait when attempting to login to a database. A single integer parameter is used to supply the number of seconds for the timeout.

```
...

import java.sql.*;
import java.io.*;
import java.util.Date;

...
    Class.forName ("jdbc.odbc.JdbcOdbcDriver");

    String url = "jdbc:odbc:msaccessdb";
    String userName = "fred';
    String passWord = "xxxxx42";

    Connection con = DriverManager.getConnection ( url,
                                                   userName,
                                                   passWord );
    DriverManager.setLoginTimeout( 60 );

...
```

Parameters

seconds—an int containing the driver login time limit

setLogStream

Declaration: `public static void setLogStream(PrintStream out)`

This method establishes a logging/tracing `PrintStream` that is used by the `DriverManager` and all loaded JDBC drivers. A single parameter is used to supply the `PrintStream` object. Passing a NULL value as a parameter will disable the logging/tracing activity.

```
...

import java.sql.*;
import java.io.*;
import java.util.Date;

...
     Class.forName ("jdbc.odbc.JdbcOdbcDriver");

     String url = "jdbc:odbc:msaccessdb";
     String userName = "fred';
     String passWord = "xxxxxx42";

     Connection con = DriverManager.getConnection ( url,
                                          userName,
                                          passWord );

      PrintStream  errorLogFile = new PrintStream(
                       new BufferedOutputStream(
                             (new FileOutputStream(

                                 "errorOutput.log" )) ));

     DriverManager.setLogStream( errorLogFile );

...
```

Parameters

`out`—a `PrintStream` object

Interface java.sql.DriverPropertyInfo

Declaration: `public class` **`DriverPropertyInfo`** `extends Object`

The `DriverProperty` class provides methods to discover and supply properties for drivers.

Variables

choices

Declaration: `public String choices[]`

If the value variable is selected from a set of values, then this set of values is supplied in this array. If there are not multiple choices available, then this array would be set to NULL.

description

Declaration: `public String description`

This variable contains a description of the property.

name

Declaration: `public String name`

This variable contains the name of the property.

required

Declaration: `public boolean required`

This `boolean` variable is set to true if a value must be supplied for this property during a `Driver` connect operation. If this variable is not set, then the `Property` is optional.

value

Declaration: `public String value`

This variable specifies the current value of the property.

This is supplied based on information from the Java environment and driver supplied default values. If no value is known then this may be a NULL value.

Constructor

DriverPropertyInfo

Declaration: `public DriverPropertyInfo(String name, String value)`

This is the initial constructor for the class. Java `String` parameters are supplied for the name of the property and the value to retrieve.

Class java.sql.NullData

Declaration: `public class NullData extends SQLWarning`

A `NullData` warning is generated when a NULL value is detected during a `getXXX` or `getObject` call. The `SQLstate` for a `NullData` is set to '01J01', a vendor-specific state.

Variables

index

Declaration: `public int index`

The index or ordinal position of the column or parameter containing the NULL value. This value may be -1 if the index is unknown. If the index is unknown, then the parameter variable `parameter` should be ignored.

```
...
    catch ( NullData nd ) {

      System.out.println( "Null data at position " + nd.index );
}
...
```

Declaration: `public boolean parameter`

This variable is set to true if the NULL value was a parameter; it is set to false if the value was not a parameter.

```
...
    catch ( NullData nd ) {

   if ( nd.parameter )
     System.out.println( "Null data in parameter " );
   else
      System.out.printn( "Null data in column" );
}
...
```

Constructor

NullData

Declaration: `public NullData()`

This method is the constructor for a `NullData` object.

Interface java.sql.PreparedStatement

Declaration: `public interface PreparedStatement extends Object extends Statement`

The `PreparedStatement` interface provides methods that allow SQL statements to be prepareted and optimized by the database engine before being executed. This improves performance for SQL statements that will be executed repeatedly.

Various 'set' methods exist for setting the IN parameter values in the SQL statement. The appropriate 'set' method must be used for the correct parameter data type. For example, if a parameter is an integer, then the `setInt` method should be used to set the value of the parameter. For parameters where there is no appropriate 'set' method, then `setObject` method should be used. The following code example demonstrates the use of this class.

```
import java.sql.*;
import java.io.*;
import java.util.Date;

class PrepTest2 {

     public static void main( String argv[] ) {

       try {

           Class.forName ("jdbc.odbc.JdbcOdbcDriver");

           String url = "jdbc:odbc:msaccessdb";

           Connection con = DriverManager.getConnection (
                                                  url, "", "");

           String qs = "select * from loadtest where col1 = ? ";
           PreparedStatement prepStmt = con.prepareStatement(
                                                         qs );

           boolean result;

           prepStmt.setInt( 1, 33 );
           ResultSet rs = prepStmt.executeQuery();
           boolean more = rs.next();
```

```
            for (; n < 2000 && more ; n++ ) {
                prepStmt.setInt( 1, n );

                rs.close();
                rs    = prepStmt.executeQuery();
                more = rs.next();

            }

         }

        catch (java.lang.Exception ex) {
        // Print description of the exception.
        System.out.println( "** Error on data select. ** " );
        ex.printStackTrace ();

        }
    }
}
```

In this example, a `PreparedStatement` object is instantiated via the `Connection` object using the method `prepareStatement`. Note that the `prepareStatement` method requires the query string to be passed as a parameter. The query string can have a number of '?' parameter place-holders for IN parameters, but this is not required.

Once the statement has been prepared, the value of the first parameter is set with the `setInt` method. The 'set' method used must match the data type being set. The prepared statement is then executed using the `executeQuery` method. This method returns a `ResultSet` object which is positioned before its first member using the `next` method.

A 'for' loop is then used to execute the query a number of times. Before each invocation of the `executeQuery` method, the `ResultSet` is closed using its `close` method. This allows the `ResultSet` object to be used again in the next call to the `executeQuery` method.

See Also: `prepareStatement`, `ResultSet`

PreparedStatement Methods

clearParameters

Declaration: `public abstract void clearParameters() throws SQLException`

This method clears all current values in a statement's parameter list. (Note that setting a parameter automatically clears its previous value.)

```
import java.sql.*;
import java.io.*;

class PrepTest {

     public static void main( String argv[] ) {

       try {

          Class.forName ("jdbc.odbc.JdbcOdbcDriver");

          String url = "jdbc:odbc:msaccessdb";

          Connection con = DriverManager.getConnection (
                                                 url, "", "");

          String qs = "update catalog set item_count = ? " +
                        " where order_num = ?  ";
          PreparedStatement prepStmt = con.prepareStatement( qs );


          prepStmt.clearParameters();
          prepStmt.setInt( 1, 10 );
          prepStmt.setInt( 2, 12345 );

          int result = prepStmt.executeUpdate();

       }

       catch (java.lang.Exception ex) {

       // Print description of the exception.
       System.out.println( "** Error on data update. ** " );
       ex.printStackTrace ();

       }
```

```
    }
}
```

execute

Declaration: `public abstract boolean execute() throws SQLException`

This method executes an SQL query. It is used primarily for the statements that return multiple results. In the event a statement returns multiple results, the methods `execute`, `getMoreResults`, `getResultSet`, and `getUpdateCount` would be used to retrieve the multiple results from the database. An example of this process is shown in the following code.

```
import java.sql.*;
import java.io.*;

class PrepTest3 {

     public static void main( String argv[] ) {

       try {

            Class.forName ("jdbc.odbc.JdbcOdbcDriver");

            String url = "jdbc:odbc:msaccessdb";

            Connection con = DriverManager.getConnection (
                                                url, "", "");

            String qs = " select * from customerView";
            PreparedStatement stmt = con.prepareStatement( qs );

            int n = 1;

            boolean more = stmt.execute();

            if ( more )
                 System.out.println( "ResultSet has been returned." );
            else {
              System.out.println( "No ResultSet has been returned." );
```

```
            System.exit( -1 );

        }

        // read the first ResultSet
        ResultSet rs = stmt.getResultSet();
        more = rs.next();
        for (; n < 2000 && more ; n++ ) {

            more = rs.next();
            System.out.println( "Col1: " + rs.getInt( 1 ) );

        }

        // read the second ResultSet

        more = stmt.getMoreResults();
        if ( !(more) ) {
            System.out.println( "No more results." );
            System.exit( -1 );
        }

        ResultSet rs1 = stmt.getResultSet();
        more = rs1.next();
        for (; n < 2000 && more ; n++ ) {

            more = rs1.next();
            System.out.println( "Col1: " + rs.getInt( 1 ) );

        }


    }

    catch (java.lang.Exception ex) {

   // Print description of the exception.
   System.out.println( "** Error on data insert. ** " );
   ex.printStackTrace ();
```

```
        }

    }

}
```

Returns

A Java `boolean` which is true if the result is a `ResultSet`, false if the result is an integer.

See Also: `execute`

executeQuery

Declaration: `public abstract ResultSet executeQuery() throws SQLException`

This method executes a prepared SQL statement, the text of which was passed to the `PreparedStatement` object when it was instantiated. The result is returned in a `ResultSet` object.

```
import java.sql.*;
import java.io.*;

class PrepTest {

     public static void main( String argv[] ) {

       try {

            Class.forName ("jdbc.odbc.JdbcOdbcDriver");

            String url = "jdbc:odbc:msaccessdb";

            Connection con = DriverManager.getConnection (
                                                 url, "", "");

            String qs = "select * from orders" +
                          " where order_num = ? ";
            PreparedStatement prepStmt = con.prepareStatement(
                                                        qs );
```

```
            prepStmt.setInt( 1, 12345 );
            ResultSet rs = prepStmt.executeQuery();

        }

        catch (java.lang.Exception ex) {

        // Print description of the exception.
        System.out.println( "** Error on data update. ** " );
        ex.printStackTrace ();

        }
    }
}
```

Returns

A ResultSet that contains the data produced by the query

executeUpdate

Declaration: public abstract int executeUpdate() throws SQLException

This method executes a prepared SQL statement that is not expected to return values—an insert, update, or delete statement or a SQL DDL statement. The method returns an integer with the count of rows affected by the update or a 0 for SQL statements that return nothing.

```
import java.sql.*;
import java.io.*;

class PrepTest {

      public static void main( String argv[] ) {

        try {

            Class.forName ("jdbc.odbc.JdbcOdbcDriver");

            String url = "jdbc:odbc:msaccessdb";

            Connection con = DriverManager.getConnection (
```

```
                                    url, "", "");

         String qs = "update orders set shipped_flag = 'S' " +
                          " where order_num = ? ";
         PreparedStatement prepStmt = con.prepareStatement( qs );

         prepStmt.setInt( 1, 12345 );
         int result = prepStmt.executeUpdate();

      }

      catch (java.lang.Exception ex) {
      // Print description of the exception.
      System.out.println( "** Error on data update. ** " );
      ex.printStackTrace ();

      }
   }
}
```

Returns

An integer row count or 0

setAsciiStream

Declaration: `public abstract void setAsciiStream(int parameterIndex, InputStream x, int length) throws SQLException`

This method sets a parameter to a Java `InputStream`. JDBC will then read from the data stream until it reaches end-of-file. For very large volumes of ASCII data, this is a more practical approach to moving the data.

Arguments are supplied for the parameter index (the ordinal position of the parameter in the parameter list) the `InputStream` (an instantiation of `java.io.InputStream`) and the length of the input stream in bytes. The driver will perform any conversion necessary to convert the data the SQL CHAR format.

```
import java.sql.*;
import java.io.*;

class PrepTest {
```

```
    public static void main( String argv[] ) {

      try {

          Class.forName ("jdbc.odbc.JdbcOdbcDriver");

          String url = "jdbc:odbc:msaccessdb";

          Connection con = DriverManager.getConnection (
                                                  url, "", "");

          String qs = "update catalog set item_desc = ? " +
                     " where order_num = ?  ";
          PreparedStatement prepStmt = con.prepareStatement( qs );

          setAsciiStream(1,
                      inpStream,
                      2500 );

          prepStmt.setInt( 2, 12345 );

          int result = prepStmt.executeUpdate();

      }

      catch (java.lang.Exception ex) {

      // Print description of the exception.
      System.out.println( "** Error on data update. ** " );
      ex.printStackTrace ();

      }
   }
}
```

Parameters

`parameterIndex`—an integer representing the parameter index
`x`—A Java `InputStream`
`length`—an integer representing the number of bytes in the stream

setBinaryStream

Declaration: `public abstract void setBinaryStream(int parameterIndex, InputStream x, int length)throws SQLException`

This method sets a parameter to a Java `InputStream`. JDBC will then read from the data stream until it reaches end-of-file. For very large volumes of binary data for a LONGVARBINARY parameter, this is a more practical approach to moving the data.

Arguments are supplied for the parameter index (the ordinal position of the parameter in the parameter list) the `InputStream` (an instantiation of `java.io.InputStream`) and the length of the input stream in bytes.

```
import java.sql.*;
import java.io.*;

class PrepTest {

     public static void main( String argv[] ) {

       try {

          Class.forName ("jdbc.odbc.JdbcOdbcDriver");

          String url = "jdbc:odbc:msaccessdb";

          Connection con = DriverManager.getConnection (
                                                url, "", "");

          String qs = "update catalog set item_desc = ? " +
                      " where order_num = ?  ";
          PreparedStatement prepStmt = con.prepareStatement( qs );

          setBinaryStream(1,
                          inpStream,
                          2500 );

          prepStmt.setInt( 2, 12345 );

          int result = prepStmt.executeUpdate();
```

```
        }

        catch (java.lang.Exception ex) {

        // Print description of the exception.
        System.out.println( "** Error on data update. ** " );
        ex.printStackTrace ();

        }
    }
}
```

Parameters

`parameterIndex`—an integer representing the parameter index
`x`—A Java `InputStream`
`length`—an integer representing the number of bytes in the stream

setBoolean

Declaration: `public abstract void setBoolean(int parameterIndex, boolean x) throws SQLException`

This method sets a parameter to a Java `boolean` value. Arguments are used indicate the parameter index and `boolean` value to set. The driver converts the `boolean` value parameter to an SQL BIT before sending it to the database.

```
import java.sql.*;
import java.io.*;

class PrepTest {

    public static void main( String argv[] ) {

      try {

        Class.forName ("jdbc.odbc.JdbcOdbcDriver");

        String url = "jdbc:odbc:msaccessdb";

        Connection con = DriverManager.getConnection (
```

```
                                        url, "", "");
        String qs = "update orders set shipped_flag = 'S' " +
                    " where shipped = ? ";
        PreparedStatement prepStmt = con.prepareStatement( qs );

        prepStmt.setBoolean( 1, true );
        int result = prepStmt.executeUpdate();

    }

    catch (java.lang.Exception ex) {

    // Print description of the exception.
    System.out.println( "** Error on data update. ** " );
    ex.printStackTrace ();

    }
  }
}
```

Parameters

`parameterIndex`—an integer representing the parameter index

`x`—the `boolean` value

setByte

Declaration: `public abstract void setByte(int parameterIndex, byte x) throws SQLException`

This method sets a parameter to a Java `byte` value. Arguments are supplied for the parameter index or ordinal position of the parameter in the parameter list and the `byte` value to set the column. The driver converts the byte value parameter to a SQL TINYINT before sending the value to the database.

```
import java.sql.*;
import java.io.*;

class PrepTest {

    public static void main( String argv[] ) {
```

```
        try {

            Class.forName ("jdbc.odbc.JdbcOdbcDriver");

            String url = "jdbc:odbc:msaccessdb";

            Connection con = DriverManager.getConnection (
                                                url, "", "");

            String qs = " select * from orders " +
                        " where tax_percent = ? ";
            PreparedStatement prepStmt = con.prepareStatement( qs );

            prepStmt.setByte( 1, 10 );
            int result = prepStmt.executeQuery();

        }

        catch (java.lang.Exception ex) {

        // Print description of the exception.
        System.out.println( "** Error on data select. ** " );
        ex.printStackTrace ();

        }
    }
}
```

Parameters

`parameterIndex`—an integer representing the parameter index
`x`—the byte value

setBytes

Declaration: `public abstract void setBytes(int parameterIndex, byte x[]) throws SQLException`

This method sets a parameter to a Java `byte` array value. Arguments are supplied for the `parameterIndex` (the ordinal position of the parameter in the parameter list) and the `byte` array value. The database converts the `byte` array value value to a SQL VARBINARY or LONGVARBINARY value before sending the parameter to the database.

```
import java.sql.*;
import java.io.*;

class PrepTest {

     public static void main( String argv[] ) {

       try {

          Class.forName ("jdbc.odbc.JdbcOdbcDriver");

          String url = "jdbc:odbc:msaccessdb";

          Connection con = DriverManager.getConnection (
                                              url, "", "");

          String qs = "update orders set flags = ? " +
                      " where order_num = ?  ";
          PreparedStatement prepStmt = con.prepareStatement( qs );

          byte y = new byte[10];
          y[1] = 1;
          y[2] = 2;
          y[3] = 3;
          prepStmt.setBytes( 1, y );
          prepStmt.setInt( 2, 12345 );

          int result = prepStmt.executeUpdate();

       }

       catch (java.lang.Exception ex) {

       // Print description of the exception.
       System.out.println( "** Error on data update. ** " );
       ex.printStackTrace ();

       }
    }
```

```
}
```

Parameters

parameterIndex—an integer representing the parameter index
x—A Java byte array

setDate

Declaration: public abstract void setDate(int parameterIndex, Date x) throws SQLException

This method sets a parameter to a Java Date value. Arguments are supplied for the parameterIndex (the ordinal position of the parameter in the parameter list) and the Date value. The database converts the Java Date value to a SQL Date value before sending the parameter to the database.

```
import java.sql.*;
import java.io.*;

class PrepTest {

     public static void main( String argv[] ) {

       try {

          Class.forName ("jdbc.odbc.JdbcOdbcDriver");

          String url = "jdbc:odbc:msaccessdb";

          Connection con = DriverManager.getConnection (
                                                url, "", "");

          String qs = "update orders set order_date = ? " +
                      " where order_num = ?  ";
          PreparedStatement prepStmt = con.prepareStatement( qs );

          Date d = Date.valueOf( "1958-01-28" );
          prepStmt.setDate( 1, d );
          prepStmt.setInt( 2, 12345 );
```

```
            int result = prepStmt.executeUpdate();

        }
        catch (java.lang.Exception ex) {

        // Print description of the exception.
        System.out.println( "** Error on data update. ** " );
        ex.printStackTrace ();

        }
    }
}
```

Parameters

parameterIndex—an integer representing the parameter index

x—A Java Date

setDouble

Declaration: public abstract void setDouble(int parameterIndex, double x) throws SQLException

This method sets a parameter to a Java double value. Arguments are supplied for the parameterIndex (the ordinal position of the parameter in the parameter list) and the Java double value. The database converts the double value to a SQL DOUBLE before sending the parameter to the database.

```
import java.sql.*;
import java.io.*;

class PrepTest {

      public static void main( String argv[] ) {

        try {

            Class.forName ("jdbc.odbc.JdbcOdbcDriver");

            String url = "jdbc:odbc:msaccessdb";

            Connection con = DriverManager.getConnection (
```

```
                                url, "", "");

            String qs = "update orders set order_amount = ? " +
                        " where order_num = ?  ";
            PreparedStatement prepStmt = con.prepareStatement( qs );

            double x = 123456.77;
            prepStmt.setDouble( 1, x );
            prepStmt.setInt( 2, 12345 );

            int result = prepStmt.executeUpdate();

        }

        catch (java.lang.Exception ex) {

        // Print description of the exception.
        System.out.println( "** Error on data update. ** " );
        ex.printStackTrace ();

        }
    }
}
```

Parameters

parameterIndex—an integer representing the parameter index
x—the double value

setFloat

Declaration: `public abstract void setFloat(int parameterIndex, float x) throws SQLException`

This method sets a parameter to a Java `float` value. Arguments are supplied for the `parameterIndex` (the ordinal position of the parameter in the parameter list) and the Java `float` value. The database converts the Java `float` value to a SQL FLOAT before sending the parameter to the database.

```
import java.sql.*;
import java.io.*;

class PrepTest {
```

```
public static void main( String argv[] ) {

  try {

     Class.forName ("jdbc.odbc.JdbcOdbcDriver");

     String url = "jdbc:odbc:msaccessdb";

     Connection con = DriverManager.getConnection (
                                   url, "", "");

     String qs = "update orders set order_amount = ? " +
                 " where order_num = ?  ";
     PreparedStatement prepStmt = con.prepareStatement( qs );

     Float x = 123456.77;
     prepStmt.setFloat( 1, x );
     prepStmt.setInt( 2, 12345 );

     int result = prepStmt.executeUpdate();

  }

  catch (java.lang.Exception ex) {

  // Print description of the exception.
  System.out.println( "** Error on data update. ** " );
  ex.printStackTrace ();

  }
 }
}
```

Parameters

parameterIndex—an integer representing the parameter index
x—a Java float value

setInt

Declaration: public abstract void setInt(int parameterIndex, int x) throws SQLException

This method sets a parameter to an integer value. Arguments are supplied for the parameter index (the ordinal position of the parameter in the parameter list) and the integer (Java int) value. The driver converts the int value to a SQL INTEGER value before sending it to the database.

```
import java.sql.*;
import java.io.*;

class PrepTest {

     public static void main( String argv[] ) {

       try {

          Class.forName ("jdbc.odbc.JdbcOdbcDriver");

          String url = "jdbc:odbc:msaccessdb";

          Connection con = DriverManager.getConnection (
                                                  url, "", "");

          String qs = "update orders set shipped_flag = 'S' " +
                      " where order_num = ? ";
          PreparedStatement prepStmt = con.prepareStatement( qs );

          prepStmt.setInt( 1, 12345 );
          int result = prepStmt.executeUpdate();

      }

      catch (java.lang.Exception ex) {

      // Print description of the exception.
```

```
        System.out.println( "** Error on data update. ** " );
        ex.printStackTrace ();

        }
    }
}
```

Parameters

parameterIndex—an integer representing the parameter index

x—the Java int value

setLong

Declaration: public abstract void setLong(int parameterIndex,long x) throws SQLException

This method sets a parameter to a Java long value. Arguments are supplied for the parameterIndex (the ordinal position of the parameter in the parameter list) and the long integer value. The database converts the long integer value to a SQL BIGINT before sending the parameter to the database.

```
import java.sql.*;
import java.io.*;

class PrepTest {
      public static void main( String argv[] ) {

        try {

            Class.forName ("jdbc.odbc.JdbcOdbcDriver");

            String url = "jdbc:odbc:msaccessdb";

            Connection con = DriverManager.getConnection (
                                              url, "", "");

           String qs = "update orders set shipped_flag = 'S' " +
                          " where order_num = ? ";
            PreparedStatement prepStmt = con.prepareStatement( qs );
```

```
            prepStmt.setLong( 1, 12345 );
            int result = prepStmt.executeUpdate();

        }

        catch (java.lang.Exception ex) {

        // Print description of the exception.
        System.out.println( "** Error on data update. ** " );
        ex.printStackTrace ();

        }
    }
}
```

Parameters

parameterIndex—an integer representing the parameter index
x—the long integer value

setNull

Declaration: `public abstract void setNull( int parameterIndex, int sqlType) throws SQLException`

This method sets the SQL parameter to a NULL value. Arguments are used to supply the index (the ordinal position) of the parameter to set and the data type of the parameter. The sqlType code is defined in java.sql.Types.

```
import java.sql.*;
import java.io.*;

class PrepTest {

     public static void main( String argv[] ) {

       try {

          Class.forName ("jdbc.odbc.JdbcOdbcDriver");

          String url = "jdbc:odbc:msaccessdb";
```

```
            Connection con = DriverManager.getConnection (
                                              url, "", "");

            String qs = "select * from orders " +
                         " where ship_date = ? ";
            PreparedStatement prepStmt = con.prepareStatement(
                                                        qs );
            prepStmt.setNull( 1, Types.DATE );
            int result = prepStmt.executeQuery();

        }

        catch (java.lang.Exception ex) {

        // Print description of the exception.
        System.out.println( "** Error on data update. ** " );
        ex.printStackTrace ();

        }
    }
}
```

Parameters

`parameterindex`—an integer representing the parameter index

`sqlType`—an integer representing the SQL data type from java.sql.Types

setNumeric

Declaration: `public abstract void setNumeric(int parameterIndex, Numeric x) throws SQLException`

This method sets a parameter to a `Numeric` value. Arguments are supplied for the `parameterIndex` (the ordinal position of the parameter in the parameter list) and the `Numeric` value. The database converts the `Numeric` value to a SQL NUMERIC before sending the parameter to the database.

```
import java.sql.*;
import java.io.*;

class PrepTest {
```

```
    public static void main( String argv[] ) {

      try {

          Class.forName ("jdbc.odbc.JdbcOdbcDriver");

          String url = "jdbc:odbc:msaccessdb";

          Connection con = DriverManager.getConnection (
                                                url, "", "");

          String qs = "update orders set order_amount = ? " +
                      " where order_num = ?  ";
          PreparedStatement prepStmt = con.prepareStatement( qs );

          Numeric x = new Numeric( "123456.77" );
          prepStmt.setNumeric( 1, x );
          prepStmt.setInt( 2, 12345 );

          int result = prepStmt.executeUpdate();

      }

      catch (java.lang.Exception ex) {

      // Print description of the exception.
      System.out.println( "** Error on data update. ** " );
      ex.printStackTrace ();

      }
   }
}
```

Parameters

`parameterIndex`—an integer representing the parameter index
`x`—a Java `Numeric` value

setObject

Declaration: `public abstract void setObject(int parameterIndex, Object x, int targetSqlType, int scale) throws SQLException`

This method sets the value of a parameter using an `Object` to supply the value. It is used primarily to pass database specific data types by using a Driver specific Java type and using a `targetSQLType` of `java.sql.types.OTHER`.

Arguments are supplied for the parameter index (the ordinal position of the parameter in the parameter list), the object, the `targetSQLType` and the scale of the object. The scale argument is used for `java.sql.Types.DECIMAL` or `java.sql.Types.NUMERIC` types; for any other data type this argument is ignored.

```
import java.sql.*;
import java.io.*;

class PrepTest {

     public static void main( String argv[] ) {

       try {

          Class.forName ("jdbc.odbc.JdbcOdbcDriver");

          String url = "jdbc:odbc:msaccessdb";

          Connection con = DriverManager.getConnection (
                                            url, "", "");

          String qs = "update catalog set item_disc = ? " +
                      " where order_num = ?  ";
          PreparedStatement prepStmt = con.prepareStatement( qs );

          setObject(1, (Object) MyObj, Types.DECIMAL, 2 );
          prepStmt.setInt( 2, 12345 );

          int result = prepStmt.executeUpdate();

     }
```

```
        catch (java.lang.Exception ex) {

        // Print description of the exception.
        System.out.println( "** Error on data update. ** " );
        ex.printStackTrace ();

        }
    }
}
```

Parameters

parameterIndex—an integer representing the parameter index

x—a Java Object containing the input parameter value

targetSqlType—the SQL type (as defined in java.sql.Types) to be sent to the database

scale—a Java int representing the scale, if needed

See Also: Types

setObject

Declaration: public abstract void setObject(int parameterIndex, Object x, int targetSqlType) throws SQLException

This method sets the value of a parameter using an Object. It is used primarily to pass database specific data types by using a Driver specific Java type and using a targetSQLType of java.sql.types.OTHER.

This method overloads setObject and unlike the alternative that passes a scale argument, this version assumes a scale of zero.

Arguments are supplied for the parameter index (the ordinal position of the parameter in the parameter list), the object and the targetSQLType.

```
import java.sql.*;
import java.io.*;

class PrepTest {

    public static void main( String argv[] ) {

        try {

            Class.forName ("jdbc.odbc.JdbcOdbcDriver");
```

```
            String url = "jdbc:odbc:msaccessdb";

            Connection con = DriverManager.getConnection (
                                                url, "", "");

           String qs = "update catalog set item_desc = ? " +
                       " where order_num = ?  ";
            PreparedStatement prepStmt = con.prepareStatement( qs );

            setObject(1, (Object) MyObj, Types.OTHER );
            prepStmt.setInt( 2, 12345 );

            int result = prepStmt.executeUpdate();

        }

        catch (java.lang.Exception ex) {

        // Print description of the exception.
        System.out.println( "** Error on data update. ** " );
        ex.printStackTrace ();

        }
    }
}
```

Parameters

`parameterIndex`—an integer representing the parameter index

`x`—a Java `Object` containing the input parameter value

`targetSqlType`—the SQL type (as defined in `java.sql.Types`) to be sent to the database

setObject

Declaration: `public abstract void setObject(int parameterIndex, Object x) throws SQLException`

This method sets the value of a parameter using an object. It is used primarily to pass database specific data types by using a Driver specific Java type and using a `targetSQLType` of `java.sql.Types.OTHER`.

This method overloads `setObject` and unlike the alternative that passes a scale argument, this version assumes a scale of zero.

Arguments are supplied for the parameter index (the ordinal position of the parameter in the parameter list) and the Java `Object`. The given argument will be converted to the SQL type (from `java.sql.Types`) for the parameter before being sent to the database.

```
import java.sql.*;
import java.io.*;

class PrepTest {

     public static void main( String argv[] ) {

       try {

          Class.forName ("jdbc.odbc.JdbcOdbcDriver");

          String url = "jdbc:odbc:msaccessdb";

          Connection con = DriverManager.getConnection (
                                                url, "", "");

          String qs = "update catalog set item_dist = ? " +
                       " where order_num = ?  ";
          PreparedStatement prepStmt = con.prepareStatement( qs );

          setObject(1, (Object) MyObj );
          prepStmt.setInt( 2, 12345 );

          int result = prepStmt.executeUpdate();

      }

      catch (java.lang.Exception ex) {

      // Print description of the exception.
      System.out.println( "** Error on data update. ** " );
      ex.printStackTrace ();
```

```
        }
    }
}
```

Parameters

parameterIndex—an integer representing the parameter index

x—a Java Object containing the input parameter value

setShort

Declaration: public abstract void setShort(int parameterIndex,short x) throws SQLException

This method sets a parameter to a Java short value. Arguments are supplied for the parameter index (the ordinal position of the parameter in the parameter list) and the short integer value. The driver converts the short integer parameter value to a SQL SMALLINT before sending it to the database.

```
import java.sql.*;
import java.io.*;

class PrepTest {

     public static void main( String argv[] ) {

       try {

          Class.forName ("jdbc.odbc.JdbcOdbcDriver");

          String url = "jdbc:odbc:msaccessdb";

          Connection con = DriverManager.getConnection (
                                          url, "", "");

          String qs = " select * from orders " +
                      " where order_num = ? ";
          PreparedStatement prepStmt = con.prepareStatement( qs );

          prepStmt.setShort( 1, 12345 );
```

```
            int result = prepStmt.executeUpdate();

        }

        catch (java.lang.Exception ex) {

        // Print description of the exception.
        System.out.println( "** Error on data update. ** " );
        ex.printStackTrace ();

        }
    }
}
```

Parameters

parameterIndex—an integer representing the parameter index
x—the short integer value

setString

Declaration: public abstract void setString(int parameterIndex, String x) throws SQLException

This method sets a parameter to a Java String value. Arguments are supplied for the parameterIndex (the ordinal position of the parameter in the parameter list) and the String value. The database converts the String value to a SQL VARCHAR or LONGVARCHAR value before sending the parameter to the database.

```
import java.sql.*;
import java.io.*;

class PrepTest {

     public static void main( String argv[] ) {

       try {

           Class.forName ("jdbc.odbc.JdbcOdbcDriver");

           String url = "jdbc:odbc:msaccessdb";
```

```
            Connection con = DriverManager.getConnection (
                                              url, "", "");

            String qs = "update orders set city = ? " +
                         " where order_num = ?  ";
            PreparedStatement prepStmt = con.prepareStatement( qs );

            String s = "Tampa";
            prepStmt.setString( 1, s );
            prepStmt.setInt( 2, 12345 );

            int result = prepStmt.executeUpdate();

        }

        catch (java.lang.Exception ex) {

        // Print description of the exception.
        System.out.println( "** Error on data update. ** " );
        ex.printStackTrace ();

        }
    }
}
```

Parameters

parameterIndex—an integer representing the parameter index

x—the String value

setTime

Declaration: `public abstract void setTime(int parameterIndex, Time x) throws SQLException`

This method sets a parameter to a Java `Time` value. Arguments are supplied for the `parameterIndex` (the ordinal position of the parameter in the parameter list) and the `Time` value. The database converts the Java `Time` value to a SQL TIME value before sending the parameter to the database.

```
import java.sql.*;
```

```
import java.io.*;

class PrepTest {

     public static void main( String argv[] ) {

       try {

          Class.forName ("jdbc.odbc.JdbcOdbcDriver");

          String url = "jdbc:odbc:msaccessdb";

          Connection con = DriverManager.getConnection (
                                                url, "", "");

          String qs = "update orders set order_time = ? " +
                     " where order_num = ?  ";
          PreparedStatement prepStmt = con.prepareStatement( qs );

          Time t = new Time( 11,22, 22 );
          prepStmt.setTime( 1, t );
          prepStmt.setInt( 2, 12345 );

          int result = prepStmt.executeUpdate();

      }

      catch (java.lang.Exception ex) {

      // Print description of the exception.
      System.out.println( "** Error on data update. ** " );
      ex.printStackTrace ();

      }
  }
```

```
}
```

Parameters

parameterIndex—an integer representing the parameter index

x—a Java Time

setTimestamp

Declaration: public abstract void setTimestamp(int parameterIndex, Timestamp x) throws SQLException

This method sets a parameter to a Java Timestamp value. Arguments are supplied for the parameterIndex (the ordinal position of the parameter in the parameter list) and the Timestamp value. The database converts the Java Timestamp value to a SQL TIMESTAMP value before sending the parameter to the database.

```
import java.sql.*;
import java.io.*;

class PrepTest {

    public static void main( String argv[] ) {

      try {

         Class.forName ("jdbc.odbc.JdbcOdbcDriver");

         String url = "jdbc:odbc:msaccessdb";

         Connection con = DriverManager.getConnection (
                                          url, "", "");

         String qs = "update orders set order_amount = ? " +
                       " where order_num = ?  ";
         PreparedStatement prepStmt = con.prepareStatement( qs );

         Timestamp ts = new Timestamp( 58, // year
                                 1, // month
                                 28, // day
                                 11, // hour
```

```
                                    22, // minutes
                                    0, // seconds
                                    0 ) // nanoseconds

            prepStmt.setTimestamp( 1, ts );
            prepStmt.setInt( 2, 12345 );

            int result = prepStmt.executeUpdate();

        }

        catch (java.lang.Exception ex) {

        // Print description of the exception.
        System.out.println( "** Error on data update. ** " );
        ex.printStackTrace ();

        }
    }
}
```

Parameters

parameterIndex–an integer representing the parameter index
x–the Timestamp value

setUnicodeStream

Declaration: public abstract void setUnicodeStream(int parameterIndex, InputStream x, int length) throws SQLException

This method sets a parameter to a Java UnicodeStream. JDBC will then read from the data stream until it reaches end-of-file. For very large volumes of Unicode data, this is a more practical approach to moving the data.

Arguments are supplied for the parameter index (the ordinal position of the parameter in the parameter list) the InputStream (an instantiation of java.io.InputStream) and the length of the input stream in bytes. The driver will perform any conversion necessary to convert the data the SQL CHAR format.

```
import java.sql.*;
import java.io.*;
```

```
class PrepTest {

      public static void main( String argv[] ) {

        try {

            Class.forName ("jdbc.odbc.JdbcOdbcDriver");

            String url = "jdbc:odbc:msaccessdb";

            Connection con = DriverManager.getConnection (
                                                url, "", "");

            String qs = "update catalog set item_desc = ? " +
                      " where order_num = ?  ";
            PreparedStatement prepStmt = con.prepareStatement( qs );

            prepStmt.getUnicodeStream(1,
                               inpStream,
                               2500 );



            prepStmt.setInt( 2, 12345 );

            int result = prepStmt.executeUpdate();

       }

       catch (java.lang.Exception ex) {

       // Print description of the exception.
       System.out.println( "** Error on data update. ** " );
       ex.printStackTrace ();

       }
    }
}
```

Interface java.sql.ResultSet

Declaration: `public interface` **`ResultSet`** `extends Object`

The `ResultSet` interface provides methods for accessing data generated by executing a `Statement`. The rows in the `ResultSet` must be retrieved in sequence but the column values in a row can be accessed in any order.

The `ResultSet` maintains a position within the set of data. Moving to the next position in the set is achieved using the `next` method. There is currently no facility to move to the previous row or to move a fixed number of row positions forward or back in the set.

Various 'get' methods are used to retrieve column data for the current row. Values can be retrieved using either the index number of the column or by using the name of the column. Column positions are numbered starting from 1. Different 'get' methods are available for each Java data type; the correct 'get' method should be used to retrieve data from the `ResultSet`.

The 'get' methods provide a means of retrieving column data using column names. These column names are case sensitive. If several columns have the same name, then the first column with that name will be retrieved.

A `ResultSet` is automatically closed when the `Statement` that created it is closed, executed again, or is used to retrieve the next result in the sequence of multiple results.

Information about a `ResultSet`'s columns is available using the `ResultSetMetaData` (`java.sql.ResultSestMetaData`) methods. An object of this class is returned by the `getMetaData` method described in this interface.

```
import java.sql.*;
import java.io.*;

class Select1 {

     public static void main( String argv[] ) {

       try {

           Class.forName ("jdbc.odbc.JdbcOdbcDriver");
           String url = "jdbc:odbc:msaccessdb";

           Connection con = DriverManager.getConnection (
                                          url, "", "");
           Statement stmt = con.createStatement();
```

```
        ResultSet rs = stmt.executeQuery(
                             "select * from orders" );
        Boolean more =    rs.next();

        while ( more ) {
                System.out.println( "Column 1: " +
                                     rs.getString( 1 ) +
                                        " - " +
                                     " Column 2: " +
                                    rs.getString( 2 ) );
                more = rs.next();
        }

       con.close();

       }

     catch (java.lang.Exception ex) {

     // Print description of the exception.
     System.out.println( "** Error on data select. ** " );
     ex.printStackTrace ();

    }
  }
}
```

In this example a `Connection` object is created using the available `DriverManager`. A `Statement` object is then created and a `ResultSet` is generated by executing a query. A call is made to the `next` method to position the cursor before the first result. A `while` loop is executed to retrieve the rows by iterating through the `ResultSet`. For each row in the `ResultSet`, a 'get' method is called to retrieve the value of each of the respective columns. In this case, the data type is assumed to be a Java `String` so the `getString` method is called for two of the columns in the table. When the `while` loop is terminated, the `close` method is called for the `Connection` object to close the connection to the database.

See Also: `executeQuery, getResultSet, ResultSetMetaData`

ResultSet Methods

clearWarnings

Declaration: `public abstract void clearWarnings() throws SQLException`

This method clears the current warnings for this `ResultSet`.

```
import java.sql.*;
import java.io.*;

class Select1 {

     public static void main( String argv[] ) {

       try {

          Class.forName ("jdbc.odbc.JdbcOdbcDriver");
          String url = "jdbc:odbc:msaccessdb";

          Connection con = DriverManager.getConnection (
                                   url, "", "");
          Statement stmt = con.createStatement();

          ResultSet rs = stmt.executeQuery(
                                     "select * from orders" );
          Boolean more =    rs.next();

          SQLWarning warn = rs.getWarnings();

          if ( warn != null )
             checkWarnings( warn );

          rs.clearWarnings();

          }
        } /
 ...
```

close

Declaration: `public abstract void close() throws SQLException`

This method releases resources associated with this `ResultSet`. (Note that a `ResultSet` is automatically closed when the `Statement` that created it is closed, re-executed, or retrieves the next result from a sequence of multiple results.)

```
...
           prepStmt.setInt( 1, n );
           ResultSet rs = prepStmt.executeQuery();
           boolean more = rs.next();
           for (; n < 2000 && more ; n++ ) {

               prepStmt.setInt( 1, n );

               // need to close the result set before
               // executing the query for this iteration
               // and returninga new result set
               rs.close();
               rs   = prepStmt.executeQuery();
               more = rs.next();

           }
...
```

findColumn

Declaration: `public abstract int findColumn(String columnName) throws SQLException`

This method returns a column index for the column name supplied. A single `String` argument is passed to the method with the column name. An integer value is returned representing the column's ordinal position in the `ResultSet`.

```
import java.sql.*;
import java.io.*;

class Select1 {

     public static void main( String argv[] ) {
```

```
        try {

            Class.forName ("jdbc.odbc.JdbcOdbcDriver");
            String url = "jdbc:odbc:msaccessdb";

            Connection con = DriverManager.getConnection (
                                       url, "", "");
            Statement stmt = con.createStatement();

            ResultSet rs = stmt.executeQuery(
                                    "select * from orders" );

            int colPosition = rs.findColumn( "order_amount");
            Boolean more =     rs.next();
            float order_value = rs.getFloat( colPosition );
            System.out.println( "order value is " + order_value );

          }
        }
```

Parameters

columnName—a Java String containing the column name

Returns

an int containing the column index

getAsciiStream

Declaration: public abstract InputStream getAsciiStream(String columnName) throws SQLException

This method allows an InputStream to be designated for a column value. This allows large data values such as LONGVARCHAR to be retrieved efficiently. (All data must be read from the stream before getting the value of any other column. The next call to a 'get' method implicitly closes the stream.)

This method returns an InputStream to a stream of ASCII characters. The method takes a single argument String with the column name.

```
import java.sql.*;
import java.io.*;
```

```
class Select1 {

    public static void main( String argv[] ) {

      try {

         Class.forName ("jdbc.odbc.JdbcOdbcDriver");
         String url = "jdbc:odbc:msaccessdb";

         Connection con = DriverManager.getConnection (
                                 url, "", "");
         Statement stmt = con.createStatement();

         ResultSet rs = stmt.executeQuery(
                               "select * from orders" );
         Boolean more =    rs.next();


         InputStream is = rs.getASCIIStream( "order_desc"
);
         }
      }
```

Parameter

columnName—a String containing the column name

Returns

A Java InputStream

getAsciiStream

Declaration: `public abstract InputStream getAsciiStream(int columnIndex) throws SQLException`

This method allows an InputStream to be designated for a column value. This allows large data values such as LONGVARCHAR to be retrieved efficiently. (All data must be read from the stream before getting the value of any other column. The next call to a 'get' method implicitly closes the stream.)This method returns an InputStream to a stream of ASCII characters.

```
import java.sql.*;
```

```
import java.io.*;

class Select1 {

     public static void main( String argv[] ) {

       try {

          Class.forName ("jdbc.odbc.JdbcOdbcDriver");
          String url = "jdbc:odbc:msaccessdb";

          Connection con = DriverManager.getConnection (
                               url, "", "");
          Statement stmt = con.createStatement();

          ResultSet rs = stmt.executeQuery(
                                  "select * from orders" );
          Boolean more =     rs.next();

          InputStream is = rs.getASCIIStream( 3 );

          ...
```

Parameters

`columnIndex`—an `int` value representing the column index

Returns

A Java `InputStream`

getBinaryStream

Declaration: `public abstract InputStream getBinaryStream(String columnName) throws SQLException`

This method allows an `InputStream` to be designated for a column value. This allows large data values such as LONGVARCHAR to be retrieved efficiently. (All data must be read from the stream before getting the value of any other column. The next call to a 'get' method implicitly closes the stream.)

This method returns an `InputStream` to a stream of `Unicode` characters. The method takes a single argument `String` with the column name.

```
import java.sql.*;
import java.io.*;

class Select1 {

     public static void main( String argv[] ) {

       try {

            Class.forName ("jdbc.odbc.JdbcOdbcDriver");
            String url = "jdbc:odbc:msaccessdb";

            Connection con = DriverManager.getConnection (
                                url, "", "");
            Statement stmt = con.createStatement();

            ResultSet rs = stmt.executeQuery(
                                 "select * from orders" );
            Boolean more =    rs.next();

            // ******************************************
            InputStream is = rs.getBinaryStream( "order_desc"
);

            }
         }
```

Parameters

`columnName`—a Java `String` containing the column name

Returns

A Java `InputStream`

getBinaryStream

Declaration: `public abstract InputStream getBinaryStream(int columnIndex) throws SQLException`

This method allows an `InputStream` to be designated for a column value. This allows large data values such as LONGVARCHAR to be retrieved efficiently. (All data must be read from the stream before getting the value of any other column. The next call to a 'get' method implicitly closes the stream.)

This method returns an InputStream to a stream of uninterpreted characters.

```
import java.sql.*;
import java.io.*;

class Select1 {

     public static void main( String argv[] ) {

       try {

          Class.forName ("jdbc.odbc.JdbcOdbcDriver");
          String url = "jdbc:odbc:msaccessdb";

          Connection con = DriverManager.getConnection (
                                url, "", "");
          Statement stmt = con.createStatement();

          ResultSet rs = stmt.executeQuery(
                               "select * from orders" );
          Boolean more =    rs.next();

          InputStream is = rs.getBinaryStream( 3 );

          ...
```

Parameters

columnIndex—an integer value representing the column index

Returns

A Java InputStream

getBoolean

Declaration: public abstract boolean getBoolean(int columnIndex) throws SQLException

This method retrieves the value of a column as a Java boolean. It receives a single integer argument for the column index (the ordinal position of the column in the result set). It returns a boolean value.

```
import java.sql.*;
import java.io.*;

class Select1 {

     public static void main( String argv[] ) {

       try {

          Class.forName ("jdbc.odbc.JdbcOdbcDriver");
          String url = "jdbc:odbc:msaccessdb";

          Connection con = DriverManager.getConnection (
                               url, "", "");
          Statement stmt = con.createStatement();

          ResultSet rs = stmt.executeQuery(
                              "select * from orders" );
          Boolean more =      rs.next();

          while ( more ) {
                  if ( rs.getBoolean( 3 ) )
                     System.out.println(
                                "Boolean value is true."  );
                  else
                     System.out.println(
                            "Boolean value is false."  );

                  more = rs.next();
          }

       }
```


Parameters

columnIndex—an integer value representing the column index

Returns

A Java boolean

getBoolean

Declaration: `public abstract boolean getBoolean(String columnName) throws SQLException`

This method returns the value of a column as a Java `boolean`. It receives a single `String` argument with the column name. It returns a Java `boolean`.

```
import java.sql.*;
import java.io.*;

class Select1 {

    public static void main( String argv[] ) {

      try {

        Class.forName ("jdbc.odbc.JdbcOdbcDriver");
        String url = "jdbc:odbc:msaccessdb";

        Connection con = DriverManager.getConnection (
                               url, "", "");
        Statement stmt = con.createStatement();

        ResultSet rs = stmt.executeQuery(
                               "select * from orders" );
        Boolean more =     rs.next();

        while ( more ) {
                if ( rs.getBoolean( "shipped" ) )
                   System.out.println(
                            "Boolean value is true."  );
                else
                   System.out.println(
                           "Boolean value is false."  );
                more = rs.next();
        }
      }
```

Parameters

`columnName`—a `String` containing the column name

Returns

A Java boolean

getByte

Declaration: public abstract byte getByte(String columnName) throws SQLException

This method returns the value of a column as a Java byte. It receives a single String argument with the column name and returns a Java byte.

```
import java.sql.*;
import java.io.*;

class Select1 {

     public static void main( String argv[] ) {

       try {

          Class.forName ("jdbc.odbc.JdbcOdbcDriver");
          String url = "jdbc:odbc:msaccessdb";

          Connection con = DriverManager.getConnection (
                                   url, "", "");
          Statement stmt = con.createStatement();

          ResultSet rs = stmt.executeQuery(
                                 "select * from orders" );
          Boolean more =       rs.next();

          while ( more ) {
                 System.out.println( "Byte value is " +

                         rs.getByte( "payment_flag ) );
                 more = rs.next();
          }
        }
```

Parameters

columnName—a String containing the column name

Returns

A Java `byte`

getByte

Declaration: `public abstract byte getByte(int columnIndex) throws SQLException`

This method returns the value of a column as a Java `byte`. It receives a single integer argument for the column index (the ordinal position of the column in the result set). It returns a Java `byte`.

```
import java.sql.*;
import java.io.*;

class Select1 {

     public static void main( String argv[] ) {

       try {

          Class.forName ("jdbc.odbc.JdbcOdbcDriver");
          String url = "jdbc:odbc:msaccessdb";

          Connection con = DriverManager.getConnection (
                                          url, "", "");
          Statement stmt = con.createStatement();

          ResultSet rs = stmt.executeQuery(
                                   "select * from orders" );
          Boolean more =     rs.next();

          while ( more ) {
                 System.out.println(
                                        "Byte value is " +

                            rs.getByte( 3 ) );
                 more = rs.next();
          }
```

```
        }
```

Parameters

columnIndex—an int value representing the column index

Returns

A Java byte

getBytes

Declaration: public abstract byte[] getBytes(String columnName) throws SQLException

This method returns the value of a column as a Java byte array. It receives a single String argument with the column name.

```
import java.sql.*;
import java.io.*;

class Select1 {

     public static void main( String argv[] ) {

       try {

          Class.forName ("jdbc.odbc.JdbcOdbcDriver");
          String url = "jdbc:odbc:msaccessdb";

          Connection con = DriverManager.getConnection (
                              url, "", "");
          Statement stmt = con.createStatement();

          ResultSet rs = stmt.executeQuery(
                              "select * from orders" );
          Boolean more =    rs.next();

          byte byteVal[] = new byte[3];
          while ( more ) {


                 byteVal = rs.getBytes( "order_flags" );
```

```
                more = rs.next();
            }
        }
```

Parameters

columnName—a String containing the column name

Returns

A Java byte array

getBytes

Declaration: public abstract byte[] getBytes(int columnIndex) throws SQLException

This method returns the value of a column as a Java byte array. It receives a single integer argument for the column index (the ordinal position of the column in the result set). It returns a Java byte array.

```
import java.sql.*;
import java.io.*;

class Select1 {

    public static void main( String argv[] ) {

      try {

         Class.forName ("jdbc.odbc.JdbcOdbcDriver");
         String url = "jdbc:odbc:msaccessdb";

         Connection con = DriverManager.getConnection (
                                   url, "", "");
         Statement stmt = con.createStatement();

         ResultSet rs = stmt.executeQuery(
                              "select * from orders" );
         Boolean more =     rs.next();

         byte byteVal[] = new byte[3];
         while ( more ) {
```

```
                byteVal = rs.getBytes( 3 );
                more = rs.next();
        }
    }
```

Parameters

columnIndex—an int value representing the column index

Returns

A Java byte array

getCursorName

Declaration: public abstract String getCursorName() throws SQLException

This method retrieves the SQL cursor name used by this ResultSet. The current row of a ResultSet can be updated/deleted using a positioned update statement referencing the cursor name. The JDBC API supports this feature using the cursor name used by a ResultSet. (If positioned update is not supported by the database, then a SQLException is thrown.)

```
...
    class PosUpd {

        public static void main( String argv[] ) {

          try {

            Class.forName ("jdbc.odbc.JdbcOdbcDriver");

            String url = "jdbc:odbc:informix5";
            Connection con =
                    DriverManager.getConnection (
                            url, "informix5", "xxxxx");

            Statement stmt1 = con.createStatement();
            ResultSet rs = stmt1.executeQuery(
                    " select * from loadtest where col1 = 5" +
                    " for update " );
```

```
                    rs.next();

// get the cursor name as a character string
                    String cursName = rs.getCursorName();

                    Statement stmt2 = con.createStatement();

                    // update stmt2 at col1 = 5 (current of cursor)
                    int result = stmt2.executeUpdate(
                         "update loadtest set col2 = '1000' " +
                         " where current of " + cursName );

               }
     ...
```

Returns

a Java string containing the `ResultSet`'s SQL cursor name

getDate

Declaration: `public abstract Date getDate(String columnName) throws SQLException`

This method returns the value of a column as a Java `Date` (`java.sql.Date`). It receives a single String argument with the column name.

```
import java.sql.*;
import java.io.*;
import java.sql.Date;

class Select1 {

     public static void main( String argv[] ) {

        try {

            Class.forName ("jdbc.odbc.JdbcOdbcDriver");
            String url = "jdbc:odbc:msaccessdb";

            Connection con = DriverManager.getConnection (
```

```
                                        url, "", "");
          Statement stmt = con.createStatement();

          ResultSet rs = stmt.executeQuery(
                                    "select * from orders" );
          Boolean more =     rs.next();

          while ( more ) {
                  System.out.println( "Date value is " +

                         rs.getDate( "order_date" ).toString() );
                  more = rs.next();
          }
        }
...
```

Parameters

columnName—a String containing the column name

Returns

A Java Date

getDate

Declaration: public abstract Date getDate(int columnIndex) throws SQLException

This method returns the value of a column as a Java Date (java.sql.Date). It receives a single integer argument for the column index (the ordinal position of the column in the result set). It returns a Java Date.

```
import java.sql.*;
import java.io.*;

import java.sql.Date;
class Select1 {

      public static void main( String argv[] ) {

        try {
```

```
        Class.forName ("jdbc.odbc.JdbcOdbcDriver");
        String url = "jdbc:odbc:msaccessdb";

        Connection con = DriverManager.getConnection (
                              url, "", "");
        Statement stmt = con.createStatement();

        ResultSet rs = stmt.executeQuery(
                              "select * from orders" );
        Boolean more =    rs.next();

        while ( more ) {
                System.out.println( "Byte value is " +

                           rs.getDate( 3 ).toString() );
                more = rs.next();
        }
      }
```

Parameters

columnIndex—an int value representing the column index

Returns

A Java Date

getDouble

Declaration: public abstract double getDouble(String columnName) throws SQLException

This method returns the value of a column as a Java double. It receives a single String argument with the column name and returns a Java double.

```
import java.sql.*;
import java.io.*;

class Select1 {

     public static void main( String argv[] ) {

       try {
```

```
        Class.forName ("jdbc.odbc.JdbcOdbcDriver");
        String url = "jdbc:odbc:msaccessdb";

        Connection con = DriverManager.getConnection (
                              url, "", "");
        Statement stmt = con.createStatement();

        ResultSet rs = stmt.executeQuery(
                              "select * from orders" );
        Boolean more =    rs.next();

        while ( more ) {
              System.out.println( "Double value is " +

                    rs.getDouble( 3).toString() ):
              more = rs.next();
        }
      }
```

Parameters

`columnName`—a `String` containing the column name

Returns

A Java `double`

getDouble

Declaration: `public abstract double getDouble(int columnIndex) throws SQLException`

This method returns the value of a column as a Java `double`. It receives a single integer argument for the column index (the ordinal position of the column in the result set). It returns a Java `double`.

```
import java.sql.*;
import java.io.*;

class Select1 {

     public static void main( String argv[] ) {
```

```
        try {

            Class.forName ("jdbc.odbc.JdbcOdbcDriver");
            String url = "jdbc:odbc:msaccessdb";

            Connection con = DriverManager.getConnection (
                                         url, "", "");
            Statement stmt = con.createStatement();

            ResultSet rs = stmt.executeQuery(
                                   "select * from orders" );
            Boolean more =     rs.next();

            while ( more ) {
                    System.out.println( "Double value is " +

                                   rs.getDouble( 3 ) );
                    more = rs.next();
            }
        }
```

Parameters

columnIndex—an int value representing the column index

Returns

A Java double

getFloat

Declaration: public abstract float getFloat(String columnName) throws SQLException

This method returns the value of a column as a Java float. It receives a single String argument with the column name and returns a Java float.

```
import java.sql.*;
import java.io.*;

class Select1 {

     public static void main( String argv[] ) {
```

```
        try {

            Class.forName ("jdbc.odbc.JdbcOdbcDriver");
            String url = "jdbc:odbc:msaccessdb";

            Connection con = DriverManager.getConnection (
                                   url, "", "");
            Statement stmt = con.createStatement();

            ResultSet rs = stmt.executeQuery(
                                   "select * from orders" );
            Boolean more =    rs.next();

            while ( more ) {
                    System.out.println( "Float value is " +

                            rs.getFloat( "order_value" ) );
                    more = rs.next();
            }
        }
```

Parameters

columnName—a String containing the column name

Returns

A Java float

getFloat

Declaration: public abstract float getFloat(int columnIndex) throws SQLException

This method returns the value of a column as a Java float. It receives a single integer argument for the column index (the ordinal position of the column in the result set). It returns a Java float.

```
import java.sql.*;
import java.io.*;

class Select1 {
```

```
public static void main( String argv[] ) {

  try {

     Class.forName ("jdbc.odbc.JdbcOdbcDriver");
     String url = "jdbc:odbc:msaccessdb";

     Connection con = DriverManager.getConnection (
                         url, "", "");
     Statement stmt = con.createStatement();

     ResultSet rs = stmt.executeQuery(
                         "select * from orders" );
     Boolean more =     rs.next();

     while ( more ) {
            System.out.println( "Float value is " +

                    rs.getFloat( 3 ) );
            more = rs.next();
     }
  }
```

Parameters

columnIndex—an int value representing the column index

Returns

A Java float

getInt

Declaration: public abstract int getInt(String columnName) throws SQLException

This method returns the value of a column as a Java int. It receives a single String argument with the column name and returns a Java int.

```
import java.sql.*;
import java.io.*;

class Select1 {
```

```
public static void main( String argv[] ) {

   try {

      Class.forName ("jdbc.odbc.JdbcOdbcDriver");
      String url = "jdbc:odbc:msaccessdb";

      Connection con = DriverManager.getConnection (
                              url, "", "");
      Statement stmt = con.createStatement();

      ResultSet rs = stmt.executeQuery(
                  "select * from orders" );
      Boolean more =    rs.next();

      while ( more ) {
              System.out.println( "Integer value is " +

                       rs.getInt( "tax_percentage") );
              more = rs.next();
      }
    }
```

Parameters

columnName—a String containing the column name

Returns

A Java int

getInt

Declaration: public abstract int getInt(int columnIndex) throws SQLException

This method returns the value of a column as a Java int. It receives a single integer argument for the column index (the ordinal position of the column in the result set). It returns a Java int.

```
import java.sql.*;
import java.io.*;
```

```
class Select1 {

    public static void main( String argv[] ) {

      try {

        Class.forName ("jdbc.odbc.JdbcOdbcDriver");
        String url = "jdbc:odbc:msaccessdb";

        Connection con = DriverManager.getConnection (
                            url, "", "");
        Statement stmt = con.createStatement();

        ResultSet rs = stmt.executeQuery(
                            "select * from orders" );
        Boolean more =    rs.next();

        while ( more ) {
                System.out.println( "Integer value is " +

                                            rs.getInt( 3 ) );
                more = rs.next();
        }
      }
```

Parameters

columnIndex—an int value representing the column index

Returns

A Java int

getLong

Declaration: public abstract long getLong(String columnName) throws SQLException

This method returns the value of a column as a Java long. It receives a single String argument with the column name and returns a Java long.

```
import java.sql.*;
import java.io.*;
```

```
class Select1 {

     public static void main( String argv[] ) {

       try {

            Class.forName ("jdbc.odbc.JdbcOdbcDriver");
            String url = "jdbc:odbc:msaccessdb";

            Connection con = DriverManager.getConnection (
                                   url, "", "");
            Statement stmt = con.createStatement();

            ResultSet rs = stmt.executeQuery(
                                     "select * from orders" );
            Boolean more =     rs.next();

            while ( more ) {
                    System.out.println( "Long value is " +

                             rs.getLong( "age" ) );
                    more = rs.next();
            }
          }
```

Parameters

`columnName`—a `String` containing the column name

Returns

A Java `long`

getLong

Declaration: `public abstract long getLong(int columnIndex) throws SQLException`

This method returns the value of a column as a Java `long`. It receives a single integer argument for the column index (the ordinal position of the column in the result set). It returns a Java `long`.

```
import java.sql.*;
import java.io.*;

class Select1 {

     public static void main( String argv[] ) {

       try {

          Class.forName ("jdbc.odbc.JdbcOdbcDriver");
          String url = "jdbc:odbc:msaccessdb";

          Connection con = DriverManager.getConnection (
                                       url, "", "");
          Statement stmt = con.createStatement();

          ResultSet rs = stmt.executeQuery(
                                   "select * from orders" );
          Boolean more =    rs.next();

          while ( more ) {
                 System.out.println( "Long value is " +

                            rs.getLong( 3 ) );

                 more = rs.next();
          }
        }
```

Parameters

columnIndex—an int value representing the column index

Returns

A Java long

getMetaData

Declaration: public abstract ResultSetMetaData getMetaData() throws SQLException

This method returns a ResultSetMetaData object for this ResultSet. This object can provide information on the number, types and properties of a ResultSet's columns.

```
import java.sql.*;
import java.io.*;

class Select1 {

     public static void main( String argv[] ) {

       try {

          Class.forName ("jdbc.odbc.JdbcOdbcDriver");
          String url = "jdbc:odbc:msaccessdb";

          Connection con = DriverManager.getConnection (
                                url, "", "");
          Statement stmt = con.createStatement();

          ResultSet rs = stmt.executeQuery(
                               "select * from orders" );

          // create a ResultSetMetaData object
          ResultSetMetaData rsmd = rs.getMetaData();

          Boolean more =    rs.next();
          String colName = null;
          while ( more ) {

               // get the column label using the metadata object
                 colName = rsmd.getColumnLabel( 1 ) +
                 System.out.println( colName + " value is " +
                     rs.getTimestamp( "order_time" ).toString() );
                 more = rs.next();
          }
       }
```

Returns

A ResultSetMetaData object

getNumeric

Declaration: `public abstract Numeric getNumeric(String columnName,int scale) throws SQLException`

`This method` returns the value of a column as a Java `Numeric`. It receives arguments for the column name and scale.

```
import java.sql.*;
import java.io.*;

class Select1 {

     public static void main( String argv[] ) {

       try {

          Class.forName ("jdbc.odbc.JdbcOdbcDriver");
          String url = "jdbc:odbc:msaccessdb";

          Connection con = DriverManager.getConnection (
                                   url, "", "");
          Statement stmt = con.createStatement();

          ResultSet rs = stmt.executeQuery(
                                   "select * from orders" );
          Boolean more =    rs.next();

          Numeric numericVal = null;
          while ( more ) {
                 numericVal = rs.getNumeric( "order_value", 2 );
                 System.out.println( "Numeric value is " +

                        numericVal.toString() );
                 more = rs.next();
          }
```

Parameters

`columnName`—a `String` containing the column name

Returns

A Java `Numeric`

getNumeric

Declaration: `public abstract Numeric getNumeric(int columnIndex, int scale) throws SQLException`

This method returns the value of a column as a Java `Numeric`. It receives arguments for the column index (the ordinal position of the column in the result set) and scale. It returns a Java `Numeric`.

```
import java.sql.*;
import java.io.*;

class Select1 {

     public static void main( String argv[] ) {

       try {

          Class.forName ("jdbc.odbc.JdbcOdbcDriver");
          String url = "jdbc:odbc:msaccessdb";

          Connection con = DriverManager.getConnection (
                                url, "", "");
          Statement stmt = con.createStatement();

          ResultSet rs = stmt.executeQuery(
                                "select * from orders" );
          Boolean more =    rs.next();

          while ( more ) {

                 System.out.println( "Numeric value is " +

                       rs.getNumeric( 3, 2 ).toString() );

                 more = rs.next();
          }
       }
```

Parameters

`columnIndex`—an `int` value representing the column index

scale—an int value representing the scale

Returns

A Numeric object

getObject

Declaration: public abstract Object getObject(String columnName) throws SQLException

This method returns the value of a column as a Java Object. A String argument is supplied for the column name.

```
import java.sql.*;
import java.io.*;

class Select1 {

     public static void main( String argv[] ) {

       try {

          Class.forName ("jdbc.odbc.JdbcOdbcDriver");
          String url = "jdbc:odbc:msaccessdb";

          Connection con = DriverManager.getConnection (
                                 url, "", "");
          Statement stmt = con.createStatement();

          ResultSet rs = stmt.executeQuery(
                                "select * from orders" );
          Boolean more =    rs.next();

          while ( more ) {
                 System.out.println( "Column 1 value is " +

                    rs.getObject( "order_desc" ).toString() );
                 more = rs.next();
          }
        }
```

Parameters

columnName—a Java String containing the column name

Returns

A java.lang.Object holding the column value.

getObject

Declaration: public abstract Object getObject(int columnIndex) throws SQLException

This method returns the value of a column as a Java Object. An argument is supplied for the column index (the ordinal position of the column in the column list).

```
import java.sql.*;
import java.io.*;

class Select1 {

    public static void main( String argv[] ) {

      try {

        Class.forName ("jdbc.odbc.JdbcOdbcDriver");
        String url = "jdbc:odbc:msaccessdb";

        Connection con = DriverManager.getConnection (
                            url, "", "");
        Statement stmt = con.createStatement();

        ResultSet rs = stmt.executeQuery(
                          "select * from orders" );
        Boolean more =    rs.next();

        while ( more ) {
              System.out.println( "Column 1 value is " +

                        rs.getObject( 1 ).toString() );
              more = rs.next();
        }
```

```
        }
```

Parameters

columnIndex—an int representing the column index

Returns

A java.lang.Object holding the column value.

getShort

Declaration: public abstract short getShort(int columnIndex) throws SQLException

This method returns the value of a column as a Java short. It receives a single integer argument for the column index (the ordinal position of the column in the result set). It returns a Java short.

```
import java.sql.*;
import java.io.*;

class Select1 {

     public static void main( String argv[] ) {

       try {

          Class.forName ("jdbc.odbc.JdbcOdbcDriver");
          String url = "jdbc:odbc:msaccessdb";

          Connection con = DriverManager.getConnection (
                                       url, "", "");
          Statement stmt = con.createStatement();

          ResultSet rs = stmt.executeQuery(
                                  "select * from orders" );
          Boolean more =     rs.next();

          while ( more ) {
                 System.out.println( "Short value is " +

                                           rs.getShort( 3 ) );
```

```
                more = rs.next();
        }

    }
```

Parameters

columnIndex—an int value representing the column index

Returns

A Java short

getShort

Declaration: public abstract short getShort(String columnName) throws SQLException

This method returns the value of a column as a Java short. It receives a single String argument with the column name and returns a Java short.

```
import java.sql.*;
import java.io.*;

class Select1 {

     public static void main( String argv[] ) {

       try {

           Class.forName ("jdbc.odbc.JdbcOdbcDriver");
           String url = "jdbc:odbc:msaccessdb";

           Connection con = DriverManager.getConnection (
                                   url, "", "");
           Statement stmt = con.createStatement();

           ResultSet rs = stmt.executeQuery(
                                      "select * from orders" );
           Boolean more =     rs.next();
           while ( more ) {
                  System.out.println( "Short integer value
is " +
```

```
                                rs.getShort( "tax percentage"
) );
                    more = rs.next();
             }
           }
```

Parameters

columnName—a String containing the column name

Returns

A Java short

getString

Declaration: public abstract String getString(int columnIndex) throws SQLException

This method retrieves the value of a column as a Java String. It receives a single integer argument for the column index (the ordinal position of the column in the result set). It returns a Java String.

```
import java.sql.*;
import java.io.*;

class Select1 {

     public static void main( String argv[] ) {

       try {

          Class.forName ("jdbc.odbc.JdbcOdbcDriver");
          String url = "jdbc:odbc:msaccessdb";

          Connection con = DriverManager.getConnection (
                                            url, "", "");
          Statement stmt = con.createStatement();

          ResultSet rs = stmt.executeQuery(
                           "select * from orders" );
          Boolean more =    rs.next();
```

```
        while ( more ) {
                System.out.println( "Column 1: " +
                                             rs.getString( 1 ) +
                                                 "—" +
                                             " Column 2: " +
                                             rs.getString( 2 ) );
                more = rs.next();
        }
        con.close();

       }
```

Parameters

columnIndex—an integer representing the column index

Returns

A Java String

getString

Declaration: public abstract String getString(String columnName) throws SQLException

This method returns the value of a column as a Java String. It receives a single String argument for the column name. It returns a Java String.

```
import java.sql.*;
import java.io.*;

class Select1 {

     public static void main( String argv[] ) {

       try {

          Class.forName ("jdbc.odbc.JdbcOdbcDriver");
          String url = "jdbc:odbc:msaccessdb";

          Connection con = DriverManager.getConnection (
                                url, "", "");
          Statement stmt = con.createStatement();
```

```
        ResultSet rs = stmt.executeQuery(
                        "select * from orders" );
        Boolean more =    rs.next();

        while ( more ) {


        // retrieve column values as strings
                System.out.println( "First name: " +
                        rs.getString( "first_name" ) +
                         "-" + " Last name: "
                         + rs.getString( "last_name" ) );
                more = rs.next();
        }

       con.close();
       }
```

Parameters

columnName—a String containing the column name

Returns

A Java String

getTime

Declaration: public abstract Time getTime(int columnIndex) throws SQLException

This method returns the value of a column as a Java Time (java.sql.Time). It receives a single integer argument for the column index (the ordinal position of the column in the result set). It returns a Java Time.

```
import java.sql.*;
import java.io.*;
import java.sql.Date;

class Select1 {

     public static void main( String argv[] ) {
```

```
try {

    Class.forName ("jdbc.odbc.JdbcOdbcDriver");
    String url = "jdbc:odbc:msaccessdb";

    Connection con = DriverManager.getConnection (
                            url, "", "");
    Statement stmt = con.createStatement();

    ResultSet rs = stmt.executeQuery(
                        "select * from orders" );
    Boolean more =    rs.next();

    while ( more ) {
            System.out.println( "Time value is " +

                    rs.getTime( 3 ).toString() );
            more = rs.next();
    }
  }
            ....
```

Parameters

columnIndex—an int value representing the column index

Returns

A Java Time value

getTime

Declaration: public abstract Time getTime(String columnName) throws SQLException

This method returns the value of a column as a Java Time value (java.sql.Time). It receives a single String argument with the column name.

```
import java.sql.*;
import java.io.*;
```

```
class Select1 {

     public static void main( String argv[] ) {

       try {

          Class.forName ("jdbc.odbc.JdbcOdbcDriver");
          String url = "jdbc:odbc:msaccessdb";

          Connection con = DriverManager.getConnection (
                                    url, "", "");
          Statement stmt = con.createStatement();

          ResultSet rs = stmt.executeQuery(
                                   "select * from orders" );
          Boolean more =     rs.next();

          while ( more ) {
                 System.out.println( "Time value is " +

                   rs.getTime( "order_time" ).toString() );
                 more = rs.next();
          }
       }
```

Parameter

columnName—a String containing the column name

Returns

A Java Time value

getTimestamp

Declaration: public abstract Timestamp getTimestamp(String columnName) throws SQLException

This method returns the value of a column as a Java Timestamp value (java.sql.Timestamp). It receives a single String argument with the column name.

```
import java.sql.*;
```

```
import java.io.*;
class Select1 {

     public static void main( String argv[] ) {

       try {

          Class.forName ("jdbc.odbc.JdbcOdbcDriver");
          String url = "jdbc:odbc:msaccessdb";

          Connection con = DriverManager.getConnection (
                                   url, "", "");
          Statement stmt = con.createStatement();

          ResultSet rs = stmt.executeQuery(
                                   "select * from orders" );
          Boolean more =    rs.next();

          while ( more ) {
                 System.out.println( "Timestamp value is " +

                    rs.getTimestamp( "order_time" ).toString() );
                 more = rs.next();
          }
       }
```

Parameter

`columnName`—a `String` containing the column name

Returns

A Java `Timestamp` value

getTimestamp

Declaration: `public abstract Timestamp getTimestamp(int columnIndex) throws SQLException`

This method returns the value of a column as a Java `Timestamp` (`java.sql.Timestamp`). It receives a single integer argument for the column index (the ordinal position of the column in the result set). It returns a Java `Timestamp` value.

```
import java.sql.*;
import java.io.*;

class Select1 {
     public static void main( String argv[] ) {

       try {

          Class.forName ("jdbc.odbc.JdbcOdbcDriver");
          String url = "jdbc:odbc:msaccessdb";

          Connection con = DriverManager.getConnection (
                                         url, "", "");
          Statement stmt = con.createStatement();

          ResultSet rs = stmt.executeQuery(
                                      "select * from orders" );
          Boolean more =    rs.next();

          while ( more ) {
                 System.out.println( "Timestamp value is " +

                         rs.getTimestamp( 3 ).toString() );
                 more = rs.next();
          }
       }
...
```

Parameters

columnIndex—an int value representing the column index

Returns

A Java Timestamp

getUnicodeStream

Declaration: `public abstract InputStream getUnicodeStream(String columnName) throws SQLException`

This method allows an InputStream to be designated for a column value. This allows large data values such as LONGVARCHAR to be retrieved efficiently. (All data must be read from the stream before getting the value of any other column. The next call to a 'get' method implicitly closes the stream.)

This method returns an `InputStream` to a stream of Unicode characters. The method takes a single argument `String` with the column name.

```
import java.sql.*;
import java.io.*;

class Select1 {

     public static void main( String argv[] ) {

        try {

           Class.forName ("jdbc.odbc.JdbcOdbcDriver");
           String url = "jdbc:odbc:msaccessdb";

           Connection con = DriverManager.getConnection (
                                    url, "", "");
           Statement stmt = con.createStatement();

           ResultSet rs = stmt.executeQuery(
                                  "select * from orders" );
           Boolean more =     rs.next();

           InputStream is = getUnicodeStream( "order_desc" );
           }
        }
```

Parameters

`columnName`—a Java `String` containing the column name

Returns

A Java `InputStream`

getUnicodeStream

Declaration: `public abstract InputStream getUnicodeStream(int columnIndex) throws SQLException`

This method allows an `InputStream` to be designated for a column value. This allows large data values such as LONGVARCHAR to be retrieved efficiently. (All data must be read from the stream before getting the value of any other column. The next call to a 'get' method implicitly closes the stream.) This method returns an `InputStream` to a stream of Unicode characters.

```
import java.sql.*;
import java.io.*;
import java.util.Date;

class Select1 {

     public static void main( String argv[] ) {

       try {

          Class.forName ("jdbc.odbc.JdbcOdbcDriver");
          String url = "jdbc:odbc:msaccessdb";

          Connection con = DriverManager.getConnection (
                            url, "", "");
          Statement stmt = con.createStatement();

          ResultSet rs = stmt.executeQuery(
                        "select * from orders" );
          Boolean more =    rs.next();

          InputStream is = rs.getUnicodeStream( 3 );
          ...
```

Parameters

`columnIndex`—an `int` value representing the column index

Returns

A Java `InputStream`

getWarnings

Declaration: `public abstract SQLWarning getWarnings() throws SQLException`

This method returns the SQLWarnings on this ResultSet. The first warning is returned; subsequent warnings are chained to the first SQLWarning. The warning chain is cleared each time a new row is returned.

```
import java.sql.*;
import java.io.*;

class Select1 {

     public static void main( String argv[] ) {

       try {

          Class.forName ("jdbc.odbc.JdbcOdbcDriver");
          String url = "jdbc:odbc:msaccessdb";

          Connection con = DriverManager.getConnection (
                                    url, "", "");
          Statement stmt = con.createStatement();

          ResultSet rs = stmt.executeQuery(
                                    "select * from orders" );
          Boolean more =    rs.next();

          SQLWarning warn = rs.getWarnings();

          if ( warn != null )
             checkWarnings( warn );
          }

       } /
 ...
```

Returns

The first SQLWarning or NULL

next

Declaration: `public abstract boolean next() throws SQLException`

This method moves to the next row in the set of rows being maintained by the ResultSet. The ResultSet is initially positioned before its first row. The first call to the next method makes the first row the current row. The method returns a boolean indicating whether or not the row being requested is valid; it returns false if there are no more rows.

```
...
public static void DisplayResults( ResultSet results )
         throws SQLException
      {
        int i;

           // Get the ResultSetMetaData and use this for
              // the column headings
              ResultSetMetaData rsmd = results.getMetaData ();

        // Get the number of columns in the result set
        int numCols = rsmd.getColumnCount ();

        // Display column headings
        for (i=1; i<=numCols; i++) {
                          if (i > 1) System.out.print("-");
          System.out.print(rsmd.getColumnLabel(i));
        }
        System.out.println("");


        // Display data, fetching until end of the result set
             // the first call to the next method positions
             // the cursor at the first result

             boolean more = results.next ();
        while (more) {

          // Loop through each column, getting the
          // column data and displaying

          for (i=1; i<=numCols; i++) {
                                  if (i > 1) System.out.print(
                                                       "-");
```

```
System.out.print(results.getString(i));
          }
          System.out.println("");

                    // Fetch the next result set row
                    // successive calls to the next method continue
to
                    // move the pointer forward in the result set
                    more = results.next ();
                 }
   }
```

Returns

A `boolean` true if the new current row is valid; false if there are no more rows.

wasNull

Declaration: `public abstract boolean wasNull() throws SQLException`

This method returns true if the *last* column read had a NULL value. (Note that you must first call the 'get' method and then immediately call the `wasNull` method to determine whether or not a NULL was retrieved.)

```
import java.sql.*;
import java.io.*;

class Select1 {

     public static void main( String argv[] ) {

       try {

          Class.forName ("jdbc.odbc.JdbcOdbcDriver");
          String url = "jdbc:odbc:msaccessdb";

          Connection con = DriverManager.getConnection (
                                           url, "", "");
          Statement stmt = con.createStatement();
```

```
ResultSet rs = stmt.executeQuery(
                    "select * from orders" );
Boolean more =    rs.next();

while ( more ) {
        System.out.println( "Column 1: " +
                            rs.getString( 1 ) +
                            "—" +
                            " Column 2: " +
                            rs.getString( 2 ) );

        if ( rs.wasNull() )
            System.out.println(
           "Last column retrieved was a NULL value. " );
        more = rs.next();
}

con.close();

}
```

Returns

A Java `boolean`

Interface java.sql.ResultSetMetaData

Declaration: `public interface` **`ResultSetMetaData`** `extends argumentObject`

The `ResultSetMetaData` interface provides access to information about the `ResultSet` that generated the object. A number of methods are available to provide various pieces of information about the `ResultSet`.

```
import java.sql.*;
import java.io.*;

class SelectGen {

     public static void main( String argv[] ) {

       try {
          Class.forName ("jdbc.odbc.JdbcOdbcDriver");
          String url = "jdbc:odbc:msaccessdb";
          Connection con = DriverManager.getConnection (
                                              url, "", "");

          String tableName = "customers";
          if ( argv.length > 0 )
             tableName = argv[0];

          String qs = "select * from " + tableName;
          Statement stmt = con.createStatement();

          ResultSet rs = stmt.executeQuery( qs );
          ResultSetMetaData rsmd = rs.getMetaData();

          int n = 0;
          boolean more = rs.next();
          while ( more ) {
                for ( n = 1; n <= rsmd.getColumnCount(); n++ )
                     System.out.println( "Col " + n +
                            " Name: " +
                            rsmd.getColumnName( n ) +
                            " value: " + rs.getString( n ) );
```

```
                    more = rs.next();
                }

            }
            catch (java.lang.Exception ex) {

            // Print description of the exception.
            System.out.println( "** Error on data select. ** " );
            ex.printStackTrace ();

            }

        }

    }
```

As this example shows, the `ResultSetMetaData` class can be used to process a query which was unknown when the application was written. This program accepts a table name from the command line. It then builds a query string using the table name, executes the query and creates a `ResultSet` object to represent the results. It creates a `ResultSetMeta` data object from the `ResultSet` and uses the information in the `ResultSetMetaData` object to intelligently process the results.

Within the `while` loop, the `getColumnCount` method is used to retrieve the column count of the `ResultSet`. This count is used to control the loop that reads each of the columns in the `ResultSet` and displays their value. The `getColumnName` method is used to print the name of the column and the `getString` method (of the `ResultSet`) is used to display the column value as a string, regardless of data type.

ResultSetMetaData Variables

columnNoNulls

Declaration: `public final static int columnNoNulls`

This value indicates that the column does **not** allow NULL values. It is a possible return value from the `isNullable` method.

columnNullable

Declaration: `public final static int columnNullable`

This value indicates that the column **does** allow NULL values. It is a possible return value from the `isNullable` method.

columnNullableUnknown

Declaration: `public final static int columnNullableUnknown`

This value indicates that it is not known whether or not a column allows NULL values. It is a possible return value from the isNullable method.

ResultSetMetaData Methods

getCatalogName

Declaration: `public abstract String getCatalogNameCatalogName(int column) throws argumentSQLException`

This method determines the catalog name for the column. It accepts an argument for the column index (ordinal position of the column in the column list) of the column to evaluate. It returns a string containing the catalog name.

```
import java.sql.*;
import java.io.*;

class SelectGen {

     public static void main( String argv[] ) {

       try {
          Class.forName ("jdbc.odbc.JdbcOdbcDriver");
          String url = "jdbc:odbc:msaccessdb";
          Connection con = DriverManager.getConnection (
                                              url, "", "");

          String qs = "select * from orders ";
          Statement stmt = con.createStatement();

          ResultSet rs = stmt.executeQuery( qs );

// get the meta-data information
          ResultSetMetaData rsmd = rs.getMetaData();

         String catalogName = rsmd.getCatalogName( 1 );
         System.out.println( "Catalog name for column is " +
```

```
                                        catalogName );

            }
          catch (java.lang.Exception ex) {

         // Print description of the exception.
         System.out.println( "** Error on data select. ** " );
         ex.printStackTrace ();

         }
      }
}
```

Parameters

column—an int value for the column index

Returns

A Java String

getColumnCount

Declaration: public abstract int getColumnCount() throws argumentSQLException

This method determines the number of columns returned in the ResultSet. It returns an integer value with the number of columns.

```
import java.sql.*;
import java.io.*;

class SelectGen {

     public static void main( String argv[] ) {

       try {
          Class.forName ("jdbc.odbc.JdbcOdbcDriver");
          String url = "jdbc:odbc:msaccessdb";
          Connection con = DriverManager.getConnection (
                                              url, "", "");

          String qs = "select * from orders ";
```

```
        Statement stmt = con.createStatement();

        ResultSet rs = stmt.executeQuery( qs );

        ResultSetMetaData rsmd = rs.getMetaData();

        int n = 0;
        boolean more = rs.next();
        while ( more ) {
                for ( n = 1; n <= rsmd.getColumnCount(); n++ )
                      System.out.println( "Col " + n +
                                   " Name: " +
                                  rsmd.getColumnName( n ) +
                                   " value: " + rs.getString( n ) );
                more = rs.next();
          }

      }
      catch (java.lang.Exception ex) {

     // Print description of the exception.
     System.out.println( "** Error on data select. ** " );
     ex.printStackTrace ();

     }

  }

}
```

Returns

An `int` containing the number of columns in the `ResultSet`

getColumnDisplaySize

Declaration: `public abstract int getColumnDisplaySize(int column) throws argumentSQLException`

This method determines the maximum width for the column in characters. It accepts an argument for the column index (ordinal position of the column in the column list) of the column to evaluate. It returns an integer value with the maximum width.

```
import java.sql.*;
import java.io.*;

class SelectGen {

      public static void main( String argv[] ) {

        try {
            Class.forName ("jdbc.odbc.JdbcOdbcDriver");
            String url = "jdbc:odbc:msaccessdb";
            Connection con = DriverManager.getConnection (
                                                url, "", "");

            String qs = "select * from orders ";
            Statement stmt = con.createStatement();

            ResultSet rs = stmt.executeQuery( qs );

// get the meta-data information
            ResultSetMetaData rsmd = rs.getMetaData();

            int MaxColumnWidth =
                        rsmd.getColumnDisplaySize( 1 );
            System.out.println(
                              "Maximum column display size is " +
                              MaxColumnWidth );

            }
        catch (java.lang.Exception ex) {

        // Print description of the exception.
        System.out.println( "** Error on data select. ** " );
        ex.printStackTrace ();

        }
    }
}
```

Parameters

column—An int value for the column index

Returns

An int value

getColumnLabel

Declaration: public abstract String getColumnLabel(int column) throws argumentSQLException

This method returns the suggested column title for the identified column. It accepts an argument for the column index (ordinal position of the column in the column list) of the column to evaluate. It returns a String containing the column label.

```
import java.sql.*;
import java.io.*;

class SelectGen {

     public static void main( String argv[] ) {

        try {
           Class.forName ("jdbc.odbc.JdbcOdbcDriver");
           String url = "jdbc:odbc:msaccessdb";
           Connection con = DriverManager.getConnection (
                                                  url, "", "");

           String qs = "select * from orders ";
           Statement stmt = con.createStatement();

           ResultSet rs = stmt.executeQuery( qs );

// get the meta-data information
           ResultSetMetaData rsmd = rs.getMetaData();

           String colLabel = rsmd.getColumnLabel( 1 );
           System.out.println( "Column label is " + colLabel );

           }
```

```
        catch (java.lang.Exception ex) {

        // Print description of the exception.
        System.out.println( "** Error on data select. ** " );
        ex.printStackTrace ();

        }
    }
}
```

Parameters

column—An int value for the column index

Returns

A Java String

getColumnName

Declaration: public abstract String getColumnName(int column) throws argumentSQLException

This method returns the name of a column. It accepts an argument for the column index (ordinal position of the column in the column list) of the column to evaluate. It returns a String containing the column name.

```
import java.sql.*;
import java.io.*;

class SelectGen {

     public static void main( String argv[] ) {

       try {
          Class.forName ("jdbc.odbc.JdbcOdbcDriver");
          String url = "jdbc:odbc:msaccessdb";
          Connection con = DriverManager.getConnection (
                                             url, "", "");

          String qs = "select * from orders ";
          Statement stmt = con.createStatement();
```

```
        ResultSet rs = stmt.executeQuery( qs );


        // get the meta-data information
        ResultSetMetaData rsmd = rs.getMetaData();

        String colName = rsmd.getColumnName( 1 );
        System.out.println( "Column name is " + colName );

        }
     catch (java.lang.Exception ex) {

    // Print description of the exception.
    System.out.println( "** Error on data select. ** " );
    ex.printStackTrace ();

    }
  }
}
```

Parameters

`column`—an `int` value for the column index

Returns

A Java `String`

getColumnType

Declaration: `public abstract int getColumnType(int column) throws argumentSQLException`

This method returns the data type of the column. It accepts an argument for the column index (ordinal position of the column in the column list) of the column to evaluate. It returns an integer representing the SQL type for the column from `java.sql.Types`.

```
import java.sql.*;
import java.io.*;

class SelectGen {

     public static void main( String argv[] ) {
```

```
        try {
            Class.forName ("jdbc.odbc.JdbcOdbcDriver");
            String url = "jdbc:odbc:msaccessdb";
            Connection con = DriverManager.getConnection (
                                                url, "", "");

            String qs = "select * from orders ";
            Statement stmt = con.createStatement();

            ResultSet rs = stmt.executeQuery( qs );

// get the meta-data information
            ResultSetMetaData rsmd = rs.getMetaData();

            String colType = rsmd.getColumnType( 1 );
            if ( colType == Types.INTEGER)
                 System.out.println(
                        "Column type is INTEGER" );

            }
        catch (java.lang.Exception ex) {

        // Print description of the exception.
        System.out.println( "** Error on data select. ** " );
        ex.printStackTrace ();

        }
    }
}
```

Parameters

column—an int value for the column index

Returns

an int

getColumnTypeName

Declaration: public abstract String getColumnTypeName(int column) throws SQLException

This method returns the data source specific type name of the column. It accepts an argument for the column index (ordinal position of the column in the column list) of the column to evaluate. It returns a `String` containing the data source specific type name for the column.

```
import java.sql.*;
import java.io.*;

class SelectGen {

     public static void main( String argv[] ) {

       try {
          Class.forName ("jdbc.odbc.JdbcOdbcDriver");
          String url = "jdbc:odbc:msaccessdb";
          Connection con = DriverManager.getConnection (
                                    url, "", "");

          String qs = "select * from orders ";
          Statement stmt = con.createStatement();

          ResultSet rs = stmt.executeQuery( qs );

          // ****************************************
          // get the meta-data information
          ResultSetMetaData rsmd = rs.getMetaData();

          String colTypeName = rsmd.getColumnTypeName( 1 );
          System.out.println( "Column type name is " +
                               colTypeName );

          }
        catch (java.lang.Exception ex) {

       // Print description of the exception.
       System.out.println( "** Error on data select. ** " );
       ex.printStackTrace ();

       }
```

```
    }
}
```

Parameters

column—an int value for the column index

Returns

A Java String

getPrecision

Declaration: public abstract int getPrecision(int column) throws argumentSQLException

This method returns the precision of a column. It accepts an argument for the column index (ordinal position of the column in the column list) of the column to evaluate. It returns an integer containing the precision of the column.

```
import java.sql.*;
import java.io.*;

class SelectGen {

     public static void main( String argv[] ) {

        try {
            Class.forName ("jdbc.odbc.JdbcOdbcDriver");
            String url = "jdbc:odbc:msaccessdb";
            Connection con = DriverManager.getConnection (
                                                  url, "", "");

            String qs = "select * from orders ";
            Statement stmt = con.createStatement();

            ResultSet rs = stmt.executeQuery( qs );

// get the meta-data information
            ResultSetMetaData rsmd = rs.getMetaData();

            int colPrecision = rsmd.getPrecision( 1 );
            System.out.println( "Column precision is " +
```

```
                                    colPrecision );

        }
       catch (java.lang.Exception ex) {

      // Print description of the exception.
      System.out.println( "** Error on data select. ** " );
      ex.printStackTrace ();

      }
   }
}
```

Parameters

column—an int value for the column index

Returns

An int

getScale

Declaration: public abstract int getScale(int column) throws argumentSQLException

This method returns the scale of a column. It accepts an argument for the column index (ordinal position of the column in the column list) of the column to evaluate. It returns an integer containing the scale of the column.

```
import java.sql.*;
import java.io.*;

class SelectGen {

      public static void main( String argv[] ) {

        try {
           Class.forName ("jdbc.odbc.JdbcOdbcDriver");
           String url = "jdbc:odbc:msaccessdb";
           Connection con = DriverManager.getConnection (
                                               url, "", "");

           String qs = "select * from orders ";
```

```
            Statement stmt = con.createStatement();

            ResultSet rs = stmt.executeQuery( qs );

// get the meta-data information
            ResultSetMetaData rsmd = rs.getMetaData();

            int colScale = rsmd.getScale( 1 );
            System.out.println( "Column scale is " + colScale );

            }
         catch (java.lang.Exception ex) {

        // Print description of the exception.
        System.out.println( "** Error on data select. ** " );
        ex.printStackTrace ();

        }
    }
}
```

Parameters

`column`—an `int` value for the column index

Returns

an `int`

getSchemaName

Declaration: `public abstract String getSchemaName(int column) throws argumentSQLException`

This method determines the schema name for the column. It accepts an argument for the column index (ordinal position of the column in the column list) of the column to evaluate. It returns a `String` containing the schema name.

```
import java.sql.*;
import java.io.*;
```

```
class SelectGen {

     public static void main( String argv[] ) {

       try {
          Class.forName ("jdbc.odbc.JdbcOdbcDriver");
          String url = "jdbc:odbc:msaccessdb";
          Connection con = DriverManager.getConnection (
                                          url, "", "");


          String qs = "select * from orders ";
          Statement stmt = con.createStatement();

          ResultSet rs = stmt.executeQuery( qs );

// get the meta-data information
          ResultSetMetaData rsmd = rs.getMetaData();

          String schemaName = rsmd.getSchemaName( 1 );
          System.out.println(
              "Schema name for column is " + schemaName );

          }
       catch (java.lang.Exception ex) {

      // Print description of the exception.
      System.out.println( "** Error on data select. ** "
);
      ex.printStackTrace ();

      }
   }
}
```

Parameters

column—an int value for the column index

Returns

A Java String

getTableName

Declaration: `public abstract String getTableName(int column) throws argumentSQLException`

This method determines the table name for the column. It accepts an argument for the column index (ordinal position of the column in the column list) of the column to evaluate. It returns a `String` containing the table name.

```
import java.sql.*;
import java.io.*;

class SelectGen {

     public static void main( String argv[] ) {

       try {
          Class.forName ("jdbc.odbc.JdbcOdbcDriver");
          String url = "jdbc:odbc:msaccessdb";
          Connection con = DriverManager.getConnection (
                                         url, "", "");

          String qs = "select * from orders ";
          Statement stmt = con.createStatement();

          ResultSet rs = stmt.executeQuery( qs );

// get the meta-data information
          ResultSetMetaData rsmd = rs.getMetaData();

          String tableName = rsmd.getTableName( 1 );
          System.out.println( "Table name for column is " +
                                   tableName );

          }
       catch (java.lang.Exception ex) {

      // Print description of the exception.
      System.out.println( "** Error on data select. ** " );
      ex.printStackTrace ();
```

```
        }
    }
}
```

Returns

A `String` containing the name of the table

isAutoIncrement

Declaration: `public abstract boolean isAutoIncrement(int column) throws argumentSQLException`

This method determines whether or not the column is automatically numbered. It accepts an argument for the column index (ordinal position of the column in the column list) of the column to evaluate. The method returns a `boolean` true if the column is automatically numbered and a `boolean` false if the column is not automatically numbered.

```
import java.sql.*;
import java.io.*;

class SelectGen {

     public static void main( String argv[] ) {

       try {
          Class.forName ("jdbc.odbc.JdbcOdbcDriver");
          String url = "jdbc:odbc:msaccessdb";
          Connection con = DriverManager.getConnection (
                                               url, "", "");

          String qs = "select * from orders ";
          Statement stmt = con.createStatement();

          ResultSet rs = stmt.executeQuery( qs );

          // get the meta-data information
          ResultSetMetaData rsmd = rs.getMetaData();

         if ( rsmd.isAutoIncrement( 1 ) )
           System.out.println(
```

```
                    "Column 1 is an auto-increment column." );

        }
        catch (java.lang.Exception ex) {

       // Print description of the exception.
       System.out.println( "** Error on data select. ** " );
       ex.printStackTrace ();

       }
    }
}
```

Parameters

`column`—An `int` value for the column index

Returns

A Java `boolean`

isCaseSensitive

Declaration: `public abstract boolean isCaseSensitive(int column) throws argumentSQLException`

This method determines whether or not a column is case sensitive. It accepts an argument for the column index (ordinal position of the column in the column list) of the column to evaluate. The method returns a `boolean` true if the column is case sensitive or a `boolean` false if the column is not case sensitive.

```
import java.sql.*;
import java.io.*;

class SelectGen {

     public static void main( String argv[] ) {

       try {
          Class.forName ("jdbc.odbc.JdbcOdbcDriver");
          String url = "jdbc:odbc:msaccessdb";
          Connection con = DriverManager.getConnection (
```

```
                                        url, "", "");

        String qs = "select * from orders ";
        Statement stmt = con.createStatement();

        ResultSet rs = stmt.executeQuery( qs );

        // get the meta-data information
        ResultSetMetaData rsmd = rs.getMetaData();

       if ( rsmd.isCaseSensitive( 1 ) )
         System.out.println(
              "Column 1 is a case sensitive column." );

     }
     catch (java.lang.Exception ex) {

    // Print description of the exception.
    System.out.println( "** Error on data select. ** " );
    ex.printStackTrace ();

    }
  }
}
```

Parameters

column—an integer value for the column index

Returns

A Java boolean

isCurrency

Declaration: public abstract boolean isCurrency(int column) throws argumentSQLException

This method determines whether or not a column is a currency value. It accepts an argument for the column index (ordinal position of the column in the column list) of the column to evaluate. The method returns a boolean true if the column is a currency value or a boolean false if the column is not.

```
import java.sql.*;
```

```
import java.io.*;

class SelectGen {

      public static void main( String argv[] ) {

        try {
            Class.forName ("jdbc.odbc.JdbcOdbcDriver");
            String url = "jdbc:odbc:msaccessdb";
            Connection con = DriverManager.getConnection (
                                                  url, "", "");

            String qs = "select * from orders ";
            Statement stmt = con.createStatement();

            ResultSet rs = stmt.executeQuery( qs );

            // get the meta-data information
            ResultSetMetaData rsmd = rs.getMetaData();

          if ( rsmd.isCurrency( 1 ) )
                System.out.println(
                       "Column 1 is a currency value column." );

        }
        catch (java.lang.Exception ex) {

       // Print description of the exception.
       System.out.println( "** Error on data select. ** " );
       ex.printStackTrace ();

       }
    }
}
```

Parameters

`column`—an `int` value for the column index

Returns

A Java `boolean`

isDefinitelyWritable

Declaration: `public abstract boolean isDefinitelyWritable(int column) throws argumentSQLException`

This method determines whether or not the column can be written by the user. It accepts an argument for the column index (ordinal position of the column in the column list) of the column to evaluate. It returns a `boolean` true if the column can be written; a `boolean` false if the column cannot be written.

```
import java.sql.*;
import java.io.*;

class SelectGen {

     public static void main( String argv[] ) {

       try {
          Class.forName ("jdbc.odbc.JdbcOdbcDriver");
          String url = "jdbc:odbc:msaccessdb";
          Connection con = DriverManager.getConnection (
                                                url, "", "");

          String qs = "select * from orders ";
          Statement stmt = con.createStatement();

          ResultSet rs = stmt.executeQuery( qs );

// get the meta-data information
          ResultSetMetaData rsmd = rs.getMetaData();

          if ( rsmd.isDefinitelyWritable( 1 ) )
             System.out.println(
                   "This column can DEFINITELY be written."  ):
            }
       catch (java.lang.Exception ex) {

     // Print description of the exception.
     System.out.println( "** Error on data select. ** " );
     ex.printStackTrace ();
```

```
        }
    }
}
```

Parameters

`column`—an `int` value for the column index

Returns

A Java `boolean`

isNullable

Declaration: `public abstract int isNullable(int column) throws argumentSQLException`

This method determines whether or not a column can be set to a NULL value. It accepts an argument for the column index (ordinal position of the column in the column list) of the column to evaluate. The method returns an integer value of `columnNoNulls`, `columnNullable`, or `columnNullableUnknown` from `java.sql.ResultSetMetaData`.

```
import java.sql.*;
import java.io.*;

class SelectGen {

     public static void main( String argv[] ) {

       try {
          Class.forName ("jdbc.odbc.JdbcOdbcDriver");
          String url = "jdbc:odbc:msaccessdb";
          Connection con = DriverManager.getConnection (
                                             url, "", "");

          String qs = "select * from orders ";
          Statement stmt = con.createStatement();

          ResultSet rs = stmt.executeQuery( qs );
          // get the meta-data information
          ResultSetMetaData rsmd = rs.getMetaData();

         if ( rsmd.isNullable( 1 ) ==
```

```
                    ResultSetMetaData.columnNullable )
              System.out.println(
                  "Column 1 can receive a NULL value." );
          else if ( rsmd.isNullable( 1 ) ==
                    ResultSetMetaData.columnNoNulls )
              System.out.println(
                  "Column 1 can NOT receive a NULL value." );
          else if ( rsmd.isNullable( 1 ) ==
                  ResultSetMetaData.columnNullableUnknown )
              System.out.println(
"It is not known whether column 1 can receive a NULL value." ); }
          catch (java.lang.Exception ex) {

          // Print description of the exception.
          System.out.println( "** Error on data select. ** " );
          ex.printStackTrace ();

          }
    }
}
```

Parameters

`column`—an integer value for the column index

Returns

An `int` value

isReadOnly

Declaration: `public abstract boolean isReadOnly(int column) throws argumentSQLException`

This method determines whether or not the column is a read-only column (not writable). It accepts an argument for the column index (ordinal position of the column in the column list) of the column to evaluate. It returns a `boolean` true if the column is read-only; a `boolean` false if the column can be written by the user.

```
import java.sql.*;
import java.io.*;

class SelectGen {
```

```
    public static void main( String argv[] ) {

      try {
          Class.forName ("jdbc.odbc.JdbcOdbcDriver");
          String url = "jdbc:odbc:msaccessdb";
          Connection con = DriverManager.getConnection (
                                            url, "", "");

          String qs = "select * from orders ";
          Statement stmt = con.createStatement();

          ResultSet rs = stmt.executeQuery( qs );

// get the meta-data information
          ResultSetMetaData rsmd = rs.getMetaData();

          if ( rsmd.isReadOnly( 1 ) )
              System.out.println(
                      "This is a read-only column."  );

          }
      catch (java.lang.Exception ex) {

     // Print description of the exception.
     System.out.println( "** Error on data select. ** " );
     ex.printStackTrace ();

     }
  }
}
```

Parameters

column—an int value for the column index

Returns

A Java boolean

isSearchable

Declaration: `public abstract boolean isSearchable(int column) throws argumentSQLException`

This method determines whether or not a column can be used in a SQL `where` clause. It accepts an argument for the column index (ordinal position of the column in the column list) of the column to evaluate. The method returns a `boolean` true if the column can be used in a `where` clause or a `boolean` false if the column cannot.

```
import java.sql.*;
import java.io.*;

class SelectGen {

      public static void main( String argv[] ) {

        try {
           Class.forName ("jdbc.odbc.JdbcOdbcDriver");
           String url = "jdbc:odbc:msaccessdb";
           Connection con = DriverManager.getConnection (
                                             url, "", "");

           String qs = "select * from orders ";
           Statement stmt = con.createStatement();

           ResultSet rs = stmt.executeQuery( qs );

           // get the meta-data information
           ResultSetMetaData rsmd = rs.getMetaData();

          if ( rsmd.isSearchable( 1 ) )
            System.out.println(
                  "Column 1 is a searchable column." );

        }
        catch (java.lang.Exception ex) {

      // Print description of the exception.
      System.out.println( "** Error on data select. ** " );
```

```
            ex.printStackTrace ();

            }
        }
}
```

Parameters

column—an int value for the column index

Returns

A Java boolean

isSigned

Declaration: public abstract boolean isSigned(int column) throws argumentSQLException

This method determines whether or not a column can contain a signed value. It accepts an argument for the column index (ordinal position of the column in the column list) of the column to evaluate. The method returns a boolean true if the column is a signed value or a boolean false if the column is not a signed value.

```
import java.sql.*;
import java.io.*;

class SelectGen {

     public static void main( String argv[] ) {

       try {
           Class.forName ("jdbc.odbc.JdbcOdbcDriver");
           String url = "jdbc:odbc:msaccessdb";
           Connection con = DriverManager.getConnection (
                                               url, "", "");

           String qs = "select * from orders ";
           Statement stmt = con.createStatement();

           ResultSet rs = stmt.executeQuery( qs );
```

```
        // get the meta-data information
        ResultSetMetaData rsmd = rs.getMetaData();

        if ( rsmd.isSigned( 1 ) )
            System.out.println( "Column 1 is signed."  );
        else
            System.out.println( "Column 1 is NOT signed."  );

          }
     catch (java.lang.Exception ex) {

    // Print description of the exception.
    System.out.println( "** Error on data select. ** "
);
    ex.printStackTrace ();

    }
  }
}
```

Parameters

`column`—an `int` value for the column index

Returns

A Java `boolean`

isWritable

Declaration: `public abstract boolean isWritable(int column) throws argumentSQLException`

This method determines whether or not the column can be written by the user. It accepts an argument for the column index (ordinal position of the column in the column list) of the column to evaluate. It returns a `boolean` true if the column can be written; a `boolean` false if the column cannot be written.

```
import java.sql.*;
import java.io.*;

class SelectGen {
```

```
        public static void main( String argv[] ) {

          try {
             Class.forName ("jdbc.odbc.JdbcOdbcDriver");
             String url = "jdbc:odbc:msaccessdb";
             Connection con = DriverManager.getConnection (
                                              url, "", "");

             String qs = "select * from orders ";
             Statement stmt = con.createStatement();

             ResultSet rs = stmt.executeQuery( qs );

// get the meta-data information
             ResultSetMetaData rsmd = rs.getMetaData();

             if ( rsmd.isWritable( 1 ) )
                System.out.println( "This column can be written." );

             }
          catch (java.lang.Exception ex) {

         // Print description of the exception.
         System.out.println( "** Error on data select. ** " );
         ex.printStackTrace ();

         }
    }
}
```

Parameters

`column`—an `int` value for the column index

Returns

a Java `boolean`

Class java.sql.SQLException


```
public class SQLException extends Exception
```

The `SQLException` interface provides information on database access errors. Information on the nature of the error, error messages, `SQLState` (as described in the XOPEN SQL specification), and vendor-specific error information are provided. Additional error messages exist as a chain to the first error message.

`SQLExceptions` are chained to the object that generated the exception; this would most likely be a `Statement` or `Connection` object. These exceptions are caught in a '`catch`' code block and the exception chain is traversed to determine the exceptions that have been generated.

```
import java.net.*;
import java.sql.*;
import java.lang.Runtime;

class ExceptionDemo {

        try {

           Class.forName ("jdbc.odbc.JdbcOdbcDriver");
           String url = "jdbc:odbc:msaccessdb";
           Connection con = DriverManager.getConnection (
                                              url, "", "");
           Statement stmt = con.createStatement();
           ResultSet rs = stmt.executeQuery(
                        "select * from orders" );

          }
         catch (SQLException ex) {

         // A SQLException was generated. Catch it and
         // display the error information. Note that there
         // could be multiple error objects chained
         // together
         System.out.println ("\n*** SQLException caught ***\n");

           while (ex != null) {
```

```
            System.out.println ("SQLState: " +
                  ex.getSQLState ());
            System.out.println ("Message:  " +
                  ex.getMessage ());
            System.out.println ("Vendor:   " +
                  ex.getErrorCode ());
            ex = ex.getNextException ();
            System.out.println ("");
          }
        }
        catch (java.lang.Exception ex) {

        // Got some other type of exception. Dump it.
        ex.printStackTrace ();
        }
```

SQLException Constructor

SQLException

Declaration: `public SQLException(String reason, String SQLState, int vendorCode)`

This is the constructor for the `SQLException` class. It accepts parameters for the reason or description of the exception, the `SQLState` the XOPEN specified code to explain the exception, and a vendor specific exception code.

Parameters

`reason`—a description of the exception

`SQLState`—an XOPEN code identifying the exception

`vendorCode`—a database vendor specific exception code

SQLException

Declaration: `public SQLException(String reason, String SQLState)`

This is the constructor for the `SQLException` class. It accepts parameters for the reason or description of the exception and the `SQLState` the XOPEN specified code to explain the exception.

Parameters

`reason`—a description of the exception

`SQLState`—an X/open code identifying the exception

SQLException

Declaration: `public SQLException(String reason)`

This is the constructor for the `SQLException` class. It accepts a single parameter for the reason or description of the exception.

Parameters

`reason`—a description of the exception

SQLException

Declaration: `public SQLException()`

This is the constructor for the `SQLException` class. This version of the constructor will create an `SQLException` object with no description, `SQLState` or vendor specific error codes.

SQLException Methods

getErrorCode

Declaration: `public int getErrorCode()`

This method returns an integer containing the vendor specific error code.

```
...
      }
         catch (SQLException ex) {

         // A SQLException was generated. Catch it and
         // display the error information. Note that there
         // could be multiple error objects chained
              // together
         System.out.println ("\n*** SQLException caught ***\n");

           while (ex != null) {
             System.out.println ("SQLState: " +
                   ex.getSQLState ());
             System.out.println ("Message:  " +
```

```
            ex.getMessage ());
    System.out.println ("Vendor:    " +

            ex.getErrorCode ());
    ex = ex.getNextException ();
    System.out.println ("");
  }
```

Returns

A Java int

getNextException

Declaration: public SQLException getNextException()

This method returns the next exception in the exception chain.

```
}
  catch (SQLException ex) {

  // A SQLException was generated. Catch it and
  // display the error information. Note that there
  // could be multiple error objects chained
      // together
  System.out.println ("\n*** SQLException caught ***\n");

    while (ex != null) {
      System.out.println ("SQLState: " +
            ex.getSQLState ());
      System.out.println ("Message:  " +
            ex.getMessage ());
      System.out.println ("Vendor:    " +
            ex.getErrorCode ());


      ex = ex.getNextException ();
      System.out.println ("");
    }
```

Returns

An SQLException representing the next SQLException in the chain.

getSQLState

Declaration: public String getSQLState()

The method returns a String containing the SQLState. The JDBC specification does not identify specific SQLState values for method exceptions.

```
...
     }
       catch (SQLException ex) {

       // A SQLException was generated. Catch it and
       // display the error information. Note that there
       // could be multiple error objects chained
            // together
       System.out.println ("\n*** SQLException caught ***\n");

         while (ex != null) {
           System.out.println ("SQLState:  " +

                 ex.getSQLState ());
           System.out.println ("Message:   " +
                 ex.getMessage ());
           System.out.println ("Vendor:    " +
                 ex.getErrorCode ());
           ex = ex.getNextException ();
           System.out.println ("");
         }
```

Returns

A Java String containing the SQLState value

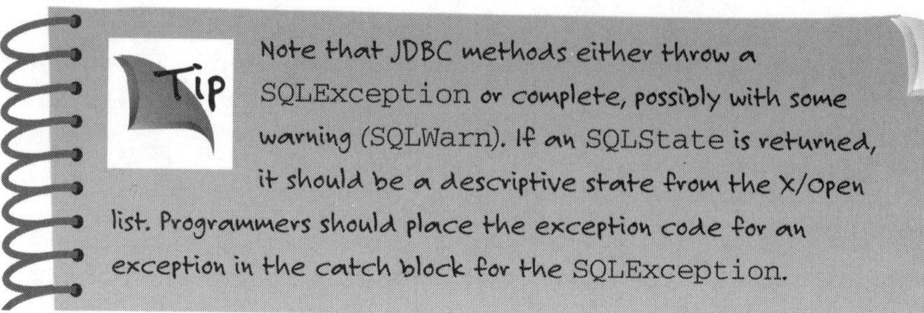

Tip
Note that JDBC methods either throw a SQLException or complete, possibly with some warning (SQLWarn). If an SQLState is returned, it should be a descriptive state from the X/Open list. Programmers should place the exception code for an exception in the catch block for the SQLException.

setNextException

Declaration: `public synchronized void setNextException(SQLException ex)`

This method adds an `SQLException` to the end of the exception chain.

```
catch (SQLException ex) {


System.out.println ("\n*** SQLException caught ***\n");

  while (ex != null) {
    System.out.println ("SQLState: " +
          ex.getSQLState ());
    System.out.println ("Message:  " +
          ex.getMessage ());
    System.out.println ("Vendor:   " +
          ex.getErrorCode ());
    ex = ex.getNextException ();
    System.out.println ("");
  }


           ex1 = new SQLException(
                          "Add a new exception."  );
           ex.setNextException( ex1 );
     }
```

Parameters

ex—the new end of the `SQLException` chain

Class java.sql.SQLWarning

`public class` **`SQLWarning`** `extends SQLException`

The `SQLWarning` class provides information on database access warnings. Warnings are silently chained to the object whose method caused it to be reported.

```
import java.net.URL;
import java.sql.*;

class Select1 {

     public static void main( String argv[] ) {

       try {

          Class.forName ("jdbc.odbc.JdbcOdbcDriver");
          String url = "jdbc:odbc:msaccessdb";
          Connection con = DriverManager.getConnection (
                                             url, "", "");
          Statement stmt = con.createStatement();
          ResultSet rs = stmt.executeQuery(
                      "select * from orders" );

          // ** check warnings **
          SQLWarning warn = con.getWarnings();

          if (warn != null) {
             System.out.println ("\n *** Warning ***\n");
             while (warn != null) {
             System.out.println ("SQLState: " +
           warn.getSQLState ());
             System.out.println ("Message:  " +
           warn.getMessage ());
             System.out.println ("Vendor:   " +
           warn.getErrorCode ());
             System.out.println ("");
                warn = warn.getNextWarning ();
             }

           }
```

See Also: `getWarnings,`

SQLWarning Constructor

SQLWarning

Declaration: `public SQLWarning(String reason, String SQLstate, int vendorCode)`

This is the constructor for the `SQLWarning` class. Arguments are supplied for the reason or description of the warning, the `SQLState` of the warning, and a vendor-specific warning code.

Parameters

`reason`—a string providing a description of the warning

`SQLState`—a string providing an XOPEN code identifying the warning

`vendorCode`—an integer providing a database vendor specific warning code

SQLWarning

Declaration: `public SQLWarning(String reason, String SQLstate)`

This is the constructor for the `SQLWarning` class. Arguments are supplied for the reason or description of the warning and the `SQLState` as specified in the X/OPEN SQL specification.

Parameters

`reason`—a string containing a description of the warning

`SQLState`—a string containing an XOPEN code identifying the warning

SQLWarning

Declaration: `public SQLWarning(String reason)`

This is the constructor for the `SQLWarning` class. An argument is supplied for the reason or description of the warning.

Parameters

`reason`—a description of the warning

SQLWarning

Declaration: `public SQLWarning()`

This is the constructor for the `SQLWarning` class.

SQLWarning Methods

getNextWarning

Declaration: `public SQLWarning getNextWarning()`

This method retrieves the next warning in the warning chain.

```
import java.net.URL;
import java.sql.*;

class Select1 {
     public static void main( String argv[] ) {

     try {

          Class.forName ("jdbc.odbc.JdbcOdbcDriver");
          String url = "jdbc:odbc:msaccessdb";
          Connection con = DriverManager.getConnection (
                                             url, "", "");
          SQLWarning = con.getWarnings();

          if (warn != null) {
             System.out.println ("\n *** Warning ***\n");
             while (warn != null) {
             System.out.println ("SQLState: " +
           warn.getSQLState ());
             System.out.println ("Message:  " +
           warn.getMessage ());
             System.out.println ("Vendor:   " +
           warn.getErrorCode ());
             System.out.println ("");
                warn = warn.getNextWarning ();
             }
...
```

Returns

An `SQLWarning` representing the next `SQLWarning` in the chain

setNextWarning

Declaration: `public void setNextWarning(SQLWarning w)`

This method adds an `SQLWarning` to the end of the warning chain.

```
import java.net.URL;
import java.sql.*;

class Select1 {

     public static void main( String argv[] ) {

     try {

          Class.forName ("jdbc.odbc.JdbcOdbcDriver");
          String url = "jdbc:odbc:msaccessdb";
          Connection con = DriverManager.getConnection (
                                               url, "", "");
          SQLWarning = con.getWarnings();

          if (warn != null) {
            System.out.println ("\n *** Warning ***\n");
            while (warn != null) {
            System.out.println ("SQLState: " +
           warn.getSQLState ());
            System.out.println ("Message:  " +
           warn.getMessage ());
            System.out.println ("Vendor:   " +
           warn.getErrorCode ());
            System.out.println ("");
                 warn = warn.getNextWarning ();
            }

          SQLWarning warn1 = new SQLWarning(
                                  "Add a new warning.");
          warn.setNextWarning( warn1 );

...
```

Parameters

w—an `SQLWarning` to add to the warning chain

Interface java.sql.Statement

Declaration: `public interface` **`Statement`** `extends Object`

The `Statement` interface provides the capability to create and execute SQL statements. Errors and warnings that may occur during execution of the SQL statement are chained to the `Statement` object.

The `Statement` object produces a `ResultSet` object. Only one `ResultSet` object can be open for a `Statement`. If multiple select and update operations must be interleaved, then two `Statement` objects with their respective `ResultSets` must be used.

```
import java.sql.*;
import java.io.*;

class Select1 {

     public static void main( String argv[] ) {

       try {

          Class.forName ("jdbc.odbc.JdbcOdbcDriver");
          String url = "jdbc:odbc:msaccessdb";
          Connection con = DriverManager.getConnection (
                                       url, "", "");

          DatabaseMetaData dmd = con.getMetaData();
          Statement stmt = con.createStatement( );

          ResultSet rs = stmt.executeQuery(
                          "select * from orders" );
          boolean more = rs.next();

          while ( more ) {
              System.out.println(
                   "Order number: " + rs.getInt(
                             "order_number" ) +
                "Units: " + rs.getInt( "order_units" ) );
                  more = rs.next();
           }
```

```
        }

        catch (java.lang.Exception ex) {

        // Print description of the exception.
        System.out.println( "** Error on data select. ** " );
        ex.printStackTrace ();

        }
    }
}
```

See Also: `createStatement, ResultSet`

Statement Methods

cancel

Declaration: `public abstract void cancel() throws SQLException`

This method allows a SQL statement to be canceled. It should be used by a separate thread, thus allowing one thread to cancel a statement being executed by another thread.

```
...
try {

        boolean cancelFlag = false;

        // any argument passed means cancel query after suspend
        if ( argv.length > 0 )
           cancelFlag = true;

        Asynch1 ASQuery = new Asynch1();


        ASQuery.start();

        Thread.sleep( 10 * 1000    );
```

```
System.out.println(
      "Query suspended for 3 seconds ... " );
ASQuery.suspend();

Thread.sleep( 3 * 1000  );

System.out.println( "Query resumed ... " );
ASQuery.resume();

if ( cancelFlag ) {
    System.out.println( "Query will be canceled ... " );
    ASQuery.prepStmt.cancel();
    ASQuery.stop();
}
...
```

clearWarnings

Declaration: `public abstract void clearWarnings() throws SQLException`

This method will clear the `SQLWarnings` on the `Statement`.

```
import java.sql.*;
import java.io.*;

class Select1 {

     public static void main( String argv[] ) {

       try {

          Class.forName ("jdbc.odbc.JdbcOdbcDriver");
          String url = "jdbc:odbc:msaccessdb";
          Connection con = DriverManager.getConnection (
                                     url, "", "");

          DatabaseMetaData dmd = con.getMetaData();
          Statement stmt = con.createStatement( );
```

```
ResultSet rs = stmt.executeQuery(
        "select * from orders" );


// clear SQLWarnings
stmt.clearWarnings();

boolean more = rs.next();

while ( more ) {
        System.out.println(
            "Order number: " + rs.getInt(
                    "order_number" ) +
            "Units: " + rs.getInt( "order_units" ) );
        more = rs.next();
 }


   stmt.close();

 }

 catch (java.lang.Exception ex) {

// Print description of the exception.
System.out.println( "** Error on data select. ** " );
ex.printStackTrace ();
}
    }
}
```

close

Declaration: `public abstract void close() throws SQLException`

This statement is used to release all the resources associated with a `Statement`. When a `Statement` is closed, its current `ResultSet` is also automatically closed. (A `Statement` is automatically closed when it is garbage collected by the Java virtual machine.)

```
import java.sql.*;
import java.io.*;

class Select1 {

     public static void main( String argv[] ) {

       try {

          Class.forName ("jdbc.odbc.JdbcOdbcDriver");
          String url = "jdbc:odbc:msaccessdb";
          Connection con = DriverManager.getConnection (
                                              url, "", "");

          DatabaseMetaData dmd = con.getMetaData();
          Statement stmt = con.createStatement( );

          ResultSet rs = stmt.executeQuery(
                   "select * from orders" );
          boolean more = rs.next();

          while ( more ) {
                   System.out.println(
                       "Order number: " + rs.getInt(
                              "order_number" ) +
                       "Units: " + rs.getInt( "order_units" ) );
                   more = rs.next();
           }

         stmt.close();

       }

       catch (java.lang.Exception ex) {

      // Print description of the exception.
      System.out.println( "** Error on data select. ** " );
```

```
            ex.printStackTrace ();

        }
    }
}
```

execute

Declaration: `public abstract execute(String sql) throws SQLException`

This method executes a SQL statement. A single `String` argument supplies the SQL statement. The `getResultSet`, `getMoreResults`, and `getUpdateCount` calls are used to navigate through multiple results. The method returns a `boolean` value of true if the result is a `ResultSet`; false if it is an integer.

```
import java.sql.*;
import java.io.*;

 class Execute2 {

   public static void main( String argv[] ) {

       try {

          Class.forName ("jdbc.odbc.JdbcOdbcDriver");
          String url = "jdbc:odbc:msaccessdb";
          Connection con = DriverManager.getConnection (
                                          url, "", "");

          String qs =
       " select * from loadtest where col1 < 200; " +
       " select * from loadtest where col1 > 200 and col1 < 300";
          Statement stmt = con.createStatement( );


          boolean more = stmt.execute( qs );

          if ( more )
              System.out.println(
```

```
            "ResultSet has been returned." );
    else {
        System.out.println(
                "No ResultSet has been returned." );
        System.exit( -1 );
    }

    // read the first ResultSet
    ResultSet rs = stmt.getResultSet();
    more = rs.next();
    int n = 1;
    for (; n < 2000 && more ; n++ ) {
        more = rs.next();
        System.out.println( "Col1: " + rs.getInt( 1 ) );
    }

    // read the second ResultSet
    more = stmt.getMoreResults();
    if ( !(more) ) {
        System.out.println( "No more results." );
        System.exit( -1 );
    }

    ResultSet rs1 = stmt.getResultSet();
    more = rs1.next();
    for (; n < 2000 && more ; n++ ) {
        more = rs1.next();
        System.out.println( "Col1: " + rs.getInt( 1 ) );
    }

    }

    catch (java.lang.Exception ex) {

   // Print description of the exception.
   System.out.println( "** Error on data insert. ** " );
   ex.printStackTrace ();

   }
```

```
        }
    }
```

Parameters

sql—A Java `String` containing a SQL statement

Returns

A boolean value

See Also: `getResultSet, getUpdateCount, getMoreResults`

executeQuery

Declaration: `public abstract ResultSet executeQuery(String sql) throws SQLException`

This method executes a SQL statement that returns a single `ResultSet`. It accepts a `String` argument with the SQL statement and returns a `ResultSet` with the results of the query.

```
import java.sql.*;
import java.io.*;

class Select1 {

      public static void main( String argv[] ) {

        try {

            Class.forName ("jdbc.odbc.JdbcOdbcDriver");
            String url = "jdbc:odbc:msaccessdb";
            Connection con = DriverManager.getConnection (
                                                  url, "", "");

            DatabaseMetaData dmd = con.getMetaData();
            Statement stmt = con.createStatement( );

ResultSet rs = stmt.executeQuery( "select * from orders" );
            boolean more = rs.next();

            while ( more ) {
                    System.out.println(
```

```
                        "Order number: " + rs.getInt(
                             "order_number" ) +
                        "Units: " + rs.getInt( "order_units" ) );
                    more = rs.next();
            }

        }

        catch (java.lang.Exception ex) {

        // Print description of the exception.
        System.out.println( "** Error on data select. ** " );
        ex.printStackTrace ();

        }
    }
}
```

Parameters

sql—a String containing the SQL statement to execute

Returns

A ResultSet containing the results of the query

executeUpdate

Declaration: `public abstract int executeUpdate(String sql) throws SQLException`

This method executes a SQL statement that performs an update operation (SQL 'update','insert', 'delete'). SQL statements that return no values such as SQL DDL statements can be executed with this method. A single String argument containing the SQL statement to execute is provided.

The method returns an integer containing the number or rows updated by the SQL operation, or a 0 for statements where a count value has no relevance such as DDL statements.

```
import java.sql.*;
import java.io.*;

class Select1 {
```

```
    public static void main( String argv[] ) {

      try {

         Class.forName ("jdbc.odbc.JdbcOdbcDriver");
         String url = "jdbc:odbc:msaccessdb";
         Connection con = DriverManager.getConnection (
                                          url, "", "");

         DatabaseMetaData dmd = con.getMetaData();
         Statement stmt = con.createStatement( );

int resultCount = stmt.executeQuery(
                              " update orders set order_count = 3 " +
                              " where order_number = '12345' " );
System.out.println( resultCount + " rows updated " );

      }

      catch (java.lang.Exception ex) {

     // Print description of the exception.
     System.out.println( "** Error on data select. ** " );
     ex.printStackTrace ();

     }
   }
}
```

Parameters

sql—a `String` containing the SQL statement to execute

Returns

An `int` value containing the row count or 0

getMaxFieldSize

Declaration: `public abstract int getMaxFieldSize() throws SQLException`

This method returns the maximum field size limit for the `Statement`. This is the maximum amount of data that can be retrieved for any BINARY,

VARBINARY, LONGVARBINARY, CHAR, VARCHAR, and LONGVARCHAR columns. If the limit is exceeded, the excess data is discarded.

```
import java.sql.*;
import java.io.*;

class Select1 {

     public static void main( String argv[] ) {

       try {

            Class.forName ("jdbc.odbc.JdbcOdbcDriver");
            String url = "jdbc:odbc:msaccessdb";
            Connection con = DriverManager.getConnection (
                                                url, "", "");

            DatabaseMetaData dmd = con.getMetaData();
            Statement stmt = con.createStatement( );


            int maxFieldSize = stmt.getMaxFieldSize();
            System.out.println( "Max field size is " +
                         maxFieldSize );

            ResultSet rs = stmt.executeQuery(
                    "select * from orders" );

            boolean more = rs.next();

            while ( more ) {
                    System.out.println(
                        "Order number: " + rs.getInt(
                              "order_number" ) +
                        "Units: " + rs.getInt( "order_units" ) );
                    more = rs.next();
            }
```

```
            stmt.close();

          }

          catch (java.lang.Exception ex) {

         // Print description of the exception.
         System.out.println( "** Error on data select. ** " );
         ex.printStackTrace ();
         }
    }
}
```

Returns

A Java `int`

getMaxRows

Declaration: `public abstract int getMaxRows() throws SQLException`

This method retrieves the maximum number of rows limit of the `ResultSet` attached to this `Statement`. The maximum rows limit is the maximum number of rows that can be retrieved from the database for a `ResultSet`. If this limit is exceeded, the remaining rows are simply not retrieved from the database. The method returns an integer value containing the maximum number of rows value for the `ResultSet`.

```
import java.sql.*;
import java.io.*;

class Select1 {

     public static void main( String argv[] ) {

       try {

          Class.forName ("jdbc.odbc.JdbcOdbcDriver");
          String url = "jdbc:odbc:msaccessdb";
          Connection con = DriverManager.getConnection (
                                                url, "", "");
```

```
        DatabaseMetaData dmd = con.getMetaData();
        Statement stmt = con.createStatement( );

        // ***********************************
        int maxRows = stmt.getMaxRows();
        System.out.println( "Max number of rows is " + maxRows );

        ResultSet rs = stmt.executeQuery(
                     "select * from orders" );

        boolean more = rs.next();

        while ( more ) {
                  System.out.println(
                     "Order number: " + rs.getInt(
                              "order_number" ) +
                     "Units: " + rs.getInt( "order_units" ) );
                  more = rs.next();
        }

stmt.close();

      }

      catch (java.lang.Exception ex) {

     // Print description of the exception.
     System.out.println( "** Error on data select. ** " );
     ex.printStackTrace ();
     }
  }
}
```

Returns

An `int` value containing the maximum number of rows allowed

getMoreResults

Declaration: `public abstract boolean getMoreResults() throws SQLException`

This method moves to the next result set in the results. It returns true if the result is a `ResultSet`; false if it is an integer. This will implicitly close the current `ResultSet` obtained with `getResultSet`.

```
import java.sql.*;
import java.io.*;

  class Execute2 {

    public static void main( String argv[] ) {

        try {

           Class.forName ("jdbc.odbc.JdbcOdbcDriver");
           String url = "jdbc:odbc:msaccessdb";
           Connection con = DriverManager.getConnection (
                                             url, "", "");

           String qs =
             " select * from loadtest where col1 < 200; " +
             " select * from loadtest where col1 > 200 and col1 <
300";
           Statement stmt = con.createStatement( );

           boolean more = stmt.execute( qs );

           if ( more )
               System.out.println(
                    "ResultSet has been returned." );
           else {
               System.out.println(
                     "No ResultSet has been returned." );
               System.exit( -1 );
           }

// read the first ResultSet
```

```
        ResultSet rs = stmt.getResultSet();
        more = rs.next();
        int n = 1;
        for (; n < 2000 && more ; n++ ) {
              more = rs.next();
              System.out.println( "Col1: " + rs.getInt( 1 ) );
        }


        // read the second ResultSet
        more = stmt.getMoreResults();
        if ( !(more) ) {
            System.out.println( "No more results." );
            System.exit( -1 );
        }

        ResultSet rs1 = stmt.getResultSet();
        more = rs1.next();
        for (; n < 2000 && more ; n++ ) {
             more = rs1.next();
             System.out.println( "Col1: " + rs.getInt( 1 ) );
        }

        }

        catch (java.lang.Exception ex) {

       // Print description of the exception.
       System.out.println( "** Error on data insert. ** " );
       ex.printStackTrace ();

       }
    }
}
```

Returns

A `boolean` value of true if the next result is a `ResultSet`; false if it is an integer

See Also: `execute`

getQueryTimeout

Declaration: `public abstract int getQueryTimeout() throws SQLException`

This method is used to set the query timeout limit for this driver. The query timeout limit is the number of seconds the driver will wait for a `Statement` to execute. If this limit is exceeded, a `SQLException` is thrown. The method returns an integer value for the number of seconds for the current query timeout value.

```
import java.sql.*;
import java.io.*;

class Select1 {

     public static void main( String argv[] ) {

        try {

            Class.forName ("jdbc.odbc.JdbcOdbcDriver");
            String url = "jdbc:odbc:msaccessdb";
            Connection con = DriverManager.getConnection (
                                                   url, "", "");

            DatabaseMetaData dmd = con.getMetaData();
            Statement stmt = con.createStatement( );

int queryTimeout = stmt.getQueryTimeout();
            System.out.println( "Query timeout is " +
                    queryTimeout );

            ResultSet rs = stmt.executeQuery(
                    "select * from orders" );

            boolean more = rs.next();

            while ( more ) {
                    System.out.println(
                        "Order number: " + rs.getInt(
                        "order_number" ) +
```

```
                    "Units: " + rs.getInt( "order_units" ) );
                more = rs.next();
            }


        stmt.close();

      }

      catch (java.lang.Exception ex) {

     // Print description of the exception.
     System.out.println( "** Error on data select. ** " );
     ex.printStackTrace ();
     }
   }
}
```

Returns

An `int` containing the current query timeout limit

getResultSet

Declaration: `public abstract ResultSet getResultSet() throws SQLException`

This method returns the current result as a `ResultSet`. It should only be called once for each result; subsequent calls for more results should be made to the `getMoreResults` method.

```
import java.sql.*;
import java.io.*;

  class Execute2 {

    public static void main( String argv[] ) {

        try {

            Class.forName ("jdbc.odbc.JdbcOdbcDriver");
            String url = "jdbc:odbc:msaccessdb";
```

```
    Connection con = DriverManager.getConnection (
                                             url, "", "");

    String qs =
" select * from loadtest where col1 < 200; " +
" select * from loadtest where col1 > 200 and col1 < 300";
    Statement stmt = con.createStatement( );

    boolean more = stmt.execute( qs );

    if ( more )
         System.out.println(
           "ResultSet has been returned." );
    else {
         System.out.println(
           "No ResultSet has been returned." );
         System.exit( -1 );
    }


    // read the first ResultSet
    ResultSet rs = stmt.getResultSet();
    more = rs.next();
    int n = 1;
    for (; n < 2000 && more ; n++ ) {
          more = rs.next();
          System.out.println( "Col1: " + rs.getInt( 1 ) );
    }

    // read the second ResultSet
    more = stmt.getMoreResults();
    if ( !(more) ) {
       System.out.println( "No more results." );
       System.exit( -1 );
    }

    ResultSet rs1 = stmt.getResultSet();
    more = rs1.next();
    for (; n < 2000 && more ; n++ ) {
```

```
                more = rs1.next();
                System.out.println( "Col1: " + rs.getInt( 1 ) );
            }

            }

            catch (java.lang.Exception ex) {

            // Print description of the exception.
            System.out.println( "** Error on data insert. ** " );
            ex.printStackTrace ();

            }
        }
    }
```

Returns

A `ResultSet`; NULL if the result is an integer

See Also: `execute`

getUpdateCount

Declaration: `public abstract int getUpdateCount() throws SQLException`

This method returns the current result as an integer value. This would be the result of an update or delete. This method should only be called once per result.

```
import java.sql.*;
import java.io.*;

  class Execute2 {

    public static void main( String argv[] ) {

        try {

            Class.forName ("jdbc.odbc.JdbcOdbcDriver");
            String url = "jdbc:odbc:msaccessdb";
            Connection con = DriverManager.getConnection (
```

```
                                url, "", "");

          String qs =
            " update stock set price = price * 1.1";
          Statement stmt = con.createStatement( );

          boolean more = stmt.execute( qs );

          if ( more )
               System.out.println(
                         "ResultSet has been returned." );
          else {
               System.out.println(
                         "No ResultSet has been returned." +
 " Will retrieve the update count." );

int updCount = stmt.getUpdateCount();
            System.out.println( updCount + " rows updated."  );
          }

          }

          catch (java.lang.Exception ex) {

         // Print description of the exception.
         System.out.println( "** Error on data insert. ** " );
         ex.printStackTrace ();

         }
      }
   }
```

Returns

An integer with the current result.

See Also: execute

getWarnings

Declaration: public abstract SQLWarning getWarnings() throws SQLException

This method returns the SQLWarnings that are currently active on this Statement. Multiple warnings are chained to the first warning returned. Warnings are automatically cleared each time a statement is executed. (Note that ResultSet warnings will be chained to the ResultSet, not the Statement.)

```
import java.sql.*;
import java.io.*;

class Select1 {

     public static void main( String argv[] ) {

       try {

            Class.forName ("jdbc.odbc.JdbcOdbcDriver");
            String url = "jdbc:odbc:msaccessdb";
            Connection con = DriverManager.getConnection (
                                                  url, "", "");

            DatabaseMetaData dmd = con.getMetaData();
            Statement stmt = con.createStatement( );

            ResultSet rs = stmt.executeQuery(
                    "select * from orders" );
// ** check warnings **
            SQLWarning warn = stmt.getWarnings();

            if (warn != null) {
               System.out.println ("\n *** Warning ***\n");
               while (warn != null) {
               System.out.println ("SQLState: " +
```

```
            warn.getSQLState ());
             System.out.println ("Message:   " +
            warn.getMessage ());
             System.out.println ("Vendor:    " +
            warn.getErrorCode ());
             System.out.println ("");
                warn = warn.getNextWarning ();
             }

          boolean more = rs.next();

          while ( more ) {
                   System.out.println(
                      "Order number: " + rs.getInt(
                            "order_number" ) +
                      "Units: " + rs.getInt( "order_units" ) );
                   more = rs.next();
           }


        stmt.close();

      }
              catch (java.lang.Exception ex) {

    // Print description of the exception.
    System.out.println( "** Error on data select. ** " );
    ex.printStackTrace ();
    }
  }
}
```

Returns

The first `SQLWarning` for the statement

setCursorName

Declaration: `public abstract void setCursorName(String name) throws SQLException`

This method sets the cursor name for use with subsequent `Statement` executes. This cursor name can then be used by positioned update and delete statements. (If the database does not support positioned update and delete statements, then this statement fails.)

Cursor names should be unique within a `Connection`. Positioned update and delete statements must be done with a different `Statement` than the one that generated the `ResultSet` being used for positioning.

```
import java.sql.*;
import java.io.*;

class PosUpd {

     public static void main( String argv[] ) {

       try {

         Class.forName ("jdbc.odbc.JdbcOdbcDriver");
         String url = "jdbc:odbc:msaccessdb";
         Connection con = DriverManager.getConnection (
                                     url, "", "");

          Statement stmt1 = con.createStatement();



          DatabaseMetaData dmd = con.getMetaData();
          if ( dmd.supportsPositionedUpdate() == false ) {
               System.out.println(
"Positioned update is not supported by this database."  );
               System.exit( -1 );
          }

          ResultSet rs = stmt1.executeQuery( "select " +
                      " * from loadtest where col1 = 5" +
                      " for update " );
          rs.next(); // look at the first row (col1=5)
```

```
            String cursName = "updcurs1";
            stmt.setCursorName( cursName );
            System.out.println( "cursor name is " + cursName );

            Statement stmt2 = con.createStatement();

            // update stmt2 at col1 = 5
            int result = stmt2.executeUpdate(
                 "update loadtest set col2 = '1000' " +
                 " where current of " + cursName );

            rs = stmt1.executeQuery(
                           "select * from loadtest " +
                " where col1 = 5 " );

            rs.next();
            System.out.println( "col1 = " + rs.getInt( 1 ) +
                                " col2 = " + rs.getInt( 2 ) );


        }

        catch (java.lang.Exception ex) {

       // Print description of the exception.
       System.out.println( "** Error on data select. ** " );
       ex.printStackTrace ();

       }
    }
}
```

Parameters

name—a `String` with the new cursor name.

setEscapeProcessing

Declaration: `public abstract void setEscapeProcessing(boolean enable) throws SQLException`

This method is used to set escape processing on for the `Statement`. If escape processing is on, then the driver will do escape substitution before sending the SQL to the database. The method receives a single `boolean` parameter; if this parameter is set to true, then escape processing is turned on.

```
import java.sql.*;
import java.io.*;

class Select1 {

     public static void main( String argv[] ) {

       try {

          Class.forName ("jdbc.odbc.JdbcOdbcDriver");
          String url = "jdbc:odbc:msaccessdb";
          Connection con = DriverManager.getConnection (
                                                url, "", "");

          DatabaseMetaData dmd = con.getMetaData();
          Statement stmt = con.createStatement( );

stmt.setEscapeProcessing( true );

          ResultSet rs = stmt.executeQuery(
                "select * from orders" );

          boolean more = rs.next();

          while ( more ) {
                 System.out.println(
                    "Order number: " + rs.getInt(
                          "order_number" ) +
                    "Units: " + rs.getInt( "order_units" ) );
                 more = rs.next();
```

```
            }

stmt.close();

        }

        catch (java.lang.Exception ex) {

       // Print description of the exception.
       System.out.println( "** Error on data select. ** " );
       ex.printStackTrace ();
       }
    }
}
```

Parameters

`enable`—a Java `boolean` value set to true to enable; false to disable

setMaxFieldSize

Declaration: `public abstract void setMaxFieldSize(int max) throws SQLException`

This method sets the maximum field size limit for the `Statement`. This is the maximum amount of data that can be retrieved for any BINARY, VARBINARY, LONGVARBINARY, CHAR, VARCHAR, and LONGVARCHAR columns. The method accepts a single integer argument for the maximum value.

```
import java.sql.*;
import java.io.*;

class Select1 {

     public static void main( String argv[] ) {

       try {

          Class.forName ("jdbc.odbc.JdbcOdbcDriver");
          String url = "jdbc:odbc:msaccessdb";
          Connection con = DriverManager.getConnection (
```

```
                                         url, "", "");

        DatabaseMetaData dmd = con.getMetaData();
        Statement stmt = con.createStatement( );

stmt.setMaxFieldSize( 2000 );
        System.out.println( "Max field size is " +
                                  stmt.getMaxFieldSize() );

        ResultSet rs = stmt.executeQuery(
                  "select * from orders" );
        boolean more = rs.next();

        while ( more ) {
                System.out.println(
                    "Order number: " + rs.getInt(
                          "order_number" ) +
                    "Units: " + rs.getInt( "order_units" ) );
                more = rs.next();
        }

stmt.close();

       }

       catch (java.lang.Exception ex) {
      // Print description of the exception.
      System.out.println( "** Error on data select. ** " );
      ex.printStackTrace ();
      }
   }
}
```

Parameters

max—an int value for the new maximum column size limit; zero means unlimited

setMaxRows

Declaration: `public abstract void setMaxRows(int max) throws SQLException`

This method allows the `maxRows` value for the `ResultSet` to be set to an integer value. The `maxRows` limit is the maximum number or rows that can be retrieved from the database for a `ResultSet`. If this limit is exceeded, the remaining rows are simply not retrieved from the database. It receives a single integer argument that is used to set the `maxRows` parameter.

```
import java.sql.*;
import java.io.*;

class Select1 {

     public static void main( String argv[] ) {

       try {

          Class.forName ("jdbc.odbc.JdbcOdbcDriver");
          String url = "jdbc:odbc:msaccessdb";
          Connection con = DriverManager.getConnection (
                                            url, "", "");

          DatabaseMetaData dmd = con.getMetaData();
          Statement stmt = con.createStatement( );


          stmt.setMaxRows( 200 );
          System.out.println( "Max number of rows is " +
                                   stmt.getMaxRows());

          ResultSet rs = stmt.executeQuery( "select * from orders"
);

          boolean more = rs.next();

          while ( more ) {
                  System.out.println(
                     "Order number: " + rs.getInt(
                           "order_number" ) +
```

```
                    "Units: " + rs.getInt( "order_units" ) );
                more = rs.next();
        }

        stmt.close();

       }

       catch (java.lang.Exception ex) {

      // Print description of the exception.
      System.out.println( "** Error on data select. ** " );
      ex.printStackTrace ();
      }
   }
}
```

Parameters

max—an int containing the maximum number of rows

setQueryTimeout

Declaration: public abstract void setQueryTimeout(int seconds) throws SQLException

This method is used to set the query timeout for the Statement. The query timeout limit is the number of seconds the driver will wait for a Statement to execute. If this limit is exceeded, a SQLException is thrown. The method receives a single integer parameter for the number of seconds.

```
import java.sql.*;
import java.io.*;

class Select1 {

     public static void main( String argv[] ) {

       try {

          Class.forName ("jdbc.odbc.JdbcOdbcDriver");
          String url = "jdbc:odbc:msaccessdb";
```

```
            Connection con = DriverManager.getConnection (
                                                 url, "", "");

            DatabaseMetaData dmd = con.getMetaData();
            Statement stmt = con.createStatement( );


            stmt.setQueryTimeout( 120 );
            System.out.println( "Query timeout is " +
                                 stmt.getQueryTimeout() );

            ResultSet rs = stmt.executeQuery( "select * from orders"
);
            boolean more = rs.next();

            while ( more ) {
                    System.out.println(
                       "Order number: " + rs.getInt(
                          "order_number" ) +
                       "Units: " + rs.getInt( "order_units" ) );
                    more = rs.next();
             }


          stmt.close();

        }

        catch (java.lang.Exception ex) {

       // Print description of the exception.
       System.out.println( "** Error on data select. ** " );
       ex.printStackTrace ();
       }
    }
}
```

Parameters

`seconds`—an integer containing the number of seconds for the time out value

Interface java.sql.Time

Declaration: `public class **Time** extends Date`

This method is used to represent SQL TIME values stored in the database. These objects store hours, minutes and seconds.

Time Constructors

Time

Declaration: `public Time(int hour, int minute, int second)`

`This method` creates a Java `Time`. It accepts integer arguments for hour, minute, and second.

Parameters

`hour`—an `int` between 0 to 23

`minute`—an `int` between 0 to 59

`second`—an `int` between 0 to 59

Methods

toString

Declaration: `public String toString()`

This method returns the `Time` value as a formatted string. The resulting `String` is formatted in the form of "hh:mm:ss".

```
import java.sql.*;
import java.util.*;
import java.sql.Time;

class t3 {

   public static void main( String args[] ){

   Time t = new Time( 11, 22, 22);
   t = t.valueOf( "01:01:01" );
   System.out.println( "Time is "+ t.toString() );

   }
```

```
}
```

Returns

a `String` with the formatted Time value

Overrides

`toString` in class Date

valueOf

Declaration: `public static Time valueOf(String stringTime)`

This method converts a `String` with a formatted `Time` value into a `Time` object. The format for the `Time` value is "hh:mm:ss" where 'hh' is hours, 'mm' is minutes and 'ss' is seconds.

```
import java.sql.*;
import java.util.*;
import java.sql.Time;

class t3 {

    public static void main( String args[] ){

    Time t = new Time( 11, 22, 22);
    t = t.valueOf( "01:01:01" );
    System.out.println( "Time is "+ t.toString() );

    }
}
```

Parameters

`stringTime`—a `String` value with the time in format "hh:mm:ss"

Returns

a `Time` value

Class java.sql.Timestamp

Declaration: `public class Timestamp extends Date`

This method allows the storage of SQL TIMESTAMP values in Java. This interface provides storage of date and time information together in a single Java object. (This class extends the standard `sun.util.date` class with nanos.)

Timestamp Constructors

Timestamp

Declaration: `public Timestamp(int year, int month, int date, int hour, int minute, int second, int nano)`

This is the constructor for the `Timestamp` value. It receives integer arguments for year, month, date, hour, minute, second, and nano seconds.

Parameters

```
year—year-1900
month—0 to 11
day—1 to 31
hour—0 to 23
minute—0 to 59
second—0 to 59
nano—0 to 999,999,999
```

Timestamp Methods

equals

Declaration: `public boolean equals(Timestamp ts)`

This method tests this `Timestamp` value against the `Timestamp` supplied as an argument. It returns a `boolean` value of true if the `Timestamps` are equal.

```
import java.sql.*;
import java.util.*;
import java.sql.Timestamp;

class t3 {

   public static void main( String args[] ){
```

```
    Timestamp ts = new Timestamp( (short) 58, 1, 28,
                                          11, 22, 22, 0 );

    ts1 = Timestamp.valueOf( "1968-01-01 01:01:01.0" );

    if ( ts.equals( ts1 ) )
        System.out.println( "Timestamp values are equal." );
    }
}
```

Parameters

`ts`–the `Timestamp` value to compare with

Returns

A Java `boolean`

getNanos

Declaration: `public int getNanos()`

This method retrieves the nanosecond `Timestamp` value. It returns the nanosecond value as an integer.

```
import java.sql.*;
import java.util.*;
import java.sql.Timestamp;

class t3 {

    public static void main( String args[] ){

    Timestamp ts = new Timestamp( (short) 58, 1, 28,
                                          11, 22, 22, 0 );

    System.out.println( "Nano seconds is " + ts.getNanos() );

System.out.println( "Timestamp is " + ts.toString() );
    }
}
```

Returns

An integer value containing the nanosecond value for the `Timestamp`

setNanos

Declaration: `public void setNanos(int n)`

`This method` sets the nanosecond value for the `Timestamp`. A single integer argument supplies the nanosecond value.

```
import java.sql.*;
import java.util.*;
import java.sql.Timestamp;

class t3 {

   public static void main( String args[] ){

   Timestamp ts = new Timestamp( (short) 58, 1, 28,
                                        11, 22, 22, 0 );

   // *********************************************
   ts.setNanos( 1000 );

   System.out.println( "Timestamp is " + ts.toString() );
   }
}
```

Parameters

`n`—an integer containing the nanosecond value

toString

Declaration: `public String toString()`

This method returns a `Timestamp` value as a formatted `String`. The `String` returned is formatted as "`yyyy-mm-dd hh:mm:ss.f`".

```
import java.sql.*;
import java.util.*;
import java.sql.Timestamp;

class t3 {

   public static void main( String args[] ){
```

```
    Timestamp ts = new Timestamp( (short) 58, 1, 28,
                                   11, 22, 22, 0 );

System.out.println( "Timestamp is " + ts.toString() );
    }
}
```

Returns

A formatted String with the Timestamp value

valueOf

Declaration: public static Timestamp valueOf(String TimestampString)

This method converts a formatted string to a Timestamp value. It takes a single String argument with a formatted string containing the Timestamp value. The Timestamp value should be in the format "yyyy-mm-dd hh:mm:ss.f".

```
import java.sql.*;
import java.util.*;
import java.sql.Timestamp;

class t3 {

   public static void main( String args[] ){

   Timestamp ts = new Timestamp( (short) 58, 1, 28,
                                  11, 22, 22, 0 );
   ts = ts.valueOf( "1968-01-01 01:01:01.0" );
   System.out.println( "Timestamp is " + ts.toString() );
   }
}
```

Parameters

TimestampString—a formatted String containing the Timestamp value

Returns

a Date value

Class java.sql.Types

Declaration: `public class` **`Types`** `extends Object`

This class defines constants that are used to identify SQL types. The actual type constant values are equivalent to those in the X/OPEN specification.

JDBC SQL Data Types

SQL type	Java Type	Description
CHAR	`String`	fixed length character string
VARCHAR	`String`	variable length character string
LONGVARCHAR	`String`	variable length character string—large (sometimes stores Blob data)
NUMERIC	`java.sql.Numeric`	numeric data type of variable precision
DECIMAL	`java.sql.Numeric`	numeric data type of variable precision and scale
BIT	`boolean`	data type with only two possible values
TINYINT	`byte`	8-bit signed integer data type
SMALLINT	`short`	16-bit signed integer data type
INTEGER	`int`	32-bit signed integer data type
BIGINT	`long`	32-bit signed integer data type
REAL	`float`	floating point number
FLOAT	`double`	double precision floating point number
DOUBLE	`double`	double precision floating point number
BINARY	`byte[]`	fixed length binary data

continued

SQL Type	Java Type	Description
VARBINARY	`byte[]`	variable length binary data
LONGVARBINARY	`byte[]`	variable length binary data
DATE	`java.sql.Date`	date data
TIME	`java.sql.Time`	time data
TIMESTAMP	`java.sql.Timestamp`	date and time data

BIGINT

Declaration: `public final static int BIGINT`

Java Type: `long`

The BIGINT data type is a four byte signed integer with a maximum value of 2,147,483,647 and a minimum value of -2,147,483,647.

BINARY

Declaration: `public final static int BINARY`

Java Type: `byte[]`

Stores fixed length binary data.

BIT

Declaration: `public final static int BIT`

Java Type: `boolean`

The `bit` data type can contain one of two values: true or false.

CHAR

Declaration: `public final static int CHAR`

Java Type: `String`

A fixed length character string. (Note that the Java `String` provides for a variable length string.)

DATE

Declaration: `public final static int DATE`

Java Type: `java.sql.Date`

Stores date information.

DECIMAL

Declaration: `public final static int DECIMAL`

Java Type: `java.sql.Numeric`

A numeric data type of variable precision.

DOUBLE

Declaration: `public final static int DOUBLE`

Java Type: `double`

A double precision floating point number.

FLOAT

Declaration: `public final static int FLOAT`

Java Type: `double`

The FLOAT is a double precision floating point number.

INTEGER

Declaration: `public final static int INTEGER`

Java Type: `int`

The INTEGER data type is a four byte signed integer with a maximum value of 2,147,483,647 and a minimum value of -2,147,483,647.

LONGVARBINARY

Declaration: `public final static int LONGVARBINARY`

Java Type: `byte[]`

Stores variable length binary data.

LONGVARCHAR

Declaration: `public final static int LONGVARCHAR`

Java Type: `String`

A variable length character string. In some databases, this is used to store Blob (binary large object) data.

NULL

Declaration: `public final static int NULL`

This constant represents the value of SQL NULL, the absence of data.

NUMERIC

Declaration: `public final static int NUMERIC`

Java Type: `java.sql.Numeric`

A numeric data type of variable precision.

OTHER

Declaration: `public final static int OTHER`

This data type indicates a database specific data type. It can be retrieved and manipulated using the `getObject` method of the `PreparedStatement`, `CallableStatement`, and `ResultSet` classes, and the `setObject` method as part of `PreparedStatement` and `CallableStatement` classes.

REAL

Declaration: `public final static int REAL`

Java Type: `float`

A floating point number.

SMALLINT

Declaration: `public final static int SMALLINT`

Java Type: `short`

The SMALLINT is a two byte integer with a maximum value of 32,767 and a minimum value of -32,767.

TIME

Declaration: `public final static int TIME`

Java Type: `java.sql.Time`

Stores time information and allows retrieval in a variety of formats.

TIMESTAMP

Declaration: `public final static int TIMESTAMP`

Java Type: `java.sql.Timestamp`

Stores date and time information and allows retrieval in a variety of formats.

TINYINT

Declaration: `public final static int TINYINT`

Java Type: `byte`

The TINYINT is a one byte integer.

VARBINARY

Declaration: `public final static int VARBINARY`

Java Type: `byte[]`

Stores variable length binary data.

VARCHAR

Declaration: public final static int VARCHAR

Java Type: `String`

A variable length character string.

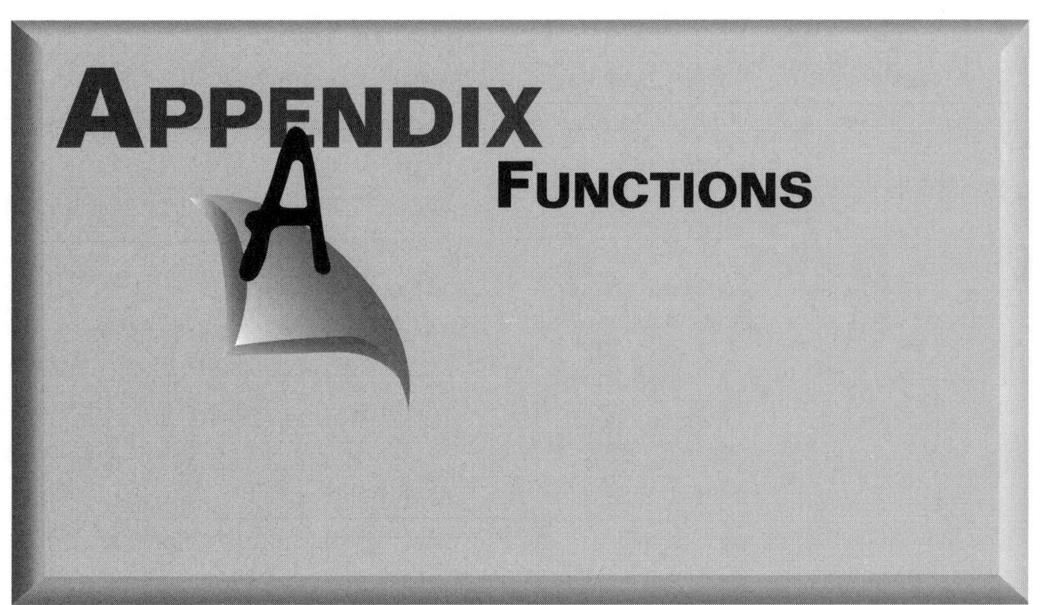

Appendix A Functions

Math Functions

Function	Description
ACOS(float)	returns the arccosine
ABS(number)	returns the absolute value
ASIN(float)	returns the arcsine
ATAN(float)	returns the arctangent
ATAN2(float1, float2)	returns the arctangent of the x and y coordinates represented by float1 and float2
CEILING(number)	returns the smallest integer greater than or equal to *number*
COS(float)	returns the cosine
COT(float)	returns the cotangent

continued

Function	Description
DEGREES(number)	returns the number of degrees
EXP(float)	returns the exponential value of float
FLOOR(number)	returns the largest integer less than or equal to *number*
LOG(float)	returns the log
LOG10(float)	returns the base 10 logarithm
MOD(integer1, integer2)	returns the modulus of *integer1* divided by *integer2*
PI()	returns the constant value of pi as a floating point number
POWER(number, power)	returns the value of number to integer power
RADIANS(number)	returns the number of radians converted from degrees
RAND(integer)	returns a random floating point value
ROUND(number, places)	returns a numeric expression rounded to integer expression places to the right of the decimal point
SIGN(number)	returns the sign of number; -1 if less than 0, 0 if number equals 0, 1 if greater than 0
SIN(float)	returns the sine
SQRT(float)	returns the square root
TAN(float)	returns the tangent
TRUNCATE(number, places)	returns the *number* of truncated *places* to the right of the decimal point

String Functions

Function	Description
ASCII(string)	returns the integer ASCII code of the leftmost character value for the character *string*

continued

Function	Description
CHAR(code)	returns the character that has the ASCII code value specified by *code*
CONCAT(string1, string2)	returns the string that is the result of concatenating *string2* to *string1*
DIFFERENCE(string1, string2)	returns an integer value that represents the difference between the SOUNDEX values of *string1* and *string2*
INSERT(string1, start, length, string2)	returns a character string where *length* characters have been deleted from *string1* beginning at *start* and where *string2* has been inserted into *string1* at *start*
LCASE(string)	returns all characters in *string* converted to lowercase
LEFT(string, count)	converts all lowercase characters in the *string* to uppercase
LENGTH(string)	returns the length of the *string* in bytes excluding trailing blanks and the string termination character
LOCATE(string1, string2, start)	locates *string1* in *string2*. Begins searching at the start of *string2* unless the optional *start* parameter is specified, in which case it would start searching at *start* position in *string2*
LTRIM(string)	eliminates leading blanks from *string*
REPEAT(string, count)	returns a string composed of *string* repeated *count* times
REPLACE(string1, string2, string3)	replaces all occurrences of *string2* in *string1* with *string3*
RIGHT(string, count)	returns the rightmost count of characters of *string*
RTRIM(string)	eliminates trailing blanks from *string*
SOUNDEX(string)	returns a data source dependent character string representing the sound of *string*

continued

Function	Description
SPACE(count)	returns a string of *count* spaces
SUBSTRING(string, start, length)	returns a substring of *string* starting at *start* and running for *length* characters
UCASE(string)	returns all characters in *string* in uppercase

Date Functions

Function	Description
CURDATE()	returns the current date
CURTIME()	returns the current time
DAYNAME(date)	returns the name of the current day (Monday, Tuesday ...)
DAYOFMONTH(date)	returns the day of the month as an integer (1-31)
DAYOFWEEK(date)	returns the day of the week as an integer (1-7)
DAYOFYEAR(date)	returns the day of the year as an integer value (0-366)
HOUR(time)	returns the hour of time as an integer value (0-23)
MINUTE(time)	returns the minute as an integer value (0-59)
MONTH(time)	returns the month as an integer value (0-1-12)
MONTHNAME(date)	returns the name of the month
NOW()	returns the current date and time as a timestamp value
QUARTER(date)	returns the quarter in date as an integer value (1-4)
SECOND(time)	returns the second in time as an integer value (0-59)
TIMESTAMPADD (interval_type, interval, timestamp)	returns the timestamp created by adding *timestamp* to *interval* of *interval_type*

continued

Function	Description
TIMESTAMPDIFF (interval_type, timestamp1, timestampt2)	returns the difference between the timestamps of type *interval_type*
WEEK(date)	returns the week number of the date as an integer (1-53)
YEAR(date)	returns the year of the date as an integer

Database Functions

Function	Description
DATABASE()	returns the name of the database corresponding to the current connection
IFNULL(expression, value)	if *expression* is null, then the *value* is returned. If the *expression* is not null, then *expression* is returned
USER()	returns the current user name

Appendix B Applet Code Example (Chapter 5)

Program 5.1 client.java

```
// Applet Package Imports
import java.awt.*;
import java.applet.Applet;
import java.sql.*;
import java.net.URL;
import java.util.*;

// will store these objects in a vector
class DBResults extends Object {

      String TextField1;
      String TextField2;
}

class DBControl {
```

continued

```
    public static  Connection conn;
    public static  Statement  stmt;
    public static  ResultSet    rs;
    public static int       currpos;
    public static int       maxrows;
    public static  Vector ResultsStorage;

}

// Main Applet
public class Client extends java.applet.Applet
{
   public Screen1_CLASS Screen1;
   // Task Object
   public Object taskdata;

   // access for screen flipping is provided here
   public CardLayout layoutManager;

   public void init()
   {
      layoutManager = new CardLayout();
      setLayout(layoutManager);

      // create an instance of the applet panels
      Screen1 = new Screen1_CLASS(this, this);

      // add the mail panel
      add("Screen1", Screen1);
   }
}


class Screen1_CLASS extends Screen
{

   public Label1_CLASS Label1;
   public Label2_CLASS Label2;
   public TextField1_CLASS TextField1;
   public TextField2_CLASS TextField2;
   public GetData_CLASS GetData;
```

continued

```
public NextRow_CLASS NextRow;
public InsertData_CLASS InsertData;
public Previous_CLASS Previous;
// Task Object
public Object taskdata;
 public Client parent;


Screen1_CLASS(Client app, Client aParent)
{
   applet = app;
   parent = aParent;

    // create instances of all subcomponents
Label1 = new Label1_CLASS(applet, this);
Label2 = new Label2_CLASS(applet, this);
TextField1 = new TextField1_CLASS(applet, this);
TextField2 = new TextField2_CLASS(applet, this);
GetData = new GetData_CLASS(applet, this);
NextRow = new NextRow_CLASS(applet, this);
InsertData = new InsertData_CLASS(applet, this);
Previous = new Previous_CLASS(applet, this);

    // add instances to the panel
    setLayout(null);
    add(Previous);
    add(InsertData);
    add(NextRow);
    add(GetData);
    add(TextField2);
    add(TextField1);
    add(Label2);
    add(Label1);

    setFont(new Font("Courier",0,8));
    move(bounds().x, 0);
    move(0, bounds().y);
resize(bounds().width, 500);
resize(500, bounds().height);
setForeground(Color.black);
setBackground(Color.lightGray);
```

continued

```
        setFont(new Font("Courier", getFont().getStyle(),
        getFont().getSize()));
        setFont(new Font(getFont().getName(), Font.PLAIN,
        getFont().getSize()));
        setFont(new Font(getFont().getName(),
        getFont().getStyle(), 15));

    }
    void initialize()
    {
    }
}

class Previous_CLASS extends Button
{
    // A class that produces a labeled button component.

    // Task Object
    public Object taskdata;
     Client applet;
     public Screen1_CLASS parent;

    Previous_CLASS(Client app, Screen1_CLASS aParent)
    {
        applet = app;
        parent = aParent;

        // create instances of all subcomponents

        // add instances to the panel
        setFont(new Font("Courier",0,8));
        setLabel("Previous ");
        move(bounds().x, 160);
        move(180, bounds().y);
        resize(bounds().width, 24);
        resize(83, bounds().height);
        setForeground(Color.black);
        setBackground(Color.lightGray);
        setFont(new Font("Courier", getFont().getStyle(),
        getFont().getSize()));
        setFont(new Font(getFont().getName(), Font.PLAIN,
        getFont().getSize()));
```

continued

```
        setFont(new Font(getFont().getName(),
        getFont().getStyle(), 15));

                }
    void initialize()
    {
    }
public boolean action(Event evt, Object what)
{
    // display the previous row
    if ( DBControl.currpos - 1 >= 1 ) {
         DBControl.currpos—;
         DBResults db = ( DBResults)
        DBControl.ResultsStorage.elementAt( DBControl.currpos );

         parent.TextField1.setText( db.TextField1 );
         parent.TextField2.setText( db.TextField2 );

   }
   else {
         DBControl.currpos = 1;
   }

    return(true);
}

}

class InsertData_CLASS extends Button
{
    // A class that produces a labeled button component.

    // Task Object
    public Object taskdata;
     Client applet;
     public Screen1_CLASS parent;

    InsertData_CLASS(Client app, Screen1_CLASS aParent)
    {
        applet = app;
        parent = aParent;
```

continued

```
    // create instances of all subcomponents

    // add instances to the panel
    setFont(new Font("Courier",0,8));
    setLabel("Insert ");
    move(bounds().x, 118);
    move(178, bounds().y);
    resize(bounds().width, 24);
    resize(80, bounds().height);
    setForeground(Color.black);
    setBackground(Color.lightGray);
    setFont(new Font("Courier", getFont().getStyle(),
    getFont().getSize()));
    setFont(new Font(getFont().getName(), Font.PLAIN,
    getFont().getSize()));
    setFont(new Font(getFont().getName(),
    getFont().getStyle(), 15));

  }
  void initialize()
  {
  }
public boolean action(Event evt, Object what)
{
  try {

  String InsertString = " insert into table1.txt values " + "(" +
                 "'" + parent.TextField1.getText() + "'" + "," +
                 "'" + parent.TextField2.getText() + "'" +
     ")";

  int Result = DBControl.stmt.executeUpdate( InsertString );

  }
  catch ( SQLException ex ) {

      System.out.println ("\n*** SQLException caught ***\n");

       while (ex != null) {
         System.out.println ("SQLState: " +
             ex.getSQLState ());
```

continued

```
            System.out.println ("Message:  " +
                  ex.getMessage ());
            System.out.println ("Vendor:   " +
                  ex.getErrorCode ());
            ex = ex.getNextException ();
            System.out.println ("");
          }

   }

   return(true);
}

}

class NextRow_CLASS extends Button
{
   // Task Object
   public Object taskdata;
    Client applet;
    public Screen1_CLASS parent;

   NextRow_CLASS(Client app, Screen1_CLASS aParent)
   {
      applet = app;
      parent = aParent;

      // create instances of all subcomponents

      // add instances to the panel
      setFont(new Font("Courier",0,8));
      setLabel("Next Row");
      move(bounds().x, 158);
      move(48, bounds().y);
      resize(bounds().width, 24);
      resize(97, bounds().height);
      setForeground(Color.black);
      setBackground(Color.lightGray);
      setFont(new Font("Courier", getFont().getStyle(),
      getFont().getSize()));
      setFont(new Font(getFont().getName(), Font.PLAIN,
      getFont().getSize()));
```

continued

```
      setFont(new Font(getFont().getName(),
      getFont().getStyle(), 15));
   }
   void initialize()
   {
   }

public boolean action(Event evt, Object what)
{

    if ( DBControl.currpos + 1 <= DBControl.maxrows ) {

       DBControl.currpos++;
       DBResults db = ( DBResults)
      DBControl.ResultsStorage.elementAt( DBControl.currpos );

       // display the results
       parent.TextField1.setText( db.TextField1 );
       parent.TextField2.setText( db.TextField2 );

     }
     else {
       DBControl.currpos = DBControl.maxrows;
     }

   return(true);
}

}

class GetData_CLASS extends Button
{
   // A class that produces a labeled button component.

   // Task Object
   public Object taskdata;
    Client applet;
    public Screen1_CLASS parent;

   GetData_CLASS(Client app, Screen1_CLASS aParent)
   {
      applet = app;
```

continued

```
        parent = aParent;

        // create instances of all subcomponents

        // add instances to the panel
        setFont(new Font("Courier",0,8));
        setLabel("Get Data");
        move(bounds().x, 120);
        move(50, bounds().y);
        resize(bounds().width, 23);
        resize(98, bounds().height);
        setForeground(Color.black);
        setBackground(Color.lightGray);
        setFont(new Font("Courier", getFont().getStyle(),
        getFont().getSize()));
        setFont(new Font(getFont().getName(), Font.PLAIN,
        getFont().getSize()));
        setFont(new Font(getFont().getName(),
        getFont().getStyle(), 15));

    }
    void initialize()
    {
    }
public boolean action(Event evt, Object what)
{
     // local variables
     String url = "jdbc:odbc:textdb";
     DBResults db;
         try {

           // Load the jdbc-odbc bridge driver
           Class.forName ("jdbc.odbc.JdbcOdbcDriver");

         // Attempt to connect to a driver.

         DBControl.conn = DriverManager.getConnection ( url, "", "");

         // get the data from the database
         DBControl.stmt = DBControl.conn.createStatement();
         String query = "select * from table1.txt";
```

continued

```
  ResultSet rs = DBControl.stmt.executeQuery( query );
  DBControl.currpos = 1;

  // store the results
  boolean more = rs.next();
  DBControl.currpos = 1;
  DBControl.ResultsStorage = new Vector();
  while ( more ) {
        db = new DBResults();
        db.TextField1 = rs.getString( 1 );
        db.TextField2 = rs.getString( 2 );
        DBControl.ResultsStorage.addElement( db );
        DBControl.currpos++;
        more = rs.next();
  }
  DBControl.maxrows = DBControl.currpos - 1;

  // display the first row
  DBControl.currpos = 1;
  DBResults dbt = ( DBResults )
DBControl.ResultsStorage.elementAt( DBControl.currpos );
  parent.TextField1.setText( dbt.TextField1 );
  parent.TextField2.setText( dbt.TextField2 );

}
catch (SQLException ex) {

  // A SQLException was generated. Catch it and
  // display the error information. Note that there
  // could be multiple error objects chained
  // together

System.out.println ("\n*** SQLException caught
***\n");

    while (ex != null) {
      System.out.println ("SQLState: " +
            ex.getSQLState ());
      System.out.println ("Message:  " +
            ex.getMessage ());
      System.out.println ("Vendor:   " +
```

continued

```
                  ex.getErrorCode ());
            ex = ex.getNextException ();
            System.out.println ("");
          }
        }

        catch (java.lang.Exception ex) {

        // Got some other type of exception. Dump it.
        ex.printStackTrace ();

      }

    return(true);
  }

  }

  class TextField2_CLASS extends TextField
  {
    // TextField is a component that allows the editing of a single
       line of text.

    // Task Object
    public Object taskdata;
     Client applet;
     public Screen1_CLASS parent;

    TextField2_CLASS(Client app, Screen1_CLASS aParent)
    {
       applet = app;
       parent = aParent;

       // create instances of all subcomponents

       // add instances to the panel
       setFont(new Font("Courier",0,8));
       move(bounds().x, 70);
       move(170, bounds().y);
       resize(bounds().width, 21);
       resize(121, bounds().height);
```

continued

```
      setForeground(Color.black);
      setBackground(Color.white);
      setFont(new Font("Courier", getFont().getStyle(),
      getFont().getSize()));
      setFont(new Font(getFont().getName(), Font.PLAIN,
      getFont().getSize()));
      setFont(new Font(getFont().getName(),
      getFont().getStyle(), 15));

   }
   void initialize()
   {
   }
}

class TextField1_CLASS extends TextField
{
   // TextField is a component that allows the editing of
      a single line of text.

   // Task Object
   public Object taskdata;
    Client applet;
    public Screen1_CLASS parent;

   TextField1_CLASS(Client app, Screen1_CLASS aParent)
   {
      applet = app;
      parent = aParent;

      // create instances of all subcomponents

      // add instances to the panel
      setFont(new Font("Courier",0,8));
      move(bounds().x, 40);
      move(170, bounds().y);
      resize(bounds().width, 21);
      resize(121, bounds().height);
      setForeground(Color.black);
      setBackground(Color.white);
      setFont(new Font("Courier", getFont().getStyle(),
      getFont().getSize()));
```

continued

```
            setFont(new Font(getFont().getName(), Font.PLAIN,
            getFont().getSize()));
            setFont(new Font(getFont().getName(),
            getFont().getStyle(), 15));

        }
        void initialize()
        {
        }
    }

    class Label2_CLASS extends Label
    {
        // A component that displays a single line of read-only text.

        // Task Object
        public Object taskdata;
         Client applet;
         public Screen1_CLASS parent;

        Label2_CLASS(Client app, Screen1_CLASS aParent)
        {
            applet = app;
            parent = aParent;
            // create instances of all subcomponents

            // add instances to the panel
            setFont(new Font("Courier",0,8));
            setText("Last Name");
            setAlignment(Label.LEFT);
            move(bounds().x, 70);
            move(50, bounds().y);
            resize(bounds().width, 19);
            resize(113, bounds().height);
            setForeground(Color.black);
            setBackground(Color.lightGray);
            setFont(new Font("Courier", getFont().getStyle(),
            getFont().getSize()));
            setFont(new Font(getFont().getName(), Font.PLAIN,
            getFont().getSize()));
            setFont(new Font(getFont().getName(),
            getFont().getStyle(), 15));
```

continued

```
   }
   void initialize()
   {
   }
}

class Label1_CLASS extends Label
{
   // A component that displays a single line of read-only text.

   // Task Object
   public Object taskdata;
    Client applet;
    public Screen1_CLASS parent;

   Label1_CLASS(Client app, Screen1_CLASS aParent)
   {
      applet = app;
      parent = aParent;

      // create instances of all subcomponents

      // add instances to the panel
      setFont(new Font("Courier",0,8));
      setText("First Name");
      setAlignment(Label.LEFT);
      move(bounds().x, 40);
      move(50, bounds().y);
      resize(bounds().width, 12);
      resize(112, bounds().height);
      setForeground(Color.black);
      setBackground(Color.lightGray);
      setFont(new Font("Courier", getFont().getStyle(),
      getFont().getSize()));
      setFont(new Font(getFont().getName(), Font.PLAIN,
      getFont().getSize()));
      setFont(new Font(getFont().getName(),
      getFont().getStyle(), 15));

    }
    void initialize()
```

continued

```
    {
    }
}

class Screen extends Panel
{
    // Task Object
    public Object taskdata;
     Client applet;
     Object parent;
    // A Panel Container class. This produces a generic
       container.

    Screen(Client app, Object aParent)
    {
       applet = app;
       parent = aParent;

       // create instances of all subcomponents

       // add instances to the panel
       setLayout(null);
       setFont(new Font("Courier",0,8));
       move(bounds().x, 0);
       move(0, bounds().y);
       resize(bounds().width, 100);
       resize(100, bounds().height);
       setForeground(Color.black);
       setBackground(Color.lightGray);
       setFont(new Font("Courier", getFont().getStyle(),
       getFont().getSize()));
       setFont(new Font(getFont().getName(), Font.PLAIN,
       getFont().getSize()));
       setFont(new Font(getFont().getName(),
       getFont().getStyle(), 15));
    }
    Screen()
    {
    }
    void initialize()
    {
    }
}
```

Appendix C RMI Code Example (Chapter 6)

DBComm.java

```
package rmiExample.DBComm;

import java.rmi.*;
import java.rmi.server.UnicastRemoteObject;
import java.util.Vector;
import java.sql.*;
import java.io.*;


public class DBComm extends  UnicastRemoteObject
          implements DBRemote {

     Vector v = new Vector();

     public DBComm() throws RemoteException {
       super();
     }

     public Vector getData( String pTableName ) {

      try {
```

continued

```
            System.out.println( "Received query.
Processing ... " );

            // get connected
            Class.forName ("sun.jdbc.odbc.JdbcOdbcDriver");
            Connection con = DriverManager.getConnection (
                             "jdbc:odbc:jdbcdsn",
                             "", "" );

            // create the statement and execute the query
            String qs = "select * from " + pTableName;
            Statement stmt = con.createStatement( );
            ResultSet rs = stmt.executeQuery( qs );
            boolean more = rs.next();

            if ( more )
               System.out.println( "Loading results ... " );

            // load the results data into a Vector
            int n = 0;
            while ( ( more ) && ( n < 100 ) ) {
                v.addElement(  rs.getObject( 1 ) );
                more = rs.next();
                n++;
            }
            System.out.println( "Returning " + n  + " rows." );

      }

  catch (java.lang.Exception ex) {

     // Print description of the exception.
     System.out.println( "** Error on data select. ** " );
     ex.printStackTrace ();

  }
  return v ;

  }


     public static void main ( String args[] ) {
```

continued

```
        // create and install a security manager
        if ( System.getSecurityManager() == null ) {

            System.setSecurityManager( new
RMISecurityManager() );
        }

        // Start the server

          try {

                DBComm obj = new DBComm();
                // Bind the object instance to the name
"JDBCServer"
                Naming.rebind( "//jserve/JDBCServer", obj );
                System.out.println( "Server has been
bound." );
          }
           catch ( Exception e ) {

                System.out.println( "JDBCServer error: " +
e.getMessage() );
                e.printStackTrace();

          }

}

}
```

DBRemote.java

```
package rmiExample.DBComm;

import java.rmi.Remote;
import java.rmi.RemoteException;
import java.util.Vector;

public interface DBRemote extends Remote {

      Vector getData( String pTable ) throws
RemoteException;

}
```

ServerTest.java

```
package rmiExample.DBComm;

import java.rmi.RemoteException;
import java.rmi.Remote;
import java.rmi.Naming;
import java.util.Vector;

public class ServerTest {

       public static void main( String argv[] ) {

       try {

         Vector v = null;

         DBComm_Stub obj = (DBComm_Stub) Naming.lookup(
                 "//jserve/JDBCServer" );

         System.out.println( "Retrieving Data." );
         v = obj.getData( "loadtest" );

         System.out.println( "Processing results." );
         int n;

         // *** need to determine the Vector call to
reveal the number
         // of elements in the vector and use that below

         for (n=0;n<50;n++)
             System.out.println( "row " + n +
" - Value: " +
                        v.elementAt( n ).toString() );

     }
      catch (Exception e) {

          System.out.println( "JDBCServer exception: " +
e.getMessage() );
        e.printStackTrace();

     }

   }
}
```

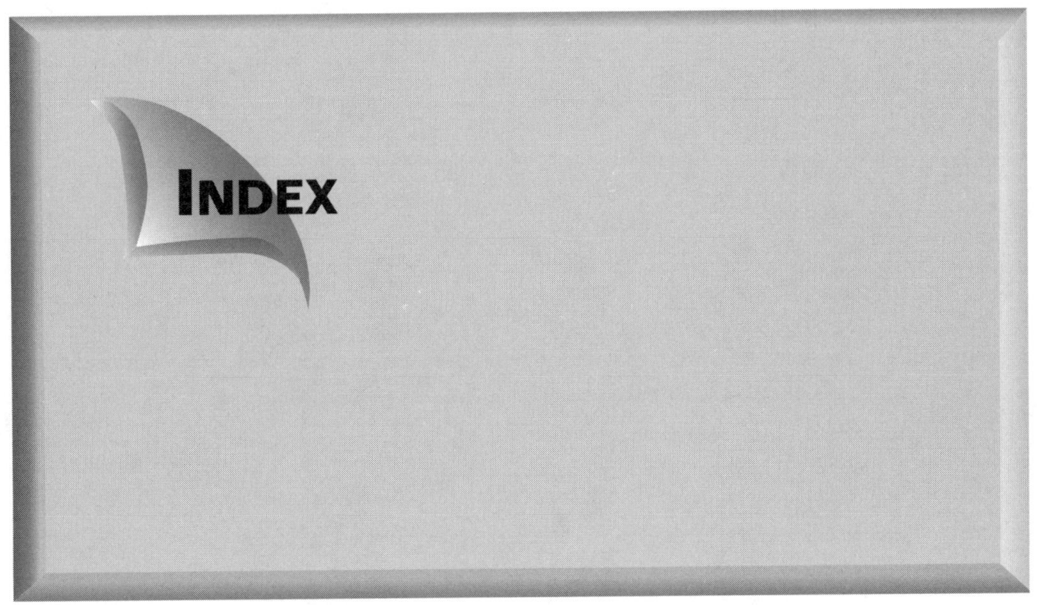

A

B

Index

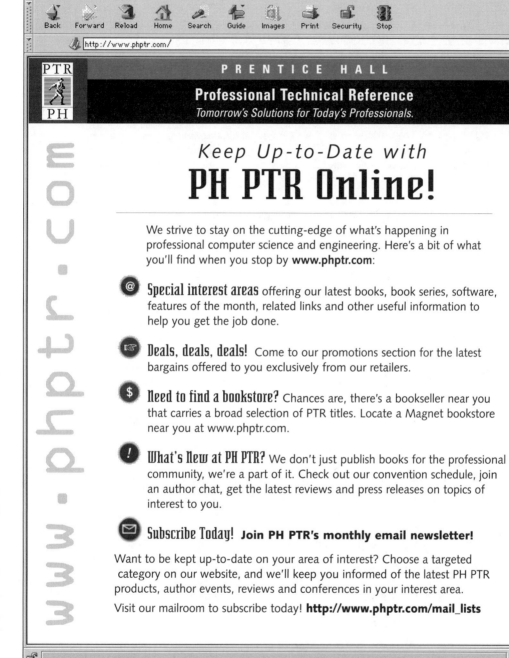

LICENSE AGREEMENT AND LIMITED WARRANTY

READ THE FOLLOWING TERMS AND CONDITIONS CAREFULLY BEFORE OPENING THIS CD PACKAGE. THIS LEGAL DOCUMENT IS AN AGREEMENT BETWEEN YOU AND PRENTICE-HALL, INC. (THE "COMPANY"). BY OPENING THIS SEALED CD PACKAGE, YOU ARE AGREEING TO BE BOUND BY THESE TERMS AND CONDITIONS. IF YOU DO NOT AGREE WITH THESE TERMS AND CONDITIONS, DO NOT OPEN THE CD PACKAGE. PROMPTLY RETURN THE UNOPENED CD PACKAGE AND ALL ACCOMPANYING ITEMS TO THE PLACE YOU OBTAINED THEM FOR A FULL REFUND OF ANY SUMS YOU HAVE PAID.

1. **GRANT OF LICENSE:** In consideration of your purchase of this book, and your agreement to abide by the terms and conditions of this Agreement, the Company grants to you a nonexclusive right to use and display the copy of the enclosed software program (hereinafter the "SOFTWARE") on a single computer (i.e., with a single CPU) at a single location so long as you comply with the terms of this Agreement. The Company reserves all rights not expressly granted to you under this Agreement.

2. **OWNERSHIP OF SOFTWARE:** You own only the magnetic or physical media (the enclosed CD) on which the SOFTWARE is recorded or fixed, but the Company and the software developers retain all the rights, title, and ownership to the SOFTWARE recorded on the original CD copy(ies) and all subsequent copies of the SOFTWARE, regardless of the form or media on which the original or other copies may exist. This license is not a sale of the original SOFTWARE or any copy to you.

3. **COPY RESTRICTIONS:** This SOFTWARE and the accompanying printed materials and user manual (the "Documentation") are the subject of copyright. The,individual programs on the CD are copyrighted by the authors of each program. Some of the programs on the CD include separate licensing agreements. If you intend to use one of these programs, you must read and follow its accompanying license agreement. You may not copy the Documentation or the SOFTWARE, except that you may make a single copy of the SOFTWARE for backup or archival purposes only. You may be held legally responsible for any copying or copyright infringement which is caused or encouraged by your failure to abide by the terms of this restriction.

4. **USE RESTRICTIONS:** You may not network the SOFTWARE or otherwise use it on more than one computer or computer terminal at the same time. You may physically transfer the SOFTWARE from one computer to another provided that the SOFTWARE is used on only one computer at a time. You may not distribute copies of the SOFTWARE or Documentation to others. You may not reverse engineer, disassemble, decompile, modify, adapt, translate, or create derivative works based on the SOFTWARE or the Documentation without the prior written consent of the Company.

5. **TRANSFER RESTRICTIONS:** The enclosed SOFTWARE is licensed only to you and may not be transferred to any one else without the prior written consent of the Company. Any unauthorized transfer of the SOFTWARE shall result in the immediate termination of this Agreement.

6. **TERMINATION:** This license is effective until terminated. This license will terminate automatically without notice from the Company and become null and void if you fail to comply with any provisions or limitations of this license. Upon termination, you shall destroy the Documentation and all copies of the SOFTWARE. All provisions of this Agreement as to warranties, limitation of liability, remedies or damages, and our ownership rights shall survive termination.

7. **MISCELLANEOUS:** This Agreement shall be construed in accordance with the laws of the United States of America and the State of New York and shall benefit the Company, its affiliates, and assignees.

8. **LIMITED WARRANTY AND DISCLAIMER OF WARRANTY:** The Company warrants that the SOFTWARE, when properly used in accordance with the Documentation, will operate in substantial conformity with the description of the SOFTWARE set forth in the Documentation. The Company does not warrant that the SOFTWARE will meet your requirements or that the operation

of the SOFTWARE will be uninterrupted or error-free. The Company warrants that the media on which the SOFTWARE is delivered shall be free from defects in materials and workmanship under normal use for a period of thirty (30) days from the date of your purchase. Your only remedy and the Company's only obligation under these limited warranties is, at the Company's option, return of the warranted item for a refund of any amounts paid by you or replacement of the item. Any replacement of SOFTWARE or media under the warranties shall not extend the original warranty period. The limited warranty set forth above shall not apply to any SOFTWARE which the Company determines in good faith has been subject to misuse, neglect, improper installation, repair, alteration, or damage by you. EXCEPT FOR THE EXPRESSED WARRANTIES SET FORTH ABOVE, THE COMPANY DISCLAIMS ALL WARRANTIES, EXPRESS OR IMPLIED, INCLUDING WITHOUT LIMITATION, THE IMPLIED WARRANTIES OF MERCHANTABILITY AND FITNESS FOR A PARTICULAR PURPOSE. EXCEPT FOR THE EXPRESS WARRANTY SET FORTH ABOVE, THE COMPANY DOES NOT WARRANT, GUARANTEE, OR MAKE ANY REPRESENTATION REGARDING THE USE OR THE RESULTS OF THE USE OF THE SOFTWARE IN TERMS OF ITS CORRECTNESS, ACCURACY, RELIABILITY, CURRENTNESS, OR OTHERWISE.

IN NO EVENT, SHALL THE COMPANY OR ITS EMPLOYEES, AGENTS, SUPPLIERS, OR CONTRACTORS BE LIABLE FOR ANY INCIDENTAL, INDIRECT, SPECIAL, OR CONSEQUENTIAL DAMAGES ARISING OUT OF OR IN CONNECTION WITH THE LICENSE GRANTED UNDER THIS AGREEMENT, OR FOR LOSS OF USE, LOSS OF DATA, LOSS OF INCOME OR PROFIT, OR OTHER LOSSES, SUSTAINED AS A RESULT OF INJURY TO ANY PERSON, OR LOSS OF OR DAMAGE TO PROPERTY, OR CLAIMS OF THIRD PARTIES, EVEN IF THE COMPANY OR AN AUTHORIZED REPRESENTATIVE OF THE COMPANY HAS BEEN ADVISED OF THE POSSIBILITY OF SUCH DAMAGES. IN NO EVENT SHALL LIABILITY OF THE COMPANY FOR DAMAGES WITH RESPECT TO THE SOFTWARE EXCEED THE AMOUNTS ACTUALLY PAID BY YOU, IF ANY, FOR THE SOFTWARE.

SOME JURISDICTIONS DO NOT ALLOW THE LIMITATION OF IMPLIED WARRANTIES OR LIABILITY FOR INCIDENTAL, INDIRECT, SPECIAL, OR CONSEQUENTIAL DAMAGES, SO THE ABOVE LIMITATIONS MAY NOT ALWAYS APPLY. THE WARRANTIES IN THIS AGREEMENT GIVE YOU SPECIFIC LEGAL RIGHTS AND YOU MAY ALSO HAVE OTHER RIGHTS WHICH VARY IN ACCORDANCE WITH LOCAL LAW.

ACKNOWLEDGMENT

YOU ACKNOWLEDGE THAT YOU HAVE READ THIS AGREEMENT, UNDERSTAND IT, AND AGREE TO BE BOUND BY ITS TERMS AND CONDITIONS. YOU ALSO AGREE THAT THIS AGREEMENT IS THE COMPLETE AND EXCLUSIVE STATEMENT OF THE AGREEMENT BETWEEN YOU AND THE COMPANY AND SUPERSEDES ALL PROPOSALS OR PRIOR AGREEMENTS, ORAL, OR WRITTEN, AND ANY OTHER COMMUNICATIONS BETWEEN YOU AND THE COMPANY OR ANY REPRESENTATIVE OF THE COMPANY RELATING TO THE SUBJECT MATTER OF THIS AGREEMENT.

Should you have any questions concerning this Agreement or if you wish to contact the Company for any reason, please contact in writing at the address below.

Robin Short

Prentice Hall PTR

One Lake Street

Upper Saddle River, New Jersey 07458

ABOUT THE CD

The enclosed CD-ROM contains the following computer-based training (CBT) course module from CBT Systems:

Java Database Connectivity.

The CD also includes a majority of the programming examples used in this book, along with Java JDK, INTERSOLV DataDirect ODBC Pack, and the Open Link Data Access Driver Suite. For more information, please refer to page xx in the front of this book.

The CD can be used on Windows® 95 and Windows NT®.

Technical Support

If you have a problem with the CBT software, please contact CBT Technical Support. In the US call 1 (800) 938-3247. If you are outside the US call 3531-283-0380.

Prentice Hall does not offer technical support for this software. However, if there is a problem with the media, you may obtain a replacement copy by e-mailing us with your problem at: disc_exchange@prenhall.com

Readers can obtain an electronic version of Appendix C from this book. To download the file, point your Web browser to:

ftp://ftp.prenhall.com/pub/ptr/unix_and_enabling_technologies.
w-048/taylorJDBC

The appendix is located in a file titled Appendix.zip, which you will need to unzip in order to use.